Bioterrorism

Guidelines for Medical and Public Health Management

Edited by
Donald A. Henderson, MD, MPH
Thomas V. Inglesby, MD
Tara O'Toole, MD, MPH

AMA Press
Vice President, Business Products: Anthony J. Frankos
Publisher: Michael Desposito
Editorial Director: Mary Lou White
Director, Production and Manufacturing: Jean Roberts
Senior Acquisitions Editor: Eileen Lynch
Project/Developmental Editor: Katharine Dvorak
Director, Marketing: J. D. Kinney
Marketing Manager: Reg Schmidt
Senior Production Coordinator: Rosalyn Carlton
Senior Print Coordinator: Ronnie Summers

JAMA
JAMA Book Liaison/Developmental Editor: Annette Flanagin, RN, MA
Editor: Catherine D. DeAngelis, MD, MPH
Executive Deputy Editor: Phil B. Fontanarosa, MD
Editorial Graphics Director: Ronna Henry Siegel, MD
Medical Illustrator: Cassio Lymn
Associate Editor: Roxanne K. Young
Assistant Editor: Jennifer Reiling
Copy Editors: Joy K. Jaeger, Beverly Stewart

Additional copies of this book may be ordered by calling 800 621-8335 or visiting www.amapress.com. Mention product number OP405502.

ISBN 1-57947-280-X

Library of Congress Cataloging-in-Publication Data

Henderson, Donald A., M.D.
Bioterrorism : guidelines for medical and public health management/
Donald A. Henderson, Thomas V. Inglesby, Tara O'Toole.
p. cm.
Includes bibliographical references and index.
ISBN 1-57947-280-X
1. Bioterrorism. I. Inglesby, Thomas V. II. O'Toole, Tara Jeanne,
1951- III. Title.
RC88.9.T47 H46 2002
363.3'2--dc21

2002008415

BP10:170-01:07/02

Cover photograph courtesy Kathleen Kuehl, USAMRIID.

CONTENTS

FOREWORD

The September 11, 2001, attacks on the World Trade Center and Pentagon changed forever our collective thinking with regard to our vulnerability to terrorist attacks. Superimposed on the events of September 11 were the first recorded cases of anthrax in the United States to result from an intentional human act. At least 5 envelopes containing *Bacillus anthracis* spores were sent to several locations via the US Postal Service, resulting in 22 confirmed or suspected cases of anthrax infection, half of which were the inhalational form of the disease. Tragically, 5 of the 11 individuals with inhalational anthrax died.

In addition to the human toll of the anthrax attacks, the fear and disruption that they engendered were extraordinary, as were the associated economic costs related to prophylactic antibiotic treatment, the law enforcement efforts, the clean up of anthrax-contaminated buildings, and other activities. Sadly, the relatively brief respite from anxiety afforded by the end of the Cold War has now been replaced by the realization that some individuals will stop at nothing to inflict pain, terror, and death on ordinary citizens. The civilian populations of countries around the world may never return to what we now know was a state of false security, of believing that some acts are so repugnant that they would never be undertaken.

The anthrax attacks of 2001, as well as credible evidence suggesting the existence of offensive bioweapons programs in at least a dozen countries, have revealed significant gaps in our overall preparedness against bioterrorism and have given a new sense of urgency to biodefense efforts. Clearly, there is a need to improve the ability to protect our citizens from potential bioterror threats, and to increase our capacity to deal with the medical and public health consequences of any future attacks. In this regard, *Bioterrorism: Guidelines for Medical and Public Health Management* provides, in one volume, state-of-the-science discussions concerning the epidemiology, microbiology, pathogenesis, prevention, and medical management of 6 potential bioterror diseases/agents (anthrax, smallpox, plague, botulinum toxin, tularemia, and hemorrhagic fever viruses) designated by the Centers for Disease Control and Prevention as "Category A" agents because of their potentially devastating impact on individuals and society. In addition, bioterrorism preparedness and response are analyzed, including the scientific and legal implications of quarantine as a possible public health tool in the event of a bioterror attack.

Much was learned from the anthrax attacks of 2001; encouragingly, the survival rate of patients with inhalational anthrax was considerably higher than previously reported, perhaps due to rapid diagnosis, aggressive therapy with multidrug antibiotic regimens, and state-of-the-art general medical supportive care. Clinicians will find the new information and insights on the pathogenesis and management of anthrax to be particularly instructive.

As discussed in this volume, acts of terrorism, including bioterrorism, generate fear and panic through their utterly unpredictable nature; the next attack could happen anywhere at any time, with any of a number of weapons, including many dangerous pathogens not included in the "Category A" list. Preparation for the next bioterrorist attack takes 2 major forms: intelligence and law enforcement activities to prevent an attack, and medical and public health activities to prepare for, respond to, and lessen the impact of attacks. The latter must be comprehensive and employ classic public health activities at the federal and local levels. These include revitalizing the capacity of hospitals and public health facilities; training "first responders"; developing and updating plans and guidelines for immediate responses at the local level; improving communications and data-sharing systems; and providing for the availability of vaccines, antibiotics, and other medical supplies for emergency. In addition, our ability to detect and counter bioterrorism depends to a large degree on the state of biomedical science. A robust commitment to basic and applied research is essential to the development of the essential tools—diagnostic tests, therapies and vaccines—needed by physicians, nurses, epidemiologists, and other public health professionals to control an outbreak of disease caused by a bioterrorist.

This volume not only gathers the best available information on major bioterror threats and appropriate medical and public health responses, but serves as a reminder that much remains to be learned, and that as a society we must continue to fortify our defenses against the next bioterror attack.

Anthony S. Fauci, MD
National Institute of Allergy and Infectious Diseases
National Institutes of Health

ACKNOWLEDGMENTS

The original objective for publishing this book was to provide a single compilation of consensus statements from the Working Group on Civilian Biodefense that could serve as a rapid resource for clinicians, public health officials, and others charged with bioterrorism planning responsibilities. The anthrax attacks of 2001 underscored the critical roles these communities would need to play in the response to future acts of bioterrorism. In the aftermath of those attacks, it was clear that case reports of the victims of those attacks should also be part of this book collection. Finally, with debate evolving in clinical, public health, and policy-maker communities about the utility, practical feasibility, ethics, and legality of various public health interventions that might be considered following a bioterrorist attack, we believed that an analysis of one such intervention (in this case, large-scale quarantine) should also be included in this book.

The editors of this collection would first like to thank the many persons who contributed to the writing of these articles, either as authors, ex officio participants, or in some other capacity. Authors, ex officio members, and persons contributing in some other capacity to a specific chapter in this book are named at the start of that chapter. All contributing authors are also named at the start of this book. It should be underscored that these articles represent the effort of a great number of otherwise extremely busy and accomplished scientists, clinicians, public health officials, and policy-makers. Without the many substantive contributions of this group, the consensus statements by the Working Group would not have been possible. We also thank Dr Anthony Fauci for taking the time from his very busy schedule to write the Foreword to this collection.

The editors of this collection are also deeply grateful and indebted to Annette Flanagin of *JAMA* who skillfully edited many of these articles in their original journal publication and committed great effort in the process of compiling them into this book. We are grateful as well to Phil Fontanarosa of *JAMA* who has also been supportive of this line of inquiry and analysis, and we are greatly appreciative of the editorial staff of *JAMA* who made many substantive contributions to these efforts in the past few years. In particular, we are appreciative of the hard work of Katharine Dvorak at AMA Press who helped to smooth the transition from journal articles to book chapters. We are grateful to Molly D'Esopo and Tim Holmes and others at the Johns Hopkins Center for Civilian Biodefense Strategies who have provided administrative or logistical assistance in completing these articles and this book.

We are grateful to Dean Al Sommer of the Johns Hopkins University School of Public Health and Dean Edward Miller of the Johns Hopkins University School of Medicine for their support of the Johns Hopkins Center for Civilian Biodefense Strategies.

Last, we are deeply appreciative of the generous foundation support that has been critical to the work of the Johns Hopkins Center for Civilian Biodefense Strategies. The Sacharuna Foundation provided early support and great wisdom. A grant from the Robert Wood Johnson foundation enabled the development of the Center's educational efforts and Web site. A gift from the Blum-Kovler Foundation made it possible to expand the Center's legislative analysis and outreach to clinicians. The Center is examining new approaches to prevention of the bioweapons threat thanks to the Nuclear Threat Initiative. And finally, the Alfred P. Sloan Foundation rescued the Center at a critical moment and has supported an array of Center projects. We are grateful and humbled by such generosity and encouragement without which much of our work would not have been possible.

Thomas V. Inglesby, MD
Tara O'Toole, MD, MPH
Donald A. Henderson, MD, MPH

CONTRIBUTORS

Olubunmi Afonja, MD
Department of Pediatrics
New York University
School of Medicine
New York, NY

Syed Ali, MD
Greater Southeast Community
Hospital
Washington, DC

Jonathan Arden, MD
Office of the Chief Medical Examiner
for the District of Columbia
Washington, DC

Isao Arita, MD
Agency for Cooperation
in International Health
Kumamoto, Japan

Stephen S. Arnon, MD
Infant Botulism Treatment
and Prevention Program
California Department of
Health Services
Berkeley

Carmina Arrastia, MD
Department of Medicine
Lenox Hill Hospital
New York, NY

Michael S. Ascher, MD
Office of Public Health Preparedness
Department of Health
and Human Services
Washington, DC

Lydia A. Barakat, MD
Griffin Hospital
Derby, Conn

Joseph Barbera, MD
Institute for Crisis and
Disaster Management
George Washington University
Washington, DC

Diane Barden, MT
Connecticut Department of Health
Hartford

John G. Bartlett, MD
Chief, Division of Infectious Diseases
Johns Hopkins University
School of Medicine
Baltimore, Md

Elise L. Berman, MD
Department of Radiology
Inova Fairfax Hospital
Falls Church, Va

Susan Bersoff-Matcha, MD
Department of Infectious Disease
Mid-Atlantic Permanente Medical
Group, Kaiser Permanente
Rockville, Md

Martin Blaser, MD
Department of Medicine
New York University
School of Medicine
New York, NY

Luciana Borio, MD
Center for Civilian Biodefense Strategies and the Schools of Public Health and Medicine
Johns Hopkins University and
National Institutes of Health
Baltimore, Md

William Borkowsky, MD
Department of Pediatrics
New York University School of Medicine
New York, NY

Joel G. Bremen, MD, DTPH
Fogarty International Center
Bethesda, Md

Jennifer Candotti
National Institutes of Health
Bethesda, Md

H. Wayne Carver II, MD
Connecticut State Medical Examiner's Office
Hartford

Donald Cerva, Jr, MD
Department of Radiology
Inova Fairfax Hospital
Falls Church, Va

Mary Wu Chang, MD
Departments of Pediatrics and Dermatology
New York University School of Medicine
New York, NY

Carlos Chiriboga, MD
Southern Maryland Hospital Center
Clinton

May Chu, PhD
Centers for Disease Control and Prevention
Fort Collins, Colo

George W. Counts, MD
Syphilis Elimination Activities
Division of STD Prevention/NCHSTP
Centers for Disease Control and Prevention
Atlanta, Ga

George Curlin, MD
National Institutes of Health
Bethesda, Md

Christopher Davis, OBE, MD, PhD
ORAQ Consultancy
Marlborough, England

Craig DeAtley, PA-C
Department of Emergency Medicine
George Washington University Medical Center
Washington, DC

Brian DeFranco, MD
Southern Maryland Hospital Center
Clinton

David T. Dennis, MD, MPH
National Center for Infectious Diseases
Centers for Disease Control and Prevention
Atlanta, Ga

Maria DeVita, MD
Section of Nephrology
Lenox Hill Hospital
New York, NY

Constance DiAngelo, MD, MS
Office of the Chief Medical Examiner for the District of Columbia
Washington, DC

Glenn Druckenbrod, MD
Department of Emergency Medicine
Inova Fairfax Hospital
Falls Church, Va

J. P. Dym, MD
Department of Medicine
Lenox Hill Hospital
New York, NY

James Earls, MD
Department of Radiology
Inova Fairfax Hospital
Falls Church, Va

Edward Eitzen, Jr, MD, MPH
US Army Medical Research Institute
of Infectious Diseases
Fort Detrick, Md

Joseph Esposito, PhD
Centers for Disease Control
and Prevention
Atlanta, Ga

Hasan Faraj, MD
Department of Medicine
Lenox Hill Hospital
New York, NY

Naaz Fatteh, MD
Department of Infectious Disease
Mid-Atlantic Permanente Medical
Group, Kaiser Permanente
Rockville, Md

Anthony S. Fauci, MD
National Institute of Allergy
and Infectious Diseases
National Institutes of Health
Bethesda, Md

Frank Fenner, MD
Australian National University
Canberra

Anne D. Fine, MD
Communicable Disease Program
New York City Department of Health
New York, NY

Steven Fochios, MD
Department of Medicine
Lenox Hill Hospital
New York, NY

David Fowler, MD
Office of the Chief Medical Examiner
for the State of Maryland
Baltimore

Dennis Frank, MD
Greater Southeast
Community Hospital
Washington, DC

Abigail Freedman, MD
Department of Pediatrics
New York University
School of Medicine
New York, NY

Arthur M. Friedlander, MD
US Army Medical Research
Institute of Infectious Diseases
Frederick, Md

Julie L. Gerberding, MD, MPH
Centers for Disease Control
and Prevention
Atlanta, Ga

Jeffrey Glick, MD
Department of Medicine
Lenox Hill Hospital
New York, NY

Larry Gostin, JD, PhD
Center for Law and the Public's Health
Georgetown University and
Johns Hopkins University
Baltimore, Md

Kevin Griffith, MD, MPH
Centers for Disease Control
and Prevention
Atlanta, Ga

Mayer Grosser, MD
Section of Emergency Medicine
Lenox Hill Hospital
New York, NY

Jeanette Guarner, MD
Centers for Disease Control
and Prevention
Atlanta, Ga

Jeanne Guillermin, PhD
Department of Sociology
Boston College
Boston, Mass

Jane Guttenberg, MD
Department of Pediatrics
New York University
School of Medicine
New York, NY

James L. Hadler, MD
Connecticut Department of Health
Hartford

Margaret A. Hamburg, MD
Office of Public Health Preparedness
Department of Health and
Human Services and Nuclear
Threat Initiative
Washington DC

Dan Hanfling, MD
Department of Emergency Medicine
Inova Fairfax Hospital
Falls Church, Va

Scott Harper, MD
Centers for Disease Control
and Prevention
Atlanta, Ga

Jerome Hauer, MPH
Office of Public Health Preparedness
Department of Health
and Human Services
Washington DC

Edward B. Hayes, MD
Centers for Disease Control
and Prevention
Atlanta, Ga

Donald A. Henderson, MD, MPH
Center for Civilian Biodefense
Strategies and the
School of Public Health
Johns Hopkins University
Baltimore, Md

Ralph Henderson, MD
World Health Organization
Geneva, Switzerland

James M. Hughes, MD
Centers for Disease Control
and Prevention
Atlanta, Ga

Thomas V. Inglesby, MD
Center for Civilian Biodefense
Strategies and the School
of Medicine
Johns Hopkins University
Baltimore, Md

Peter B. Jahrling, PhD
US Army Medical Research Institute
of Infectious Diseases
Frederick, Md

John A. Jernigan, MD
Centers for Disease Control
and Prevention
Atlanta, Ga

Karl M. Johnson, MD
Center for Civilian Biodefense
Strategies and
Departments of Microbiology
and Neuroscience
Johns Hopkins University
Baltimore, Md

Richard T. Johnson, MD
University of New Mexico
Albuquerque

Irina Kaplounova, MD
Department of Medicine
Lenox Hill Hospital
New York, NY

Katherine Kelley, PhD
Connecticut Department of Health
Hartford

David L. Kirschke, MD
Centers for Disease Control
and Prevention
Atlanta, Ga

Robert Knouss, MD
Office of Emergency Preparedness
Department of Health
and Human Services
Rockville, Md

John F. Koerner, MPH, CIH
President, JF Koerner Consulting, Inc.
Operations Director, WMD Response
Washington, DC

Jeffrey P. Koplan, MD, MPH
Centers for Disease Control
and Prevention
Atlanta, Ga

Christopher M. Krol, MD
Department of Radiology
Lenox Hill Hospital
New York, NY

Thomas Ksiazek, DVM, PhD
Centers for Disease Control
and Prevention
Atlanta, Ga

Frank Kuepper
Charité of the Humboldt
University of Berlin
Berlin, Germany

Agnieszka Kwapniewski, MD
Department of Medicine
Lenox Hill Hospital
New York, NY

Gigi Kwik, PhD
Center for Civilian Biodefense
Strategies
Johns Hopkins University
Baltimore, Md

H. Clifford Lane, MD
National Institute of Allergy
and Infectious Diseases
National Institutes of Health
Bethesda, Md

Marcelle Layton, MD
Communicable Disease Program
New York City Department of Health
New York, NY

Herb Lazarus, MD
Department of Pediatrics
New York University
School of Medicine
New York, NY

Jacqueline Lee, MD
Office of the Chief Medical Examiner
for the District of Columbia
Washington, DC

Scott Lillibridge, MD
Centers for Disease Control
and Prevention
Atlanta, Ga

Dan Lucey, MD
Washington Hospital Center
Washington, DC

Anthony Macintyre, MD
Department of Emergency Medicine
George Washington University
Medical Center
Washington, DC

Brian Mahy, PhD, ScD
Centers for Disease Control
and Prevention
Atlanta, Ga

Brian Malkin, Esq
Hyman, Phelps & McNamara, PC
Washington DC

Venkat Mani, MD
Southern Maryland Hospital Center
Clinton

Chung Marston
Centers for Disease Control
and Prevention
Atlanta, Ga

Eric E. Mast, MD, MPH
Centers for Disease Control
and Prevention
Atlanta, Ga

Henry Masur, MD
Critical Care Medicine Department
Clinical Center
National Institutes of Health
Bethesda, Md

Thom A. Mayer, MD
Department of Emergency Medicine
Inova Fairfax Hospital
Falls Church, Va

Donald Mayo, ScD
Connecticut Department of Health
Hartford

Joseph McDade, PhD
Centers for Disease Control
and Prevention
Atlanta, Ga

Richard F. Meyer, PhD
Centers for Disease Control
and Prevention
Atlanta, Ga

Andrea Meyerhoff, MD
Office of the Commissioner
US Food and Drug Administration
Rockville, Md

Bushra Mina, MD
Section of Critical Care Medicine
Lenox Hill Hospital
New York, NY

Jeffrey Moses, MD
Section of Interventional Cardiology
Lenox Hill Hospital
New York, NY

Farzad Mostashari, MD
Department of Health
New York University
School of Medicine
New York, NY

Cecele Murphy, MD
Department of Emergency Medicine
Inova Fairfax Hospital
Falls Church, Va

Gary J. Nabel, MD, PhD
Vaccine Research Center
National Institutes of Health
Bethesda, Md

Ashna Nayyar, MS, PA-C
Department of Emergency Medicine
Inova Fairfax Hospital
Falls Church, Va

Michael Nguyen, MD
Departments of Infectious Disease and Internal Medicine
Mid-Atlantic Permanente Medical Group, Kaiser Permanente
Rockville, Md

Stuart L. Nightingale, MD
Office of the Assistant Secretary for Planning and Evaluation and Office of the Deputy Assistant Secretary for International and Refugee Health
Office of the Secretary
Department of Health and Human Services
Washington, DC

Michael T. Osterholm, PhD, MPH
Center for Infectious Disease Research and Policy
University of Minnesota
Minneapolis

Tara O'Toole, MD, MPH
Center for Civilian Biodefense Strategies and the School of Public Health
Johns Hopkins University
Baltimore, Md

Gerald Parker, PhD, DVM
US Army Medical Research and Materiel Command
Fort Detrick, Md

Denis Pauze, MD
Department of Emergency Medicine
Inova Fairfax Hospital
Falls Church, Va

Guillermo Perez-Perez, MD
Department of Medicine
New York University School of Medicine
New York, NY

Trish M. Perl, MD, MSc
Johns Hopkins University Hospital
Baltimore, Md

C. J. Peters, MD
Center for Biodefense
University of Texas Medical Branch
Galveston

Paul A. Pham, PharmD
Johns Hopkins University
Baltimore, Md

Michael Pollanen, MD, PhD
Office of the Chief Medical Examiner for the District of Columbia
Washington, DC

Tanja Popovic, MD, PhD
Centers for Disease Control and Prevention
Atlanta, Ga

Howard L. Quentzel, MD
Griffin Hospital
Derby, Conn

William Raub, PhD
Office of Assistant Secretary for Planning and Evaluation
Department of Health and Human Services
Washington, DC

David Reagan, MD
Greater Southeast Community Hospital
Washington, DC

Athena Remolina, MD
Section of Cardiology
Lenox Hill Hospital
New York, NY

Karen Rexroth
Southern Maryland Hospital Center
Clinton, Md

Thomas Robin, M(ASCP)
Microbiology Laboratory
Lenox Hill Hospital
New York, NY

Jonathan Rosenthal, MD
Department of Infectious Disease
Mid-Atlantic Permanente Medical
Group, Kaiser Permanente
Rockville, Md

Mary Ripple, MD
Office of the Chief Medical Examiner
for the State of Maryland
Baltimore

Philip K. Russell, MD
Center for Civilian Biodefense
Strategies and the School
of Public Health
Johns Hopkins University
Baltimore, Md

Robert Schacht, MD
Department of Pediatrics
New York University
School of Medicine
New York, NY

Robert Schechter, MD
Infant Botulism Treatment
and Prevention Program
California Department
of Health Services
Berkeley

Alan L. Schmaljohn, PhD
US Army Medical Research Institute
of Infectious Diseases
Frederick, Md

Monica Schoch-Spana, PhD
Center for Civilian Biodefense
Strategies
Johns Hopkins University
Baltimore, Md

Wun-Ju Shieh, MD, PhD
Centers for Disease Control
and Prevention
Atlanta, Ga

Mridula Singh, MD
Southern Maryland Hospital Center
Clinton

Stephen M. Spear, MD
Griffin Hospital
Derby, Conn

David S. Stephens, MD
Emory University School of Medicine
Atlanta, Ga

Anthony Suffredini, MD
National Institutes of Health
Bethesda, Md

David L. Swerdlow, MD
Clinical Outcomes Section
Division of HIV/AIDS Prevention
National Center for HIV, STD,
TB Prevention
Centers for Disease Control
and Prevention
Atlanta, Ga

Michael L. Tapper, MD
Section of Infectious Disease
Lenox Hill Hospital
New York, NY

Jack Titus, MD
Office of the Chief Medical Examiner
for the State of Maryland
Baltimore

Kevin Tonat, DrPH, MPH
Office of Emergency Preparedness
Department of Health
and Human Services
Rockville, Md

Timothy Townsend, MD
Johns Hopkins University
Baltimore, Md

Michael Traister, MD
Department of Pediatrics
New York University
School of Medicine
New York, NY

Raymond Tso, MD
Department of Medicine
Lenox Hill Hospital
New York, NY

Ljiljana Vasovic, MD
Department of Pathology
Lenox Hill Hospital
New York, NY

Jane Wong, MS
California Department of Health
Berkeley

Brad Wood, MD
National Institutes of Health
Bethesda, Md

Sherif R. Zaki, MD, PhD
Centers for Disease Control
and Prevention
Atlanta, Ga

Why Understanding Biological Weapons Matters to Medical and Public Health Professionals

Tara O'Toole, MD, MPH; Thomas V. Inglesby, MD; Donald A. Henderson, MD, MPH

This book is intended to guide medical and public health management following a biological weapons attack on civilian populations. It is hoped that the information in this book will be of particular use to professionals who might be called on to provide medical care for those exposed to future bioterrorist attacks, or who are charged with creating and operating public health epidemic response systems. The chapters are papers previously published in the *Journal of the American Medical Association* (*JAMA*) that have been subsequently reviewed and updated for this book.

With the publication of the consensus statement on viral hemorrhagic fevers in 2002, the Working Group on Civilian Biodefense completed the charge it set in 1998: to identify the pathogens that, if used as bioweapons against civilian populations, might cause illness and death on a large scale; to gather and distill available information on these agents to aid medical and public health professionals who might be called on to respond to such attacks; and to make consensus recommendations regarding key medical and public health issues that would follow bioweapons attacks with these agents.[1-7]

In 1998, the Working Group, comprising of leaders from academia and government, concluded that 5 specific bioweapons agents and 1 group of viruses—the agents of viral hemorrhagic fever (VHF)—had the potential to cause such mass disruption, illness, or death in a large biological attack that merited priority attention. A number of characteristics were considered in this judgment: high morbidity or mortality, transmissibility from person to person, lack of effective or available vaccine, lack of effective or available treatment, possible infectivity by aerosol, wide-scale availability of the pathogen or toxin, feasibility of large-scale production of the pathogen or toxin, and capacity for aerosol delivery of the pathogen or toxin. While no single agent exhibits all of these characteristics, the agents fulfilled many of these criteria. These specific agents—anthrax, smallpox, plague, tularemia, botulinum toxin, and the agents of VHF—are the same as those identified as Class A agents in the subsequent analysis by the Centers for Disease Control and Prevention (CDC).[8]

It is understood by the Working Group that this list of bioweapons agents of greatest concern as well as the scientific and clinical understanding of their manifestations and treatment will need to be revised and updated in accord with the evolution of our understanding of the bioterrorism threat, scientific research, and clinical experience. Consistent with this, the Working Group consensus statement on anthrax in this book is a recently revised and published version of the original statement,[1,2] reflecting the knowledge gleaned from the anthrax attacks of 2001 through the US postal system. The smallpox consensus statement published in this volume has also been revised to reflect current information, as has the statement on botulinum toxin, which here contains an addendum highlighting the important interval changes that have occurred since the time of that paper's original publication in 2001.

This book also contains 5 case reports describing in detail a number of the individual anthrax cases resulting from the 2001 attacks.[9-13] As these reports make clear, the experience of caring for the 22 patients who contracted cutaneous or inhalational anthrax generated important new information and highlighted aspects of historical clinical data.

Before October 2001, understanding of inhalational anthrax was based primarily on old clinical case series and the reports of the illnesses that followed the 1979 release of anthrax powder from the Soviet bioweapons facility at Sverdlovsk in Russia. The clinical presentations that followed the 2001 attacks underscore the heterogeneity of the possible initial signs and symptoms of inhalational anthrax. In the 2001 series of cases, early manifestations were nonspecific and included severe headache, abdominal pain, drenching sweats, and tachycardia out of proportion to fever. While 7 of the first 10 patients presenting with inhalational anthrax following the 2001 attacks had a widened mediastinum, all 10 patients had a chest radiograph abnormality of some form. Pleural effusions had been reported previously, but in 2001 it was a striking finding—8 of 10 patients with inhalation anthrax had pleural effusion, with many requiring thoracentesis.[14] Survival among the 2001 cases reached 55%—a much better outcome than was anticipated even by a recent reanalysis of available Sverdlovsk data.[15] Early diagnosis and treatment with appropriate antibiotics before patients became gravely ill appeared to be associated with survival.[14]

An overriding lesson from the medical and public health response to the 2001 anthrax attacks stands out: it is essential that medical practitioners, laboratories, and public health professionals are linked in a robust communication network that enables rapid exchange of scientific knowledge, clinical observations, and epidemiologic data. The index case of inhalational anthrax of the 2001 attacks was initially diagnosed by an alert physician and local laboratorians who had recently completed CDC-sponsored bioterrorism preparedness training.[16,17] Many of the important clinical observations in the outbreak were made by clinicians who then disseminated them among colleagues and to public health agencies.

The anthrax attacks of 2001 underscored the critical role of public health agencies in responding to bioterrorist attacks. Public health officials' ability to identify and deliver antibiotics to large numbers of potentially exposed individuals almost certainly prevented additional deaths[18] and may have helped quell public anxiety. These attacks—which resulted in a total of 22 cases—imposed severe stress on the public health agencies in the affected states and Washington, DC. Laboratories were pressed to identify thousands of samples of suspicious powders in addition to analyzing clinical specimens. The United States Army Research Institute for Infectious Disease (USAMRIID) performed 19 000 anthrax assays in the weeks following the mailings (E. Eitzen, oral communication, March 6, 2002). State and local health departments were also inundated with requests for analyses of environmental samples, nasal swabs, and clinical specimens. Thirty-three thousand people were initially placed on antibiotics; 10 000 were eventually urged by public health officials to complete a 60-day course of prophylaxis (J. L. Gerberding, oral communication). Environmental surveys at a large and as yet undefined number of post offices and downstream mailrooms were carried out. Public health authorities were forced to assign additional staff to anthrax response activities, thus pulling people from their regular duties. Federal, state, and local public health officials all worked long hours through weekends, vacations, and holidays.

The 22 cases of anthrax resulting from the 2001 attacks were enormously disruptive and costly. Mail delivery to the US Capitol was interrupted for weeks; the Hart Senate office building remained closed for over three months. The bill for decontamination of the Hart building alone is estimated to exceed $23 million.

As is often the case in crises that demand action on the basis of incomplete information and professional judgment, the anthrax mailings highlighted the importance of distinguishing what is known from what is uncertain and unknown. For example, before the 2001 mailings, it was not anticipated that powdered anthrax contained in sealed, unopened envelopes would pose a danger to individuals handling such material. During this crisis, public health recommendations regarding postexposure antibiotic prophylaxis and vaccination as well as the risk of acquiring anthrax through environmental exposure were based on information that evolved as events unfolded. As is noted in the revised anthrax consensus statement,[1] there was no information available that showed *Bacillus anthracis* spores of "weapons grade" quality could leak out the edges of envelopes or through the pores of envelopes. When it became clear that the first case of anthrax in Florida was likely caused by a *B anthracis*–contaminated letter that had been opened, evaluation of the postal workers who might have handled or processed the unopened letter showed no illness. When anthrax cases were discovered in New York City, each was believed linked to the handling of an unopened letter containing anthrax spores. However, in one case the letter was not identified. Judgments based, in part, on these facts were then revised when illness was first discovered in persons handling or processing unopened letters.

The relatively small number of anthrax cases resulting from the 2001 mailings might lead some to reason that the threat of bioterrorism has been overblown. The number of persons who became sick or died from anthrax in 2001 was far less than the number of those who died following the World Trade Center and

Pentagon attacks or from naturally occurring infectious diseases in the United States and around the world. But such comparisons do not address more serious fundamental concerns provoked by these anthrax attacks, and do not take up the larger implications.

The tragic events of September 11, 2001, and the subsequent dissemination of anthrax through the US mail demonstrated that terrorists are willing and able to use advanced technologies to kill noncombatant civilians on a large scale. The argument advanced by some analysts that biological weapons simply would not or could not be used is now proven false. While all that can be done should be done in the name of the nation states forswearing and banning this class of weapons, at least for the present, measures must be taken to prepare for such future attacks.

Biological weapons and bioweapons development programs are present in the world. All states named by the US State Department as state sponsors of terrorism are believed either to possess or to be actively pursuing biological weapons. Anthrax is one of the most studied of the Class A agents and is, arguably, the simplest and most accessible bioweapons pathogen. The Soviet bioweapons program manufactured tons of anthrax in powder form.[19] Iraq admitted to producing 8 000 liters of concentrated anthrax powder, although the United Nations believes the actual quantities were much higher.[20] Al Queda laboratories intending to make anthrax bioweapons were recently discovered.[21] But anthrax is only one of many possible bioweapons threats.

Future bioweapons attacks could have wide-ranging and serious effects on the US health care system. The medical and public health ramifications of the attacks of 2001 are highlighted in this book. The US mail system became the unlikely delivery system for a biological weapon. But what would have been the outcome had there been a more widespread attack? As has been stated in multiple presentations and publications, the US health care system, or any nation's health care system, is not prepared to cope with a sudden surge of hundreds or thousands of patients with inhalational anthrax requiring intensive medical care. Financial pressures on the US health care system have caused most hospitals to adopt just-in-time staffing and supply models, significantly limiting the ability to respond to sudden surges in patient demand. Before the 2001 attacks, most hospitals and health care delivery organizations had not been much involved in bioterrorism planning and preparedness activities. The federal bioterrorism preparedness funds now being distributed through state health departments will enable health care organizations to undertake needs assessments and begin to implement measures needed for epidemic response. Similarly, the resources now being made available to public health agencies across the nation will enable greater capacity to respond to and investigate disease outbreaks, to strengthen the laboratory network, to improve communication between and among key public health and medical institutions, and to provide a variety of other important critical enhancements.

Finally, responding to a large-scale bioweapon-initiated contagious disease outbreak would require an emergency response and decision-making quite distinct from that demanded by naturally occurring outbreaks or other forms of terrorist attack. The chapter, "Large-Scale Quarantine Following Biological Terrorism in the United States," at the end of this book, highlights the importance of thinking through the difficult decisions that would be necessary to manage a bioterrorist attack employing contagious disease.[22] In medieval times, quarantine of ships or whole towns was sometimes imposed in attempt to halt the spread of transmissible disease. Although one can imagine circumstances in which such actions might again become necessary, it is important to recognize that there is a range of interventions that might be more appropriate and effective at interrupting contagion in modern society. It is critical that decision-makers begin to consider the complexities and potential adverse effects of implementing disease containment measures.

As physicians and public health professionals, we are deeply disturbed by the prospect that the ancient scourge of infectious disease, enabled by modern science and technologies, might be used to create weapons of mass lethality. It is the unfortunate responsibility of those who would count themselves among the healing professions to think carefully about such possibilities, to do what is possible to prevent such horrors, and to take steps to lessen the death and suffering that would result from a large bioterrorism attack should prevention fail.

References

1. Inglesby TV, O'Toole T, Henderson DA, et al. Anthrax as a biological weapon, 2002: updated recommendations for management. *JAMA.* 2002;287:2236-2252.
2. Inglesby TV, Henderson DA, Bartlett JG, et al. Anthrax as a biological weapon: medical and public health management. *JAMA.* 1999;281:1735-1745.
3. Henderson DA, Inglesby TV, Bartlett JG, et al. Smallpox as a biological weapon: medical and public health management. *JAMA.* 1999;281:2127-2137.
4. Inglesby TV, Dennis DT, Henderson DA, et al. Plague as a biological weapon: medical and public health management. *JAMA.* 2000;283:2281-2290.
5. Arnon SA, Schecter R, Inglesby TV, et al. Botulinum toxin as a biological weapon: medical and public health management. *JAMA.* 2001;285:1059-1070.
6. Dennis DT, Inglesby TV, Henderson DA, et al. Tularemia as a biological weapon: medical and public health management. *JAMA.* 2001;285:2763-2773.
7. Borio L., Inglesby T, Peters CJ, et al. Hemorrhagic fever as a biological weapons: medical and public health management. *JAMA.* 2002;287:2391-2405.
8. Rotz LD, Kahn AS, Lillibridge SR, et al. Public health assessment of potential biological terrorism agents. *Emerg Infect Dis.* 2002;8:225-230.
9. Mayer TA, Bersoff-Matcha S, Murphy C, et al. Clinical presentation of inhalational anthrax following bioterrorism exposure: report of 2 surviving patients. *JAMA.* 2001;286:2549-2553.
10. Borio L, Frank D, Mani V, et al. Death due to bioterrorism-related inhalational anthrax: report of 2 patients. *JAMA.* 2001;286:2554-2559.
11. Mina B, Dym J, Kuepper F, et al. Fatal inhalational anthrax with unknown source of exposure in a 61-year-old woman in New York City. *JAMA.* 2002;287:858-862.
12. Barakat L, Quentzel H, Jernigan J, et al. Fatal inhalational anthrax in a 94-year-old Connecticut woman. *JAMA.* 2002;287:863-868.
13. Freedman A, Afonja O, Chang M, et al. Cutaneous anthrax associated with microangiopathic hemolytic anemia and coagulopathy in a 7-month-old infant. *JAMA.* 2002;287:869-874.
14. Jernigan J, Stephens D, Ashford D, et al. Bioterrorism-related inhalation anthrax: the first 10 cases reported in the United States. *Emerg Infect Dis.* 2001;7:933-944.
15. Brookmeyer R, Blades N, Hugh-Jones M, et al. The statistical analysis of truncated data: application to the Sverdlovsk anthrax outbreak. *Biostatistics.* 2001;2:233-247.

16. Bush LM, Abrams BH, Beall A, et al. Index case of fatal inhalational anthrax due to bioterrorism in the United States. *N Engl J Med.* 2001;345: 1607-1610.

17. Lane HC, Fauci AS. Bioterrorism on the home front: a new challenge for American medicine. *JAMA.* 2001;286:2595-2597.

18. Brookmeyer R, Blades N. Prevention of inhalational anthrax in the US outbreak. *Science.* 2002; 295:1861.

19. Alibek K, Handelman S. *Biohazard: The Chilling True Story of the Largest Covert Biological Weapons Program in the World—Told From Inside by the Man Who Ran It.* New York, NY: Random House; 1999.

20. Zilinskas RA. Iraq's biological weapons: the past as future? *JAMA.* 1997;278:418-424.

21. Gordon MR. US says it found Al Queda lab being built to produce anthrax. *New York Times.* March 23, 2002:A1.

22. Barbera J, Macintyre A, Gostin L, et al. Large-scale quarantine following biological terrorism in the United States: scientific examination, logistic and legal limits, and possible consequences. *JAMA.* 2001;286:2711-2717.

Bioterrorism on the Home Front

A New Challenge for American Medicine

H. Clifford Lane, MD; Anthony S. Fauci, MD

On October 4, 2001, it was announced that a 63-year-old man had been hospitalized in Palm Beach County, Florida, with inhalational anthrax.[1] This was the first recognized case of inhalational anthrax in the United States since 1976, and the first in US history to result from an intentional human act. As such, it ushered in a new era for the United States, one in which the hypothetical threat of lethal bioterrorism has become a stark reality. Importantly, the juxtaposition of this event with the vicious terrorist attacks on the World Trade Center and the Pentagon, despite no proven connection at this time, has resulted in a heightened state of concern in the United States and in other countries.

Since October 4 and as of December 7, the Centers for Disease Control and Prevention (CDC) has confirmed a total of 11 cases of inhalational anthrax and 7 cases of cutaneous anthrax. There have been 4 cases of suspected cutaneous anthrax.[2] All but 1 of these cases appear to have been directly linked to the US postal system. The epidemiologic link of the apparently isolated case of the 61-year-old Bronx resident and employee of a Manhattan hospital who died of inhalational anthrax remains a mystery. Clinical cases of cutaneous or inhalational anthrax have clustered in the Boca Raton, Fla, New York City/New Jersey, and Washington, DC, areas. However, traces of anthrax spores, which likely are secondary contamination from identified primary sources of anthrax spores, have been found in distant locations such as Indianapolis, Ind. and Kansas City, Mo. More than 30 000 people are estimated to have received antibiotics as a consequence of possible exposure to anthrax spores.[2] The need for continual reevaluation of conventional wisdom regarding this disease as well as other potential bioterrorist threats has been made clear from these recent experiences. In this regard, the cross-contamination of mail and the special vulnerability of postal workers are 2 of the most unexpected epidemiologic findings thus far.

The 4 patients described by Mayer and colleagues[3] and Borio and colleagues[4] in the 2 chapters that follow this chapter provide a graphic account of the serious clinical consequences of inhalational anthrax. While one needs to be cautious in drawing generalizations from a handful of cases, several points can be made at this time from the available information. First, it is quite clear that with early recognition and rapid, aggressive initiation of appropriate antibiotic treatment, inhalational anthrax is a serious but nonetheless treatable disease. Of the 11 cases of inhalational anthrax reported from this outbreak, 5 patients have died, 3 have been released from the hospital continuing successful treatment, and 3 (including the 2 patients in the report by Mayer et al) are recovering while continuing to receive therapy. The fact that 6 of these patients have survived provides hope that the previously published mortality rates of 86% to 97% for inhalational anthrax[8] may not be accurate in the year 2001. Second, although there did not appear to be any clear-cut signs of early anthrax infection, certain characteristics were common among all 4 cases reported by Mayer et al and Borio et al. These included tachycardia disproportionate to the degree of fever, normal or elevated white blood cell counts, and abnormalities on chest radiographs or chest computed tomographic (CT) images. Among the radiographic changes were evidence of a widened mediastinum, pulmonary infiltrates, and pleural effusions. Abdominal pain or chest discomfort was noted in 3 of the 4 cases.

Based on these observations, primary care clinicians should be encouraged to obtain chest radiographs and consider chest CT scanning to aid in the diagnostic workup of patients in whom inhalational anthrax is a diagnostic consideration.[6] During influenza season, it is likely that frontline physicians will be faced with the dilemma of attempting to rule out a diagnosis of early anthrax in patients with influenza or other viral illnesses. The combination of a careful history ascertainment with attention to potential environmental exposure and the use of appropriate radiologic studies should be able to reduce the inevitable widespread use of antibiotics during the upcoming influenza season. Moreover, although chest radiography and rapid diagnostic kits for influenza might prove helpful as adjuncts to other diagnostic tools, these should not be used as definitive diagnostic tests, particularly if they yield negative results. Viral diseases other than influenza A or B can present with “flulike” symptoms, and the chest radiograph may be read as normal early in the course of inhalational anthrax.

Importantly, strong weight should be placed on the epidemiologic setting within which the patient presents. Of note, all 4 patients described by Mayer and colleagues[3] and Borio and colleagues[4] in the following 2 chapters worked at the Brentwood postal distribution center just outside of Washington, DC, and, thus, were possibly exposed to the same source of anthrax. The 2 patients who survived were admitted on October 19 and 20, while the 2 patients who died were admitted on October 21 and 22.[7] Thus, the index of suspicion of the clinicians within the context of the epidemiologic setting should play an important role in guiding decisions regarding further diagnostic testing and therapeutic interventions.

Bacillus anthracis is a spore-forming, nonhemolytic, nonmotile gram-positive rod. The organisms that have been identified thus far during the current outbreak appear indistinguishable and have uniformly been susceptible to ciprofloxacin, doxycycline, chloramphenicol, clindamycin, rifampin, vancomycin, clarithromycin, penicillin, and amoxicillin.[7] The *B anthracis* genome includes both a cephalosporinase and an inducible penicillinase. For this reason, it is not advisable to rely on either cephalosporins or penicillins alone for treatment. In late 2001, CDC recommendations for initial treatment of inhalational anthrax[7] included intravenous ciprofloxacin or doxycycline along with 1 or 2 additional agents. The successful regimen of ciprofloxacin, rifampin, and clindamycin used by Mayer and colleagues[3] was in keeping with these recommendations. While there are no prior published data regarding the use of clindamycin to treat inhalational anthrax in humans, it has been suggested that clindamycin may provide both an antimicrobial as well as an antitoxin activity.[3] The recommended duration of therapy for inhalational or cutaneous anthrax is 60 days.[7,8]

Nonhuman primate data[9,10] and data from the 1979 Sverdlovsk outbreak[11] have indicated that *B anthracis* spores can retain their ability to germinate for an extended period following inhalation. Based on these data, the current CDC recommendation is that all individuals exposed to anthrax spores receive a 60-day course of antibiotics as postexposure prophylaxis.[12] The lack of anthrax cases thus far among the individuals exposed to the contaminated letter in the US Senate office building suggests that this approach is effective. Current recommendations by the CDC[7] for postexposure prophylaxis regimens in adults include either ciprofloxacin, 500 mg orally every 12 hours, or doxycycline, 100 mg orally twice per day, with dose adjustments in children (ciprofloxacin, 15 mg/kg orally every 12 hours, or doxycycline, 2.2 mg/kg orally twice daily for children ≤45 kg). The US Food and Drug Administration (FDA) has approved these 2 drugs as well as procaine penicillin for this indication. Given the adverse effects of ciprofloxacin and doxycycline in children, the CDC also recommends that if the isolate is determined to be sensitive to penicillin, children should be switched to amoxicillin, 80 mg/kg (not to exceed 500 mg per dose) orally every 8 hours. Additional work is needed to expand the range of antibiotics approved by the FDA for this indication.

Bacillus anthracis has several characteristics that make it a particularly virulent organism.[13,14] These include an antiphagocytic poly-D-glutamic acid capsule and 2 toxins, lethal toxin and edema toxin. These 2 toxins are formed when the respective toxin factors, lethal factor or edema factor, bind to the protective antigen protein. Immunity to anthrax appears to be antibody mediated and has been conferred in animal studies by immunization with either a cell-free culture supernatant of *B anthracis* absorbed to aluminum hydroxide (anthrax vaccine adsorbed [AVA]) or recombinant protective antigen. The AVA vaccine is currently in use by the US military. The efficacy of this vaccine in preventing inhalational anthrax in humans was established in the mid-1950s in a cohort of 1249 mill workers in New Hampshire and Pennsylvania who processed raw imported goat hair.[15] The recombinant protective antigen vaccines are currently under development.

The recent outbreaks of inhalational and cutaneous anthrax have brought an ancient disease into the arena of high-tech medicine. This juxtaposition is an important reminder on the one hand of the levels of sophistication of the currently available armamentarium of diagnostics and therapeutics, and on the other hand of the importance of the fundamentals of sound clinical medicine. Because of the advances in imaging, microbiology, antibiotics, and critical care, certain patients have survived who, in a different era, almost certainly would have succumbed to this disease. However, this might not have been possible without the insight gained from taking a careful history, including an occupational and environmental history, and having a high index of suspicion for a rare disease. Rapid dissemination of information via the Internet also has been invaluable in keeping the public informed and physicians aware of the latest developments and recommendations in a rapidly evolving story. The CDC's bioterrorism Website (http://www.bt.cdc.gov) has been a consistent source of the latest information and recommendations.

There is no reason to believe this will be an isolated act of bioterrorism. In fact, it is likely that additional attacks involving *B anthracis* and perhaps other pathogens will occur. Each will present the health care community with a new set of challenges and a need for rapid dissemination of reliable, up-to-date information. To successfully deal with these challenges, prompt sharing of information among law enforcement authorities, public health officials, and frontline health care providers will continue to be essential. The alertness, open-mindedness, and sound clinical judgment of physicians and other health care professionals will be critical to the successful public health response to current and future threats.

References

1. Fla. anthrax case confirmed 63-year-old man hospitalized. *Associated Press.* October 4, 2001.
2. Centers for Disease Control and Prevention. Investigation of bioterrorism-related anthrax. Connecticut, 2001. *MMWR Morb Mortal Wkly Rep.* 2001;50:1077-1079.
3. Mayer TA, Bersoff-Matcha S, Murphy C, et al. Clinical presentation of inhalational anthrax following bioterrorism exposure: report of 2 surviving patients. *JAMA.* 2001;286:2549-2553.
4. Borio L, Frank D, Mani V, et al. Death due to bioterrorism-related inhalational anthrax: report of 2 patients. *JAMA.* 2001;286:2554-2559.
5. Use of anthrax vaccine in the United States: recommendations of the Advisory Committee on Immunization Practices. *Clin Toxicol.* 2001;39:85-100.
6. Centers for Disease Control and Prevention. Investigation of bioterrorism related anthrax and interim guidelines for clinical evaluation of persons with possible anthrax. *MMWR Morb Mortal Wkly Rep.* 2001;50:941-948.
7. Centers for Disease Control and Prevention. Investigation of bioterrorism-related anthrax and interim guidelines for exposure management and antimicrobial therapy. *MMWR Morb Mortal Wkly Rep.* 2001;50:909-919.
8. Inglesby TV, Henderson DA, Bartlett JG, et al, for the Working Group on Civilian Biodefense. Anthrax as a biological weapon: medical and public health management. *JAMA.* 1999;281:1735-1745.
9. Henderson DW, Peacock S, Belton FC. Observations on the prophylaxis of experimental pulmonary anthrax in the monkey. *J Hyg.* 1956;54:28-36.
10. Friedlander AM, Welkos SL, Pitt ML, et al. Postexposure prophylaxis against experimental inhalation anthrax. *J Infect Dis.* 1993;167:1239-1242.
11. Meselson M, Guillemin J, Hugh-Jones M, et al. The Sverdlovsk anthrax outbreak of 1979. *Science.* 1994;266:1202-1208.
12. Centers for Disease Control and Prevention. Investigation of anthrax associated with intentional exposure and interim public health guidelines. *MMWR Morb Mortal Wkly Rep.* 2001;50:889-893.
13. Dixon TC, Meselson M, Guillemin J, Hanna PC. Anthrax. *N Engl J Med.* 1999;341:815-826.
14. Little SF, Ivins BE. Molecular pathogenesis of Bacillus anthracis infection. *Microbes Infect.* 1999;1:131-139.
15. Brachman PS, Gold H, Plotkin SA, Fekety FR, Werrin M, Ingraham NR. Field evaluation of a human anthrax vaccine. *Am J Public Health.* 1962;56:632-645.

Clinical Presentation of Inhalational Anthrax Following Bioterrorism Exposure

Report of 2 Surviving Patients

Thom A. Mayer, MD; Susan Bersoff-Matcha, MD; Cecele Murphy, MD; James Earls, MD; Scott Harper, MD; Denis Pauze, MD; Michael Nguyen, MD; Jonathan Rosenthal, MD; Donald Cerva, Jr, MD; Glenn Druckenbrod, MD; Dan Hanfling, MD; Naaz Fatteh, MD; Ashna Nayyar, MS, PA-C; Elise L. Berman, MD

The use of anthrax as a weapon of biological terrorism has moved from theory to reality. This report describes the clinical presentation, diagnostic workup, and initial therapy of 2 patients with inhalational anthrax. The clinical course is in some ways different from what has been described as the classic pattern for inhalational anthrax. A high degree of clinical suspicion, coupled with abnormal findings on chest radiographs and non–contrast-enhanced computed tomography (CT) imaging of the chest led to a presumptive diagnosis of inhalational anthrax in both cases, later confirmed by blood cultures and polymerase chain reaction (PCR) testing. Timely intervention with antibiotic therapy, including ciprofloxacin, rifampin, and clindamycin, and supportive therapy appears to have slowed the progression of inhalational anthrax and has resulted to date in improved clinical outcome.

Until 2001, inhalational anthrax was a rare disease, with the last case in the United States reported in 1976. The potential use of anthrax as a bioterrorism agent has been described for more than 75 years, and nearly 20 countries are known to have investigated its use as a biological weapon.[1, 2] Current understanding of the clinical course and presentation of inhalational anthrax has been largely shaped by 3 sources: the unintentional anthrax exposure in Sverdlovsk in the former Soviet Union in 1979[3]; scattered outbreaks of the disease, usually among wool sorters or laboratory workers[4, 5]; and experimental animal models.[6, 7]

We diagnosed and treated documented inhalational anthrax in 2 patients in 2001 whose clinical symptoms, diagnostic workup, and clinical course suggest that some redefinition of the natural history of inhalational anthrax in its initial presentation is warranted, at least in the setting of a bioterrorism event.

Background

On October 15, 2001, a staff member of a US senator's office opened a tightly sealed envelope and noticed a "small burst of dust."[8] The following day, the letter was shown to contain *Bacillus anthracis* by PCR testing. While criminal and epidemiologic research indicated a discrete area of exposure at the US Capitol, postal workers outside this area were not known to be at risk.

Patient 1

On October 19, 2001, a 56-year-old male postal worker from the Brentwood facility in Washington, DC, presented to the emergency department. He had been well until 3 days prior to admission, when he developed low-grade fever, chills, cough, dyspnea on exertion, and generalized malaise. The cough was initially productive of clear sputum until the night of admission, when it became blood tinged. The dyspnea was progressive and accompanied on the day of admission by a feeling of midsternal, nonradiating, pleuritic chest tightness.

On review of systems, the patient noted myalgias, arthralgias, anorexia, and a sore throat. There was no congestion or other nasal symptoms. The patient had a childhood history of asthma but had been asymptomatic since adolescence. He denied any history of smoking tobacco. His primary duties at work involved distribution of express mail letters from the Brentwood and Baltimore-Washington-International Airport postal centers to government agencies, including the Senate office building.

The patient's initial vital signs were temperature of 37.5°C, pulse of 110/min, respirations of 18/min, blood pressure of 157/75 mm Hg, and oxygen saturation of 98% in room air. The physical examination revealed a thin but otherwise healthy patient in no apparent distress. The only abnormality on physical examination was a decrease in breath sounds in the left lower lung base, without dullness, percussion, or egophony. The white blood cell count was 7500/µL (segmented neutrophils, 76; bands, 8; lymphocytes, 7; monocytes, 7). Serum chemistry results were normal, with the exception of creatine kinase, which was 207 U/L, with a creatine kinase–MB fraction of 1 U/L. Arterial blood gas analysis showed pH of 7.45, $PaCO_2$ of 27 mm Hg, PaO_2 of 80.3 mm Hg, and oxygen saturation of 97% in room air.

A posterior-anterior and lateral chest radiograph depicted a minimally widened mediastinum (most notable in the right paratracheal region), bilateral hilar masses, a moderate right pleural effusion, a suggestion of a left subpulmonic effusion, and a slight right lower lobe air-space opacity (**Figure 1A**). A noncontrast spiral CT of the chest showed profuse and slightly hyperattenuating paratracheal, anterior-posterior window, subcarinal, hilar, and azygoesophageal recess adenopathy (**Figure 1B**). The largest lymph node was in the subcarinal region and measured 4.2 cm in maximal transverse diameter (upper limit of normal, 1.0-1.5 cm). In addition, there was evidence of diffuse infiltrating mediastinal edema, bilateral moderate-sized pleural effusions, bibasilar air-space disease, and thickened peribronchial tissue.

Figure 1. Imaging Characteristics of Patient 1

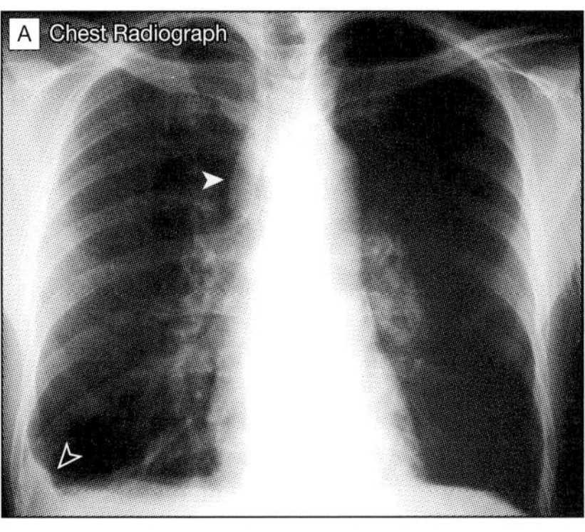

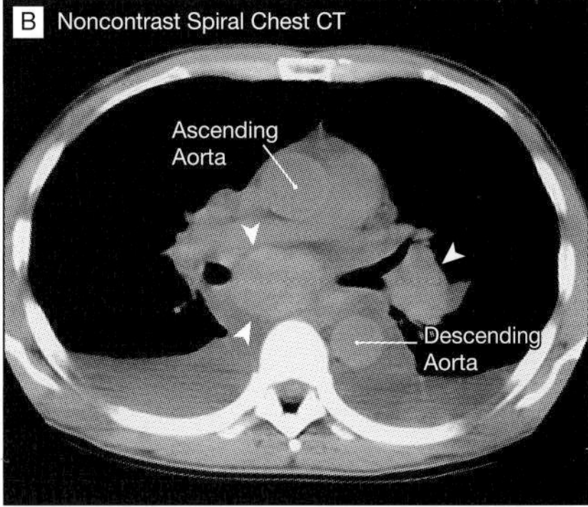

A, Chest radiograph depicts a minimally widened mediastinum (white arrowhead), bilateral hilar adenopathy, moderate right pleural effusion (black arrowhead), and a subtle left lower lobe air-space opacity. B, Large hyperdense lymph nodes (arrowheads) are depicted in the subcarinal space and left hilum on this noncontrast spiral computed tomography (CT) image. The density of the lymph nodes is equal to that of blood in the adjacent ascending and descending aorta. Bilateral pleural effusions and edema of the mediastinal fat are also present.

Figure 2. Gram Stain of Blood Culture at 11 Hours of Growth Showing Prominent Gram-Positive Rods, Later Confirmed as *Bacillus anthracis*

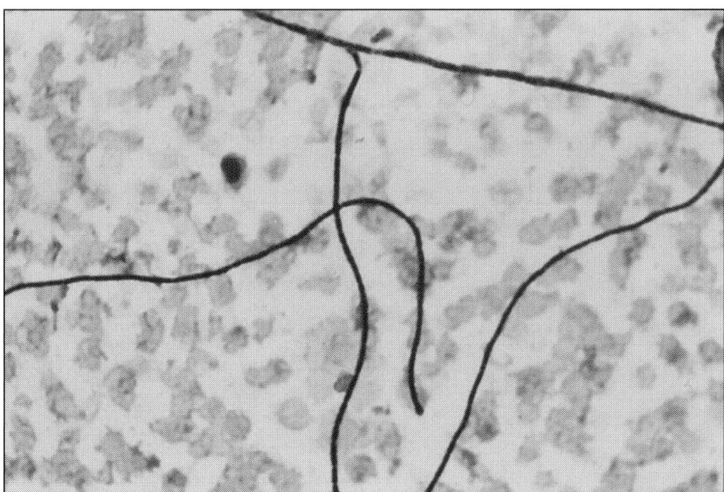

Original magnification ×40.

Blood cultures obtained at the time of admission showed prominent gram-positive rods on Gram stain at 11 hours, consistent with *B anthracis* (**Figure 2**). The patient was given parenteral ciprofloxicin, 400 mg every 8 hours; rifampin, 300 mg every

12 hours; and clindamycin, 900 mg every 8 hours. He was admitted to the hospital for further therapy, where he was in serious but stable condition on the 20th hospital day. *Bacillus anthracis* was confirmed as the etiologic organism at the Virginia State Health Laboratory and the Centers for Disease Control and Prevention (CDC) by PCR on October 21.

Patient 2

On October 20, 2001, a 56-year-old man who worked at the Brentwood post office in the mail sorting center presented to the emergency department with a progressively worsening headache of 3 days' duration, described as gradual in onset, global, and constant. He also complained of nausea, chills, and night sweats, but denied fevers, vomiting, photophobia, visual complaints, nuchal rigidity, slurred speech, or weakness. He had no respiratory complaints other than a mild sore throat, and the remainder of his review of systems was negative.

The patient's vital signs were temperature 37.6°C, pulse of 127/min, respirations of 20/min, blood pressure of 133/87 mm Hg, and oxygen saturation of 94% in room air. Physical examination revealed a well-developed man in no acute distress whose neurologic examination result was completely normal. The remainder of physical examination was notable only for diffuse rhonchi and decreased breath sounds in both lung bases.

His white blood cell count was 9700/μL with a normal differential, and the remainder of his laboratory studies yielded normal results. A noncontrast head CT image was normal. He underwent a lumbar puncture, which showed 20 red blood cells per high-power field, 4 white blood cells per high-power field, cerebrospinal fluid glucose level of 92 mg/dL (5.1 mmol/L), and no organisms on Gram stain. Culture and Gram stain of the cerebrospinal fluid were negative. Serum electrolytes were normal.

Anterior-posterior chest radiograph showed a widened mediastinum and low lung volumes, along with bilateral hilar masses, a right pleural effusion, and bilateral perihilar air-space disease (**Figure 3A**). A noncontrast spiral chest CT showed profuse and slightly hyperattenuating paratracheal, AP window, subcarinal, hilar, and azygoesophageal recess adenopathy, although to a lesser extent than in patient 1 (**Figure 3B**). Diffuse mediastinal edema, bilateral pleural effusions, bibasilar air-space disease, and thickened peribronchial tissue were noted.

Because of the markedly abnormal chest radiograph and CT scans, a presumptive diagnosis of inhalational anthrax was made and the patient was given parenteral ciprofloxacin, 400 mg every 8 hours; rifampin, 300 mg every 12 hours; and clindamycin, 900 mg every 8 hours. *Bacillus anthracis* grew from the blood at 15 hours and was confirmed by PCR by the Virginia Department of Health and the CDC. The patient remained stable on the 21st hospital day.

Comment

The medical literature on inhalational anthrax has stressed the rarity of this disease but has also emphasized several important features.[9-14] First, it has

Figure 3. Imaging Characteristics of Patient 2

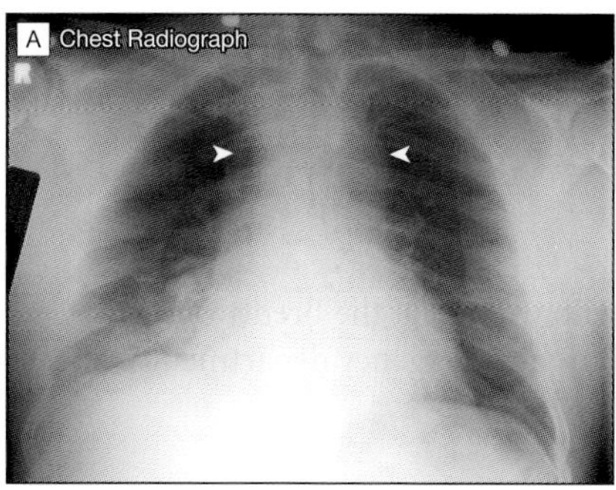

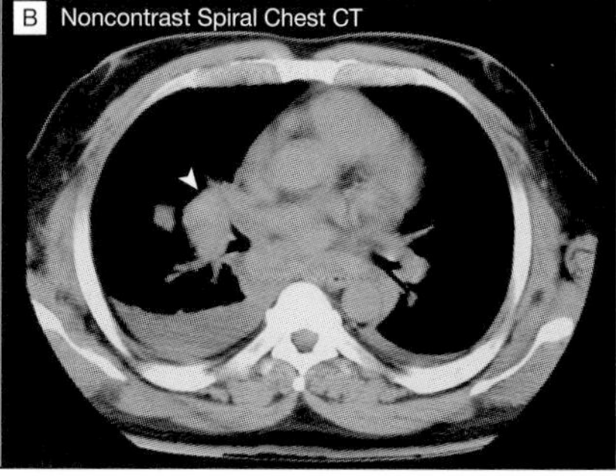

A, Portable chest radiograph depicts a widened mediastinum (arrowheads), bilateral hilar fullness, a right pleural effusion, and bilateral perihilar air-space disease. B, Noncontrast spiral computed tomography (CT) depicts an enlarged and hyperdense right hilar lymph node (arrowhead), bilateral pleural effusions, and edema of the mediastinal fat.

been emphasized that early diagnosis of inhalational anthrax is exceedingly difficult, particularly if there is not a clearly defined exposure known to the clinicians treating a patient. It has been suggested that syndromic surveillance could be an important component in raising clinical suspicion of the disease, since it has been presumed that identification of an increase in flulike syndromes leading to clinical deterioration and death would be a harbinger in identifying the disease.[10-13]

Second, the illness previously has been characterized as having a 2-stage clinical course, with early nonspecific respiratory symptoms followed in 24 to 72 hours by the abrupt onset of fever, dyspnea, profound respiratory distress, and shock, with death occurring in 80% to 90% of patients.[11-15] Third, radiographic findings of a widened or abnormal mediastinum in previously healthy patients with flulike symptoms have been considered pathognomonic of inhalational anthrax.[9, 11-15] However, these radiographic signs have been described as a relatively late finding associated with a poor prognosis.[9, 11, 12] The 1999 consensus statement from the Working Group on Civilian Biodefense indicated that "treatment at this stage would be unlikely to alter the outcome of the illness."[9]

These features of the disease are derived not only from previous cases of inhalational anthrax but also because of what is known of the pathophysiology of the disease. Inhalational anthrax occurs following deposition of a sufficient number of spores into the alveolar space. These 1- to 5-μm spores are then ingested by macrophages, which are transported by the lymphatic system to the mediastinal lymph nodes. Germination of the spore into the *B anthracis* organism typically occurs within 1 to 3 days, but may occur as long as 60 days following transport to the lymph nodes.[3, 14] Once the bacteria replicate, anthrax toxin is released, comprising 3 proteins: protective antigen, lethal factor, and edema factor. Lethal factor and protective antigen bind to form lethal toxin, which is the predominant virulence factor of the disease. Once production of lethal toxin has occurred, apoptosis and hemorrhagic necrosis of the mediastinal lymph nodes occur rapidly, producing a clinical cascade of hemorrhagic mediastinitis and edema. When hemorrhagic necrosis extends to the pleura, bloody pleural effusions occur. Hematogenous spread of the bacteria and the toxin results in systemic disease, with profound shock, dyspnea, respiratory distress, and, in the majority of cases, death.[11-15]

The 2 cases we report add to what is known about the natural history of inhalational anthrax and the initial presentation of the disease. Neither of the cases were known at the time of clinical presentation to have been exposed to anthrax or to be at high risk of the disease. In both cases, the treating physicians had a high clinical index of suspicion regarding the disease, based partly on the known *B anthracis* exposures in the Senate office building, although the association of the disease with postal workers was not clearly known at the time the first patient presented to the emergency department. Both patients had an increased pulse rate, elevated out of proportion to either symptoms or fever, and an abnormal chest radiograph with bilateral pleural effusions and mediastinal lymphadenopathy. The second patient presented with a different clinical picture, with severe headache, low-grade fever, night sweats, and nausea. The chest radiograph showed a right pleural effusion and a widened mediastinum; these findings were considered highly suggestive of inhalational anthrax and led to obtaining the chest CT image, which further confirmed the clinical suspicion of the disease.

Both patients were treated with ciprofloxacin, rifampin, and clindamycin and did not develop the classic findings of high-grade fever, dyspnea, profound respiratory distress, and shock. Ciprofloxacin was chosen because of its presumed effect on patients with inhalational anthrax, as evidenced by the fact that it is recommended as first-line therapy for treatment of inhalational anthrax.[8] Rifampin was used to provide additional gram-positive coverage and because of its primarily intracellular mechanism of action.[16] Clindamycin was added because of its ability to prevent expression of toxin in patients with streptococcal disease.[17] This activity was believed to be of theoretical advantage in anthrax, in which toxin production is a major cause of morbidity and mortality.

These reports suggest that early diagnosis and treatment may improve the prognosis of inhalational anthrax. Both patients had substantial mediastinal pathologic findings at the time of their clinical presentation, yet aggressive therapy resulted in a good clinical outcome at this stage of their illness. Other possibilities are that these patients were exposed to a lower, sublethal dose of spores or that the strain of *B anthracis* was of a lower virulence than previously reported. However, the presence of substantial mediastinal lymphadenopathy and pleural effusions indicate a substantial degree of disease at the time of initial presentation. This suggests that early diagnosis and intervention interrupted what has primarily been described as a 2-stage cycle of the disease, in which mediastinal necrosis and hemorrhage progress to widespread toxin release and death, with reported mortality rates of 80% to 90%.[9-14]

Reports of the radiographic findings of inhalational anthrax before 2001 were limited to descriptions of chest radiographs in a small number of cases.[12, 18, 19] As the cases presented here illustrate, prior publications have reported widened mediastinum, adenopathy, pleural effusions, and parenchymal infiltrates. While these findings may make a dramatic presentation, there is nothing specific about this constellation of radiographic findings that would, by itself, lead to a diagnosis of inhalational anthrax. Nonetheless, the presence of pleural effusions in the presence of a clinical history of potential exposure should raise suspicion of inhalational anthrax.

We found chest CT studies to be substantially useful. Prior to this report, there were no published reports of the CT findings of inhalational anthrax, and there were no cases of inhalational anthrax with correlative CT imaging accessioned at the Armed Forces Institute of Pathology in Washington, DC (Jeffrey R. Galvin, MD, Armed Forces Institute of Pathology, Washington DC, written communication, October 23, 2001). Both of the cases reported herein had an unusual combination of findings that may prove to be helpful in diagnosing inhalational anthrax, namely, the presence of hyperdense enlarged mediastinal adenopathy and diffuse mediastinal edema. Although pathological correlation was not obtained in these cases, the hyperdensity in the lymph nodes is likely due to the presence of localized hemorrhage, which is known to be present based on prior reports.[20, 21] To optimally depict the presence of hyperdense adenopathy, noncontrast CT images may be more useful than contrast-enhanced images. Each patient presented with abnormal findings on chest radiographs, but CT of the chest showed much more dramatic evidence of mediastinal lymph node enlargement, suggesting that the chest radiograph substantially understates the degree of disease compared with chest CT.

At our institution, symptomatic patients with known or suspected exposure to anthrax spores receive a chest radiograph. If pleural effusion, mediastinal lymphadenopathy, or mediastinal widening is found, a non–contrast-enhanced CT study of the chest is obtained. For patients with normal chest radiographs but who have a substantial clinical suspicion of inhalational anthrax, chest CT also is obtained because this study may reveal important clinical information in such cases.

Our experience with 2 patients with inhalational anthrax resulting from a bioterrorism event suggests that a high degree of clinical suspicion, diagnostic workup including chest CT, and early intervention with appropriate antibiotics may reduce the previously reported mortality of 80% to 90% in inhalational anthrax.[9, 11-15] Although it is unfortunate that inhalational anthrax has reemerged as a distinct clinical entity rather than a theoretical bioterrorism agent, it is extremely important that clinicians be aware of this clinical presentation and be prepared to evaluate and appropriately treat such patients. Unfortunately, only further experience with this devastating disease can clarify its precise natural history and optimal treatment.

Acknowledgments: We are grateful to the 2 patients who graciously provided permission to publish this information for the medical community.

References

1. Christopher GW, Cieslak TJ, Pavlin JA, Eitzen EM. Biological warfare: a historical perspective. *JAMA.* 1997;278:412-417.

2. Brownlee S. Clear and present danger. *Washington Post Magazine.* October 28, 2001.

3. Meselson M, Guillemin J, Hugh-Jones M, et al. The Sverdlovsk anthrax outbreak of 1979. *Science.* 1994;266:1202-1208.

4. Brachman PS. Inhalational anthrax. *Ann N Y Acad Sci.* 1980;353:83-93.

5. Brachman PS, Kaufman AF, Dalldorf FG. Industrial inhalational anthrax. *Bacteriol Rev.* 1966;30: 646-659.

6. Fritz DL, Jaax NK, Lawrence WB, et al. Pathology of experimental inhalation anthrax in the rhesus monkey. *Lab Invest.* 1995;73:691-702.

7. Gleiser CA, Berdjis CC, Hartman HA, Gochenour WS. Pathology of experimental respiratory anthrax in macaca mulatta. *Br J Exp Pathol.* 1963;44: 416-426.

8. Centers for Disease Control and Prevention. Investigation of bioterrorism-related anthrax and interim guidelines for exposure management and antimicrobial therapy. *MMWR Morb Mortal Wkly Rep.* 2001;50:909-919.

9. Inglesby TV, Henderson DA, Bartlett JG, et al, for the Working Group on Civilian Biodefense. Anthrax as a biological weapon: medical and public health management. *JAMA.* 1999;281:1735-1745.

10. Centers for Disease Control and Prevention. Bioterrorism alleging use of anthrax and interim guidelines for management. *MMWR Morb Mortal Wkly Rep.* 1999;48:69-74.

11. Pile JC, Malone JD, Eitzen EM, Friedlander AM. Anthrax as a potential biological warfare agent. *Arch Intern Med.* 1998;158:429-434.

12. Shafazand S, Doyle R, Ruoss S, et al. Inhalational anthrax: epidemiology, diagnosis, and management. *Chest.* 1999;116:1369-1376.

13. Dixon TC, Meselson M, Guillemin J, Hanna PC. Anthrax. *N Engl J Med.* 1999;341:815-826.

14. Lew DP. Bacillus anthracis (anthrax). In: Mandell GL, Bennett JE, Dolin R, eds. *Principles and Practice of Infectious Diseases.* 5th ed. Philadelphia, Pa: Churchill Livingstone; 2000:2215-2220.

15. Franz DR, Jahrling PB, Friedlander A, et al. Clinical recognition and management of patients exposed to biological warfare agents. *JAMA.* 1997;278: 399-411.

16. Farr BM. Rifamycins. In: Mandell GL, Bennett JE, Dolin R, eds. *Principles and Practice of Infectious Diseases.* 5th ed. Philadelphia, Pa: Churchill Livingstone; 2000:348-356.

17. Jriskandan S, McKee A, Hall L, et al. Comparative effects of clindamycin and ampicillin on superantigenic activity of Streptococcus pyogenes. *J Antimicrob Chemother.* 1997;40:275-277.

18. Abramova FA, Grinberg LM, Yampolskaya OV, Walker DH. Pathology of inhalational anthrax in 42 cases from the Sverdlovsk outbreak of 1979. *Proc Natl Acad Sci U S A.* 1993;90:2291-2294.

19. Vessal K, Yeganehdoust J, Dutz W, Kohout E. Radiological changes in inhalation anthrax. a report of radiological and pathological correlation in two cases. *Clin Radiol.* 1975;26:471-474.

20. Fritz DL, Jaax NK, Lawrence WB, et al. Pathology of experimental inhalation anthrax in the rhesus monkey. *Lab Invest.* 1995;73:691-702.

21. Grinberg LM, Abramova FA, Yampolskaya OV, Walker DH, Smith JH. Quantitative pathology of inhalational anthrax, I: quantitative microscopic findings. *Mod Pathol.* 2001;14:482-495.

Death Due to Bioterrorism-Related Inhalational Anthrax

Report of 2 Patients

Luciana Borio, MD; Dennis Frank, MD; Venkat Mani, MD; Carlos Chiriboga, MD; Michael Pollanen, MD, PhD; Mary Ripple, MD; Syed Ali, MD; Constance DiAngelo, MD, MS; Jacqueline Lee, MD; Jonathan Arden, MD; Jack Titus, MD; David Fowler, MD; Tara O'Toole, MD, MPH; Henry Masur, MD; John G. Bartlett, MD; Thomas V. Inglesby, MD

On October 9, 2001, a letter containing anthrax spores was mailed to a US senator's office in Washington, DC.[1] That letter was processed at the Brentwood postal facility, one of the largest in the Washington, DC, metropolitan area, and eventually opened by the senator's staff 6 days later. As of October 30, 2001, 5 postal workers who worked at or handled bulk mail from that facility had been hospitalized with confirmed inhalational anthrax. Two of them died shortly after admission to area hospitals. These 2 fatal cases are reported here to educate clinicians about the clinical presentation and course of illness of inhalational anthrax following exposure to anthrax spores.

Patient 1

On October 16 (day 1), a 47-year-old male postal worker who worked in the mail sorting area of the Brentwood facility developed nausea, abdominal pain, and "flulike" symptoms. He attributed his symptoms to "food poisoning" and continued to work despite ongoing symptoms. On October 20 (day 5), while in church, he had a brief, self-limited syncopal episode. By the time paramedics arrived, he felt better. He went home, did not eat, and immediately went to bed, unlike his usual routine. He reported to work that evening and on October 21 (day 6), at 2 AM, he developed worsening nausea, vomiting, abdominal pain, and profuse sweating and drove to an emergency department. On arrival, he also complained of lightheadedness and diaphoresis and denied dyspnea and chest pain. He had no significant medical history. His only chronic medical problem was asthma, and salmeterol was his only medication.

The patient's temperature was 36.1°C, blood pressure was 82/59 mm Hg, pulse was 95/min, respirations were 18/min, and oxygen saturation was 99% in room air. Physical examination was unremarkable. Laboratory data revealed mild leukocytosis and hemoconcentration. Chest radiograph (**Figure 1A**) showed a subtle and ill-defined area of increased density in the right subhilar region; follow-up with computed tomography (CT) was suggested. After treatment with intravenous fluids, promethazine, and famotidine, his symptoms resolved. At 4 AM, vital signs were as follows: temperature, 36.6°C; blood pressure, 109/68 mm Hg; pulse, 86/min; and respirations, 20/min. He was discharged to home at approximately 5 AM with a presumptive diagnosis of gastroenteritis and instructions to see his primary care physician the following day.

Throughout the day of October 21 (day 6), the patient's gastrointestinal symptoms progressed and he developed dyspnea and diaphoresis. On October 22 (day 7) at 4:45 AM, his wife found him slumped in the bathroom. He was taken to a hospital by ambulance. On arrival, he reported nausea, vomiting, and lightheadedness and denied dyspnea or chest pain but was ill-appearing and in respiratory distress. Temperature was 35.5°C, blood pressure was 76/46 mm Hg, pulse was 152/min, respirations were 28/min, and oxygen saturation was 96% in room air. Physical examination revealed regular tachycardia, decreased breath sounds at the lung bases, diffuse wheezes and rhonchi, mild abdominal tenderness, and mottled and cool skin.

Figure 1. Chest Radiographs for Patient 1

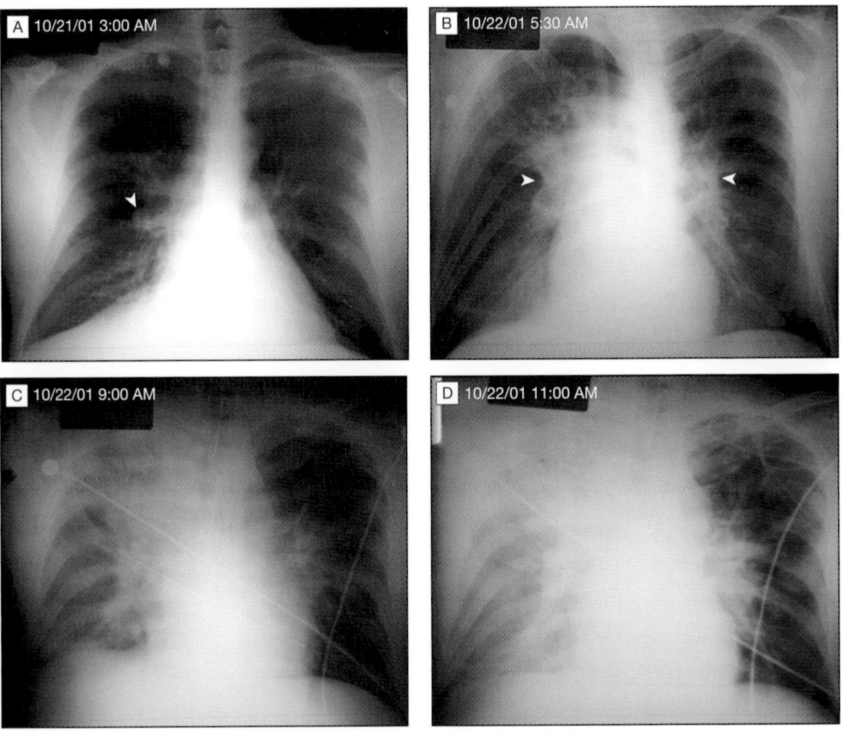

A, Initially, only subtle bilateral hilar prominence (arrowhead) and right perihilar infiltrate was noted, but subsequent images (B-D) revealed a progressively widened mediastinum (B, arrowheads) and marked perihilar infiltrates, peribronchial cuffing, and air bronchograms.

A working diagnosis of inhalational anthrax was made because of reports in the news media that 2 postal workers had been hospitalized in the Washington, DC, metropolitan area with inhalational anthrax.[2] Laboratory data (**Table 1**) showed leukocytosis, hemoconcentration, azotemia, and an elevated amylase level. Chest radiographs (**Figure 1B, C, and D**) revealed progressive pulmonary infiltrates and, compared with the radiograph of October 21, new pleural effusions and a widened mediastinum. A Gram stain of the admission peripheral blood buffy coat revealed numerous large, gram-positive bacilli (**Figure 2**). At that time, a Gram stain was requested on blood that had been incubated for 1 hour in BD Bactec (BD, Sparks, Md) culture media. The long chains of gram-positive bacilli (**Figure 3A**) and the "jointed bamboo-rod" appearance (**Figure 3B**) were considered typical of *Bacillus anthracis*. Anthrax was confirmed by the Centers for Disease Control and Prevention (CDC) in the following days[3] (the CDC confirms *B anthracis* in culture when 2 tests are positive: polymerase chain reaction and gamma phage lysis).

Table 1. Laboratory Findings*

	Patient 1			Patient 2	
	10/21/01 2:35 AM	10/22/01 8:31 AM	10/22/01 11:47 AM	10/21/01 6:40 AM	10/22/01 2:00 PM
White blood cells, /μL	13 300	31 200	47 000	18 800	. . .
Neutrophils, %	78.3	78	. . .	79.8	. . .
Hematocrit, %	51.4	62	42.4	55.3	. . .
Platelets, /μL	207 000	250 000	223 000	141 000	. . .
Sodium, mEq/L	139	148	150	130	137
Potassium, mEq/L	4.7	4.8	4.1	5.3	4.8
Chloride, mEq/L	106	109	122	99	108
Bicarbonate, mEq/L	22	18	12	14	12
Serum urea nitrogen, mg/dL	20	52	44	22	42
Creatinine, mg/dL	1.2	2.8	1.9	1.6	2.4
Glucose, mg/dL	124	. . .	163	425	531
Calcium, mg/dL	7.9	8.5	4.4	8.5	7.8

continued

Table 1. ***Continued***

	Patient 1			Patient 2	
Magnesium, mg/dL	2.1	. . .	1.3	. . .	2.5
Arterial blood gases					
Fraction of inspired oxygen	. . .	1.0	. . .	2L, NC	100%, mask
pH	. . .	7.13	. . .	7.42	7.40
Pco2, mm Hg	. . .	36	. . .	25	24
Po2, mm Hg	. . .	150	. . .	66	71
Oxygen saturation, %	. . .	. . .	. . .	93	100
Creatine phosphokinase U/L	115	. . .	51	107	. . .
Creatine kinase, U/L	. . .	. . .	. . .	1.3	. . .
Troponin I, ng/mL	0	. . .	0.2	<0.3	0.6
Prothrombin time, s	12.3	. . .	22.1	. . .	13.2
Partial thromboplastin time, s	27.1	. . .	96	. . .	27.9
Total protein, g/dL	. . .	4.5	. . .	6.8	. . .
Albumin, g/dL	3.6	2.9	. . .	3.1	. . .
Alkaline phosphatase, U/L	119	197	. . .	116	. . .
Total bilirubin, mg/dL	0.4	0.2	. . .	0.9	. . .
Aspartate aminotrans-ferase, U/L	39	47	. . .	76	. . .
Alanine aminotrans-ferase, U/L	44	33	. . .	77	. . .
Amylase, U/L	. . .	318	. . .	. . .	. . .

*To convert creatinine from mg/dL to μmol/L, multiply by 88.4. To convert glucose from mg/dL to mmol/L, multiply by 0.05551. To convert calcium from mg/dL to mmol/L, multiply by 0.25. To convert magnesium from mg/dL to mmol/L, multiply by 0.4114. To convert bilirubin from mg/dL to μmol/L, multiply by 17.1. Ellipses indicate test not done; NC, nasal cannula.

Figure 2. Gram Stain of Peripheral Blood Buffy Coat for Patient 1

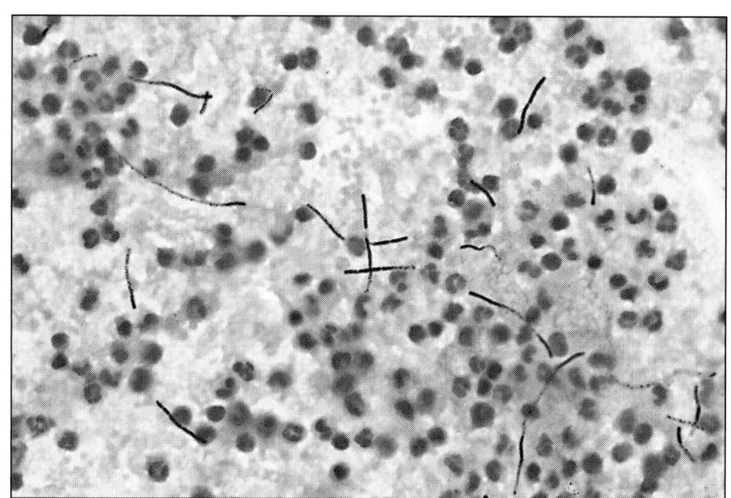

Gram-positive bacilli in short chains (original magnification ×40).

Figure 3. Gram Stain of Blood in Culture Media for Patient 1

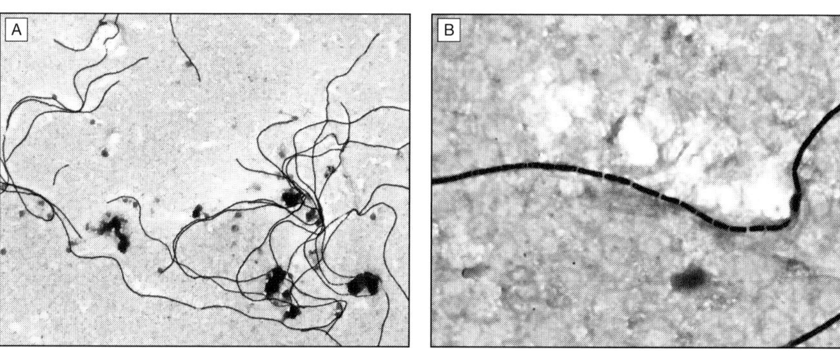

A, Gram-positive bacilli in long chains (original magnification ×20). B, Enlargement showing typical "jointed bamboo-rod" appearance of *Bacillus anthracis* (original magnification ×100).

Despite prompt initiation of therapy with one 500-mg dose of parenteral levofloxacin; penicillin G, 3 million U every 4 hours; one 2-g dose of ceftriaxone; and one 600-mg dose of rifampin, the patient developed progressive hypoxemic respiratory failure and marked hypotension. Mechanical ventilation and vasopressor therapy was instituted. Gram stain of an endotracheal aspirate showed few white blood cells and rare large gram-positive bacilli. A cotton swab from the nose was obtained for culture at admission, plated on sheep blood agar, and read at 24 hours, and was negative for *B anthracis*. The patient developed abdominal

Figure 4. Abdominal and Chest Computed Tomography (CT) Images for Patient 1

A Abdominal CT With Intravenous Contrast

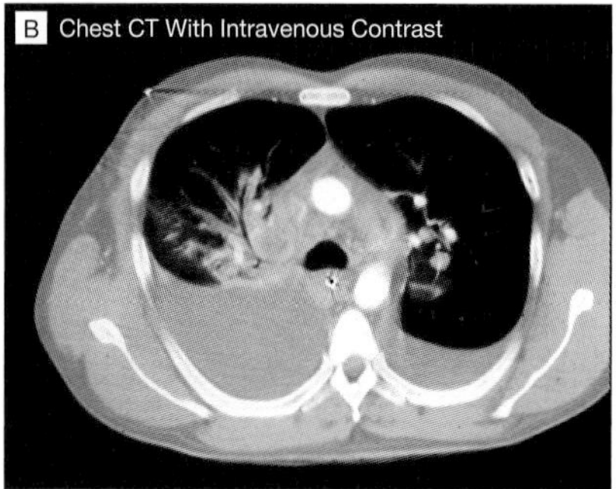

A, Abdominal CT scan with intravenous contrast showing moderate amount of ascites, small-bowel wall edema, and intramural pneumatosis (arrowheads), consistent with a necrotizing enteritis. Other CT windows showed air within the hepatic branches of the portal venous system. B, Chest CT scan with intravenous contrast showing large bilateral perihilar infiltrates, perihilar lymphadenopathy, and widened mediastinum. Other CT windows showed high-attenuation mediastinal lymphadenopathy and blood in the mediastinum, consistent with hemorrhagic lymphadenopathy and hemorrhagic mediastinitis.

distention; a CT scan with intravenous contrast revealed moderate ascites and small-bowel intramural pneumatosis (**Figure 4A**). A chest CT image revealed parenchymal infiltrates, pleural effusions, and a widened mediastinum (**Figure 4B**). On October 22 (day 7), 5 hours after admission, the patient developed ventricular tachycardia followed by refractory bradycardia and asystole and died despite attempts at cardiac resuscitation.

At autopsy, there were multifocal hemorrhagic foci in the mediastinum with extension along hilar and parenchymal bronchi and blood vessels. There was hilar lymphadenopathy (2.5 cm) and hemorrhagic necrotizing hilar lymphadenitis; microscopic examination showed effacement of the nodal architecture, acute hemorrhagic necrosis, abundant karyorrhectic debris, and infiltration of polymorphonuclear leukocytes. Brown and Brenn stain of the hilar soft tissue and lymph nodes showed abundant gram-positive bacilli. There was no gross or microscopic evidence of pneumonia but there were large serous pleural effusions bilaterally (right, 250 cc; left, 500 cc).

There was a large amount of ascites (2500 cc). The small bowel was edematous and multifocal mesenteric soft tissue hemorrhage was present. A portion of the ileum showed hemorrhage and necrotizing infection without visible mucosal ulceration. Microscopic examination of the involved section of the ileum showed serosal and submucosal acute and chronic inflammation extending into the lamina propria. Brown and Brenn stain of the ileum showed abundant gram-positive bacilli. The mesenteric lymph nodes, terminal ileum, and large bowel were grossly unremarkable. Brain and cerebrospinal fluid were not examined. The cause of death was certified as inhalational anthrax. The manner of death was certified as homicide.

Patient 2

On October 17 (day 1), a 55-year-old male postal worker who worked as a distribution clerk in the mail sorting area of the Brentwood facility and who had hypertension, diabetes mellitus, and remote history of sarcoidosis sought outpatient medical attention for myalgias, weakness, and fever of 1 day's duration. He was diagnosed as having a viral syndrome and sent home. His symptoms persisted. On October 21 (day 5) at 6 AM, he presented to an emergency department (of a different hospital than that of patient 1) complaining of severe dyspnea, myalgias, weakness, retrosternal chest pressure, high fever, chills, nausea, vomiting, and a cough productive of scant greenish sputum.

On initial physical examination, the patient was alert, well-appearing, and in no acute respiratory distress. Temperature was 38.9°C, blood pressure was 119/73 mm Hg, pulse was 150/min, respirations were 20/min, and oxygen saturation was 94% in room air. The remainder of the examination was notable for rales and decreased breath sounds at the right lung base and an irregular tachycardia. Electrocardiogram showed atrial fibrillation.

Laboratory data (see Table 1) revealed marked leukocytosis, profound hemoconcentration, metabolic acidosis, hyperglycemia, azotemia, and hypoxemia. The admission chest radiograph is shown in **Figure 5A**.

Because the health care staff were aware through news media reports that 2 postal workers had been hospitalized in the local metropolitan area with inhalational anthrax, the patient was admitted with a diagnosis of suspected inhalational anthrax. He was given prompt treatment with one 500-mg dose of parenteral levofloxacin. Within 13 hours of admission, he developed marked hypotension requiring institution of vasopressors and progressive hypoxemic respiratory failure requiring endotracheal intubation. Shortly thereafter, he developed

Figure 5. Chest Radiograph and Gram Stain of Blood in Culture Media for Patient 2

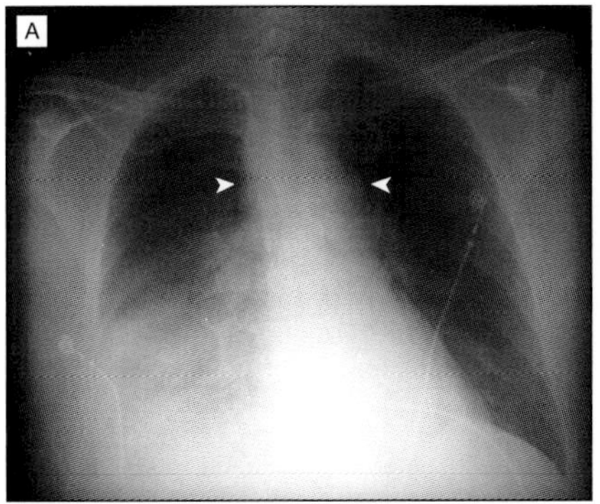

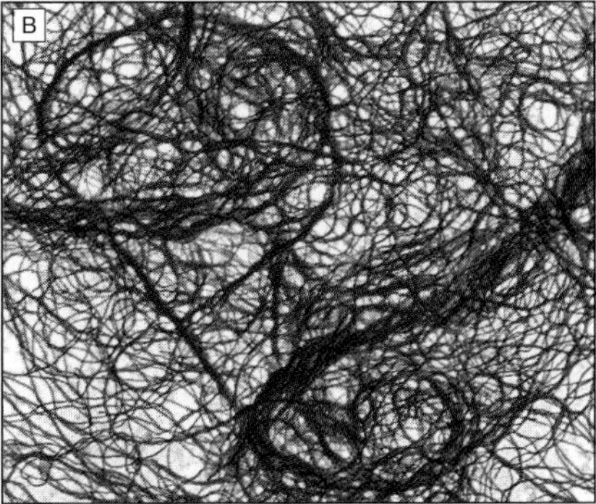

A, Chest radiograph shows widened mediastinum (arrowheads) with mediastinal and hilar lymphadenopathy, air-space disease of the right middle and lower lobes, and bilateral pleural effusions. B, Gram stain of blood in culture media shows very long chains of gram-positive bacilli (original magnification × 20).

bradycardia and asystole and died despite attempts at cardiac resuscitation. The case was reported to the medical examiner.

A Gram stain of blood incubated in BD Bactec culture media (**Figure 5B**) was recognized to have gram-positive rods the next morning, 24 hours after the patient's admission. The CDC subsequently confirmed the organism to be *B anthracis*.[3]

At autopsy, there was marked acute hemorrhagic mediastinitis, hemorrhagic necrotizing lymphadenitis of the hilar and mediastinal lymph nodes (3-5 cm in diameter), and bilateral serosanguinous pleural effusion (right, 1300 cm^3; left, 700 cm^3). Bilateral acute subpleural hemorrhage was present at the hilum of both lungs with extension along the adventitia of the intraparenchymal branches of the pulmonary arteries. Microscopic examination of the lymph nodes revealed effacement of the nodal architecture, acute hemorrhagic necrosis, infiltration by polymorphonuclear leukocytes, and numerous bacilli. There was no evidence of pneumonia or meningitis. The cause of death was certified as inhalational anthrax. The manner of death was certified as homicide.

Comment

Inhalational anthrax presents with nonspecific symptoms that cannot be distinguished from many more common diseases based on early clinical manifestations or routine laboratory tests. Both patients in this report sought medical care for apparently mild, nonspecific illnesses and were sent home. Only after the news media reported cases of inhalational anthrax involving 2 postal workers from the local mail facility did these patients' physicians consider the possibility that they could have inhalational anthrax. At that point, the patients had been ill for 7 days (patient 1) and 5 days (patient 2). The courses of their illness are similar to that reported in an outbreak of anthrax that occurred in Sverdlovsk in 1979.[4] Despite aggressive medical therapy, both patients developed rapidly progressive disease and died.

These patients received antimicrobial therapy at the discretion of their physicians, before the CDC released formal guidelines on October 26, 2001.[3] These guidelines recommend combination therapy for inhalational anthrax and complicated cutaneous anthrax. Ciprofloxacin or doxycycline are recommended in conjunction with another active antimicrobial drug, such as rifampin or clindamycin. Even though all isolates tested were susceptible to penicillin, ß-lactamases were identified in these isolates, and penicillin monotherapy for treatment of systemic infection is not recommended. Susceptibility testing also revealed intermediate sensitivity to ceftriaxone and presence of a cephalosporinase. Cephalosporins, therefore, are not indicated for the treatment of *B anthracis* infection.

These 2 cases emphasize that in the event of serious outbreaks of infectious diseases, such as those that occurred following the handling of anthrax-containing letters at the Brentwood postal facility, rapid communication of epidemiologic data to frontline medical care providers (especially emergency physicians and primary care clinicians) is essential so they may initiate appropriate diagnostic procedures and therapies. Efforts should be made to enhance communications systems between public health agencies and clinicians.[5]

A presumptive diagnosis of *B anthracis* can be made readily by most microbiology laboratories. The organism grows readily, can be safely evaluated in a biosafety level 2 facility, has characteristic Gram stain morphology, and should be suspected anytime a nonmotile, nonhemolytic gram-positive rod is identified in the setting of a compatible clinical syndrome. Communicating presumptive diagnostic information throughout the public health and clinical community must be a priority. Nasal swab cultures cannot reliably rule out exposure to *B anthracis*, as stated by the CDC[3] and exemplified by patient 1, who, despite severe clinical disease, had a negative nasal swab culture. Whether the culture would have been positive if a Dacron swab had been used, if a more rigorous culturing technique was used, or if a deeper site had been sampled is unknown.

These 2 case reports also emphasize the importance of having microbiology laboratory capacity to more conclusively identify anthrax and other diseases that may be caused by bioterrorism in the clinical settings where these diseases will present. Rapid diagnostic tests to distinguish early anthrax infection from other diseases of similar clinical appearance should be a high priority on a national research agenda to respond to the threat of bioterrorism. There are distressingly few health care facilities that can provide comprehensive diagnostic services and expert consultative support.

The clinical presentations of these 2 patients provide key information about the clinical presentations and clinical courses of these homicides. Clinicians throughout the country in the full range of health science disciplines must rapidly increase their knowledge about agents of bioterrorism and work collaboratively with governmental, academic, and private organizations to ensure that their communities have the resources and expertise necessary to manage these assaults expeditiously and efficiently.

Acknowledgments: We thank the following for their invaluable assistance in preparing the manuscript: David Reagan, MD, Greater Southeast Community Hospital, Washington, DC; Mridula Singh, MD, Bryan DeFranco, MD, and Karen Rexroth, Southern Maryland Hospital Center, Clinton, Md; Dan Lucey, MD, Washington Hospital Center, Washington, DC; Constance DiAngelo, MD, MS, Jacqueline Lee, MD, Jonathan Arden, MD, and their technical staff, Office of the Chief Medical Examiner for the District of Columbia, Washington, DC; and Anthony Suffredini, MD, Brad Wood, MD, and Jennifer Candotti, National Institutes of Health, Bethesda, Md.

We are grateful to the families of these 2 patients for providing permission to publish this important information for the medical community.

References

1. Revkin AC. The odyssey of an anthrax-tainted envelope and a trail of death. *New York Times.* October 31, 2001:B8.

2. CNN. Anthrax: new case of inhalation. October 22, 2001. Available at: http://www.cnn.com/2001/US/10/21/anx.anthrax.facts/ index.html. Accessed November 6, 2001.

3. Centers for Disease Control and Prevention. Investigation of bioterrorism-related anthrax and interim guidelines for exposure management and antimicrobial therapy. *MMWR Morb Mortal Wkly Rep.* 2001;50:909-919.

4. Grinberg LM, Abramova FA, Yampolskaya OV, Walker DH, Smith JH. Quantitative pathology of inhalational anthrax, I: quantitative microscopic findings. *Mod Pathol.* 2001;14:482-495.

5. Inglesby TV, Henderson DA, Bartlett JG, et al, for the Working Group on Civilian Biodefense. Anthrax as a biological weapon: medical and public health management. *JAMA.* 1999;281:1735-1745.

Bioterrorism Preparedness and Response

Clinicians and Public Health Agencies as Essential Partners

Julie L. Gerberding, MD, MPH; James M. Hughes, MD; Jeffrey P. Koplan, MD, MPH

Beginning in mid-September 2001, the United States experienced unprecedented biological attacks involving the intentional distribution of *Bacillus anthracis* spores through the postal system.[1] The full impact of this bioterrorist activity has not been assessed, but already the toll is large. A total of 22 persons developed anthrax and 5 died as a direct result.[2-5] More than 10 000 persons were advised to take postexposure prophylactic treatment because they were at known or potential risk for inhalational anthrax; in addition, more than 20 000 others started such treatment until the investigation provided reassurance that exposure was unlikely and treatment could be stopped; thousands more were affected by hoaxes or false alarms, and still more were worried coworkers, friends, and family members of those directly affected.[6] The impact was not limited to the United States. Hoaxes involving threatening letters or powder-containing envelopes were reported from several countries; mail cross-contaminated with *B anthracis* was distributed to some US embassies, and persons in remote corners of the world were advised to take prophylactic antimicrobial treatment.

Three patients who acquired anthrax as a consequence of these attacks are described in detail in the 3 chapters that follow.[7-9] They are unique from the other patients infected with anthrax during the attacks of 2001 in that their infection cannot be directly linked to an occupational exposure. At the time they first sought medical attention, none could provide a history suggestive of exposure to *B anthracis*, and other causes were considered more likely to explain their illnesses. In retrospect, the source of the infant's exposure was inferred when anthrax spores were found in his mother's workplace. (See "Cutaneous Anthrax Associated With Microangiopathic Hemolytic Anemia and Coagulopathy in a 7-Month-Old Infant" later in this book.) For the other 2 patients, exposure to cross-contaminated mail remains a plausible but unproven hypothesis. Despite intensive investigations, the sources of their infections may never be known. These stories teach the important lesson that anyone—active elderly persons, healthy infants, and hard-working private citizens—could be infected during a bioterrorist event. Hence, the safety of all persons, regardless of age, health status, location, or occupation, must be addressed in bioterrorism preparedness and response programs.

From the public health perspective, recognition and response to the bioterrorist attacks of 2001 have evolved in a series of overlapping phases at each location. The initial phase involved detection and then confirmation of a case of anthrax or a powder-containing envelope, followed by rapid deployment of public health and law enforcement personnel and other needed resources to the site. The second phase has been characterized by full-scale investigations as well as interventions to prevent additional cases. Longer-term consequence management, including follow-up of affected individuals and remediation of contaminated sites that could pose an occupational health risk, are major follow-up activities. In all these phases, clinicians have proven to be essential partners, which is a lesson that must be incorporated into future bioterrorism preparedness and response efforts and professional education programs.

In most situations, alert clinicians actually initiated the first phase of the response by obtaining the appropriate laboratory tests, recognizing that a patient might have anthrax, and notifying health officials. Emergency physicians, outpatient primary care physicians and other practitioners, dermatologists, and pediatricians participated in the early recognition of infected patients, illustrating their critical role in surveillance for bioterrorism. Radiologists, infectious diseases specialists, pulmonologists, surgeons, hospitalists, critical care specialists, laboratorians, pathologists, and many other specialists also contributed to the diagnosis and management. Together, these clinicians have created a remarkably effective detection system for identifying and reporting cases. Their collective efforts provided an early warning to public health and law enforcement agencies that signaled the need for large-scale interventions to protect thousands of others at risk.

For this frontline surveillance system to function at its best, all clinicians, regardless of their specialty, must have enough basic information about the clinical manifestations of infections caused by the select agents of bioterrorism to raise their suspicion when they see a patient with a compatible illness. In addition, clinicians must know how to diagnose these conditions and when and how to report their suspicion to local public health and law enforcement officials. In the 2001 response scenario, obtaining an accurate occupational history was vital in assessing anthrax risk; all clinicians need this skill to be prepared for similar scenarios in the future.

Enhancing the knowledge and skills of clinicians is not just a matter of 1-time educational programs. Bioterrorism-related infections hopefully will remain rare events, and creative ongoing strategies will be required to sustain attention to potential new cases when the current phase of alarm and interest ebbs. Furthermore, better systems are needed for public health agencies to alert all clinicians when an attack is suspected or documented, facilitate real-time reporting, and disseminate credible information required for optimal exposure risk assessment, diagnosis, and treatment. Such efforts will simultaneously result in an improved capacity to detect and respond to naturally occurring emerging and reemerging infectious diseases.

Frontline clinicians faced a challenge that often was even more difficult than diagnosing anthrax—that of excluding the diagnosis among the many worried patients with concerns about potential exposure or among those who sought care for rashes or illnesses suggestive of the diagnosis. In the absence of clinical algorithms or rapid diagnostic tests, their clinical judgment helped reassure patients and avert the distraction that initiating unneeded response efforts would have otherwise entailed. For the future, developing clinical algorithms and laboratory testing protocols and reagents that rapidly and accurately identify all pathogens in the differential diagnosis of the suspicious illness, not just the select agents of bioterrorism, is important but will take time.

Primary care clinicians certainly have played a key role in managing postexposure prophylactic treatment interventions and their complications in the second phase of the response to the recent bioterrorist attacks. The initial distribution of antimicrobial drugs was usually coordinated through public health agencies, but often involved local clinicians as well. Those in outpatient settings have provided adherence counseling and advice about managing adverse events and other complications. Some clinicians also helped patients make decisions about their personal risk and the need for anthrax vaccine or additional days of antimicrobial prophylaxis. Patients with special concerns or underlying illnesses have solicited consultation about antimicrobial treatment from their obstetricians, pediatricians, and other medical specialists.

Many of the individualized preventive treatment decisions had to be made in the context of an inadequate or evolving evidence base. Input from clinicians directly involved in the affected areas and from professional medical societies and other organizations proved to be extremely useful for the development of the Centers for Disease Control and Prevention's interim treatment guidelines.[10-16] Clinicians also assisted many patients with decisions about anthrax vaccine treatment options, even though they had little advance warning or information about the program. Mechanisms to anticipate and more quickly respond to the needs of those caring for the diverse population of affected patients is another priority for enhancing bioterrorism response capacity as part of preparation for future events.

Clinicians are actively engaged in the follow-up phase of the response (long-term consequence management and remediation) and are likely to be even more engaged in the future. The possibility of late onset of inhalational anthrax among exposed persons, even though considered unlikely by most experts, requires heightened concern about febrile illnesses, chest pain, sweats, profound fatigue, and other symptoms in persons who were exposed to *B anthracis*. Likewise, clinicians must be alert to the possibility of long-term adverse events attributable to antimicrobial treatment and vaccination. Prophylactic anitimicrobial treatment is not likely to cause frequent serious late-onset adverse events, but there is inadequate experience with 60 or more days of antimicrobial treatment and anthrax vaccine among the diverse populations represented in the treated group. During the next 2 years, the Centers for Disease Control and Prevention plan to survey the health status of the 10 000 people whose exposure history suggested a need for prolonged prophylactic antimicrobial treatment, but local clinicians will be the most important resource for detecting adverse events, recognizing their association with prophylactic treatment for anthrax, and reporting them to health officials and the Food and Drug Administration. Other occupational and mental health issues that will require the services of additional medical specialists may emerge among exposed persons over the next months to years.

Although it is tempting to respond as if the anthrax threat of 2001 has ended, the criminal(s) who perpetrated these acts of bioterrorism has not been apprehended. The country and the world remain at risk for additional exposures and infections with this deadly pathogen and perhaps with other agents. The importance of individual clinicians in bioterrorism preparedness and response was not fully appreciated by many until the anthrax attacks of 2001 occurred. Hopefully, the lessons learned from these attacks will motivate local health departments, health care organizations, and clinicians to engage in collaborative programs to enhance their communication and local preparedness and response capabilities. Knowledgeable clinicians, operating in the framework of a health care delivery system that is fully prepared to support the necessary diagnostic and treatment modalities to manage affected patients, and seamless linkages to local public health agencies will provide a strong foundation for detecting, responding to, and combating bioterrorism and other infectious disease threats to public health in the future.

References

1. Recognition of illness associated with the intentional release of a biologic agent. *MMWR Morb Mortal Wkly Rep*. 2001;50:893-897.
2. Jernigan JA, Stephens DS, Ashford DA, et al. Bioterrorism-related inhalational anthrax. *Emerg Infect Dis*. 2001;7:933-944.
3. Borio L, Frank D, Mani V, et al. Death due to bioterrorism-related inhalational anthrax: report of 2 patients. *JAMA*. 2001;286:2554-2559.
4. Mayer TA, Bersoff-Matcha S, Murphy C, et al. Clinical presentation of inhalational anthrax following bioterrorism exposure. *JAMA*. 2001;286:2549-2553.
5. Bush LM, Abrams BH, Beall A, Johnson CC. Index case of fatal inhalational anthrax due to bioterrorism in the United States. *N Engl J Med*. 2001;345:1607-1610.
6. Update: investigation of bioterrorism-related anthrax and adverse events from antimicrobial prophylaxis. *MMWR Morb Mortal Wkly Rep*. 2001;50:973-976.
7. Mina B, Dym JP, Kuepper F, et al. Fatal inhalational anthrax with unknown source of exposure in a 61-year-old woman in New York City. *JAMA*. 2002;287:858-862.
8. Freedman A, Afonja O, Chang MW, et al. Cutaneous anthrax associated with microangiopathic hemolytic anemia and coagulopathy in a 7-month-old infant. *JAMA*. 2002;287:869-874.
9. Barakat LA, Quentzel HL, Jernigan JA, et al. Fatal inhalational anthrax in a 94-year-old Connecticut woman. *JAMA*. 2002;287:863-868.
10. Update: investigation of anthrax associated with intentional exposure and interim public health guidelines, October 2001. *MMWR Morb Mortal Wkly Rep*. 2001;50:889-893.
11. Update: investigation of bioterrorism-related anthrax and interim guidelines for exposure management and antimicrobial therapy, October 2001. *MMWR Morb Mortal Wkly Rep*. 2001;50:909-919.
12. Update: investigation of bioterrorism-related anthrax and interim guidelines for clinical evaluation of persons with possible anthrax. *MMWR Morb Mortal Wkly Rep*. 2001;50:941-948.
13. Updated recommendations for antimicrobial prophylaxis among asymptomatic pregnant women after exposure to Bacillus anthracis. *MMWR Morb Mortal Wkly Rep*. 2001;50:960.
14. Interim guidelines for investigation of and response to *Bacillus anthracis* exposures. *MMWR Morb Mortal Wkly Rep*. 2001;50:987-990.
15. Update: interim recommendations for antimicrobial prophylaxis for children and breastfeeding mothers and treatment of children with anthrax. *MMWR Morb Mortal Wkly Rep*. 2001;50:1014-1016.
16. Bell DM, Kozarsky PE, Stephens DS. Clinical issues in the prophylaxis, diagnosis, and treatment of antrhax. *Emerg Infect Dis*. 2002;8:222-225.

Fatal Inhalational Anthrax With Unknown Source of Exposure in a 61-Year-Old Woman in New York City

Bushra Mina, MD; J. P. Dym, MD; Frank Kuepper; Raymond Tso, MD; Carmina Arrastia, MD; Irina Kaplounova, MD; Hasan Faraj, MD; Agnieszka Kwapniewski, MD; Christopher M. Krol, MD; Mayer Grosser, MD; Jeffrey Glick, MD; Steven Fochios, MD; Athena Remolina, MD; Ljiljana Vasovic, MD; Jeffrey Moses, MD; Thomas Robin, M(ASCP); Maria DeVita, MD; Michael L. Tapper, MD

Anthrax is caused by the bacterium *Bacillus anthracis* and was used as an agent of bioterrorism in the United States in the fall of 2001.[1,2] The *B anthracis* spores lead to the disease by entering the body cavity through skin contact, ingestion, or inhalation.[3] Pulmonary anthrax is the most lethal form of the disease.[4] Along with smallpox, tularemia, plague, and botulism, anthrax is now at the forefront in the age of biological warfare.[5-7]

As of January 9, 2002, a total of 22 cases of anthrax had been reported to the Centers for Disease Control and Prevention (CDC) as a result of the anthrax attacks of 2001: 11 cases were confirmed inhalational anthrax and 12 cases (7 confirmed and 4 suspected) were cutaneous anthrax.[8] An estimated 32 000 people were prescribed prophylactic antibiotic therapy between October 9 and November 9, 2001.[9] Anthrax spores were found at government buildings, post offices, and news media centers in Florida, Washington, DC, New Jersey, and New York, NY. In this chapter, we report the first case of inhalational anthrax in New York City, a 61-year-old hospital employee who had none of the exposure risks previously described in this cluster of cases.

Case Report

On October 28, 2001, a 61-year-old Vietnamese woman was brought into the emergency department of Lenox Hill Hospital in New York City complaining of weakness, chest heaviness, dyspnea, malaise, cough, and chills for the preceding 3 days. On the day prior to admission, the cough was associated with pink-tinged sputum. The patient previously had been in her usual state of health and had worked until 2 days prior to admission. The patient denied headache, neck pain, fever, sore throat, or rash. The patient had a medical history of hypertension controlled with amlodipine and fosinopril. The patient was a nonsmoker and denied

Figure 1. Chest Radiograph on Admission

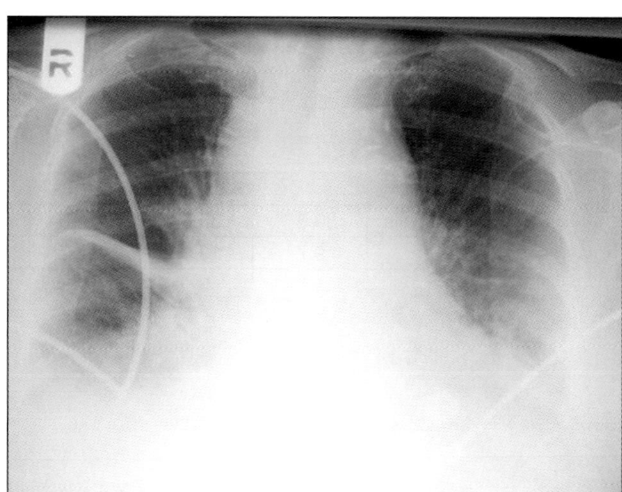

Chest radiograph shows marked widening of the paratracheal stripe and superior mediastinum. There are moderate bilateral effusions with fluid in the minor fissure and bilateral perihilar infiltrates.

alcohol use or recreational drug use. She had immigrated to the United States from Vietnam 20 years earlier but had no recent travel. She worked in the central supply room of a Manhattan hospital in a space shared with a mail receiving and sorting room.

On physical examination, the patient had a respiratory rate of 38/min and was in respiratory distress. Blood pressure was 128/60 mm Hg, pulse was 86/min, and temperature was 97°F (36°C). Head examination results were normal without scleral icterus or oral thrush. The neck was supple with no bruits or jugular venous distension, and the trachea was midline. There was no evidence of cervical or axillary adenopathy. Chest examination revealed inspiratory rales and decreased breath sounds bilaterally. Heart examination revealed regular rate and rhythm, with normal S_1 and S_2 and no S_3, S_4, or murmurs. The abdomen was soft, nontender, and nondistended, and no organomegaly was evident. There were no neurological deficits. No skin lesions were detected.

The initial portable view of the chest obtained shortly after presentation demonstrated marked widening of the superior mediastinum, with moderate bilateral pleural effusions, fluid in the minor fissure, and bilateral perihilar infiltrates (**Figure 1**). An electrocardiogram showed sinus tachycardia at a rate of 101/min without any signs of myocardial ischemia. Arterial blood gas values obtained while the patient was receiving supplemental oxygen (100% nonrebreather face mask) were pH, 7.41; partial pressure of carbon dioxide, 40 mm Hg; partial pressure of oxygen, 122 mm Hg; and oxygen saturation, 99%. Laboratory values on hospital admission are shown in **Table 1**. A bedside echocardiogram showed normal left ventricular function and wall motion, slight aortic

Table 1. Laboratory Data*

Variables	Values			
	Day 1	**Day 2**	**Day 3**	**Day 4**
Hematologic				
White blood cell count, $\times 10^3/\mu L$	11.4	23.9	25.4	15.8
Differential cell count, %				
Polymorphonuclear cells	83.6	80.6	81.9	88.6
Lymphocytes	9.7	13.1	13.7	7.1
Monocytes	6.7	6.1	4.0	4.2
Hemoglobin, g/dL	15.5	16.2	9.7	10.4
Hematocrit, %	46.3	47.1	28.3	29.3
Platelet count, $\times 10^3/\mu L$	135	59	37	68
Serum chemistry				
Glucose, mg/dL	179	129	278	163
Sodium, mEq/L	134	134	150	148
Potassium, mEq/L	3.5	5.1	3.6	3.7
Chloride, mEq/L	96	100	100	104
Bicarbonate, mEq/L	26	22	30	27
Serum urea nitrogen, mg/dL	18	39	56	68
Creatinine, mg/dL	0.8	1.9	4.0	4.4
Calcium, mg/dL	7.6	6.1	4.6	6.5
Albumin, g/dL	3.3	2.0	1.5	2.5
Alkaline phosphatase, U/L	96	96	56	92
Lactate dehydrogenase, U/L	1370	4788	6109	. . .
Lactate, mg/dL	. . .	75	. . .	. . .
Aspartate aminotransferase, U/L	240	471	10044	10888
Alanine aminotransferase, U/L	263	660	6100	4494
Total bilirubin, mg/dL	. . .	0.1	1.3	2.2
Creatine kinase, U/L	74	198	. . .	. . .
Troponin	Negative			
Coagulation				
Prothrombin time, s	10.3	11.5	23.5	. . .
International normalized ratio	0.8	1.0	4.2	. . .
Partial thromboplastin time, s	23.8	29.3	60.0	. . .
Dimerized plasmin fragment D, mg/L	. . .	. . .	>4000	>4000

* Ellipses indicate value not available. To convert glucose from mg/dL to mmol/L, multiply by 0.05551. To convert urea nitrogen from mg/dL to mmol/L, multiply by 0.357. To convert creatinine from mg/dL to µmol/L, multiply by 88.4. To convert calcium from mg/dL to mmol/L, multiply by 0.25. To convert bilirubin from mg/dL to µmol/L, multiply by 17.1.

regurgitation, a small pericardial effusion, and an aneurysm of the ascending aorta. Blood cultures were drawn and were submitted in aerobic and anaerobic culture bottles (BioMerieux, Raleigh-Durham, NC). The patient was initially treated presumptively for congestive heart failure with 20 mg of intravenous furosemide. Empirical intravenous levofloxacin, 500 mg/d, was administered for community-acquired pneumonia and the possibility of inhalational anthrax.

The patient was admitted to the medical intensive care unit. Her respiratory and hemodynamic status deteriorated rapidly, and she was immediately intubated because of tachypnea, respiratory distress, and oxygen desaturation. Frothy pink secretions were suctioned from the endotracheal tube. Pulmonary artery catheterization revealed right atrial pressure of 4 mm Hg (reference range, 0-6 mm Hg), right ventricular pressure of 17/5 mm Hg (reference range, 20-30/0-5 mm Hg), and pulmonary artery pressure of 20/10 mm Hg (reference range, 20-30/5-15 mm Hg), but pulmonary artery wedge pressures could not be measured. After unsuccessful crystalloid resuscitation, vasopressor therapy (norepinephrine, phenylephrine, and, later, vasopressin) was initiated. The differential diagnosis included dissecting ascending aortic aneurysm with leakage, severe community-acquired pneumonia, vasculitis (Wegener granulomatosis), and inhalational anthrax. Rifampin, 300 mg intravenously every 8 hours, and clindamycin, 800 mg every 8 hours, were added to the antibiotic regimen, and the levofloxacin dosage was increased to 500 mg every 12 hours.

Repeat chest radiograph revealed progressive widening of the mediastinum, and the tip of the pulmonary artery catheter was positioned in the main pulmonary artery trunk. Spiral computed tomography of the chest demonstrated large bilateral pleural effusions, a small amount of blood layering in the dependent portion of the right pleural space, and a large amount of edema and hemorrhage in the soft tissues surrounding the trachea, bronchi, and hilar regions bilaterally, with complete infiltration of the mediastinal fat planes, bronchial mucosal thickening, and encasement and compression of the hilar vessels (**Figure 2A**). An intact 4.2-cm aneurysm of the ascending aorta was incidentally noted. Delayed images at 20 minutes demonstrated multiple confluent ringlike areas of enhancement with hypodense centers compatible with hemorrhagic lymph node necrosis involving the subcarinal, paratracheal, subaortic, and azygoesophageal recess nodes (**Figure 2B**). A high-density pericardial effusion, suggesting hemorrhage, was also present.

Bilateral chest tubes were inserted and each drained more than 1 L of serosanguinous fluid. Pleural fluid analysis produced the following values: glucose, 147 mg/dL (8.2 mmol/L); total protein, 4.2 g/dL; lactic dehydrogenase, 1264 U/L; white blood cell count, $3.0 \times 10^3/\mu L$; and red blood cell count, $0.073 \times 10^6/\mu L$. At the time of admission to the intensive care unit, the patient had an Acute Physiology and Chronic Health Evaluation III score of 143, with predicted intensive care unit and hospital mortality of 80% and 89%, respectively.

On the second hospital day, fiberoptic bronchoscopy revealed severe hemorrhagic tracheobronchitis with oozing of bloody fluid from the mucosal surfaces and easy sloughing of the mucosa. The patient developed worsening hepatic function with increasing aminotransferases, nonoliguric renal failure with creatinine

Figure 2. Spiral Computed Tomography of the Chest and 20-Minute Delayed Image

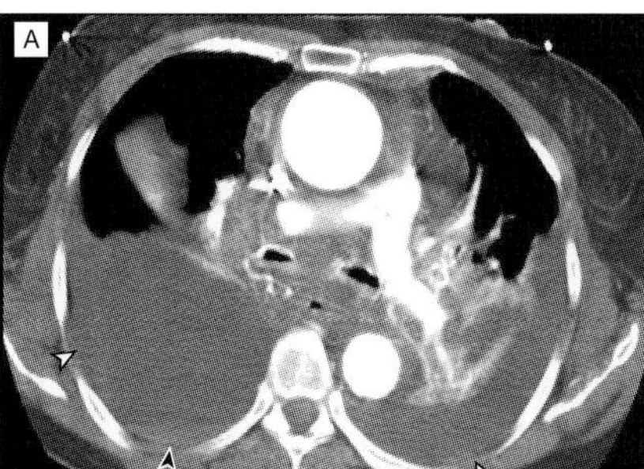

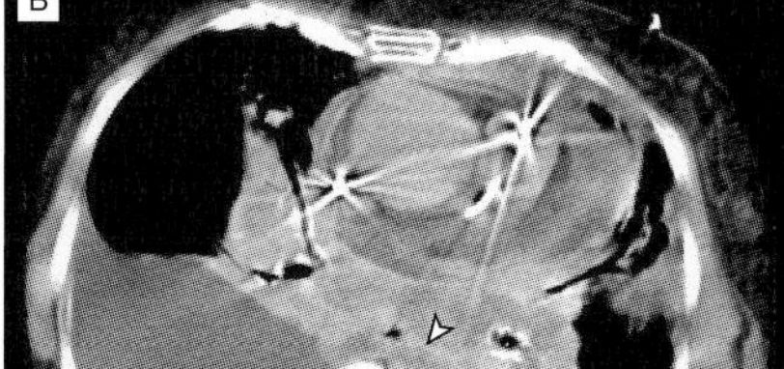

A, Computed tomographic image demonstrates large bilateral pleural effusions (white arrowheads) with a small amount of hemorrhagic debris (black arrowhead) in the dependent portion of the right pleural space. There is a large amount of edema and high-density soft tissue surrounding the trachea, bronchi, and hilar regions bilaterally, with obliteration of the mediastinal fat planes. There is marked bronchial mucosal edema and compression of the hilar vessels. B, This image demonstrates multiple confluent ringlike areas of enhancement with hypodense centers, consistent with subcarinal and mediastinal hemorrhagic lymphadenopathy (white arrowhead). There is additional involvement of the paratracheal, subaortic, and azygoesophageal recess nodes. A high-density hemorrhagic pericardial effusion is also present.

level increasing to 1.9 mg/dL (168 μmol/L), lactic acidosis (lactate, 75 mg/dL), leukocytosis ($23.9 \times 10^3/\mu L$), and disseminated intravascular coagulopathy (Table 1). A continuous infusion of furosemide was initiated and multiple blood products were transfused. Blood cultures obtained on admission became positive for large gram-positive bacilli after 20 hours of incubation (**Figure 3**). Smears of the broth were Gram stained and revealed gram-positive rods in extremely long chains. Examination of a wet preparation of the blood culture broth demonstrated that the organism was nonmotile. Blood, pleural fluid, and bronchial wash specimens were sent for DNA amplification by polymerase chain reaction (PCR). A repeat echocardiogram confirmed a slight increase in the amount of pericardial fluid.

On the third hospital day, phenylephrine was tapered off and the norepinephrine dose was decreased by 50%. The patient's respiratory status deteriorated, with worsening oxygenation and ventilation. The blood culture isolate was confirmed as *B anthracis* by gamma phage lysis and direct fluorescent antibody testing against capsular and cell wall antigens at the New York City Department of Health and the CDC. Blood, pleural fluid, and bronchial washings were also positive by PCR for *B anthracis* at the same laboratories. Levofloxacin was discontinued and ciprofloxacin, 400 mg every 12 hours, was initiated. Repeat echocardiogram confirmed an increase in the size of the pericardial effusion and mild-to-moderate right atrial and ventricular collapse during early diastole. Cardiac index was 2.6 L/(min/m^2) (reference range, 2.4-4.0 L/[min/m^2]), systemic vascular resistance was 1131 (dynes • s • m^2)/ cm^5 (reference range, 900-1400

Figure 3. Gram Stain of Blood Culture Obtained on Admission

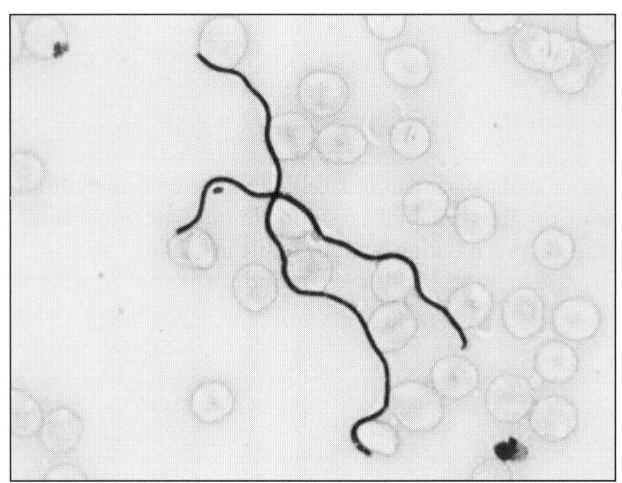

Gram stain of blood culture shows gram-positive bacilli (original magnification ×1000).

[dynes • s • m^2]/cm^5), and a pulmonary capillary wedge pressure was 13 mm Hg (reference range, 6-12 mm Hg), with no evidence of equalization of pressures. A follow-up echocardiogram 5 hours later documented further increase in the pericardial fluid with evidence of collapse of the right atrium and ventricle.

The patient's respiratory status deteriorated further, and blood gas analysis revealed a pH of 7.49, a partial pressure of carbon dioxide of 37 mm Hg, a partial pressure of oxygen of 59 mm Hg, and an oxygen saturation of 92% with pressure-control ventilation, with pressure control of 20 cm H_2O, 100% oxygen, and positive end-expiratory pressure of 5 cm H_2O. Because of her deteriorating hemodynamic status and inability to maintain adequate oxygenation, a bedside echocardiographically guided pericardiocentesis was attempted unsuccessfully by the interventional cardiology service. The patient decompensated further, with worsening oxygenation and refractory hypotension with vasopressors, and she became bradycardic and pulseless. Cardiopulmonary resuscitation was unsuccessful and the patient died on the fourth hospital day. Repeat blood cultures from the second and fourth hospital days were negative for any pathogens.

An autopsy performed at the office of the chief medical examiner of the city of New York confirmed marked hemorrhagic mediastinitis. The hilar and peribronchial lymph nodes were enlarged, necrotic, and replaced by hematoma. Touch prep revealed few scattered gram-positive bacilli. There was a large hemorrhagic pericardial effusion and extensive pulmonary edema. There was no meningitis, bronchopneumonia, splenomegaly, or mesenteric lymphadenopathy. There were no hemorrhagic lesions of the liver or kidney. The cause of death was inhalational anthrax and the manner of death was homicide (James Gill, MD, New York City Medical Examiner Office, oral communication, January 14, 2002).

Comment

For the patient presented herein, there were no obvious links to any of the settings previously associated with either naturally occurring or bioterrorism-associated anthrax. Inhalational anthrax was considered in this patient from the time of admission because of the widespread publicity surrounding previous cutaneous anthrax cases in New York City and the alerts issued to the medical community by the New York City Department of Health. Despite early institution of antibiotics, the disease progressed rapidly, resulting in multiple organ failure and large pericardial effusion precipitating hemodynamic instability.

The clinical presentation of inhalational anthrax in this patient was typical. Several days of a nonspecific prodrome of malaise, generalized weakness, chills, and occasional chest pain preceded complete respiratory failure, septic shock, a large pleural effusion, and multiple organ dysfunction. Hemorrhagic mediastinitis and hemorrhagic pericardial effusion may have contributed to respiratory failure. Death occurred 7 days after the onset of symptoms, similar to that reported by Dixon et al.[4]

The anthrax bacillus is a gram-positive, aerobic, spore-forming microorganism. Aerosolized anthrax spores can be trapped in the upper airways, although spores of 2 to 3 μm can pass through the bronchi to the alveoli. The spores are engulfed by macrophages, which carry them to the peribronchial and mediastinal lymph nodes, where they germinate and replicate into vegetative bacilli. This leads to hemorrhagic lymphadenitis and the enlarged mediastinum that is observed on radiographic images.[4,7] Mediastinal hemorrhage with high-density adenopathy in an acutely ill patient with no history of trauma should raise concern for inhalational anthrax infection.

Inhalational anthrax is not considered a true pneumonia, and death results from septicemia, toxemia, or pulmonary complications and usually occurs within 36 hours.[4] As of November 7, 2001, 5 of the 11 patients with inhalational anthrax associated with bioterrorism in the United States had died. The 6 survivors were treated in the prodromal phase of the disease; none of the patients who required intubation or who became hemodynamically unstable have survived.[10] Early suspicion and initiation of antibiotic therapy while awaiting culture results may improve the prognosis.[1]

The initial diagnosis of anthrax is usually made by positive cultures of blood, cerebrospinal fluid, or skin lesion (vesicular fluid or eschar).[3] Rapid identification of the growing organism can be made by direct fluorescent antibody testing and gamma phage lysis. DNA amplification from body fluids by PCR may help in early diagnosis of the disease. Antibody testing by enzyme-linked immunosorbent assay may yield positive results in convalescent serum specimens.[4] Currently, such tests are available only in local and state public health laboratories or at the CDC.

Following the anthrax attacks of 2001, 7 cases of cutaneous anthrax and 1 case of inhalational anthrax were reported in New York City. All of the cutaneous cases occurred among employees or persons directly associated with the news media; 2 were NBC employees, 1 was a CBS employee, 3 were from the *New York Post*, and 1 was the infant of an ABC employee. Environmental samples from these companies' buildings were positive for anthrax spores.

The patient presented in this case report differed from other reported cases of inhalational anthrax in that no clear risk for exposure has yet been determined. Extensive environmental samples from the patient's residence and workplace were negative for *B anthracis* by PCR and conventional bacterial cultures. Nasal cultures taken from personal contacts and coworkers in the same workplace environment were also negative for *B anthracis.* Environmental samples from surfaces and an air filtration system from the subway route that the patient rode daily were also negative for anthrax (New York City Department of Health and CDC).[8, 11-13]

It has been postulated that infection from a cross-contaminated envelope may have been the source of anthrax transmission in this patient.[8] However, it is unclear why she is the only patient in New York City to date who has developed inhalational anthrax. Nonetheless, even patients without obvious sources of possible anthrax exposure may be at risk for bioterrorism-associated diseases. Heightened public health and health care facility surveillance efforts, increased awareness by the public, and health care professional education are needed to ensure that the unusual clinical presentations of such rare infections do not go unrecognized.

Acknowledgments: We thank Rita Neilan, RN, RPh, PhD, for help with the manuscript; Robert Phillips, MD, PhD, for reviewing the manuscript; Joel Ackelsberg, MD, of the New York City Department of Health for assistance with details of the epidemiologic investigation; and James Gill, MD, of the New York City Medical Examiner Office for providing the autopsy report.

Following discussion with the hospital administrator and human resources department at the patient's place of employment and investigations by the social work department, there is no known living family member, next of kin, or legally authorized representative of this patient to obtain consent for publication.

References

1. Mayer TA, Bersoff-Matcha S, Murphy C, et al. Clinical presentation of inhalational anthrax following bioterrorism exposure: report of 2 surviving patients. *JAMA.* 2001;286:2549-2553.
2. Borio L, Frank D, Mani V, et al. Death due to bioterrorism-related inhalational anthrax: report of 2 patients. *JAMA.* 2001;286:2554-2559.
3. Swartz MN. Recognition and management of anthrax—an update. *N Engl J Med.* 2001;345:1621-1626.
4. Dixon BS, Meselson M, Guillemin J, Hanna PC. Anthrax. *N Engl J Med.* 1999;341:815-826.
5. Pile JC, Malone JD, Eitzen EM, et al. Anthrax as a potential biological warfare agent. *Arch Intern Med.* 1998;158:429-434.
6. Inglesby TV, Henderson DA, Bartlett JG, et al, for the Working Group on Civilian Biodefense. Anthrax as a biological weapon: medical and public health management. *JAMA.* 1999;281:1735-1745.
7. Shafazand S, Doyle R, Ruoss S, Weinacker A, Raffin TA. Inhalational anthrax-epidemiology, diagnosis, and management. *Chest.* 1999;116:1369-1376.
8. Centers for Disease Control and Prevention. Update: investigation of bioterrorism-related anthrax—Connecticut, 2001. *MMWR Morb Mortal Wkly Rep.* 2001;50:1077-1079.
9. Centers for Disease Control and Prevention. Investigation of bioterrorism-related anthrax, 2001. *MMWR Morb Mortal Wkly Rep.* 2001;50:1008-1010.

10. Jernigan JA, Stephens DS, Ashford DA, et al. Bioterrorism related inhalational anthrax: the first 10 cases reported in the United States. *Emerg Infect Dis.* 2001;7:933-944.

11. Centers for Disease Control and Prevention. Update: investigation of bioterrorism-related anthrax and interim guidelines for clinical evaluation of persons for possible anthrax. *MMWR Morb Mortal Wkly Rep.* 2001;50:941-948.

12. Press release. New York, NY: Office of Public Affairs, New York City Department of Health; October 31, 2001.

13. Press release. New York, NY: Office of Public Affairs, New York City Department of Health; November 20, 2001.

Fatal Inhalational Anthrax in a 94-Year-Old Connecticut Woman

Lydia A. Barakat, MD; Howard L. Quentzel, MD; John A. Jernigan, MD; David L. Kirschke, MD; Kevin Griffith, MD, MPH; Stephen M. Spear, MD; Katherine Kelley, PhD; Diane Barden, MT; Donald Mayo, ScD; David S. Stephens, MD; Tanja Popovic, MD, PhD; Chung Marston; Sherif R. Zaki, MD, PhD; Jeanette Guarner, MD; Wun-Ju Shieh, MD, PhD; H. Wayne Carver II, MD; Richard F. Meyer, PhD; David L. Swerdlow, MD; Eric E. Mast, MD, MPH; James L. Hadler, MD; for the Anthrax Bioterrorism Investigation Team

On October 4, 2001, a diagnosis of inhalational anthrax in a news media outlet employee in Florida marked the recognition of the first confirmed outbreak of anthrax associated with bioterrorism in the United States. Between October 4 and November 20, 2001, inhalational anthrax was identified in 11 persons who lived or worked in Florida, New York, New Jersey, the District of Columbia, and Connecticut.[1] The first 10 inhalational anthrax patients associated with this outbreak have been described previously.[2-5] Direct exposure to envelopes containing *Bacillus anthracis* or to contaminated postal equipment was likely in the first 9 patients. The 10th reported patient was a resident of New York, NY, and the nature of her exposure is currently unknown. The 11th patient with bioterrorism-related inhalational anthrax was identified in Connecticut and is described in this chapter.

Case Report

On November 16, 2001, a 94-year-old woman from Oxford, Connecticut, with fever, fatigue, myalgias, dry cough, and shortness of breath of approximately 3 days' duration was evaluated at her local hospital. During the preceding 2 months, following the death of a close friend, she had experienced depressive symptoms, including decreased appetite and increased general fatigue. On the day before admission, family members noted that she was confused. There was no recent history of headache, chills, sweats, sore throat, rhinorrhea, hemoptysis, chest pain, abdominal pain, nausea, vomiting, or diarrhea. She had chronic obstructive pulmonary disease. She had a 22-pack-year smoking history but had not smoked in 30 years. She also had hypertension and chronic renal insufficiency. Her medications included montelukast, irbesartan, loratadine, alprazolam, inhaled salmeterol xinafoate/fluticasone propionate, and azelastine nasal spray. Her only nonprescription medication was a multivitamin tablet, and she rarely drank alcohol. Her diet was unremarkable. The patient had lived alone since the death of her husband 22 years earlier. She had previously worked as a legal secretary. She had no recent travel and had no pets. Additional history obtained following admission revealed that she did not remember opening any mail containing powder. On admission, the patient's vital signs were a temperature of 102.3°F (39.1°C), blood pressure of 106/50 mm Hg with no orthostatic changes, pulse of 119/min, and respiratory rate of 18/min. Oxygen saturation was 93% while breathing room air. She was alert and oriented, there were no signs of meningeal irritation, and the remainder of the physical examination, including skin, was unremarkable.

Laboratory findings included a total white blood cell count of 8.1 × 10^3/μL (78% neutrophils, 15% lymphocytes, and 7% monocytes) and normal hematocrit and platelet counts. Serum urea nitrogen level was 39 mg/dL (13.9 mmol/L), serum creatinine level was 1.3 mg/dL (115 μmol/L), and serum electrolyte levels were within normal ranges, except for a sodium level of 134 mEq/L. Serum chemistry levels were normal except for an aspartate aminotransferase of 45 U/L. Urinalysis showed 3 to 5 white blood cells per high-power field and moderate bacteria. Posterior-anterior and lateral chest radiographs were initially interpreted as having no evidence of pulmonary infiltrates, widened mediastinum, or pleural effusion (**Figure 1A**). However, later comparison with films obtained 3 years previously suggested possible interval enlargement of the left hilum and a possible small left pleural effusion. Computed tomography of the chest was not performed.

Blood and urine cultures were obtained, and the patient was admitted to the hospital with a diagnosis of viral syndrome and dehydration. Initial treatment included intravenous hydration and observation. Antibiotic therapy was not initiated on the day of admission.

On the morning of November 17, the patient was febrile but clinically stable. Using a colorimetric detection system (BacT/Alert, Organon Technica Corp, Durham, NC), growth of gram-positive bacilli in chains was detected in all 4 blood culture bottles after 14 hours of incubation (**Figure 1B**). The urine culture grew more than 100 000 colony-forming units/mL of *Escherichia coli* that were susceptible to ampicillin. Approximately 24 hours after presentation, the patient received a single 2-g dose of ceftazidime, and vancomycin, 1 g/d intravenously, was begun. Oral ciprofloxacin, 500 mg every 12 hours, and ampicillin/sulbactam, 3 g intravenously every 6 hours, were added. Blood cultures obtained 3 hours after initiation of antibiotics were sterile.

On November 18, the patient developed respiratory distress. Her white blood cell count was 13.3 × 10^3/μL (80% neutrophils, 11% lymphocytes, and 9% monocytes) and her oxygen saturation decreased to 90% while receiving 2 L/min of oxygen via nasal cannula. A chest radiograph showed clear evidence of a left pleural effusion (**Figure 2A**). Intravenous vancomycin and oral ciprofloxacin were continued, ampicillin/sulbactam was discontinued, and intravenous erythromycin (500 mg every 6 hours) was initiated in the early hours of November 19.

On November 19, review of the preliminary microbiologic analysis of the blood isolate raised suspicion for anthrax; therefore, the Connecticut Department

Figure 1. Admission Chest Radiograph and Gram Stain of Blood Culture

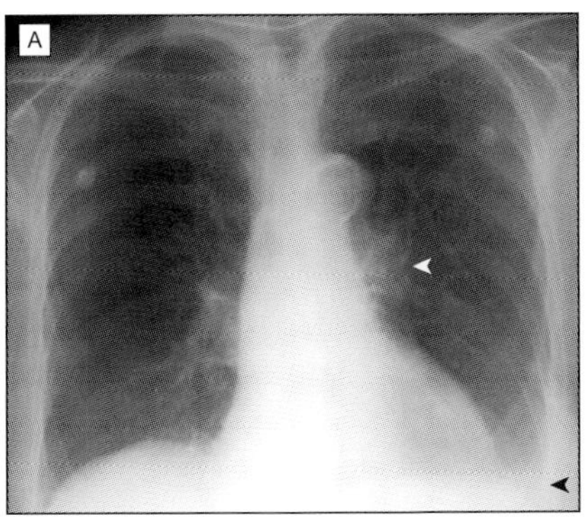

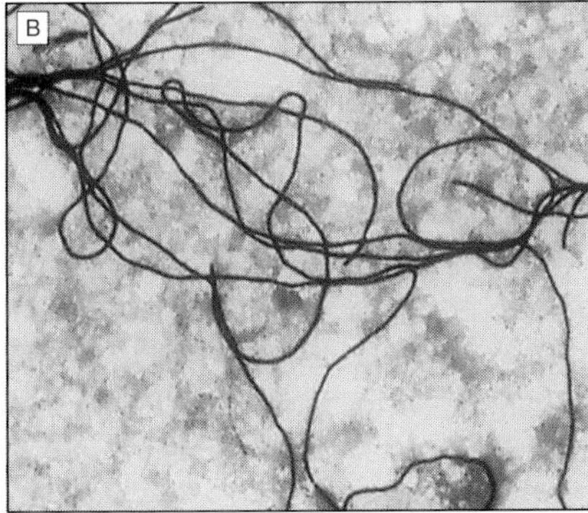

A, Admission posterior-anterior chest radiograph shows possible left hilar enlargement (white arrowhead) and blunting of the left costophrenic angle (black arrowhead), possibly due to a small left pleural effusion. B, Gram stain of blood culture isolate showing gram-positive rods in chains (original magnification ×100).

of Public Health was notified about the positive blood culture results, and assistance in ruling out *B anthracis* was requested. The patient's condition deteriorated with worsening hypoxemia and renal function (serum urea nitrogen and serum creatinine levels of 43 mg/dL [15.4 mmol/L] and 2.6 mg/dL [230 μmol/L], respectively). Her white blood cell count was $25.0 \times 10^3/\mu L$ (83% segmented neutrophils, 8% band forms, and 8% lymphocytes). Chest radiograph showed progression of the left pleural effusion. A left thoracentesis yielded 800 mL of serosanguinous fluid, with 4224 red blood cells, 1463 white blood cells, a pH of 7.12, lactate dehydrogenase level of 611 U/L, glucose level of 259 mg/dL (14.4 mmol/L), and protein level of 3.4 g/dL. No organisms were seen on the Gram stain of the pleural fluid, and bacterial culture of the fluid did not grow, but subsequent testing at the Centers for Disease Control and Prevention showed that the *B anthracis*–specific polymerase chain reaction (PCR) assay was positive. The patient required endotracheal intubation and mechanical ventilation. In addition to vancomycin, clindamycin, 900 mg intravenously every 6 hours, was begun, erythromycin was discontinued, and the route of ciprofloxacin administration was changed from oral to intravenous. Methylprednisolone, 40 mg intravenously every 8 hours, was initiated.

On November 20, the isolate was identified as *B anthracis* by the Connecticut state laboratory, with confirmation at the Centers for Disease Control and Prevention the following day. Confirmatory testing of the isolate included gamma phage lysis and detection of capsule and cell-wall antigens by direct fluorescent antibody assays. In addition, PCR showed that the isolates contained *B anthracis*-specific DNA. The isolates were susceptible to ciprofloxacin, tetracycline, penicillin, and a number of other antibiotics. The antibiotic susceptibilities were identical to the isolates obtained from other patients during this bioterrorism-related

Figure 2. Portable Chest Radiographs

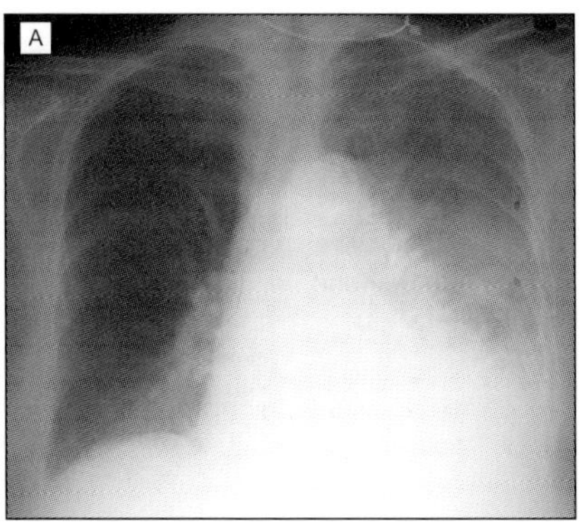

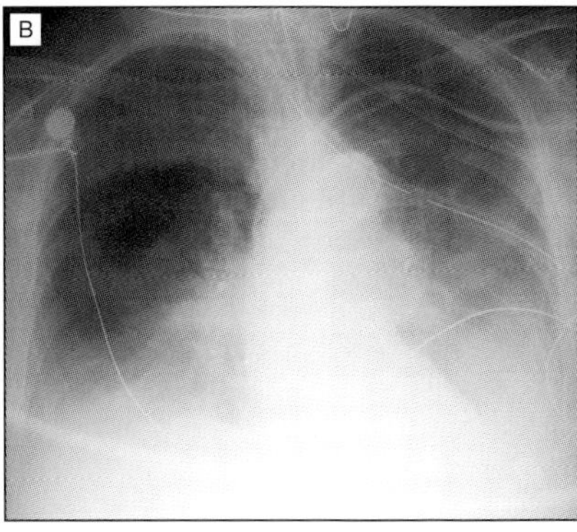

A, Portable chest radiograph shows bilateral lower lung consolidation, left greater than right, and hazy opacity in the left chest, suggestive of pleural effusion. B, Supine portable chest radiograph demonstrates extensive consolidation in both lower lungs and bilateral hazy opacities, suggesting pleural effusion.

anthrax outbreak.[6] Subsequent multiple-locus variable-number tandem repeat analysis revealed that the isolate was also genetically indistinguishable compared with the other strains from cases of bioterrorism-related anthrax.[1,6,7]

Between November 19 and 21, the patient remained febrile with a maximum temperature of 101.5°F (38.6°C). She developed hypotension requiring treatment with vasopressors and required high levels of supplemental oxygen (80% fraction of inspired oxygen) to maintain adequate oxygenation. Chest radiographs revealed progressive consolidation and a new right pleural effusion (**Figure 2B**). A chest tube was placed in the left pleural space. Total white blood cell count increased to $43.6 \times 10^3/\mu L$ (83% segmented neutrophils, 12% lymphocytes, and 5% monocytes) and serum creatinine level increased to 3.7 mg/dL (327 μmol/L). Hematocrit, platelet count, liver enzymes, and coagulation profile remained normal, with the exception of an aspartate aminotransferase level of 61 U/L. The patient's condition continued to deteriorate, and she died on November 21.

The case was reported to the state medical examiner. An autopsy was performed 8 hours after death. More than 1 L of serosanguinous fluid was present in the right pleural cavity, and the right lung had areas of patchy consolidation. A chest tube was noted within the left pleural space. There was no evidence of a primary cutaneous lesion. The mediastinal lymph nodes were enlarged and hemorrhagic. The central nervous system was unremarkable, and, except for small, granular, and cystic kidneys, the abdominal organs were grossly normal. Microscopic examination demonstrated extensive necrosis and hemorrhage of mediastinal lymph nodes (**Figure 3A**), intra-alveolar and interstitial edema with focal hemorrhage and fibrin deposition in the lungs, and splenic necrosis. There was no histopathologic evidence of pneumonia.

Figure 3. Mediastinal Lymph Nodes

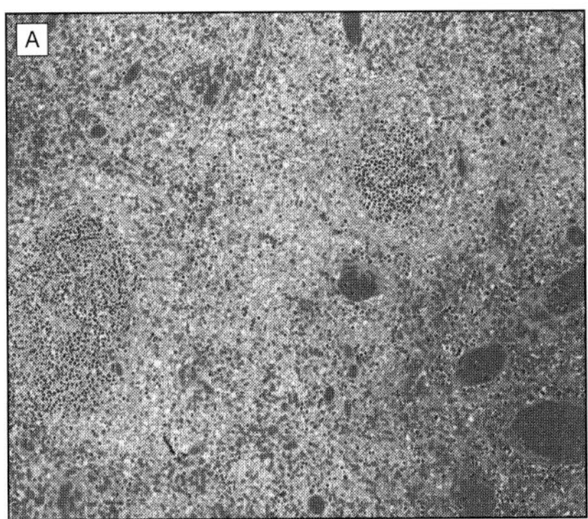

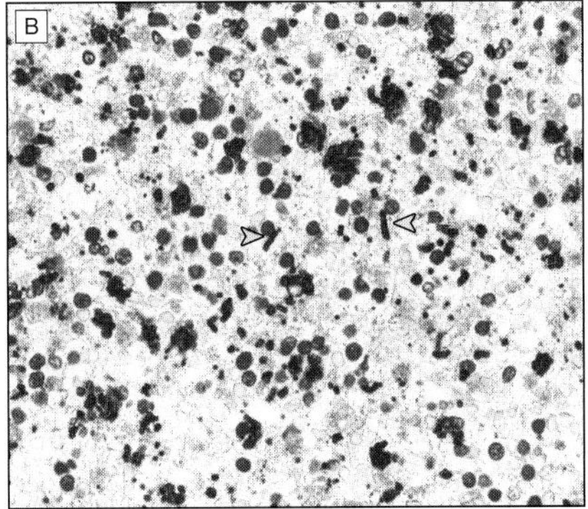

A, Photomicrograph of a postmortem mediastinal lymph node shows hemorrhage, necrosis, and nodular collections of immunoblasts (hematoxylin-eosin stain, original magnification ×25).
B, Photomicrograph of an immunohistochemical assay of a mediastinal lymph node shows *Bacillus anthracis* bacilli (arrows), numerous red staining polymorphic particles, and red-purple dust. The polymorphic particles and red-purple dust represent bacterial fragments and antigens that are being processed by inflammatory cells. The fragments and antigens that seem more compact, as if they were staining the cytoplasm of cells, are considered intracellular while those that appear single or as red-purple dust are mostly extracellular (immunohistochemical assay with a mouse monoclonal anti–*B anthracis* cell wall antibody and detection with alkaline phosphatase and naphthol fast red, original magnification ×100).

Immunohistochemical staining using *B anthracis* capsule and cell-wall monoclonal antibodies showed abundant bacilli and granular staining in the mediastinal lymph nodes (**Figure 3B**), cellular fraction of the pleural effusion, visceral and parietal pleura, and pulmonary interstitium. No pathologic or immunopathologic evidence of *B anthracis* was identified in the abdominal organs or central nervous system using tissue Gram stains or immunohistochemical stains. Postmortem blood; pleural fluid; and spleen, lung, liver, and mediastinal lymph node tissue specimens were inoculated onto bacteriologic media for culture and tested for *B anthracis*–specific DNA using PCR. Growth of *B anthracis* was detected only from the mediastinal lymph node; all other postmortem specimens were sterile. The mediastinal lymph node tissue was also the only postmortem specimen from which *B anthracis* DNA was detected by PCR assay. The cause of death was certified as inhalational anthrax.

Serial serum samples obtained on November 16, 17, 18, and 19 were tested for IgG antibody to the protective antigen component of the anthrax toxins by enzyme-linked immunosorbent assay; all samples were nonreactive.

Comment

This report describes the 11th patient with bioterrorism-related inhalational anthrax identified from the anthrax attacks in the United States during 2001. The *B anthracis* isolate from the patient's bloodstream was indistinguishable by molecular typing and by antibiotic susceptibilities from isolates from the other recently identified patients with inhalational and cutaneous anthrax,[1] indicating an epidemiologic relationship with the recent bioterrorism-related outbreak. The source of the exposure for this patient has not been identified.[8] Extensive environmental sampling of the patient's home and all other locations she was known to have visited in the 60 days prior to onset of symptoms failed to find *B anthracis*. Environmental sampling performed at the southern Connecticut postal processing and distribution center that processed her mail identified *B anthracis* spores in 3 high-speed mail sorters.[8] No direct exposure to mail known to contain *B anthracis* spores has been identified for this patient, but at least 1 resident of her community is known to have received a *B anthracis*–contaminated envelope that was likely to have become cross-contaminated as it passed through the postal system.[8] These findings do not provide definitive evidence of the route of exposure for the patient reported here, but they are consistent with the hypothesis that the exposure to *B anthracis* may have resulted from receipt of mail that was cross-contaminated with spores.

Host factors, including advanced age, underlying lung disease, and medication use, may have played a role in this patient's susceptibility to inhalational anthrax. Advanced age is associated with changes in the immune system that may increase susceptibility to a variety of infections.[9, 10] The absence of deaths reported among persons younger than 24 years in the Sverdlovsk outbreak in Russia and the paucity of childhood cases in Russian home industry-based inhalational anthrax during the early part of last century have been interpreted as evidence that increased age may be an important risk factor for this disease,[11, 12] although it is possible that younger age groups were less likely to be exposed in these settings.

Underlying chronic illness, such as emphysema, is associated with an increased risk of respiratory infection in elderly persons.[9] Previously, Brachman et al[13, 14] hypothesized that underlying pulmonary disease may also predispose to inhalational anthrax. Two of the 18 US cases of inhalational anthrax reported in the 20th century had underlying lung disease; 1 had beryllium exposure and chronic pulmonary fibrosis and the other had underlying pulmonary sarcoidosis.[13, 14] The only known exposure for the patient with sarcoidosis was that he walked by the open door of a tannery known to be contaminated with *B anthracis*. No cases of inhalational anthrax were reported among those who worked in the tannery, raising the hypothesis that his underlying pulmonary disease made him susceptible to infection by exposure to a small number of spores.

The incubation period for this patient's illness could not be determined, but her onset of symptoms was 56 days after letters containing *B anthracis* were mailed to New York City news media outlets, 35 days after letters containing *B anthracis* were mailed to US senators, and 3 weeks after onset of illness in the 10th patient with bioterrorism-related inhalational anthrax following the 2001 attacks. These findings suggest that the incubation period of the patient described herein could have been longer than that observed among earlier patients. In nonhuman primates, the incubation period ranges from 2 to 98 days among animals not vaccinated or treated with antibiotics, and evidence suggests that the duration of the incubation period is inversely related to the number of *B anthracis*-bearing particles to which the animals are exposed (ie, smaller doses result in longer incubation periods).[15-17]

The hypothesis that the dose of spores is inversely related to incubation period in humans is supported by the Sverdlovsk experience; individuals who died of inhalational anthrax who both lived and worked outside the area of highest calculated dose had a prolonged median incubation period of 21 days. In contrast, those who both lived and worked within the high-dose area had a median incubation period of only 10 days.[18] In addition, the incubation period for a laboratory worker who acquired inhalational anthrax after exposure to a massive number of aerosolized *B anthracis* spores was approximately 1 day (G. Briggs Phillips, PhD, oral communication, January 18, 2002). The onset of illness in this patient is consistent with the hypothesis that infection may have resulted from exposure to small numbers of *B anthracis* spores.

The presenting signs, symptoms, and laboratory findings for this patient were similar to those reported for the other 10 patients with bioterrorism-related inhalational anthrax following the attacks of 2001.[2] The nonspecific nature of the findings presented herein makes an accurate presumptive diagnosis difficult. The diagnosis became apparent only after growth of *B anthracis* was detected in blood cultures. The clinical features of her initial illness were relatively mild despite evidence of high-level *B anthracis* bacteremia at presentation; growth in blood cultures was detected after 14 hours of incubation. Rapid growth of *B anthracis* in blood or cerebrospinal fluid cultures was also observed in previously reported patients with bioterrorism-related anthrax who had not received prior antibiotics.[2] Of interest, blood cultures obtained from this patient 3 hours following the initiation of antibiotic therapy revealed no growth. Antibiotic therapy appears to rapidly sterilize the bloodstream and greatly diminishes the sensitivity of blood cultures as a diagnostic test for inhalational anthrax,[2] emphasizing the importance of obtaining blood cultures prior to initiation of antibiotic therapy for patients suspected to have anthrax.

This patient's admission chest radiograph was interpreted as normal. However, in retrospect, subtle changes were present in comparison with earlier films. In 2 of the previous cases of inhalational anthrax from the 2001 attacks, the presenting chest radiograph was initially interpreted as normal, but in both cases, subsequent review indicated the presence of abnormalities in the hila, mediastinum, parenchyma, or pleural spaces.[2] The combined experience with bioterrorism-related inhalational anthrax from the 2001 attacks suggests that while abnormalities are usually present on the initial chest radiograph, the changes may be difficult to detect. Chest computed tomographic images may be helpful in characterizing abnormalities of the lungs and mediastinum and revealing mediastinal lymphadenopathy.[2]

The hospital course of the patient described in this chapter was characterized by fever followed by the onset of respiratory distress with the development of bilateral pleural effusions, progressive respiratory insufficiency, and, ultimately, hypotension and death. Multidrug antibiotic therapy initiated prior to onset of the fulminant phase of the illness was not successful in this patient in contrast with 6 other recent cases of bioterrorism-related anthrax.[2] Although the bacteremia was rapidly cleared, histopathology and postmortem culture of mediastinal lymph node tissue indicated the presence of viable *B anthracis*, suggesting suboptimal bactericidal activity or tissue penetration with the regimen used in this patient. Further study is needed to determine which antimicrobial regimens are most effective in treating this disease. Use of rifampin in combination with other agents may offer some benefit; 4 of the 6 survivors of inhalational anthrax from the attacks of 2001 were treated with combinations that included both a fluoroquinolone and rifampin. Persistence and reaccumulation of pleural effusions, interstitial edema, and respiratory distress were reported to be difficult problems in the other patients with inhalational anthrax following the 2001 attacks.[2]

The postmortem findings of hemorrhagic lymphadenopathy and necrosis in this patient were consistent with reports of other cases of bioterrorism-related inhalational anthrax in 2001, with the exception that the pathologic, immunopathologic, and microbiological evidence of *B anthracis* was predominately confined to the thorax. In other fatal cases of bioterrorism-related inhalational anthrax, immunohistochemical staining showed *B anthracis* bacilli in multiple organs.[2] The presence of abundant *B anthracis* in the pleural surface and pleural fluid in this and previous cases highlights the important role of the pleural space in the pathogenesis of anthrax and the value of pleural fluid in the diagnosis of inhalational anthrax. In patients suspected of having inhalational anthrax but in whom the diagnosis is unconfirmed, pleural fluid studies should be obtained and evaluated by bacterial culture, *B anthracis*–specific PCR, and immunohistologic staining of the pleural fluid cell block.[2]

In summary, we describe the 11th case of bioterrorism-related inhalational anthrax reported in the United States following the anthrax attacks of 2001. The source of exposure to *B anthracis* in this patient is not known. Exposure to mail that was cross-contaminated as it passed through postal facilities contaminated with *B anthracis* spores is one hypothesis under investigation. The presenting clinical features of this patient were subtle and nondistinctive. The diagnosis was recognized because blood cultures were obtained prior to the administration of antibiotics, emphasizing the importance of this diagnostic test in evaluating ill patients who have been exposed to *B anthracis*. New approaches to early diagnosis and more effective treatment of the pulmonary complications of inhalational anthrax are clearly warranted.

Acknowledgments: We thank the patient's family for providing permission to publish information about this case for the medical community. We also acknowledge the valuable contribution of the following to this work: Jeanine Bartlett, Tara Ferebee-Harris, Patricia Greer, James Gruden, Gale Jaccabacci, Jeltley Montague, Tim Morken, Chalanda Smith, Kay Vydareny, and the microbiology laboratory and medical housestaff of Griffin Hospital.

Members of the Anthrax Bioterrorism Investigation Team: Greg Armstrong, Kenneth Bell, Mike Bowen, Joe Bresee, Dave Brownell, Joe Burkhart, Greg Burr, Matt Cartter, Nicole Coffin, Richard Collins, Larry Cseh, Scott Deitchman, Timothy Dignam, Rick Ekenberg, Marc Fischer, Julie Gerberding, Mike Grout, Jennifer Hamborsky, Alex Hoffmaster, James Hughes, Max Kiefer, Bradley King, Jacob Kool, Leslye LaClaire, Neil Lustig, Jennifer McClellan, Paul Mead, Bruce Newton, Stephanie Noviello, Otilio Oyervides, John Painter, Christopher Paddock, Umesh Parashar, Bradley Perkins, Joseph Perz, Conrad Quinn, Renee Ridzon, Ron Sanders, Charles Schable, Karen Spago, Adrian Stoica, David Sylvain, Kathi Tatti, Eyasu Teshale, Rob Weyant, Alcia Williams, Jennifer Williams, Scott Wright, Heather Wurtzel, and Ronald Zabrocki.

References

1. Keim P, Price L, Klevytska A, et al. Multiple-locus variable-number tandem repeat analysis reveals genetic relationships with *Bacillus anthracis*. *J Bacteriol.* 2000;182:2928-2936.
2. Jernigan J, Stephens D, Ashford D, et al. Bioterrorism-related inhalational anthrax: the first 10 cases reported in the United States. *Emerg Infect Dis.* 2001;7:933-944.
3. Mayer TA, Bersoff-Matcha S, Murphy C, et al. Clinical presentation of inhalational anthrax following bioterrorism exposure: report of 2 surviving patients. *JAMA.* 2001;286:2549-2553.
4. Borio L, Frank D, Mani V, et al. Death due to bioterrorism-related inhalational anthrax: report of 2 patients. *JAMA.* 2001;286:2554-2559.
5. Bush LM, Abrams BH, Beall A, Johnson CC. Index case of fatal inhalational anthrax due to bioterrorism in the United States. *N Engl J Med.* 2001;345:1607-1610.
6. Centers for Disease Control and Prevention. Update: investigation of bioterrorism-related anthrax and interim guidelines for exposure management and antimicrobial therapy, October 2001. *MMWR Morb Mortal Wkly Rep.* 2001;50:909-919.
7. Centers for Disease Control and Prevention. Update: investigation of bioterrorism-related inhalational anthrax—Connecticut, 2001. *MMWR Morb Mortal Wkly Rep.* 2001;50:1049-1051.
8. Centers for Disease Control and Prevention. Update: investigation of bioterrorism-related anthrax—Connecticut, 2001. *MMWR Morb Mortal Wkly Rep.* 2001;50:1077-1079.
9. Castle S. Clinical relevance of age-related immune dysfunction. *Clin Infect Dis.* 2000;31:578-585.
10. Miller R. The aging immune system: primer and prospectus. *Science.* 1996;273:70-74.
11. Walker D, Yampolskaya O, Grinberg L. Death at Sverdlovsk: what have we learned? *Am J Pathol.* 1994;144:1135-1141.
12. Dixon T, Meselson M, Guillemin J, Hanna P. Anthrax. *N Engl J Med.* 1999;341:815-826.
13. Brachman P, Pagano J, Albrink W. Two cases of fatal inhalation anthrax, one associated with sarcoidosis. *N Engl J Med.* 1961;265:203-208.
14. Brachman P. Inhalation anthrax. *Ann N Y Acad Sci.* 1980;353:83-93.
15. Gleiser C, Berdjis C, Hartman H, Gochenour W. Pathology of experimental respiratory anthrax in *Macaca mulatta*. *Br J Exp Pathol.* 1963;44:416-426.
16. Glassman H. Discussion. *Bacteriol Rev.* 1966;30:657-659.
17. Brachman P, Kaufmann A, Dalldorf F. Industrial inhalation anthrax. *Bacteriol Rev.* 1966;30:646-659.
18. Meselson M, Guillemin J, Hugh-Jones M, et al. The Sverdlovsk anthrax outbreak of 1979. *Science.* 1994;266:1202-1208.

Cutaneous Anthrax Associated With Microangiopathic Hemolytic Anemia and Coagulopathy in a 7-Month-Old Infant

Abigail Freedman, MD; Olubunmi Afonja, MD; Mary Wu Chang, MD; Farzad Mostashari, MD; Martin Blaser, MD; Guillermo Perez-Perez, MD; Herb Lazarus, MD; Robert Schacht, MD; Jane Guttenberg, MD; Michael Traister, MD; William Borkowsky, MD

Anthrax infection is caused by *Bacillus anthracis*, an aerobic, spore-forming, gram-positive rod found throughout the world, and presents in 3 forms: -cutaneous, inhalational, and gastrointestinal. The term *anthrax*, from the Greek anthrakos, meaning coal, derives from the characteristic lesion of the cutaneous form, a black eschar. Cutaneous anthrax accounts for approximately 95% of cases,[1] while inhalational anthrax, the traditional woolsorter's disease, is less common, and gastrointestinal anthrax is rare.[2, 3] However, all forms can lead to bacteremia, sepsis, meningitis, and death, and all of these manifestations can occur in children.

Anthrax remains endemic in many parts of the world, including Asia, Africa, South America, and Australia, and it is estimated that up to 20 000 cases occur annually.[4] In contrast, 224 cases of cutaneous anthrax were reported in the United States from 1944 to 2000, and only 5 between 1984 and 2000.[5,6] Furthermore, only 18 cases of inhalational anthrax occurred in the United States during the 20th century, the last in 1976, and cases of gastrointestinal anthrax have not been reported in the United States.[2] None of these 20th-century cases were reported in children.

Following the bioterrorist anthrax attacks of 2001, the epidemiological picture of anthrax changed considerably. In addition to bioterrorism-related exposures to anthrax spores in various locations around the country, verified cases of both pulmonary and cutaneous anthrax were reported, including several deaths. With 3 exceptions, all cases occurred in adults, whose exposure took place in the context of their work in journalism, government, or postal service.[7] We report a case of cutaneous anthrax with systemic complications that occurred in a 7-month-old infant. This chapter includes detailed clinical information describing this patient's complicated course.

Case Report

A 7-month-old, previously healthy, white male infant was admitted to the hospital on October 1, 2001. Two days prior to admission he was noted to have a painless red macule on the proximal medial aspect of the left upper extremity with associated swelling. During the next 24 hours, the arm became increasingly edematous, the macule evolved to a papule, and a serous drainage was evident. However, the patient remained afebrile and without apparent pain or other systemic symptoms. His primary pediatricians treated him with amoxicillin/clavulanate potassium for presumed cellulitis, but he required admission to the hospital after

Table 1. Laboratory Findings, Maximal Daily Temperature, and Therapy of a 7-Month-Old Infant With Cutaneous Anthrax, Microangiopathic Hemolytic Anemia, and Coagulopathy

	Illness Day				
	3	4	5	6	7
Temperature, °C	99	102.5	101	101	100.8
Hematologic					
White blood cells, x $10^3/\mu L$	28	16	16.7	17.6	25.1
Neutrophil, %	47	28	24		
Segmented cells, %					10
Band form, %				23	17
Hematocrit, %	42.5	37.3	29.9	23.3	18.7*
Reticulocytes, %				2.2	4.4
Platelet, x $10^3/\mu L$	409	19	73	53	56
Coagulation					
Prothrombin time, s					12.1
Partial thromboplastin time, s					24.2
Thrombin time, s					
Fibrinogen, mg/dL					93
D-dimers, ng/mL					>1000
Fibrin degradation products, µg/mL					>20
Chemistry					
Lactate dehydrogenase, U/L					5504
Sodium, mEq/L	128	120	132	131	
Potassium, mEq/L	4.9	4.8			
Serum urea nitrogen, mg/dL†	14	12			
Creatinine, mg/dL‡	0.6	0.3			
Urinalysis					
Blood		Negative			
Protein, mg/dL		Negative			
Type of antibiotic	Ampicillin-sulbactam	Ampicillin-sulbactam and clindamycin	Ampicillin-sulbactam and clindamycin	Clindamycin and cephalexin	Clindamycin and cephalexin
Corticosteroid therapy	No	No	No	No	No

* Value from smear of schistocytes and fragmented red blood cells

† To convert to mmol/L, multiply by 0.357.

‡ To convert to µmol/L, multiply by 88.4.

the third dose, due to increased swelling and drainage of the lesion, and his difficulty in tolerating oral medication.

The infant did not have a significant medical history but he had recently played outdoors in a New York park and had also visited his mother at her workplace, the offices of a national television news organization, for an hour the day before his symptoms began. Anthrax spores were subsequently found at his mother's workplace.

On admission, the infant was alert, afebrile, and in no apparent distress. Laboratory studies revealed significant leukocytosis and hyponatremia (**Table 1**).

Illness Day								
8	**9**	**10**	**11**	**12**	**14**	**15**	**17**	**20**
99.6	99.2	98.1	98	98	98	98	101.8	98
25.3	29.8	30.4	18.2	17.6	15.1	12.7	11.4	7.3
20	24	14	22	18	21		39	11
22	23	27	49	14	14		5	2
14.3	23.6	19.5	36.2	32.5	33.9	28.8	31	34
7.5		10	10.1		20			
96	43	60	61	52	66	103	181	265
13.1	13.6	12.6					12.1	12
26.5	24.1	23.6					33.8	26
				40.9	67.7			
58	56	117					216	280
>1000		>1000						
>5, <20		>20						>40
		4820		5670			2805	
133	132	135		133	134			
2.9	2.5	3.3		3.9	3.6			
26	21	15		20	13			
0.9	0.9	0.8		0.7	0.4			
Moderate		Large	Large	Large		Large		
30		>299	>299	>299		100		
None	None	None	None	None	None	None	Ciprofloxacin	Ciprofloxacin
Yes	Yes	Yes	Yes	Yes	Yes	Yes	No	No

Blood was not sent for culture, but intravenous ampicillin/sulbactam was initiated. Surgical incision and drainage performed with the patient under local anesthesia revealed no underlying abscess, but dark red fluid was expressed from the lesion. Bacterial cultures were not performed.

On hospital day 2, the left arm showed massive, nonpitting, nontender edema with a dark red macule approximately 2 to 3 cm in diameter. There was copious, yellow serous drainage from the wound and paler erythema extending across the anterior thorax to the sternum. No axillary adenopathy was palpable. The hyponatremia was managed with fluid restriction and clindamycin was added to the antibiotic regimen. An infectious disease consultation was obtained. A gram stain of the wound drainage showed neither white blood cells nor organisms. Differential diagnoses considered were infection of bone, soft tissue, or both; arachnid bite; and obstructive mass lesion. Ultrasound of the left upper extremity revealed diffuse inflammation without abscess, and minimal axillary lymphadenopathy. Doppler studies excluded deep vein thrombosis or other vascular compromise to the limb. Later that day, the patient became febrile (39.2°C) and developed significant thrombocytopenia.

During the next 2 days, the arm edema decreased slightly, a 3-mm area of central necrosis was noted at the wound site, and petechiae appeared on the left anterosuperior thorax and axilla. The patient's hematocrit decreased to 23.3%, and low-grade fever, hyponatremia, thrombocytopenia, and leukocytosis persisted, now with a significant number of band forms. Due to loss of intravenous access, the antibiotic regimen was changed to oral cephalexin and clindamycin.

By hospital day 5, the fever resolved and the arm edema had decreased considerably. The lesion appeared as a circumscribed erythematous plaque (4.5 × 5 cm) with a central eschar of less than 1 cm (**Figure 1**). A magnetic resonance image of the upper extremity (previously published[8]) revealed extensive soft tissue inflammation extending from the left lateral chest wall to the hand, but there was no bone involvement, soft tissue gas or fluid collection, or mass lesion. The hematocrit decreased to 18.7%. The glucose-6-phosphate dehydrogenase enzyme level was normal, but the peripheral blood smear revealed schistocytes and fragmented red blood cells. A serum lactate dehydrogenase level of greater than 5000 U/L, along with evidence of mild increases in serum urea nitrogen and creatinine levels, supported a diagnosis of microangiopathic hemolytic anemia.

At this point, the working diagnosis was cutaneous and systemic loxoscelism, as the clinical course and the evolution of the skin lesion (Figure 1) seemed more consistent with envenomation than an infectious process. Dermatologic consultation concurred with this diagnosis. Oral prednisolone was begun and antibiotics were discontinued.

While the patient's arm edema improved and he remained afebrile, his hematologic status worsened during the next few days. The hematocrit decreased to 14.3% with accompanying tachycardia, necessitating 2 transfusions of 15 mL/kg of packed red blood cells. Coagulopathy was evident, with ongoing thrombocytopenia and elevated D-dimer levels and fibrin degradation products. A persistent hypofibrinogenemia required transfusion of 4 U of cryoprecipitate. Renal

Figure 1. The Lesion of Cutaneous Anthrax at Hospital Day 5

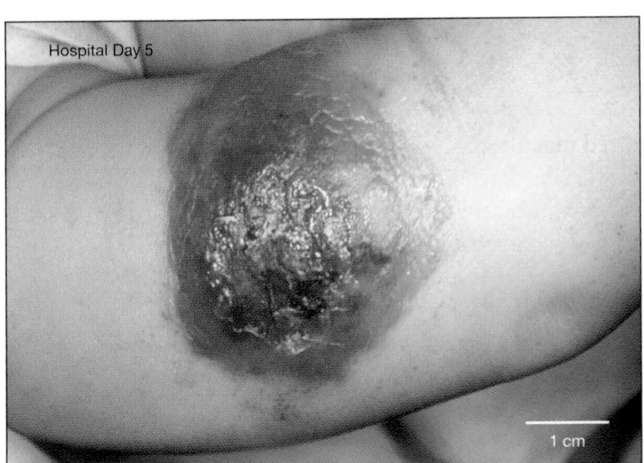

Figure 2. The Lesion of Cutaneous Anthrax at Hospital Day 12

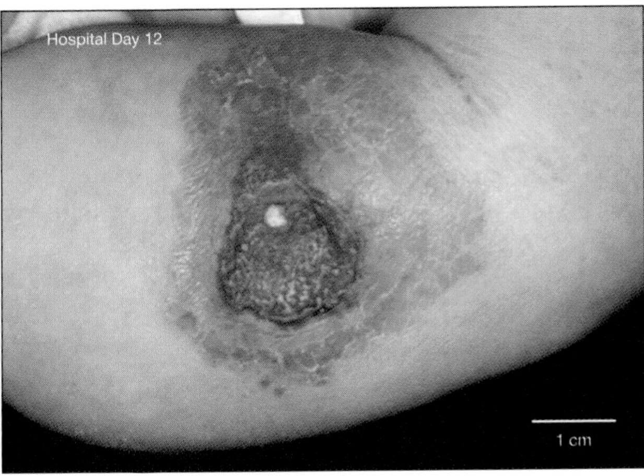

insufficiency, with elevated serum urea nitrogen, hematuria, proteinuria, transient oliguria, and hypertension (systolic blood pressure of 130 mm Hg and diastolic blood pressure of 85 mm Hg) were present. By hospital day 12, these laboratory abnormalities were resolving and the patient was clinically stable. However, a 2-cm black eschar was present in the center of the cutaneous lesion (**Figure 2**).

That day, the first case of cutaneous anthrax in New York was reported and the New York Department of Health was notified that this infant was potentially infected with anthrax. Two skin biopsies of the lesion were performed the next day, and these, as well as blood obtained on hospital day 2, were sent to the Centers for Disease Control and Prevention for polymerase chain reaction diagnosis and

Figure 3. IgM and IgG Response to Anthrax Lysate (Western Blot)

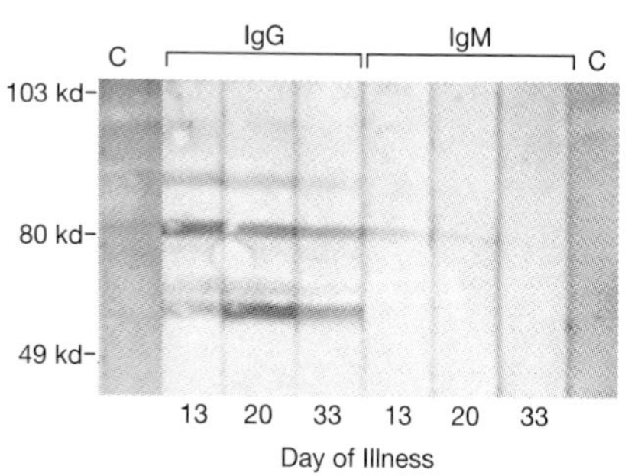

Band at 83 kd, protective factor; and at 89 to 93 kd, edema and lethal factors. Bottom 2 bands are thought to indicate a breakdown product of the antigens.

immunohistology, respectively. Two days later, these tests were reported as positive for *B anthracis*, with significant anthrax DNA present in the serum sample and immunohistochemical detection of fragmented anthrax bacilli in the biopsy tissue. Western blot testing of serum samples from day 13 of illness revealed both an IgM response to the 83-kd protective factor and an IgG response (**Figure 3**).

On day 20 of the patient's illness, the IgM response decreased but the IgG response intensified and extended to the edema and lethal factors band of 89 to 93 kd. The patient was discharged home on day 17 of illness, receiving oral ciprofloxacin, the treatment recommended by the Centers for Disease Control and Prevention. His platelet count and fibrinogen level were normal, but evidence of a mild hemolysis persisted. After 2 weeks of ciprofloxacin, when the other anthrax isolates were shown to be susceptible to penicillin, amoxicillin was used as the antibiotic. Hematuria, anemia, and elevated D-dimer levels slowly resolved over the next 2 weeks, 30 days after admission. Serum urea nitrogen and creatinine levels were normal at 12 days after admission and the skin lesion healed with evidence of scarring by day 60 (**Figure 4**).

Comment

Cutaneous anthrax is primarily a local infection and may resolve spontaneously. Untreated cutaneous anthrax may cause systemic disease with up to 20% mortality,[9] although with antibiotic treatment the mortality rate is less than 1%.[10] Antibiotic treatment has been reported to sterilize the skin lesion within 24 hours[10]; thus, prompt institution of antibiotics appears to limit hematogenous spread of the organism, but does not change the local, toxin-mediated effects. Signs of systemic infection may range from fever and leukocytosis to septic shock, meningitis, and death.

Cutaneous anthrax in children is reported less frequently than in adults; a review of MEDLINE revealed 30 case reports between 1967 and 2001, mostly in rural settings in developing nations. The disease has been reported in neonates,

Figure 4. The Lesion of Cutaneous Anthrax 2 Months After Discharge

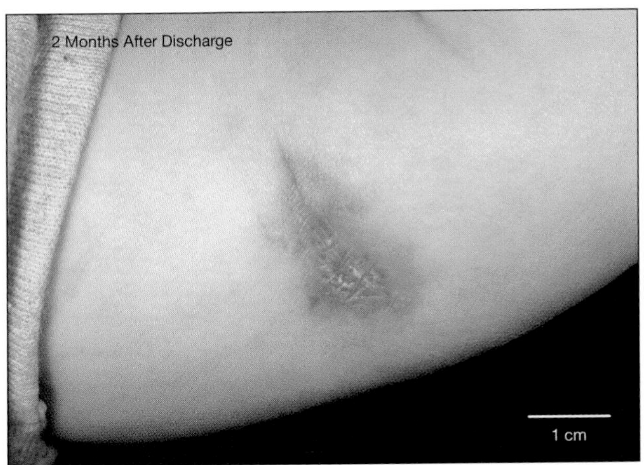

children, and adolescents. While infants and young children may acquire anthrax from infected bedding or other fomites, 2 reports suggest that skin-to-skin contact may be an important route of transmission in this age group. One case involved an infant whose mother had an anthrax lesion on her cheek,[11] the other involved 2 young children who slept in the same bed.[12] In another case series of 11 patients with periocular anthrax, 6 children were younger than 6 years. The authors speculate that young children may be more likely to rub their eyes with spore-contaminated fingers or to have spore-carrying insects swarm on their eyelids.[13] The origin of cutaneous anthrax in the infant described in this chapter is probably related to the finding of anthrax spores at the mother's workplace. One possible scenario is that spores present on the hands of someone in the workplace who lifted or held the child may have contacted an exposed or possibly abraded area of the child's skin.

The clinical presentation of cutaneous anthrax in children as reported in the literature is similar to that in adults, with an initial painless papulovesicular lesion surrounded by massive interstitial edema, which develops an eschar within 2 to 5 days. Children also can develop systemic symptoms, such as fever and leukocytosis, particularly if treatment is delayed and bacteremia develops. A review of cases from the first half of the 20th century reveals that more than half of anthrax meningitis cases in children were preceded by cutaneous disease.[14] While the patient described in this chapter had a fairly typical clinical course with respect to the cutaneous lesion, several features of this case have not, to our knowledge, been described previously in the context of cutaneous anthrax.

First, this child's illness was complicated by severe hematologic abnormalities requiring multiple transfusions of blood products. Between admission and hospital day 6, he developed a severe microangiopathic hemolytic anemia with significant thrombocytopenia, renal involvement, and coagulopathy. To date, there has been only 1 case report of coagulopathy resulting from cutaneous anthrax. In this case, a 20-year-old Iranian woman with cutaneous anthrax developed septic shock associated with thrombocytopenia, hypofibrinogenemia, elevated fibrin degradation products, and elevated prothrombin time,[9] with associated hematuria, hypoproteinemia, and hyperkalemia. In another report, involving a 57-year-old British man, the patient had a normal hematologic profile but developed elevated creatine kinase levels and renal failure.[15] Neither of these patients exhibited the combination of acute hemolysis, coagulopathy, and renal insufficiency found in the patient described here.

Second, the patient developed persistent hyponatremia, which required careful fluid management during his hospital course. Electrolyte abnormalities, particularly hyperkalemia, occasionally have been described in patients with cutaneous anthrax, usually in connection with severe sepsis and shock. Mild hyponatremia was reported in 5 of the first 10 individuals with bioterrorism-related inhalational anthrax following the attacks of 2001.[16] Hyponatremia in this infant coincided with the massive edema of his left upper extremity and was probably related to the degree of fluid shift in his 7-month-old body, something that might not be seen in a larger child or an adult. The hyponatremia began to resolve with the administration of corticosteroids, which have been reported to be beneficial in the treatment of the edema associated with anthrax.[17]

Third, the patient had severe systemic symptoms despite timely institution of antibiotic and corticosteroid therapy. Most case reports suggest that cutaneous anthrax in children is, for the most part, a mild infection, with few serious consequences provided that treatment with antibiotics is provided.[18, 19] Mortality and significant morbidity are consistently described as the result of delay in treatment and are proportional to the clinical status of the patient at presentation. Occasionally, bacteremia or meningitis occurs in children with cutaneous disease.[2] In this patient, systemic signs occurred 36 to 48 hours after antibiotics were started. Bacterial DNA was detected in a peripheral blood sample suggesting that significant bacteremia or circulating toxin was already present, despite the patient remaining afebrile and having largely normal laboratory values. The role of surgical debridement in the dissemination of bacteria or toxin is unclear.

Fourth, many of the signs and symptoms, including edema, fever, leukocytosis, thrombocytopenia, hemolysis, renal failure, and disseminated intravascular coagulation, while rarely associated with cutaneous anthrax, are associated with envenomations, particularly that of *Loxosceles reclusa*.[20, 21] Although this spider has rarely been found in New York, cutaneous anthrax had never before been diagnosed in an infant prior to October 200l.

Possibly the most useful clinical features for distinguishing anthrax from other diagnoses, such as cellulitis or insect bite, are the relatively large extent of the associated edema and the painlessness of the lesion. The culture of the organism from a site of inflammation prior to the initiation of antibiotics is a diagnostic response. Serological responses to anthrax toxins, particularly the protective antigen, have previously been used to define infection in humans and animals. One study in humans found that only 24% of infected individuals had detectable antiprotective antigen antibodies within the first week of infection.

This increased to 83% when a serum sample was obtained after the first week.[22] Only 1 report has compared serological responses in children and adults.[23] In this case, antibodies were seen in 8 of 17 adults and in 2 of 8 children, with much lower titer levels in children, suggesting that they may be less responsive than adults. The infant in this chapter had evidence of an evolving primary immune response, particularly to the protective antigen, by day 13 of illness on Western blot. We hypothesized that the prolonged evidence of hemolysis may have been due to the absence of antibody production to the toxins. The kinetics of the response did correlate with the increase in platelets but not with the ongoing hemolysis.

As this case illustrates, cutaneous anthrax in an infant or child may quickly progress to a severe systemic disease; thus, if the diagnosis is suspected, the patient should be admitted to the hospital, electrolyte and hematological status should be monitored carefully, and intravenous antibiotics should be instituted. A presumptive diagnosis can be made by blood culture or Gram stain prior to initiating antibiotics, or more definitively by serum polymerase chain reaction and skin biopsy. Although the strain of anthrax recovered from the infections following the attacks of 2001 is susceptible to penicillin, doxycycline, and fluoroquinolones, the use of the latter 2 drugs in young children is potentially problematic. After this infant was diagnosed, it was recommended that he be treated with ciprofloxacin for the remainder of the 60 days from the onset of infection, as per the initial recommendations of the Centers for Disease Control and Prevention.[24]

Fluoroquinolones are theoretically toxic to developing cartilage but the American Academy of Pediatrics recommends their use, as the benefits outweigh the risks.[25] Doxycycline is another option despite its propensity to stain the enamel of developing teeth. The Centers for Disease Control and Prevention subsequently recommended that a second antibiotic be added to the initial therapy of systemic disease.[7] The addition of clindamycin to this infant's therapy may have provided additional benefit. Although ciprofloxacin was initiated once the diagnosis was established, therapy was changed to amoxicillin after a week because of concerns about potential toxicity and since the organism was sensitive to this agent.[26]

In this new era of bioterrorism, anthrax should be considered in the differential diagnosis of acute progressive inflammatory disorders of the skin as well as the other syndromes with which it is associated.

Acknowledgments: We are grateful to the patient's mother for granting permission to publish this information about her son for the medical community.

References

1. Dixon TC, Meselson M, Guillemin J, Hanna PC. Anthrax. *N Engl J Med.* 1999;341:815-826.

2. Inglesby TV, Henderson DA, Bartlett JG, et al. Anthrax as a biological weapon: medical and public health management. *JAMA.* 1999;281: 1735-1745.

3. Centers for Disease Control and Prevention. Human ingestion of *Bacillus anthracis:* contaminated meat: Minnesota, August 2000. *MMWR Morb Mortal Wkly Rep.* Cited in *JAMA.* 2000;284: 1644-1646.

4. Edwards MS. Anthrax. In: Feigen RD, Cherry JD, eds. Textbook of Pediatric Infectious Diseases. Vol 1. Philadelphia, Pa: WB Saunders Co; 1998: 1176-1179.

5. Centers for Disease Control and Prevention. Summary of notifiable diseases: 1945-1994. *MMWR Morb Mortal Wkly Rep.* 1994;43:70-78.

6. Centers for Disease Control and Prevention. Summary of notifiable diseases: United States, 1999. *MMWR Morb Mortal Wkly Rep.* 1999;48:82-89.

7. Centers for Disease Control and Prevention. Update: investigation of bioterrorism-related anthrax and interim public health guidelines for exposure management and antimicrobial therapy, October 2001. *MMWR Morb Mortal Wkly Rep.* 2001;50:909-919.

8. Roche KJ, Chang MW, Lazarus H. Cutaneous anthrax infection. *N Engl J Med.* 2001;345:1611.

9. Khajehdehi P. Toxemic shock, hematuria, hypokalemia, and hypoproteinemia in a case of cutaneous anthrax. *Mt Sinai J Med.* 2001;68: 213-215.

10. Manios S, Kavaliotis I. Anthrax in children: a long forgotten, potentially fatal infection. *Scand J Infect Dis.* 1979;11:203-206.

11. Arya LS, Saidalo A, Qureshi MA, Singh M. Anthrax in infants and children in Afghanistan. *Indian J Pediatr.* 1982;49:529-534.

12. Thappa DM. Cutaneous anthrax in two siblings. *Indian J Pediatr.* 2001;68:573-574.

13. Yorsten D, Foster A. Cutaneous anthrax leading to corneal scarring from cicatricial ectropion. *Br J Ophthalmol.* 1989;73:809-811.

14. Tahernia AC, Hashemi G. Survival in anthrax meningitis. *Pediatrics.* 1972;50:329-333.

15. Mallon E, McKee PH. Extraordinary case report: cutaneous anthrax. *Am J Dermatopathol.* 1997; 19:79-82.

16. Jernigan JA, Stephens DS, Ashford DA, et al. Bioterrorism-related inhalational anthrax: the first 10 cases reported in the United States. *Emerg Infect Dis.* 2001;7:933-944.

17. Doust JY, Sarkarzadeh A, Kavoossi K. Corticosteroid in treatment of malignant edema of chest wall and neck (anthrax). *Dis Chest.* 1968;53: 773-774.

18. Smego Jr RA, Geberian B, Desmangels G. Cutaneous manifestations of anthrax in rural Haiti. *Clin Infect Dis.* 1998;26:97-102.

19. Tahernia AC. Treatment of anthrax in children. *AJDC.* 1967;42:181-182.

20. Williams ST, Khare VK, Johnston GA, Blackall DP. Severe intravascular hemolysis associated with brown recluse spider envenomation: a report of two cases and review of the literature. *Am J Clin Pathol.* 1995;104:463-467.

21. Wright SW, Wrenn KD, Murray L, Seger D. Clinical presentation and outcome of brown recluse spider bite. *Ann Emerg Med.* 1997;30:28-32.

22. Turnbull PCB, Doganay M, Lindeque PM, Aygen B, McLaughlin J. Serology and anthrax in humans, livestock and Etosha National Park wildlife. *Epidemiol Infect.* 1992;108:299-213.

23. Heyworth B, Ropp ME, Voos UG, Meinel HI, Darlow HM. Anthrax in the Gambia: an epidemiological study. *BMJ.* 1975:4:79-82.

24. CDC update: notice to readers: interim recommendations for antimicrobial prophylaxis for children and breastfeeding mothers and treatment of children with anthrax. *MMWR Morb Mortal Wkly Rep.* 2001;50:1014-1016.

25. American Academy of Pediatrics. *AAP 2000 Red Book: Report of the Committee on Infectious Diseases.* Elk Grove Village, Ill: American Academy of Pediatrics; 2000.

26. CDC update: investigation of bioterrorism-related anthrax and interim guidelines for exposure management and antimicrobial therapy. *MMWR Morb Mortal Wkly Rep.* 2001;50:909-919.

Anthrax as a Biological Weapon

Updated Recommendations for Management

Thomas V. Inglesby, MD; Tara O'Toole, MD, MPH; Donald A. Henderson, MD, MPH; John G. Bartlett, MD; Michael S. Ascher, MD; Edward Eitzen, MD, MPH; Arthur M. Friedlander, MD; Julie L. Gerberding, MD, MPH; Jerome Hauer, MPH; James M. Hughes, MD; Joseph McDade, PhD; Michael T. Osterholm, PhD, MPH; Gerald Parker, PhD, DVM; Trish M. Perl, MD, MSc; Philip K. Russell, MD; Kevin Tonat, DrPH, MPH; for the Working Group on Civilian Biodefense

Of the biological agents that may be used as weapons, the Working Group on Civilian Biodefense identified a limited number of organisms that, in worst-case scenarios, could cause disease and deaths in sufficient numbers to gravely impact a city or region. *Bacillus anthracis*, the bacterium that causes anthrax, is one of the most serious of these.

Several countries are believed to have offensive biological weapons programs, and some independent terrorist groups have suggested their intent to use biological weapons. Because the possibility of a terrorist attack using bioweapons is especially difficult to predict, detect, or prevent, it is among the most feared terrorism scenarios.[1] In September 2001, *B anthracis* spores were sent to several locations via the US Postal Service. Twenty-two confirmed or suspect cases of anthrax infection resulted. Eleven of these were inhalational cases, of whom 5 died; 11 were cutaneous cases (7 confirmed, 4 suspected).[2] In this chapter, these attacks are termed *the anthrax attacks of 2001*. The consequences of these attacks substantiated many findings and recommendations in the Working Group on Civilian Biodefense's previous consensus statement published in 1999[3]; however, the new information from these attacks warrants updating the previous statement.

Before the anthrax attacks of 2001, modern experience with inhalational anthrax was limited to an epidemic in Sverdlovsk, Russia, in 1979 following an unintentional release of *B anthracis* spores from a Soviet bioweapons factory and to 18 occupational exposure cases in the United States during the 20th century. Information about the potential impact of a large, covert attack using *B anthracis* or the possible efficacy of postattack vaccination or therapeutic measures remains limited. Policies and strategies continue to rely partially on interpretation and extrapolation from an incomplete and evolving knowledge base.

Consensus Methods

The working group for this article comprised 23 representatives from academic medical centers; research organizations; and government, military, public health, and emergency management institutions and agencies. For the original consensus statement,[3] we searched MEDLINE databases from January 1966 to April 1998 using Medical Subject Headings of *anthrax*, *Bacillus anthracis*, *biological weapon*, *biological terrorism*, *biological warfare*, and *biowarfare*. Reference review identified work published before 1966. Working group members identified unpublished sources.

The first consensus statement, published in 1999,[3] followed a synthesis of the information and revision of 3 drafts. We reviewed anthrax literature again in January 2002, with special attention to articles following the anthrax attacks of 2001. Members commented on a revised document; proposed revisions were incorporated with the working group's support for the final consensus document.

The assessment and recommendations provided herein represent our best professional judgment based on current data and expertise. The conclusions and recommendations need to be regularly reassessed as new information develops.

History of Current Threat

For centuries, *B anthracis* has caused disease in animals and serious illness in humans.[4] Research on anthrax as a biological weapon began more than 80 years ago.[5] Most national offensive bioweapons programs were terminated following widespread ratification or signing of the Biological Weapons Convention (BWC) in the early 1970s[6]; the US offensive bioweapons program was terminated after President Nixon's 1969 and 1970 executive orders. However, some nations continued offensive bioweapons development programs despite ratification of the BWC. In 1995, Iraq acknowledged producing and weaponizing *B anthracis* to the United Nations Special Commission.[7] The former Soviet Union is also known to have had a large *B anthracis* production program as part of its offensive bioweapons program.[8] A recent analysis reports that there is clear evidence of or widespread assertions from nongovernmental sources alleging the existence of offensive biological weapons programs in at least 13 countries.[6]

The anthrax attacks of 2001 have heightened concern about the feasibility of large-scale aerosol bioweapons attacks by terrorist groups. It has been feared that independent, well-funded groups could obtain a manufactured weapons product or acquire the expertise and resources to produce the materials for an attack. However, some analysts have questioned whether "weapons-grade" material such as that used in the 2001 attacks (ie, powders of *B anthracis* with characteristics such as high spore concentration, uniform particle size, low electrostatic charge, treated to reduce clumping) could be produced by those not supported by the resources of a nation-state. The US Department of Defense recently reported that 3 defense employees with some technical skills but without expert knowledge of bioweapons manufactured a simulant of *B anthracis* in less than a month for

$1 million.[9] It is reported that Aum Shinrikyo, the cult responsible for the 1995 release of sarin nerve gas in a Tokyo subway station,[10] dispersed aerosols of anthrax and botulism throughout Tokyo at least 8 times.[11] Forensic analysis of the *B anthracis* strain used in these attacks revealed that this isolate most closely matched the Sterne 34F2 strain, which is used for animal vaccination programs and is not a significant risk to humans.[12] It is probable that the cult attacks produced no illnesses for this and other technical reasons. Al Quaeda also has sought to acquire bioweapons in its terrorist planning efforts, although the extent to which they have been successful is not reported.[13]

In the anthrax attacks of 2001, *B anthracis* spores were sent in at least 5 letters to Florida, New York City, and Washington, DC. Twenty-two confirmed or suspected cases resulted. All of the identified letters were mailed from Trenton, NJ. The *B anthracis* spores in all the letters were identified as the Ames strain. The specific source (provenance) of *B anthracis* cultures used to create the spore-containing powder remains unknown at the time of this publication.

It is now recognized that the original Ames strain of *B anthracis* did not come from a laboratory in Ames, Iowa, rather from a laboratory in College Station, Tex. Several distinct Ames strains have been recognized by investigating scientists, which are being compared with the Ames strain used in the attack. At least 1 of these comparison Ames strains was recovered from a goat that died in Texas in 1997.[14]

Senator Daschle's letter reportedly had 2 g of *B anthracis*–containing powder; the quantity in the other envelopes has not been disclosed. The powder has been reported to contain between 100 billion to 1 trillion spores per gram[15] although no official analysis of the concentration of spores or the chemical composition of the powder has been published.

The anthrax attacks of 2001 used 1 of many possible methods of attack. The use of aerosol-delivery technologies inside buildings or over large outdoor areas is another method of attack that has been studied. In 1970, the World Health Organization[16] and, in 1993, the Office of Technology Assessment[17] analyzed the potential scope of larger attacks. The 1979 Sverdlovsk accident provides data on the only known aerosol release of *B anthracis* spores resulting in an epidemic.[18]

An aerosol release of *B anthracis* would be odorless and invisible and would have the potential to travel many kilometers before dissipating.[16, 19] Aerosol technologies for large-scale dissemination have been developed and tested by Iraq[7] and the former Soviet Union[8] Few details of those tests are available. The US military also conducted such trials over the Pacific Ocean in the 1960s. A US study near Johnston Atoll in the South Pacific reported a plane "sprayed a 32-mile-long line of agent that traveled for more then 60 miles before it lost its infectiousness."[20]

In 1970, the World Health Organization estimated that 50 kg of *B anthracis* released over an urban population of 5 million would sicken 250 000 and kill 100 000.[16] A US Congressional Office of Technology assessment analysis from 1993 estimated that between 130 000 and 3 million deaths would follow the release of 100 kg of *B anthracis*, a lethality matching that of a hydrogen bomb.[17]

Epidemiology of Anthrax

Naturally occurring anthrax in humans is a disease acquired from contact with anthrax-infected animals or anthrax-contaminated animal products. The disease most commonly occurs in herbivores, which are infected after ingesting spores from the soil. Large anthrax epizootics in herbivores have been reported.[21] A published report states that anthrax killed 1 million sheep in Iran in 1945[22]; this number is supported by an unpublished Iranian governmental document.[23] Animal vaccination programs have reduced drastically the animal mortality from the disease.[24] However, *B anthracis* spores remain prevalent in soil samples throughout the world and cause anthrax cases among herbivores annually.[22, 25, 26]

Anthrax infection occurs in humans by 3 major routes: inhalational, cutaneous, and gastrointestinal. Naturally occurring inhalational anthrax is now rare. Eighteen cases of inhalational anthrax were reported in the United States from 1900 to 1976; none were identified or reported thereafter. Most of these cases occurred in special-risk groups, including goat hair mill or wool or tannery workers; 2 of them were laboratory associated.[27]

Cutaneous anthrax is the most common naturally occurring form, with an estimated 2000 cases reported annually worldwide.[26] The disease typically follows exposure to anthrax-infected animals. In the United States, 224 cases of cutaneous anthrax were reported between 1944 and 1994.[28] One case was reported in 2000.[29] The largest reported epidemic occurred in Zimbabwe between 1979 and 1985, when more than 10 000 human cases of anthrax were reported, nearly all of them cutaneous.[30]

Although gastrointestinal anthrax is uncommon, outbreaks are continually reported in Africa and Asia[26, 31, 32] following ingestion of insufficiently cooked contaminated meat. Two distinct syndromes are oral-pharyngeal and abdominal.[31, 33, 34] Little information is available about the risks of direct contamination of food or water with *B anthracis* spores. Experimental efforts to infect primates by direct gastrointestinal instillation of *B anthracis* spores have not been successful.[35] Gastrointestinal infection could occur only after consumption of large numbers of vegetative cells, such as what might be found in raw or undercooked meat from an infected herbivore, but experimental data is lacking.

Inhalational anthrax is expected to account for most serious morbidity and most mortality following the use of *B anthracis* as an aerosolized biological weapon. Given the absence of naturally occurring cases of inhalational anthrax in the United States since 1976, the occurrence of a single case is now cause for alarm.

Microbiology

B anthracis derives from the Greek word for coal, *anthrakis*, because of the black skin lesions it causes. *B anthracis* is an aerobic, gram-positive, spore-forming, nonmotile *Bacillus* species. The nonflagellated vegetative cell is large (1-8 μm long, 1-1.5 μm wide). Spore size is approximately 1 μm. Spores grow readily on all ordinary laboratory media at 37°C, with a "jointed bamboo-rod" cellular appearance (**Figure 1**) and a unique "curled-hair" colonial appearance. Experienced micro-

Figure 1. Gram Stain of Blood in Culture Media

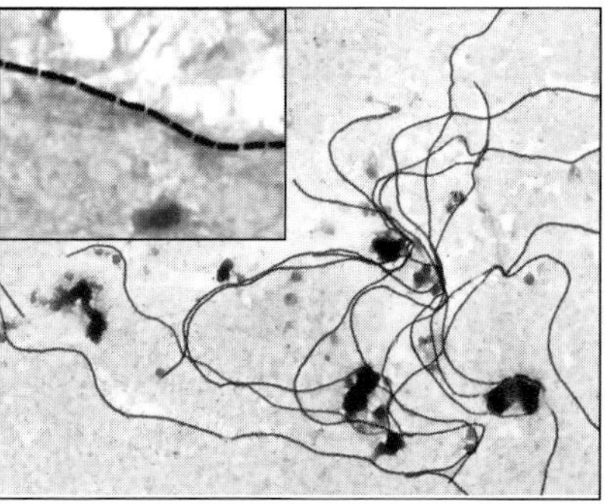

Gram-positive bacilli in long chains (original magnification ×20). Enlargement shows typical "jointed bamboo-rod" appearance of *Bacillus anthracis* (original magnification ×100). Reproduced with permission from Borio et al.[36]

biologists should be able to identify this cellular and colonial morphology; however, few practicing microbiologists outside the veterinary community have seen *B anthracis* colonies beyond what they may have seen in published material.[37] *B anthracis* spores germinate when they enter an environment rich in amino acids, nucleosides, and glucose, such as that found in the blood or tissues of an animal or human host. The rapidly multiplying vegetative *B anthracis* bacilli, on the contrary, will only form spores after local nutrients are exhausted, such as when anthrax-infected body fluids are exposed to ambient air.[22] Vegetative bacteria have poor survival outside of an animal or human host; colony counts decline to being undetectable within 24 hours following inoculation into water.[22] This contrasts with the environmentally hardy properties of the *B anthracis* spore, which can survive for decades in ambient conditions.[37]

Pathogenesis and Clinical Manifestations

Inhalational Anthrax

Inhalational anthrax follows deposition into alveolar spaces of spore-bearing particles in the 1- to 5-μm range.[38,39] Macrophages then ingest the spores, some of which are lysed and destroyed. Surviving spores are transported via lymphatics to mediastinal lymph nodes, where germination occurs after a period of spore dormancy of variable and possibly extended duration.[35,40,41] The trigger(s) responsible for the transformation of *B anthracis* spores to vegetative cells is not fully understood.[42] In Sverdlovsk, cases occurred from 2 to 43 days after exposure.[18] In experimental infection of monkeys, fatal disease occurred up to 58 days[40] and 98 days[43] after exposure. Viable spores were demonstrated in the mediastinal lymph nodes of 1 monkey 100 days after exposure.[44]

Once germination occurs, clinical symptoms follow rapidly. Replicating *B anthracis* bacilli release toxins that lead to hemorrhage, edema, and necrosis.[32,45]

In experimental animals, once toxin production has reached a critical threshold, death occurs even if sterility of the bloodstream is achieved with antibiotics.[27] Extrapolations from animal data suggest that the human LD_{50} (ie, dose sufficient to kill 50% of persons exposed to it) is 2500 to 55 000 inhaled *B anthracis* spores.[46] The LD_{10} was as low as 100 spores in 1 series of monkeys.[43] Recently published extrapolations from primate data suggest that as few as 1 to 3 spores may be sufficient to cause infection.[47] The dose of spores that caused infection in any of the 11 patients with inhalational anthrax in 2001 could not be estimated, although the 2 cases of fatal inhalational anthrax in New York City and Connecticut provoked speculation that the fatal dose, at least in some individuals, may be quite low.

A number of factors contribute to the pathogenesis of *B anthracis*, which makes 3 toxins—*protective antigen*, *lethal factor*, and *edema factor*—that combine to form 2 toxins: lethal toxin and edema toxin (**Figure 2**). The protective antigen allows the binding of lethal and edema factors to the affected cell membrane and facilitates their subsequent transport across the cell membrane. Edema toxin impairs neutrophil function in vivo and affects water homeostasis leading to edema, and lethal toxin causes release of tumor necrosis factor α and interleukin 1 ß, factors that are believed to be linked to the sudden death in severe anthrax infection.[48] The molecular target of lethal and edema factors within the affected cell is not yet elucidated.[49] In addition to these virulence factors, *B anthracis* has a capsule that prevents phagocytosis. Full virulence requires the presence of both an antiphagocytic capsule and the 3 toxin components.[37] An additional factor contributing to *B anthracis* pathogenesis is the high concentration of bacteria occurring in affected hosts.[49]

Inhalational anthrax reflects the nature of acquisition of the disease. The term *anthrax pneumonia* is misleading because typical bronchopneumonia does not occur. Postmortem pathological studies of patients from Sverdlovsk showed that all patients had hemorrhagic thoracic lymphadenitis, hemorrhagic mediastinitis, and pleural effusions. About half had hemorrhagic meningitis. None of these autopsies showed evidence of a bronchoalveolar pneumonic process, although 11 of 42 patient autopsies had evidence of a focal, hemorrhagic, necrotizing pneumonic lesion analogous to the Ghon complex associated with tuberculosis.[50] These findings are consistent with other human case series and experimentally induced inhalational anthrax in animals.[40, 51, 52] A recent reanalysis of pathology specimens from 41 of the Sverdlovsk patients was notable primarily for the presence of necrotizing hemorrhagic mediastinitis; pleural effusions averaging 1700 mL in quantity; meningitis in 50%; arteritis and arterial rupture in many; and the lack of prominent pneumonitis. *B anthracis* was recovered in concentrations of up to 100 million colony-forming units per milliliter in blood and spinal fluid.[53]

In animal models, physiological sequelae of severe anthrax infection have included hypocalcemia, profound hypoglycemia, hyperkalemia, depression and paralysis of respiratory center, hypotension, anoxia, respiratory alkalosis, and terminal acidosis,[54, 55] suggesting that besides the rapid administration of antibiotics,

Figure 2. Pathogenesis of *Bacillus anthracis*

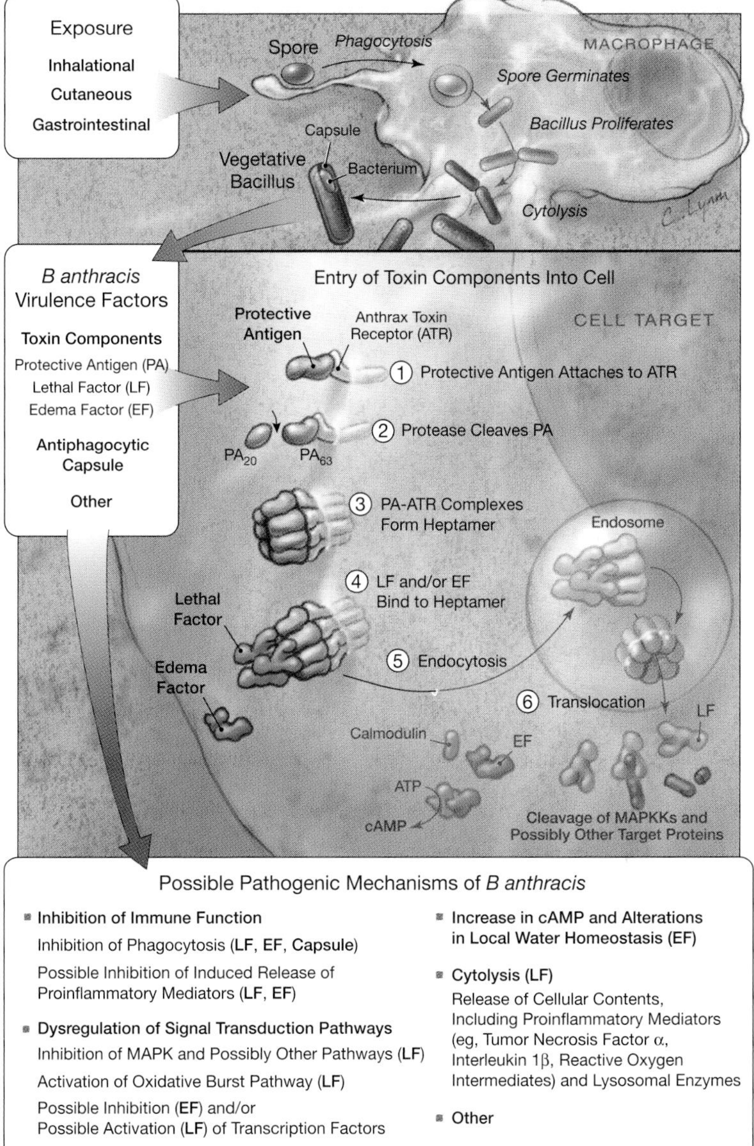

The major known virulence factors of *B anthracis* include the exotoxins edema toxin (PA and EF) and lethal toxin (PA and LF) and the antiphagocytic capsule. Although many exact molecular mechanisms involved in the pathogenicity of the anthrax toxins are uncertain, they appear to inhibit immune function, interrupt intracellular signaling pathways, and lyse cell targets causing massive release of proinflammatory mediators. ATP indicates adenosine triphosphate; cAMP, cyclic adenosine monophosphate; MAPKK, mitogen-activated protein kinase kinase; and MAPK, mitogen-activated protein kinase.

survival might improve with vigilant correction of electrolyte disturbances and acid-based imbalance, glucose infusion, and early mechanical ventilation and vasopressor administration.

Historical Data. Early diagnosis of inhalational anthrax is difficult and requires a high index of suspicion. Prior to the 2001 attacks, clinical information was limited to a series of 18 cases reported in the 20th century and the limited data from Sverdlovsk. The clinical presentation of inhalational anthrax had been described as a 2-stage illness. Patients reportedly first developed a spectrum of nonspecific symptoms, including fever, dyspnea, cough, headache, vomiting, chills, weakness, abdominal pain, and chest pain.[18, 27] Signs of illness and laboratory studies were nonspecific. This stage of illness lasted from hours to a few days. In some patients, a brief period of apparent recovery followed. Other patients progressed directly to the second, fulminant stage of illness.[4, 27, 56]

This second stage was reported to have developed abruptly, with sudden fever, dyspnea, diaphoresis, and shock. Massive lymphadenopathy and expansion of the mediastinum led to stridor in some cases.[57, 58] A chest radiograph most often showed a widened mediastinum consistent with lymphadenopathy.[57] Up to half of patients developed hemorrhagic meningitis with concomitant meningismus, delirium, and obtundation. In this second stage, cyanosis and hypotension progressed rapidly; death sometimes occurred within hours.[4, 27, 56]

In the 20th-century series of US cases, the mortality rate of occupationally acquired inhalational anthrax was 89%, but the majority of these cases occurred before the development of critical care units and, in most cases, before the advent of antibiotics.[27] At Sverdlovsk, it had been reported that 68 of the 79 patients with inhalational anthrax died.[18] However, a separate report from a hospital physician recorded 358 ill with 45 dead; another recorded 48 deaths among 110 patients.[59] A recent analysis of available Sverdlovsk data suggests there may have been as many as 250 cases with 100 deaths.[60] Sverdlovsk patients who had onset of disease 30 or more days after release of organisms had a higher reported survival rate than those with earlier disease onset. Antibiotics, antianthrax globulin, corticosteroids, mechanical ventilation, and vaccine were used to treat some residents in the affected area after the accident, but how many were given vaccine and antibiotics is unknown, nor is it known which patients received these interventions or when. It is also uncertain if the *B anthracis* strain (or strains) to which patients were exposed was susceptible to the antibiotics used during the outbreak. However, a community-wide intervention about the 15th day after exposure did appear to diminish the projected attack rate.[60] In fatal cases, the interval between onset of symptoms and death averaged 3 days. This is similar to the disease course and case fatality rate in untreated experimental monkeys, which have developed rapidly fatal disease even after a latency as long as 58 days.[40]

2001 Attacks Data. The anthrax attacks of 2001 resulted in 11 cases of inhalational anthrax, 5 of whom died. Symptoms, signs, and important laboratory data from these patients are listed in **Table 1**. Several clinical findings from the first 10 patients with inhalational anthrax deserve emphasis.[36, 61-66] Malaise and fever

Table 1. Initial Symptoms, Physical Findings, and Test Results in Patients With Inhalational Anthrax Following US Anthrax Attacks in October and November 2001*

Symptoms (N = 10)	
Fever and chills	10
Sweats, often drenching	7
Fatigue, malaise, lethargy	10
Cough, minimal or nonproductive	9
Nausea or vomiting	9
Dyspnea	8
Chest discomfort or pleuritic pain	7
Myalgias	6
Headache	5
Confusion	4
Abdominal pain	3
Sore throat	2
Rhinorrhea	1
Physical Findings	
Fever >37.8˚C	7
Tachycardia, heart rate >100/min	8
Hypotension, <110 mm Hg	1
Laboratory Results	
White blood cell count, median	9800 × 10^3/µL
Differential neutrophilia, >70%	7
Neutrophil band forms, >5%	4[†]
Elevated transaminases, SGOT or SPGT >40 U/L[‡]	9
Hypoxemia, alveolar-arterial oxygen gradient >30 mm Hg on room air oxygen saturation <94%	6
Metabolic acidosis	2
Elevated creatinine, >1.5 mg/dL (132.6 µmol/L)	1
Chest X-ray Film Findings	
Any abnormality	10
Mediastinal widening	7
Infiltrates or consolidation	7
Pleural effusion	8
Chest Computed Tomographic Findings[§]	
Any abnormality	8
Mediastinal lymphadenopathy, widening	7
Pleural effusion	8
Infiltrates or consolidation	6

* Adapted with permission from Jernigan et al.[61]

† Five persons had laboratory results measuring neutrophil band forms.

‡ SGOT indicates serum glutamic oxalacetic transaminase; SGPT, serum glutamic pyruvic transaminase.

§ Eight persons had computed tomographic scan results.

were presenting symptoms in all 10 cases. Cough, nausea, and vomiting were also prominent. Drenching sweats, dyspnea, chest pain, and headache were also seen in a majority of patients. Fever and tachycardia were seen in the majority of patients at presentation, as were hypoxemia and elevations in transaminases.

Importantly, all 10 patients had abnormal chest x-ray film results: 7 had mediastinal widening, 7 had infiltrates, and 8 had pleural effusions. Chest computed tomographic (CT) scans showed abnormal results in all 8 patients who had this test: 7 had mediastinal widening; 6, infiltrates; 8, pleural effusions.

Data are insufficient to identify factors associated with survival, although early recognition and initiation of treatment and use of more than 1 antibiotic have been suggested as possible factors.[61] For the 6 patients for whom such information is known, the median period from presumed time of exposure to the onset of symptoms was 4 days (range, 4-6 days). Patients sought care a median of 3.5 days after symptom onset. All 4 patients exhibiting signs of fulminant illness prior to antibiotic administration died.[61] Of note, the incubation period of the 2 fatal cases from New York City and Connecticut is not known.

Cutaneous Anthrax

Historically, cutaneous anthrax has been known to occur following the deposition of the organism into skin; previous cuts or abrasions made one especially susceptible to infection.[30, 67] Areas of exposed skin, such as arms, hands, face, and neck, were the most frequently affected. In Sverdlovsk, cutaneous cases occurred only as late as 12 days after the original aerosol release; no reports of cutaneous cases appeared after prolonged latency.[18]

After the spore germinates in skin tissues, toxin production results in local edema. An initially pruritic macule or papule enlarges into a round ulcer by the second day. Subsequently, 1- to 3-mm vesicles may appear that discharge clear or serosanguinous fluid containing numerous organisms on Gram stain. As shown in **Figure 3**, development of a painless, depressed, black eschar follows, often associated with extensive local edema. The anthrax eschar dries, loosens, and falls off in the next 1 to 2 weeks. Lymphangitis and painful lymphadenopathy can occur with associated systemic symptoms. Differential diagnosis of eschars includes tularemia, scrub typhus, rickettsial spotted fevers, rat bite fever, and ecthyma gangrenosum.[68] Noninfectious causes of eschars include arachnid bites[63] and vasculitides. Although antibiotic therapy does not appear to change the course of eschar formation and healing, it does decrease the likelihood of systemic disease. Without antibiotic therapy, the mortality rate has been reported to be as high as 20%; with appropriate antibiotic treatment, death due to cutaneous anthrax has been reported to be rare.[4]

Following the anthrax attacks of 2001, there have been 11 confirmed or probable cases of cutaneous anthrax. One case report of cutaneous anthrax resulting from these attacks has been published (Figure 3).[63] This child had no reported evidence of prior visible cuts, abrasions, or lesions at the site of the cutaneous lesion that developed. The mean incubation period for cutaneous anthrax cases diagnosed in 2001 was 5 days, with a range of 1 to 10 days, based on estimated

Figure 3. Lesion of Cutaneous Anthrax Associated With Microangiopathic Hemolytic Anemia and Coagulopathy in a 7-Month-Old Infant

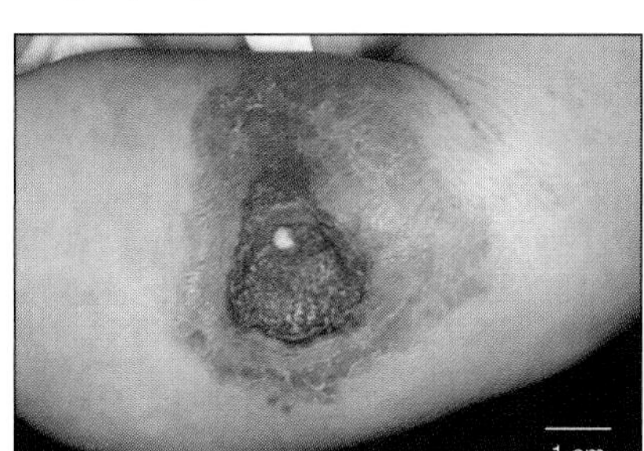

By hospital day 12, a 2-cm black eschar was present in the center of the cutaneous lesion. Reproduced with permission from Freedman et al.[63]

dates of exposure to *B anthracis*–contaminated letters. Cutaneous lesions occurred on the forearm, neck, chest, and fingers.[69]

The only published case report of cutaneous anthrax from the attacks of 2001 is notable for the difficulty in recognition of the disease in a previously healthy 7-month-old, the rapid progression to severe systemic illness despite hospitalization, and clinical manifestations that included microangiopathic hemolytic anemia with renal involvement, coagulopathy, and hyponatremia.[63] Fortunately, this child recovered, and none of the cutaneous cases of anthrax diagnosed after the 2001 attacks were fatal.

Gastrointestinal Anthrax

Some think gastrointestinal anthrax occurs after deposition and germination of spores in the upper or lower gastrointestinal tract. However, considering the rapid transit time in the gastrointestinal tract, it seems more likely that many such cases must result from the ingestion of large numbers of vegetative bacilli from poorly cooked infected meat rather than from spores. In any event, the oral-pharyngeal form of disease results in an oral or esophageal ulcer and leads to the development of regional lymphadenopathy, edema, and sepsis.[31,33] Disease in the lower gastrointestinal tract manifests as primary intestinal lesions occurring predominantly in the terminal ileum or cecum,[50] presenting initially with nausea, vomiting, and malaise and progressing rapidly to bloody diarrhea, acute abdomen, or sepsis. Massive ascites has occurred in some cases of gastrointestinal anthrax.[34] Advanced infection may appear similar to the sepsis syndrome occurring in either inhalational or cutaneous anthrax.[4] Some authors suggest that aggressive medical intervention, as would be recommended for inhalational anthrax, may reduce mortality. Given the difficulty of early diagnosis of gastrointestinal anthrax, however, mortality may be high.[4] Postmortem examinations in Sverdlovsk showed gastrointestinal submucosal lesions in 39 of 42 patients,[50] but all of these patients were also found to have definitive pathologic evidence of an inhalational source of

Table 2. Diagnosis of Inhalational Anthrax Infection*

Category	Findings
Epidemiology	Sudden appearance of several cases of severe acute febrile illness with fulminant course and death or Acute febrile illness in persons identified as being at risk following a specific attack (eg, those in the 2001 attacks: postal workers, members of the news media, and politicians and their staff)
Diagnostic tests	Chest radiograph: widened mediastinum, infiltrates, pleural effusion Chest computed tomographic scan: hyperdense hilar and mediastinal nodes, mediastinal edema, infiltrates, pleural effusion Thoracentesis: hemorrhagic pleural effusions
Microbiology	Peripheral blood smear: gram-positive bacilli on blood smear Blood culture growth of large gram-positive bacilli with preliminary identification of *Bacillus* species†
Pathology	Hemorrhagic mediastinitis, hemorrhagic thoracic lymphadenitis, hemorrhagic meningitis; DFA stain of infected tissues

* See Table 1 for list of febrile illness symptoms and signs.

† Most rapid assays are available only at laboratories participating in the Laboratory Response Network.

infection. There were no gastrointestinal cases of anthrax diagnosed in either the Sverdlovsk series or following the anthrax attacks of 2001.

Diagnosis

Table 2 lists the epidemiology, diagnostic tests, microbiology, and pathology for a diagnosis of inhalational anthrax infection. Given the rarity of anthrax infection, the first clinical or laboratory suspicion of an anthrax illness must lead to early initiation of antibiotic treatment pending confirmed diagnosis and should provoke immediate notification of the local or state public health department, local hospital epidemiologist, and local or state public health laboratory. In the United States, a Laboratory Response Network (LRN) has been established through a collaboration of the Association of Public Health Laboratories and the CDC (details are available at www.bt.cdc.gov/LabIssues/index.asp). Currently 81 clinical laboratories in the LRN can diagnose bioweapons pathogens. Several preliminary diagnostic tests for *B anthracis* can be performed in hospital laboratories using routine procedures. *B anthracis* is a gram-positive, nonhemolytic, encapsulated, penicillin-sensitive, spore-forming bacillus. Confirmatory tests such as immunohistochemical staining, gamma phage, and polymerase chain reaction assays must still be performed by special reference laboratories in the LRN.

The determination of individual patient exposure to *B anthracis* on the basis of environmental testing is complex due to the uncertain specificity and sensitivity

Figure 4. Chest Radiograph and Computed Tomography (CT) Image

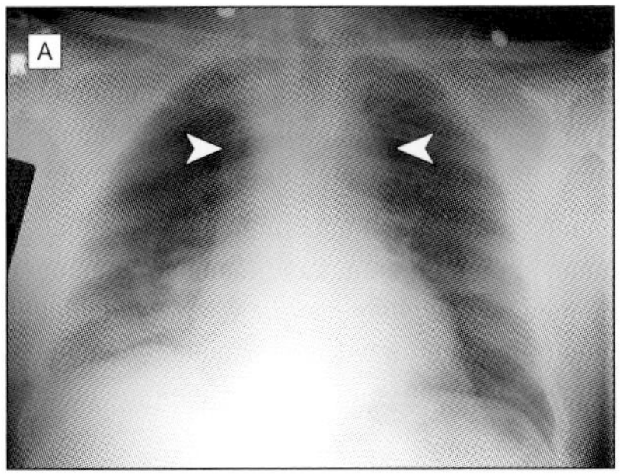

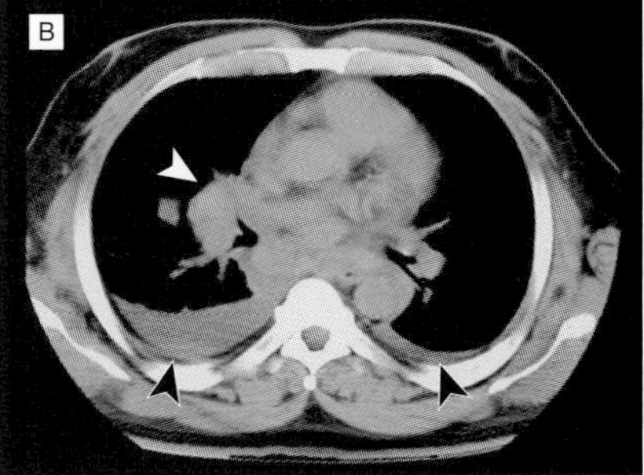

A, Portable chest radiograph of 56-year-old man with inhalational anthrax depicts a widened mediastinum (white arrowheads), bilateral hilar fullness, a right pleural effusion, and bilateral perihilar air-space disease. B, Noncontrast spiral CT scan depicts an enlarged and hyperdense right hilar lymph node (white arrowhead), bilateral pleural effusions (black arrowheads), and edema of the mediastinal fat. Reproduced with permission from Mayer et al.[66]

of rapid field tests and the difficulty of assessing individual risks of exposure. A patient (or patients) seeking medical treatment for symptoms of inhalational anthrax will likely be the first evidence of a clandestine release of *B anthracis* as a biological weapon. The appearance of even a single previously healthy patient who becomes acutely ill with nonspecific febrile illness and symptoms and signs consistent with those listed in Table 1 and whose condition rapidly deteriorates should receive prompt consideration for a diagnosis of anthrax infection. The recognition of cutaneous cases of anthrax may also be the first evidence of an anthrax attack.[70]

The likely presence of abnormal findings on either chest x-ray film or chest CT scan is diagnostically important. Although anthrax does not cause a classic bronchopneumonia pathology, it can cause widened mediastinum, massive pleural effusions, air bronchograms, necrotizing pneumonic lesions, and/or consolidation, as has been noted above.[36, 55, 56, 61, 64-66] The result can be hypoxemia and chest imaging abnormalities that may or may not be clinically distinguishable from pneumonia. In the anthrax attacks of 2001, each of the first 10 patients had abnormal chest x-ray film results and each of 8 patients for whom CT scans were obtained had abnormal results. These included widened mediastinum on chest radiograph and effusions on chest CT scan (**Figure 4**). Such findings in a previously healthy patient with evidence of overwhelming febrile illness or sepsis would be highly suggestive of advanced inhalational anthrax.

The bacterial burden may be so great in advanced inhalational anthrax infection that bacilli are visible on Gram stain of peripheral blood, as was seen following the 2001 attacks. The most useful microbiologic test is the standard blood culture, which should show growth in 6 to 24 hours. Each of the 8 patients who had blood cultures obtained prior to initiation of antibiotics had positive blood cultures.[61] However, blood cultures appear to be sterilized after even 1 or 2 doses of antibiotics, underscoring the importance of obtaining cultures prior to initiation of antibiotic therapy (J.L.G., oral communication, March 7, 2002). If the laboratory has been alerted to the possibility of anthrax, biochemical testing and review of colonial morphology could provide a preliminary diagnosis 12 to 24 hours after inoculation of the cultures. Definitive diagnosis could be promptly confirmed by an LRN laboratory. However, if the clinical laboratory has not been alerted to the possibility of anthrax, *B anthracis* may not be correctly identified. Routine procedures customarily identify a *Bacillus* species in a blood culture approximately 24 hours after growth, but some laboratories do not further identify *Bacillus* species unless specifically requested. This is because the isolation of *Bacillus* species most often represents growth of the common contaminant *Bacillus cereus.*[71] Given the possibility of future anthrax attacks, it is recommended that routine clinical laboratory procedures be modified, so *B anthracis* is specifically excluded, after identification of a *Bacillus* species bacteremia unless there are compelling reasons not to do so. If it cannot be excluded then the isolate should be transferred to an LRN laboratory.

Sputum culture and Gram stain are unlikely to be diagnostic of inhalational anthrax, given the frequent lack of a pneumonic process.[37] Gram stain of sputum was reported positive in only 1 case of inhalational anthrax in the 2001 series. If cutaneous anthrax is suspected, a Gram stain and culture of vesicular fluid should be obtained. If the Gram stain is negative or the patient is taking antibiotics already, punch biopsy should be performed, and specimens sent to a laboratory with the ability to perform immunohistochemical staining or polymerase chain reaction assays.[69,70] Blood cultures should be obtained and antibiotics should be initiated pending confirmation of the diagnosis of inhalational or cutaneous anthrax.

Nasal swabs were obtained in some persons believed to be at risk of inhalational anthrax following the anthrax attacks of 2001. Although a study has shown the presence of *B anthracis* spores in nares of some monkeys following experimental exposure to *B anthracis* spores for some time after exposure,[72] the predictive value of the nasal swab test for diagnosing inhalational anthrax in humans is unknown and untested. It is not known how quickly antibiotics make spore recovery on nasal swab tests impossible. One patient who died from inhalational anthrax had a negative nasal swab.[36] Thus, the CDC advised in the fall of 2001 that the nasal swab should not be used as a clinical diagnostic test. If obtained for an epidemiological purpose, nasal swab results should not be used to rule out infection in a patient. Persons who have positive nasal swab results for *B anthracis* should receive a course of postexposure antibiotic prophylaxis since a positive swab would indicate that the individual had been exposed to aerosolized *B anthracis.*

Antibodies to the protective antigen (PA) of *B anthracis,* termed *anti-PA IgG,* have been shown to confer immunity in animal models following anthrax vaccination.[73,74] Anti-PA IgG serologies have been obtained from several of those involved in the 2001 anthrax attacks, but the results of these assays are not yet published. Given the lack of data in humans and the expected period required to develop an anti-PA IgG response, this test should not be used as a diagnostic test for anthrax infection in the acutely ill patient but may be useful for epidemiologic purposes.

Postmortem findings are especially important following an unexplained death. Thoracic hemorrhagic necrotizing lymphadenitis and hemorrhagic necrotizing mediastinitis in a previously healthy adult are essentially pathognomonic of inhalational anthrax.[50, 58] Hemorrhagic meningitis should also raise strong suspicion of anthrax infection.[32, 50, 58, 75] However, given the rarity of anthrax, a pathologist might not identify these findings as caused by anthrax unless previously alerted to this possibility.

If only a few patients present contemporaneously, the clinical similarity of early inhalational anthrax infection to other acute febrile respiratory infections may delay initial diagnosis although probably not for long. The severity of the illness and its rapid progression, coupled with unusual radiological findings, possible identification of *B anthracis* in blood or cerebrospinal fluid, and the unique pathologic findings , should serve as an early alarm. The index case of inhalational anthrax in the 2001 attacks was identified because of an alert clinician who suspected the disease on the basis of large gram-positive bacilli in cerebrospinal fluid in a patient with a compatible clinical illness, and as a result of the subsequent analysis by laboratory staff who had recently undergone bioterrorism preparedness training.[65]

Vaccination

The US anthrax vaccine, named anthrax vaccine adsorbed (AVA), is an inactivated cell-free product, licensed in 1970, and produced by Bioport Corp, Lansing, Mich. The vaccine is licensed to be given in a 6-dose series. In 1997, it was mandated that all US military active- and reserve-duty personnel receive it.[76] The vaccine is made from the cell-free filtrate of a nonencapsulated attenuated strain of *B anthracis*.[77] The principal antigen responsible for inducing immunity is the PA.[26, 32] In the rabbit model, the quantity of antibody to PA has been correlated with the level of protection against experimental anthrax infection.[78]

Preexposure vaccination with AVA has been shown to be efficacious against experimental challenge in a number of animal studies.[78-80] A similar vaccine was shown in a placebo-controlled human trial to be efficacious against cutaneous anthrax.[81]The efficacy of postexposure vaccination with AVA has been studied in monkeys.[40] Among 60 monkeys exposed to 8 LD_{50} of *B anthracis* spores at baseline, 9 of 10 control animals died, and 8 of 10 animals treated with vaccine alone died. None of 29 animals died while receiving doxycycline, ciprofloxacin, or penicillin for 30 days; 5 developed anthrax once treatment ceased. The remaining 24 all died when rechallenged. The 9 receiving doxycycline for 30 days plus vaccine at baseline and day 14 after exposure did not die from anthrax infection even after being rechallenged.[40]

The safety of the anthrax vaccine has been the subject of much study. A recent report reviewed the results of surveillance for adverse events in the Department of Defense program of 1998-2000.[82] At the time of that report, 425 976 service members had received 1 620 793 doses of AVA. There were higher rates of local reactions to the vaccine in women than men, but "no patterns of unexpected local or systemic adverse events" were identified.[82] A recent review of safety of AVA anthrax vaccination in employees of the United States Army Medical Research Institute of Infectious Diseases (USAMRIID) over the past 25 years reported that 1583 persons had received 10 722 doses of AVA.[83] One percent of these inoculations (101/10 722) were associated with 1 or more systemic events (defined as headache, malaise, myalgia, fever, nausea, vomiting, dizziness, chills, diarrhea, hives, anorexia, arthralgias, diaphoresis, blurred vision, generalized itching, or sore throat). The most frequently reported systemic adverse event was headache (0.4% of doses). Local or injection site reactions were reported in 3.6%. No long-term sequelae were reported in this series.

The Institute of Medicine (IOM) recently published a report on the safety and efficacy of AVA,[84] which concluded that AVA is effective against inhalational anthrax and concluded that if given with appropriate antibiotic therapy, it may help prevent the development of disease after exposure. The IOM committee also concluded that AVA was acceptably safe. Committee recommendations for new research include studies to describe the relationship between immunity and quantitative antibody levels; further studies to test the efficacy of AVA in combination with antibiotics in preventing inhalational anthrax infection; studies of alternative routes and schedules of administration of AVA; and continued monitoring of reported adverse events following vaccination. The committee did not evaluate the production process used by the manufacturer.

A recently published report[85] analyzed a cohort of 4092 women at 2 military bases from January 1999 to March 2000. The study compared pregnancy rates and adverse birth outcomes between groups of women who had been vaccinated with women who had not been vaccinated and the study found that anthrax vaccination with AVA had no effect on pregnancy or adverse birth outcomes.

A human live attenuated vaccine has been produced and used in countries of the former Soviet Union.[86] In the Western world, live attenuated vaccines have been considered unsuitable for use in humans because of safety concerns.[86]

Current vaccine supplies are limited, and the US production capacity remains modest. Bioport is the single US manufacturing facility for the licensed anthrax vaccine. Production has only recently resumed after a halt required the company to alter production methods so that it conformed to the US Food and Drug Administration (FDA) Good Manufacturing Practice standard. Bioport has a contract to produce 4.6 million doses of vaccine for the US Department of Defense that cannot be met until at least 2003 (D.A.H., oral communication, February 2002).

The use of AVA was not initiated immediately in persons believed to have been exposed to *B anthracis* during the 2001 anthrax attacks for a variety of reasons, including the unavailability of vaccine supplies. Subsequently, near the end of the 60-day period of antibiotic prophylaxis, persons deemed by investigating public health authorities to have been at high risk for exposure were offered postexposure AVA series (3 inoculations at 2-week intervals, given on days 1, 14, and 28) as an adjunct to prolonged postexposure antibiotic prophylaxis. This group of affected persons was also offered the alternatives of continuing a prolonged course of antibiotics or of receiving close medical follow-up without vaccination or additional antibiotics.[87] This vaccine is licensed for use in the preexposure setting, but because it had not been licensed for use in the postexposure context, it was given under investigational new drug procedures.

The working group continues to conclude that vaccination of exposed persons following a biological attack in conjunction with antibiotic administration for 60 days following exposure provide optimal protection to those exposed. However, until ample reserve stockpiles of vaccine are available, reliance must be placed on antibiotic administration. To date, there have been no reported cases of anthrax infection among those exposed in the 2001 anthrax attacks who took prophylactic antibiotics, even in those persons not complying with the complete 60-day course of therapy.

Preexposure vaccination of some persons deemed to be in high-risk groups should be considered when substantial supplies of vaccine become available. A fast-track program to develop recombinant anthrax vaccine is now under way. This may lead to more plentiful vaccine stocks as well as a product that requires fewer inoculations.[88] Studies to evaluate intramuscular vs subcutaneous routes of administration and less frequent dosing of AVA are also under way (J.M.H., oral communication, February 2002).

Therapy

Recommendations for antibiotic and vaccine use in the setting of an aerosolized *B anthracis* attack are conditioned by a very small series of cases in humans, a limited number of studies in experimental animals, and the possible necessity of treating large numbers of casualties. A number of possible therapeutic strategies have yet to be explored experimentally or to be submitted for approval to the FDA. For these reasons, the working group offers consensus recommendations based on the best available evidence. The recommendations do not necessarily represent uses currently approved by the FDA or an official position on the part of any of the federal agencies whose scientists participated in these discussions and will need to be revised as further relevant information becomes available.

Given the rapid course of symptomatic inhalational anthrax, early antibiotic administration is essential. A delay of antibiotic treatment for patients with anthrax infection may substantially lessen chances for survival.[89, 90] Given the difficulty in achieving rapid microbiologic diagnosis of anthrax, all persons in high-risk groups who develop fever or evidence of systemic disease should start receiving therapy for possible anthrax infection as soon as possible while awaiting the results of laboratory studies.

There are no controlled clinical studies for the treatment of inhalational anthrax in humans. Thus, antibiotic regimens commonly recommended for empirical treatment of sepsis have not been studied. In fact, natural strains of *B anthracis* are resistant to many of the antibiotics used in empirical regimens for sepsis treatment, such as those regimens based on the extended-spectrum cephalosporins.[91, 92] Most naturally occurring *B anthracis* strains are sensitive to penicillin, which historically has been the preferred anthrax therapy. Doxycycline is the preferred option among the tetracycline class because of its proven efficacy in monkey studies[56] and its ease of administration. Other members of this class of antibiotics are suitable alternatives. Although treatment of anthrax infection with ciprofloxacin has not been studied in humans, animal models suggest excellent efficacy.[40, 56, 93] In vitro data suggest that other fluoroquinolone antibiotics would have equivalent efficacy although no animal data using a primate model of inhalational anthrax are available.[92] Penicillin and doxycycline are approved by the FDA for the treatment of anthrax. Although neither penicillin, doxycycline, nor ciprofloxacin are specifically approved by the FDA for the treatment of inhalational anthrax, these drugs may be useful when given in combination with other antimicrobial drugs. (See Table 3.)* Other drugs that are usually active in vitro include clindamycin, rifampin, imipenem, aminoglycosides, chloramphenicol, vancomycin, cefazolin, tetracycline, linezolid, and the macrolides.

Reports have been published of a *B anthracis* strain that was engineered to resist the tetracycline and penicillin classes of antibiotics.[94] Balancing considerations of treatment efficacy with concerns regarding resistance, the working group in 1999 recommended that ciprofloxacin or other fluoroquinolone therapy be initiated in adults with presumed inhalational anthrax infection.[3] It was advised that antibiotic resistance to penicillin- and tetracycline-class antibiotics should be assumed following a terrorist attack until laboratory testing demonstrated otherwise. Once the antibiotic susceptibility of the *B anthracis* strain of the index case had been determined, the most widely available, efficacious, and least toxic antibiotic was recommended for patients requiring treatment and persons requiring postexposure prophylaxis. Since the 1999 consensus statement publication, a study[95] demonstrated the development of in vitro resistance of an isolate of the Sterne strain of *B anthracis* to ofloxacin (a fluoroquinolone closely related to ciprofloxacin) following subculturing and multiple cell passage.

Following the anthrax attacks of 2001, the CDC[96] offered guidelines advocating use of 2 or 3 antibiotics in combination in persons with inhalational anthrax based on susceptibility testing with epidemic strains. Limited early information following the attacks suggested that persons with inhalational anthrax treated intravenously with 2 or more antibiotics active against *B anthracis* had a greater chance of survival.[61] Given the limited number of persons who developed inhalational anthrax, the paucity of comparative data, and other uncertainties, it remains unclear whether the use of 2 or more antibiotics confers a survival advantage, but combination therapy is a reasonable therapeutic approach in the face of life-threatening illness. Another factor supporting the initiation of combi-

* This statement and subsequent statements marked with an asterisk throughout this chapter have been changed from the original published paper (Anthrax as a Biological Weapon, 2002, Updated Recommendations for Management. *JAMA*. 2002;287:2236-2252.) based on subsequent clarification of FDA and CDC policy statements on these issues.

nation antibiotic therapy for treatment of inhalational anthrax is the possibility that an engineered strain of B *anthracis* resistant to 1 or more antibiotics might be used in a future attack. Some infectious disease experts have also advocated the use of clindamycin, citing the theoretical benefit of diminishing bacterial toxin production, a strategy used in some toxin-mediated streptococcal infections.[97] There are no data as yet that bear specifically on this question. Central nervous system penetration is another consideration; doxycycline or fluoroquinolone may not reach therapeutic levels in the cerebrospinal fluid. Thus, in the aftermath of the anthrax attacks, some infectious disease authorities recommended preferential use of ciprofloxacin over doxycycline, plus augmentation with chloramphenicol, rifampin, or penicillin when meningitis is established or suspected.

The B *anthracis* isolate recovered from patients with inhalational anthrax was susceptible to all of the antibiotics expected in a naturally occurring strain.[96] This isolate showed an inducible ß-lactamase in addition to a constitutive cephalosporinase. The importance of the inducible ß-lactamase is unknown; these strains are highly susceptible to penicillin in vitro, with minimum inhibiting concentrations less than 0.06 µg/mL. A theoretical concern is that this sensitivity could be overcome with a large bacterial burden. For this reason, the CDC advised that patients with inhalational anthrax should not be treated with penicillin or amoxicillin as monotherapy and that ciprofloxacin or doxycycline be considered the standards based on in vitro activity, efficacy in the monkey model, and FDA's approval of ciprofloxacin, doxycycline, and penicillin G procaine for postexposure prophylaxis of inhalational anthrax.*

In the contained casualty setting (a situation in which a modest number of patients require therapy), the working group supports these new CDC antibiotic recommendations[96] and advises the use of intravenous antibiotic administration (**Table 3**). These recommendations will need to be revised as new data become available.

If the number of persons requiring therapy following a bioterrorist attack with anthrax is sufficiently high (ie, a mass casualty setting), the working group recognizes that combination drug therapy and intravenous therapy may no longer be possible for reasons of logistics and/or exhaustion of equipment and antibiotic supplies. In such circumstances, oral therapy may be the only feasible option (**Table 4**). The threshold number of cases at which combination and parenteral therapy become impossible depends on a variety of factors, including local and regional health care resources.

In experimental animals, antibiotic therapy during anthrax infection has prevented development of an immune response.[40, 94] This suggests that even if the antibiotic-treated patient survives anthrax infection, the risk of recurring disease may persist for a prolonged period because of the possibility of delayed germination of spores. Therefore, we recommend that antibiotic therapy be continued for at least 60 days postexposure, with oral therapy replacing intravenous therapy when the patient is clinically stable enough to take oral medication.

Cutaneous anthrax historically has been treated with oral penicillin. For reasons articulated above, the working group recommends that oral fluoroquinolone or

Table 3. Recommended Therapy for Inhalational Anthrax Infection in the Contained Casualty Setting[a,b]

Category	Initial IV Therapy[c,d]	Duration
Adults	Ciprofloxacin, 400 mg every 12 h or Doxycycline, 100 mg every 12 h[f] and 1 or 2 additional antimicrobials[d]	IV treatment initially[e] before switching to oral antimicrobial therapy when clinically appropriate: Ciprofloxacin 500 mg every 12h or Doxycycline 100 mg every 12h Continue oral or IV treatment for 60 days[k]
Children	Ciprofloxacin 10 mg/kg dose every 12 h (max 400 mg/dose)[g,h,i] or Doxycycline[f,j] for those weighing: >45 kg: 100 mg every 12h ≤45 kg: 2.2 mg/kg every 12h and 1 or 2 additional antimicrobials[d]	IV treatment initially[e] before switching to oral antimicrobial therapy when clinically appropriate: Ciprofloxacin 15 mg/kg every 12h (max 500 mg/dose)[h] or Doxycycline[i] for those weighing: >45 kg: 100 mg every 12h ≤45 kg: 2.2 mg/kg every 12h and 1 or 2 additional antimicrobials[d] Continue oral and IV treatment for 60 days[k]
Pregnant women[l]	Same for nonpregnant adults	IV treatment initially before switching to oral antimicrobial therapy when clinically appropriate[b]; oral therapy regimens are the same for nonpregnant adults
Immuno-compromised persons	Same for nonimmunocompromised adults and children	

[a] This table is adapted with permission from the *Morbidity and Mortality Weekly Report.*[96] For gastrointestinal and oropharyngeal anthrax, use regimens recommended for inhalational anthrax.

[b] Ciprofloxacin or doxycycline should be considered an essential part of first-line therapy for inhalational anthrax.

[c] Steroids may be considered as an adjunct therapy for patients with severe edema and for meningitis based on experience with bacterial meningitis of other etiologies.

[d] Other agents with in vitro activity include rifampin, vancomycin, penicillin, ampicillin, chloramphenicol, imipenem, clindamycin, and clarithromycin. Because of concerns of constitutive and inducible ß-lactamases in *Bacillus anthracis*, penicillin and ampicillin should not be used alone. Consultation with an infectious disease specialist is advised.

[e] Initial therapy may be altered based on clinical course of the patient; 1 or 2 antimicrobial agents may be adequate as the patient improves.

Table 3 footnotes continued on next page.

[f] If meningitis is suspected, doxycycline may be less optimal because of poor central nervous system penetration.

[g] If intravenous (IV) ciprofloxacin is not available, oral ciprofloxacin may be acceptable because it is rapidly and well absorbed from the gastrointestinal tract with no substantial loss by first-pass metabolism. Maximum serum concentrations are attained 1 to 2 hours after oral dosing but may not be achieved if vomiting or ileus is present.

[h] In children, ciprofloxacin dosage should not exceed 1 g/d.

[i] These statements have been changed from the original published paper (Anthrax as a Biological Weapon, 2002: Updated Recommendations for Management. *JAMA*. 2002;287: 2236-2252.) based on clarification of FDA and CDC policy statements on these issues.[98]

[j] The American Academy of Pediatrics recommends treatment of young children with tetracyclines for serious infections (ie, Rocky Mountain spotted fever).

[k] Because of the potential persistence of spores after an aerosol exposure, antimicrobial therapy should be continued for 60 days.

[l] Although tetracyclines are not recommended during pregnancy, their use may be indicated for life-threatening illness. Adverse effects on developing teeth and bones of fetus are dose related; therefore, doxycycline might be used for a short time (7-14 days) before 6 months of gestation. The high death rate from the infection outweighs the risk posed by the antimicrobial agent.

doxycycline in the adult dosage schedules described in **Table 5** be used to treat cutaneous anthrax until antibiotic susceptibility is proven. Amoxicillin is a suitable alternative if there are contraindications to fluoroquinolones or doxycycline such as pregnancy, lactating mother, age younger than 18 years, or antibiotic intolerance. For cutaneous lesions associated with extensive edema or for cutaneous lesions of the head and neck, clinical management should be conservative as per inhalational anthrax treatment guidelines in Table 3. Although previous guidelines have suggested treating cutaneous anthrax for 7 to 10 days,[32,71] the working group recommends treatment for 60 days postexposure in the setting of bioterrorism, given the presumed concomitant inhalational exposure to the primary aerosol. Treatment of cutaneous anthrax generally prevents progression to systemic disease although it does not prevent the formation and evolution of the eschar. Topical therapy is not useful.[4]

In addition to penicillin, the fluoroquinolones, and the tetracycline class of antibiotics, other antibiotics effective in vitro include chloramphenicol, clindamycin, extended-spectrum penicillins, macrolides, aminoglycosides, vancomycin, cefazolin, and other first-generation cephalosporins.[91,101] The efficacy of these antibiotics has not yet been tested in humans or in animal studies. The working group recommends the use of these antibiotics only to augment fluoroquinolones or tetracyclines or if the preferred drugs are contraindicated, not available, or inactive in vitro in susceptibility testing. *B anthracis* strains exhibit natural resistance to sulfamethoxazole, trimethoprim, cefuroxime, cefotaxime sodium, aztreonam, and ceftazidime.[91,92,101] Therefore, these antibiotics should not be used.

Pleural effusions were present in all of the first 10 patients with inhalational anthrax in 2001. Seven needed drainage of their pleural effusions, 3 required chest tubes.[69] Future patients with inhalational anthrax should be expected to have pleural effusions that will likely require drainage.

Table 4. Recommended Therapy for Inhalational Anthrax Infection in the Mass Casualty Setting or for Postexposure Prophylaxis*

Category	Initial Oral Therapy†	Alternative Therapy If Strain Is Proved Susceptible	Duration After Exposure, d
Adults	Ciprofloxacin, 500 mg orally every 12 h	Doxycycline, 100 mg orally every 12 h‡ Amoxicillin, 500 mg orally every 8 h§	60
Children	Ciprofloxacin 15 mg/kg/ dose po every 12h (max 500 mg/dose)‖,¶	Weight ≥20 kg: amoxicillin, 500 mg orally every 8 h§ Weight <20 kg: amoxicillin, 80 mg/kg/day taken orally in 3 divided doses every 8 h§,¶,100	60
Pregnant women#	Ciprofloxacin, 500 mg orally every 12 h	Amoxicillin, 500 mg orally every 8 h§	60
Immuno-suppressed persons	Same as for nonimmunosuppressed adults and children		

* Some of these recommendations are based on animal studies or in vitro studies and are not approved by the US Food and Drug Administration.

† In vitro studies suggest ofloxacin (400 mg orally every 12 hours, or levofloxacin, 500 mg orally every 24 hours) could be substituted for ciprofloxacin. In addition, 400 mg of gatifloxicin or moxifloxacin, both fluoroquinolones with mechanisms of action consistent with ciprofloxacin, taken orally daily could be substituted.

‡ In vitro studies suggest that 500 mg of tetracycline orally every 6 hours could be substituted for doxycycline.

§ According to the CDC recommendations for the bioterrorist attacks in 2001, in which *B anthracis* was susceptible to penicillin, amoxicillin was a suitable alternative for postexposure prophylaxis in infants, children, and pregnant and breastfeeding women. Amoxicillin was also a suitable alternative for completion of 60 days of antibiotic therapy for patients in these groups with cutaneous or inhalational anthrax whose clinical illness had resolved after treatment with a ciprofloxacin or doxycycline based regimen (14-21 days for inhalational or complicated cutaneous anthrax; 7-10 days for uncomplicated cutaneous anthrax). Such patients required prolonged therapy because they were presumably exposed to aerosolized *B anthracis*.* [98, 99]

‖ Doxycycline could also be used if antibiotic susceptibility testing, exhaustion of drug supplies, adverse reactions preclude use of ciprofloxacin. For children heavier than 45 kg, adult dosage should be used. For children lighter than 45 kg, 2.2 mg/kg of doxycycline orally every 12 hours should be used.

¶ These statements have been changed from the original published paper (Anthrax as a Biological Weapon, 2002: Updated Recommendations for Management. *JAMA*. 2002;287: 2236-2252.) based on clarification of FDA and CDC policy statements on these issues.[98]

See "Management of Special Groups" for details.

Postexposure Prophylaxis

Guidelines for which populations would require postexposure prophylaxis to prevent inhalational anthrax following the release of a *B anthracis* aerosol as a

Table 5. Recommended Therapy for Cutaneous Anthrax Infection Associated With a Bioterrorism Attack*

Category	Initial Oral Therapy†	Duration, d‡
Adults	Ciprofloxacin, 500 mg every 12h† or Doxycycline, 100 mg every 12h†	60
Children§	Ciprofloxacin, 15 mg/kg/dose every 12h (max 500 mg/dose)§ or Doxycycline for those weighing‖ >45 kg: 100 mg every 12h ≤45 kg: 2.2 mg/kg every 12h	60
Pregnant women¶	Ciprofloxacin, 500 mg every 12h or Doxycycline, 100 mg every 12h	60
Immuno-compromised persons	Same for nonimmunocompromised adults and children	

* Adapted with permission from the *Morbidity and Mortality Weekly Report.*[96] Cutaneous anthrax with signs of systemic involvement, extensive edema, or lesions on the head or neck require intravenous therapy, and a multidrug approach is recommended (Table 3).

† Ciprofloxacin or doxycycline should be considered first-line therapy. Amoxicillin can be substituted if a patient cannot take a fluoroquinolone or tetracycline class drug. Adults are recommended to take 500 mg of amoxicillin orally 3 times a day. For children, 80 mg/kg of amoxicillin to be divided into 3 doses in 8-hour increments is an option for completion of therapy after clinical improvement. Oral amoxicillin dose is based on the need to achieve appropriate minimum inhibitory concentration levels.

‡ Previous guidelines have suggested treating cutaneous anthrax for 7 to 10 days, but 60 days is recommended for bioterrorism attacks, given the likelihood of exposure to aerosolized *Bacillus anthracis.*

§ These statements have been changed from the original published paper (Anthrax as a Biological Weapon, 2002: Updated Recommendations for Management. *JAMA.* 2002;287: 2236-2252.) based on clarification of FDA and CDC policy statements on these issues.[98]

‖ The American Academy of Pediatrics recommends treatment of young children with tetracyclines for serious infections (eg, Rocky Mountain spotted fever).

¶ Although tetracyclines or ciprofloxacin are not recommended during pregnancy, their use may be indicated for life-threatening illness. Adverse effects on developing teeth and bones of a fetus are dose related; therefore, doxycycline might be used for a short time (7-14 days) before 6 months of gestation.

biological weapon will need to be developed by public health officials depending on epidemiological circumstances. These decisions would require estimates of the timing, location, and conditions of the exposure.[102] Ongoing case monitoring would be needed to define the high-risk groups, to direct follow-up, and to guide the addition or deletion of groups requiring postexposure prophylaxis.

Ciprofloxacin, doxycycline, and penicillin G procaine are approved by the FDA for postexposure prophylaxis of inhalational anthrax.*[103] Therefore, for postexposure prophylaxis, we recommend the same antibiotic regimen as that recommended for treatment of mass casualties; prophylaxis should be continued for at least 60 days postexposure (Table 4). Preliminary analysis of US postal workers who were advised to take 60 days of antibiotic prophylaxis for exposure to *B anthracis* spores following the anthrax attacks of 2001 showed that 2% sought medical attention because of concern of possible severe allergic reactions related to the medications, but no persons required hospitalization because of an adverse drug reaction.[104] Many persons did not begin or complete their recommended antibiotic course for a variety of reasons, including gastrointestinal tract intolerance, underscoring the need for careful medical follow-up during the period of prophylaxis.[104] In addition, given the uncertainties regarding how many weeks or months spores may remain latent in the period following discontinuation of postexposure prophylaxis, persons should be instructed to report immediately flulike symptoms or febrile illness to their physicians who should then evaluate the need to initiate treatment for possible inhalational anthrax. As noted above, postexposure vaccination is recommended as an adjunct to postexposure antibiotic prophylaxis if vaccine is available.

Management of Special Groups

Consensus recommendations for special groups as set forth herein reflect the clinical and evidence-based judgments of the working group and at this time do not necessarily correspond with FDA-approved use, indications, or labeling.

Children. It has been recommended that ciprofloxacin and other fluoroquinolones not be used in children younger than 16 to 18 years because of a link to permanent arthropathy in adolescent animals and transient arthropathy in a small number of children. However, the FDA has concluded that the risk-benefit assessment indicates that administration of ciprofloxacin to pediatric patients for postexposure prophylaxis of inhalational anthrax is appropriate.* [105] The Working Group recommends that ciprofloxacin be used as a component of combination therapy for children with inhalational anthrax. For postexposure prophylaxis or following a mass casualty attack, monotherapy with fluoroquinolones is recommended by the Working Group pending susceptibility testing. For postexposure prophylaxis of children, amoxicillin is suitable if susceptibility testing allows[96] (Table 4).

The American Academy of Pediatrics has recommended that doxycycline not be used in children younger than 9 years because the drug has resulted in retarded skeletal growth in infants and discolored teeth in infants and children.[106] However, the serious risk of infection following an anthrax attack supports the consensus recommendation that doxycycline, instead of ciprofloxacin, be used in children if antibiotic susceptibility testing, exhaustion of drug supplies, or adverse reactions preclude use of ciprofloxacin.

According to the CDC recommendations for the bioterrorist attacks in 2001, in which *B anthracis* was susceptible to penicillin, amoxicillin was a suitable alternative for postexposure prophylaxis in infants, children, and breastfeeding women. Amoxicillin was also a suitable alternative for completion of 60 days of antibiotic therapy for patients in these groups with cutaneous or inhalational anthrax whose clinical illness had resolved after treatment with a ciprofloxacin or doxycycline based regimen (14-21 days for inhalational or complicated cutaneous anthrax; 7-10 days for uncomplicated cutaneous anthrax). Such patients required prolonged therapy because they were presumably exposed to aerosolized *B anthracis*.* [98, 99] In a contained casualty setting, the working group recommends that children with inhalational anthrax receive intravenous antibiotics (Table 3). In a mass casualty setting and as postexposure prophylaxis, the working group recommends that children receive oral antibiotics (Table 4).

The US anthrax vaccine is licensed for use only in persons aged 18 to 65 years because studies to date have been conducted exclusively in this group.[77] No data exist for children, but based on experience with other inactivated vaccines, it is likely that the vaccine would be safe and effective.

Pregnant Women. Fluoroquinolones are not generally recommended during pregnancy because of their known association with arthropathy in adolescent animals and small numbers of children. Animal studies have discovered no evidence of teratogenicity related to ciprofloxacin, but no controlled studies of ciprofloxacin in pregnant women have been conducted. Balancing these possible risks against the concerns of anthrax due to engineered antibiotic-resistant strains, the working group recommends that pregnant women receive ciprofloxacin as part of combination therapy for treatment of inhalational anthrax (Table 3). We also recommend that pregnant women receive fluoroquinolones in the usual adult dosages for postexposure prophylaxis or monotherapy treatment in the mass casualty setting (Table 4). The tetracycline class of antibiotics has been associated with both toxic effects in the liver in pregnant women and fetal toxic effects, including retarded skeletal growth.[106]

Balancing the risks of anthrax infection with those associated with doxycycline use in pregnancy, the working group recommends that doxycycline can be used as an alternative to ciprofloxacin as part of combination therapy in pregnant women for treatment of inhalational anthrax. For postexposure prophylaxis or in mass casualty settings, doxycycline can also be used as an alternate to ciprofloxacin in pregnant women. If doxycycline is used in pregnant women, periodic liver function testing should be performed. No adequate controlled trials of penicillin or amoxicillin administration during pregnancy exist. However, the CDC recommends penicillin for the treatment of syphilis during pregnancy and amoxicillin as a treatment alternative for chlamydial infections during pregnancy.[106] According to the CDC recommendations for the bioterrorist attacks in 2001, in which *B anthracis* was susceptible to penicillin, amoxicillin was a suitable alternative for postexposure prophylaxis in pregnant and breastfeeding women. Amoxicillin was also a suitable alternative for completion of 60 days of antibiotic therapy for patients in these groups with cutaneous or inhalational anthrax whose clinical illness had resolved after treatment with a ciprofloxacin- or doxycycline-based regimen (14-21 days for inhalational or complicated cutaneous anthrax; 7-10 days for uncomplicated cutaneous anthrax). Such patients required prolonged therapy because they were presumably exposed to aerosolized *B anthracis*.* [98, 99]

Ciprofloxacin (and other fluoroquinolones), penicillin, and doxycycline (and other tetracyclines) are each excreted in breast milk. Therefore, a breastfeeding woman should be treated or given prophylaxis with the same antibiotic as her infant based on what is most safe and effective for the infant.

Immunosuppressed Persons. The antibiotic treatment or postexposure prophylaxis for anthrax among those who are immunosuppressed has not been studied in human or animal models of anthrax infection. Therefore, the working group consensus recommends administering antibiotics in the same regimens recommended for immunocompetent adults and children.

Infection Control

There are no data to suggest that patient-to-patient transmission of anthrax occurs and no person-to-person transmission occurred following the anthrax attacks of 2001.[18,67] Standard barrier isolation precautions are recommended for hospitalized patients with all forms of anthrax infection, but the use of high-efficiency particulate air filter masks or other measures for airborne protection are not indicated.[107] There is no need to immunize or provide prophylaxis to patient contacts (eg, household contacts, friends, coworkers) unless a determination is made that they, like the patient, were exposed to the aerosol or surface contamination at the time of the attack.

In addition to immediate notification of the hospital epidemiologist and state health department, the local hospital microbiology laboratories should be notified at the first indication of anthrax so that safe specimen processing under biosafety level 2 conditions can be undertaken as is customary in most hospital laboratories.[56] A number of disinfectants used for standard hospital infection control, such as hypochlorite, are effective in cleaning environmental surfaces contaminated with infected bodily fluids.[22,107]

Proper burial or cremation of humans and animals who have died because of anthrax infection is important in preventing further transmission of the disease. Serious consideration should be given to cremation. Embalming of bodies could be associated with special risks.[107] If autopsies are performed, all related instruments and materials should be autoclaved or incinerated.[107] The CDC can provide advice on postmortem procedures in anthrax cases.

Decontamination

Recommendations for decontamination in the event of an intentional aerosolization of *B anthracis* spores are based on evidence concerning aerosolization techniques, predicted spore survival, environmental exposures at Sverdlovsk and among goat hair mill workers, and environmental data collected following the anthrax attacks of 2001. The greatest risk to humans exposed to an aerosol of *B anthracis* spores occurs when spores first are made airborne, the period called *primary aerosolization*. The aerobiological factors that affect how long spores remain airborne include the size of the dispersed particles and their hydrostatic properties.[102] Technologically sophisticated dispersal methods, such as aerosol release from military aircraft of large quantities of *B anthracis* spores manipulated for use in a weapon, are potentially capable of exposing high numbers of victims over large areas. Recent research by Canadian investigators has demonstrated that even "low-tech" delivery systems, such as the opening of envelopes containing powdered spores in indoor environments, can rapidly deliver high concentrations of spores to persons in the vicinity.[108] In some circumstances, indoor airflows, activity patterns, and heating, ventilation, and air conditioning systems may transport spores to other parts of the building.

Following the period of primary aerosolization, *B anthracis* spores may settle on surfaces, possibly in high concentrations. The risk that *B anthracis* spores might pose by a process of secondary aerosolization (resuspension of spores into the air) is uncertain and is likely dependent on many variables, including the quantity of spores on a surface; the physical characteristics of the powder used in the attack; the type of surface; the nature of the human or mechanical activity that occurs in the affected area; and host factors.

A variety of rapid assay kits are available to detect *B anthracis* spores on environmental surfaces. None of these kits has been independently evaluated or endorsed by the CDC, FDA, or Environmental Protection Agency, and their functional characteristics are not known.[109] Many false-positive results occurred following the anthrax attacks of 2001. Thus, any result using currently available rapid assay kits does not necessarily signify the presence of *B anthracis*; it is simply an indication that further testing is required by a certified microbiology laboratory. Similarly, the sensitivity and false-negative rate of disease kits are unknown.

At Sverdlovsk, no new cases of inhalational anthrax developed beyond 43 days after the presumed date of release. None were documented during the months and years afterward, despite only limited decontamination and vaccination of 47 000 of the city's 1 million inhabitants.[59] Some have questioned whether any of the cases with onset of disease beyond 7 days after release might have represented illness following *secondary aerosolization* from the ground or other surfaces. It is impossible to state with certainty that secondary aerosolizations did not occur in Sverdlovsk, but it appears unlikely. The epidemic curve reported is typical for a common-source epidemic,[3, 60] and it is possible to account for virtually all confirmed cases having occurred within the area of the plume on the day of the accident. Moreover, if secondary aerosolization had been important, new cases would have likely continued well beyond the observed 43 days (**Figure 5**).

Although persons working with animal hair or hides are known to be at increased risk of developing inhalational or cutaneous anthrax, surprisingly few occupational exposures in the United States have resulted in disease. During the first half of the 20th century, a significant number of goat hair mill workers were heavily exposed to aerosolized spores. Mandatory vaccination became a requirement for working in goat hair mills only in the 1960s. Prior to that, many unvaccinated person-years of high-risk exposure had occurred, but only 13 cases of inhalational anthrax were reported.[27, 54] One study of environmental exposure,

Figure 5. Day of Onset of Inhalational Anthrax Following Sverdlovsk Accident

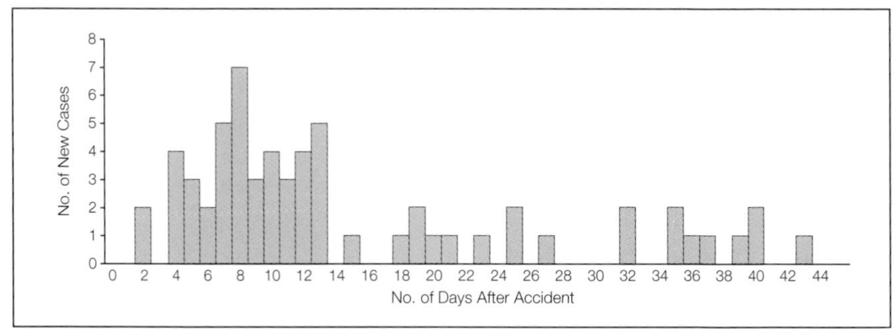

Figure is based on data from Guillermin.[59]

conducted at a Pennsylvania goat hair mill, showed that workers inhaled up to 510 *B anthracis* particles of at least 5 μm in diameter per person per 8-hour shift.[54] These concentrations of spores were constantly present in the environment during the time of this study, but no cases of inhalational anthrax occurred.

Field studies using *B anthracis*–like surrogates have been carried out by US Army scientists seeking to determine the risk of secondary aerosolization. One study concluded that there was no significant threat to personnel in areas contaminated by 1 million spores per square meter either from traffic on asphalt-paved roads or from a runway used by helicopters or jet aircraft.[110] A separate study showed that in areas of ground contaminated with 20 million *Bacillus subtilis* spores per square meter, a soldier exercising actively for a 3-hour period would inhale between 1000 and 15 000 spores.[111]

Much has been written about the technical difficulty of decontaminating an environment contaminated with *B anthracis* spores. A classic case is the experience at Gruinard Island, Scotland. During World War II, British military undertook explosives testing with *B anthracis* spores. Spores persisted and remained viable for 36 years following the conclusion of testing. Decontamination of the island occurred in stages, beginning in 1979 and ending in 1987 when the island was finally declared fully decontaminated. The total cost is unpublished, but materials required included 280 tons of formaldehyde and 2000 tons of seawater.[112]

Following the anthrax attacks of 2001, substantial efforts were undertaken to decontaminate environmental surfaces exposed to *B anthracis* spores. Sections of the Hart Senate office building in Washington, DC, contaminated from opening a letter laden with *B anthracis*, were reopened only after months of decontamination procedures at an estimated cost of $23 million.[113] Decontamination efforts at many other buildings affected by the anthrax attacks of 2001 have not yet been completed.

Prior to the anthrax attacks of 2001, there had been no recognition or scientific study showing that *B anthracis* spores of "weapons-grade" quality would be capable of leaking out the edges of envelopes or through the pores of envelopes, with resulting risk to the health of those handling or processing those letters.

When it became clear that the Florida case of anthrax was likely caused by a letter contaminated with *B anthracis*, assessment of postal workers who might have handled or processed that letter showed no illness.[69] When the anthrax cases were discovered, each was linked to a letter that had been opened. At first, there was no evidence of illness among persons handling or processing unopened mail. This fact influenced the judgment that persons handling or processing unopened *B anthracis* letters were not at risk. These judgments changed when illness was discovered in persons who had handled or processed unopened letters in Washington, DC. Much remains unknown about the risks to persons handling or processing unopened letters containing *B anthracis* spores. It is not well understood how the mechanical systems of mail processing in a specific building would affect the risk of disease acquisition in a worker handling a contaminated letter in that facility. It is still uncertain what the minimum dose of spores would be to cause infection in humans, although it may theoretically be as few as 1 to 3 spores.[47] The mechanisms of disease acquisition in the 2 fatal inhalational anthrax cases in New York City and in Connecticut remain unknown, although it is speculated that disease in these 2 cases followed the inhalation of small numbers of spores present in some manner in "cross-contaminated" mail.

The discovery of *B anthracis* spores in a contaminated letter in the office of Senator Daschle in the Hart office building led the Environmental Protection Agency to conduct tests in this office to assess the risk of secondary aerosolization of spores. Prior to the initiation of decontamination efforts in the Hart building, 17 blood agar gel plates were placed around the office and normal activity in the office was simulated. Sixteen of the 17 plates yielded *B anthracis.* Although this experiment did not allow conclusions about the specific risk of persons developing anthrax infection in this context, it did demonstrate that routine activity in an environment contaminated with *B anthracis* spores could cause significant spore resuspension.[114]

Given the above considerations, if an environmental surface is proved to be contaminated with *B anthracis* spores in the immediate area of a spill or close proximity to the point of release of *B anthracis* biological weapons, the working group believes that decontamination of that area would likely decrease the risk of acquiring anthrax by secondary aerosolization. However, as has been demonstrated in environmental decontamination efforts following the anthrax attacks of 2001, decontamination of buildings or parts of buildings following an anthrax attack is technically difficult. For these reasons, the working group would advise that decisions about methods for decontamination following an anthrax attack follow full expert analysis of the contaminated environment and the anthrax weapon used in the attack and be made in consultation with experts on environmental remediation. If vaccines were available, postexposure vaccination might be a useful intervention for those working in highly contaminated areas, because it could further lower the risk of anthrax infection.

In the setting of an announced alleged *B anthracis* release, such as the series of anthrax hoaxes occurring in many areas of the United States in 1998[115] and following the anthrax attacks of 2001, any person coming in direct physical contact with a substance alleged to be containing *B anthracis* should thoroughly wash the exposed skin and articles of clothing with soap and water.[116] In addition, any person in direct physical contact with the alleged substance should receive post-exposure antibiotic prophylaxis until the substance is proved not to be *B anthracis*. The anthrax attacks of 2001 and new research[108] have shown that opening letters containing substantial quantities of *B anthracis* spores in certain conditions can confer risk of disease to persons at some distance from the location of where the letter was opened. For this reason, when a letter is suspected of containing (or proved to contain) *B anthracis*, immediate consultation with local and state public health authorities and the CDC for advised medical management is warranted.

Additional Research

Development of a recombinant anthrax vaccine that would be more easily manufactured and would require fewer doses should remain a top priority. Rapid diagnostic assays that could reliably identify early anthrax infection and quickly distinguish from other flulike or febrile illnesses would become critical in the event of a large-scale attack. Simple animal models for use in comparing antibiotic prophylactic and treatment strategies are also needed. Operational research to better characterize risks posed by environmental contamination of spores, particularly inside buildings, and research on approaches to minimize risk in indoor environments by means of air filters or methods for environmental cleaning following a release are also needed. A better understanding of the genetics and pathogenesis of anthrax, as well as mechanisms of virulence and immunity, will be of importance in the prospective evaluation of new therapeutic and diagnostic strategies. Novel therapeutic approaches with promise, such as the administration of competitors against the protective antigen complex,[117] should also be tested in animals and developed where evidence supports this. Recent developments such as the publishing of the *B anthracis* genome and the discovery of the crystalline structure of the lethal and edema factor could hold great clinical hope for both the prevention and treatment of anthrax infection.[118]

Ex Officio Participants in the Working Group on Civilian Biodefense: George Curlin, MD, National Institutes of Health, Bethesda, Md; Margaret Hamburg, MD, Nuclear Threat Initiative, Washington, DC; Stuart Nightingale, MD, Office of Assistant Secretary for Planning and Evaluation, DHHS, Washington, DC; William Raub, PhD, Office of Public Health Preparedness, DHHS, Washington, DC; Robert Knouss, MD, Office of Emergency Preparedness, DHHS, Rockville, Md; Marcelle Layton, MD, Office of Communicable Disease, New York City Health Department, New York, NY; and Brian Malkin, formerly of FDA, Rockville, Md.

Funding/Support: Funding for this study primarily was provided by each participant's institution or agency.

Disclaimers: In many cases, the indication and dosages and other information are not consistent with current approved labeling by the US Food and Drug Administration (FDA). The recommendations on the use of drugs and vaccine for uses not approved by the FDA do not represent the official views of the FDA or of any of the federal agencies whose scientists participated in these discussions. Unlabeled uses of the products recommended are noted in the sections of this article in which these products are discussed.

Where unlabeled uses are indicated, information used as the basis for the recommendation is discussed. The views, opinions, assertions, and findings contained herein are those of the authors and should not be construed as official US Department of Health and Human Services, US Department of Defense, or US Department of Army positions, policies, or decisions unless so designated by other documentation.

Acknowledgments: The working group wishes to thank Jeanne Guillemin, PhD, Matthew Meselson, PhD, Timothy Townsend, MD, Martin Hugh-Jones, MA, VetMB, MPH, PhD, and Philip Brachman, MD, for their review and commentary on the originally published manuscript, and Molly D'Esopo for her efforts in the preparation of the revised manuscript.

References

1. Carter A, Deutsch J, Zelicow P. Catastrophic terrorism. *Foreign Aff.* 1998;77:80-95.
2. Investigation of bioterrorism-related anthrax: Connecticut, 2001. *MMWR Morb Mortal Wkly Rep.* 2001;50:1077-1079.
3. Inglesby TV, Henderson DA, Bartlett JG, et al. Anthrax as a biological weapon. *JAMA.* 1999;281:1735-1745.
4. Lew D. *Bacillus anthracis.* In: Mandell GL, Bennett JE, Dolin R, eds. *Principles and Practice of Infectious Disease.* New York, NY: Churchill Livingstone Inc; 1995:1885-1889.
5. Christopher G, Cieslak T, Pavlin J, Eitzen E. Biological warfare: a historical perspective. *JAMA.* 1997;278:412-417.
6. Monterey Institute for International Studies chemical and biological weapons resource page. *Chemical and Biological Weapons.* Monterey, Calif: Monterey Institute for International Studies; 2001. Available at: http://cns.miis.edu/research/cbw/possess.htm.
7. Zilinskas RA. Iraq's biological weapons. *JAMA.* 1997;278:418-424.
8. Alibek K, Handelman S. *Biohazard: The Chilling True Story of the Largest Covert Biological Weapons Program in the World.* New York, NY: Random House; 1999.
9. Miller J. A germ-making plant. *New York Times.* September 4, 2001:A1.
10. Public Health Service Office of Emergency Preparedness. *Proceedings of the Seminar on Responding to the Consequences of Chemical and Biological Terrorism.* Washington, DC: US Dept of Health and Human Services; 1995.
11. WuDunn S, Miller J, Broad W. How Japan germ terror alerted world. *New York Times.* May 26, 1998:A1, 6.
12. Keim P, Smith K, Keys C, Takahashi H, Kurata T, Kaufmann A. Molecular investigation of the Aum Shinrikyo anthrax release in Kameido, Japan. *J Clin Microbiol.* 2001;39:4566-4567.
13. Washington File. New CIA report documents global weapons proliferation trends. Washington, DC: US Dept of State; February 1, 2002. Available at: http://usinfo.state.gov/products/washfile. Accessed February 1, 2002.
14. Enserink M. Microbial genomics: TIGR begins assault on the anthrax genome. *Science.* 2002;295:1442-1443.
15. Kennedy H. Daschle letter bombshell billions of anthrax spores. *New York Daily News.* October 31, 2001:5.
16. *Health Aspects of Chemical and Biological Weapons.* Geneva, Switzerland: World Health Organization; 1970.
17. Office of Technology Assessment, US Congress. *Proliferation of Weapons of Mass Destruction.* Washington, DC: US Government Printing Office; 1993. Publication OTA-ISC-559.
18. Meselson M, Guillemin J, Hugh-Jones M, et al. The Sverdlovsk anthrax outbreak of 1979. *Science.* 1994;266:1202-1208.
19. Simon J. Biological terrorism: preparing to meet the threat. *JAMA.* 1997;278:428-430.
20. Regis E. *The History of America's Secret Germ Warfare Project.* New York, NY: Random House; 1999.
21. Kohout E, Sehat A, Ashraf M. Anthrax: a continuous problem in south west Iran. *Am J Med Sci.* 1964;247:565.
22. Titball R, Turnbull P, Hutson R. The monitoring and detection of *Bacillus anthracis* in the environment. *Soc Appl Bacteriol Symp Ser.* 1991; 20:9S-18S.

23. l'agriculture Pdmd. Premiere Partie. I-la fievre charbonneuse en Iran.1-historique-especes atteintes; 1946. Located at: Archives De L'institute D'hessarek, Teheran, Iran.

24. Pienaar U. Epidemiology of anthrax in wild animals and the control on anthrax epizootics in the Kruger National Park, South Africa. *Fed Proc.* 1967;26:1496-1591.

25. Dragon D, Rennie R. The ecology of anthrax spores. *Can Vet J.* 1995;36:295-301.

26. Brachman P, Friedlander A. Anthrax. In: Plotkin S, Orenstein W, eds. *Vaccines.* 3rd ed. Philadelphia, Pa: WB Saunders Co; 1999:629-637.

27. Brachman P, Friedlander A. Inhalation anthrax. *Ann N Y Acad Sci.* 1980;353:83-93.

28. Summary of notifiable diseases, 1945-1994 . *MMWR Morb Mortal Wkly Rep.* 1994;43:70-78.

29. Human anthrax associated with an epizootic among livestock. *MMWR Morb Mortal Wkly Rep.* 2001;50:677-680.

30. Myenye K, Siziya S, Peterson D. Factors associated with human anthrax outbreak in the Chikupo and Ngandu villages of Murewa district in Mashonaland East Province, Zimbabwe. *Cent Afr J Med.* 1996; 42:312-315.

31. Sirisanthana T, Nelson K, Ezzell J, Abshire T. Serological studies of patients with cutaneous and oral-pharyngeal anthrax from northern Thailand. *Am J Trop Med Hyg.* 1988;39:575-581.

32. Friedlander A. Anthrax. In: Zajtchuk R, Bellamy R, eds. *Textbook of Military Medicine: Medical Aspects of Chemical and Biological Warfare.* Washington, DC: Office of the Surgeon General, US Dept of the Army; 1997:467-478.

33. Sirisanthana T, Navachareon N, Tharavichitkul P, Sirisanthana V, Brown AE. Outbreak of oral-pharyngeal anthrax. *Am J Trop Med Hyg.* 1984;33:144-150.

34. Dutz W, Saidi F, Kouhout E. Gastric anthrax with massive ascites. *Gut.* 1970;11:352-354.

35. Lincoln R, Hodges D, Klein F, et al. Role of the lymphatics in the pathogenesis of anthrax. *J Infect Dis.* 1965;115:481-494.

36. Borio L, Frank D, Mani V, et al. Death due to bioterrorism-related inhalational anthrax. *JAMA.* 2001;286:2554-2559.

37. Williams R. *Bacillus anthracis* and other spore forming bacilli. In: Braude AI, Davis LE, Fierer J, eds. *Infectious Disease and Medical Microbiology.* Philadelphia, Pa: WB Saunders Co; 1986:270-278.

38. Druett H, Henderson D, Packman L, Peacock S. Studies on respiratory infection. *J Hyg.* 1953;51:359-371.

39. Hatch T. Distribution and deposition of inhaled particles in respiratory tract. *Bacteriol Rev.* 1961;25:237-240.

40. Friedlander AM, Welkos SL, Pitt ML, et al. Postexposure prophylaxis against experimental inhalation anthrax. *J Infect Dis.* 1993;167:1239-1242.

41. Ross JM. The pathogenesis of anthrax following the administration of spores by the respiratory route. *J Pathol Bacteriol.* 1957;73:485-495.

42. Hanna PC, Ireland JA. Understanding *Bacillus anthracis* pathogenesis. *Trends Microbiol.* 1999;7:180-182.

43. Glassman H. Industrial inhalation anthrax. *Bacteriol Rev.* 1966;30:657-659.

44. Henderson DW, Peacock S, Belton FC. Observations on the prophylaxis of experimental pulmonary anthrax in the monkey. *J Hyg.* 1956;54:28-36.

45. Smith H, Keppie J. Observations on experimental anthrax. *Nature.* 1954;173:869-870.

46. *Soviet Biological Warfare Threat.* Washington, DC: Defense Intelligence Agency, US Dept of Defense; 1986. Publication DST-161OF-057-86.

47. Peters CJ, Hartley DM. Anthrax inhalation and lethal human infection. *Lancet.* 2002;359: 710-711.

48. Dixon TC, Meselson M, Guillemin J, Hanna PC. Anthrax. *N Engl J Med.* 1999;341:815-826.

49. Friedlander AM. Microbiology: tackling anthrax. *Nature.* 2001;414:160-161.

50. Abramova FA, Grinberg LM, Yampolskaya O, Walker DH. Pathology of inhalational anthrax in 42 cases from the Sverdlovsk outbreak in 1979. *Proc Natl Acad Sci U S A.* 1993;90:2291-2294.

51. Dalldorf F, Kaufmann AF, Brachman PS. Woolsorters' disease. *Arch Pathol.* 1971;92:418-426.

52. Gleiser CA, Berdjis CC, Harman HA, Gochenour WS. Pathology of experimental respiratory anthrax in *Macaca mulatta. Br J Exp Pathol.* 1963;44: 416-426.

53. Grinberg LM, Abramova FA, Yampolskaya OV, et al. Quantitative pathology of inhalational anthrax, I. *Mod Pathol.* 2001;14:482-495.

54. Dahlgren CM, Buchanan LM, Decker HM, et al. *Bacillus anthracis* aerosols in goat hair processing mills. *Am J Hyg.* 1960;72:24-31.

55. Walker JS, Lincoln RE, Klein F. Pathophysiological and biochemical changes in anthrax. *Fed Proc.* 1967;26:1539-1544.

56. Franz DR, Jahrling PB, Friedlander A, et al. Clinical recognition and management of patients exposed to biological warfare agents. *JAMA.* 1997;278: 399-411.

57. Vessal K, Yeganehdoust J, Dutz W, Kohout E. Radiologic changes in inhalation anthrax. *Clin Radiol.* 1975;26:471-474.

58. Albrink WS, Brooks SM, Biron RE, Kopel M. Human inhalation anthrax. *Am J Pathol.* 1960;36: 457-471.

59. Guillemin J. *Anthrax: The Investigation of a Deadly Outbreak.* Berkeley: University of California Press; 1999.

60. Brookmeyer R, Blades N, Hugh-Jones M, Henderson D. The statistical analysis of truncated data: application to the Sverdlovsk anthrax outbreak. *Biostatistics.* 2001;2:233-247.

61. Jernigan J, Stephens D, Ashford D, Omenaca C, et al. Bioterrorism-related inhalation anthrax: the first 10 cases reported in the United States. *Emerg Infect Dis.* 2001;7:933-944.

62. Barakat LA, Quentzel HL, Jernigan JA, et al. Fatal inhalational anthrax in a 94-year-old Connecticut woman. *JAMA.* 2002;287:863-868.

63. Freedman A, Afonja O, Chang M, et al. Cutaneous anthrax associated with microangiopathic hemolytic anemia and coagulopathy in a 7-month-old infant. *JAMA.* 2002;287:869-874.

64. Mina B, Dym JP, Kuepper F, et al. Fatal inhalational anthrax with unknown source of exposure in a 61-year-old woman in New York City. *JAMA.* 2002; 287:858-862.

65. Bush LM, Abrams BH, Beall A, Johnson CC. Index case of fatal inhalational anthrax due to bioterrorism in the United States. *N Engl J Med.* 2001;345:1607-1610.

66. Mayer TA, Bersoff-Matcha S, Murphy C, et al. Clinical presentation of inhalational anthrax following bioterrorism exposure. *JAMA.* 2001;286:2549-2553.

67. Pile JC, Malone JD, Eitzen EM, Friedlander A. Anthrax as a potential biological warfare agent. *Arch Intern Med.* 1998;158:429-434.

68. Kaye E, Kaye K. Fever and rash. In: Braunwalde, Fauci AS, Isselbacher KJ, et al, eds. *Harrison's Textbook of Medicine.* New York, NY: McGraw-Hill; 2001.

69. Investigation of bioterrorism-related anthrax and interim guidelines for clinical evaluation of persons with possible anthrax. *MMWR Morb Mortal Wkly Rep.* 2001;50:941-948.

70. Carucci JA, McGovern TW, Norton SA, et al. Cutaneous anthrax management algorithm. *J Am Acad Dermatol.* 2001; Nov 21. Available at: http://www.harcourthealth.com/scripts/om.dll/serve ?arttype = full&article = a121613.

71. Penn C, Klotz S. Anthrax. In: Gorbach S, Bartlett J, Blacklow N, eds. *Infectious Diseases.* Philadelphia, Pa: WB Saunders Co; 1998:1575-1578.

72. Hail A, Rossi C, Ludwig G, Ivins B, Tammariello R, Henchal E. Comparison of noninvasive sampling sites for early detection of *Bacillus* anthrax spores from rhesus monkeys after aerosol exposure. *Mil Med.* 1999;164:833-837.

73. Pitt M, Little S, Ivins B, et al. In vitro correlate of immunity in a rabbit model of inhalational anthrax. *Vaccine.* 2001;19:4768-4773.

74. Welkos S, Little S, Friedlander A, Fritz D, Fellows P. The role of antibodies to *Bacillus anthracis* and anthrax toxin components in inhibiting the early stages of infection by anthrax spores. *Microbiology.* 2001;147(pt 6):1677-1685.

75. Brachman P. Anthrax. In: Hoeprich PD, Jordan MC, Ronald AR, eds. *Infectious Diseases.* Philadelphia, Pa: JB Lippincott; 1994:1003-1008.

76. Anthrax vaccine, military use in Persian Gulf region [press release]. Washington, DC: US Dept of Defense; September 8, 1998.

77. Michigan Department of Public Health. *Anthrax Vaccine Adsorbed.* Lansing: Michigan Dept of Public Health; 1978.

78. Pitt M, Little S, Ivins B, et al. In vitro correlate of immunity in an animal model of inhalational anthrax. *J Appl Microbiol.* 1999;87:304.

79. Ivins BE, Fellows P, Pitt ML, et al. Efficacy of standard human anthrax vaccine against Bacillus anthracis aerosol spore challenge in rhesus monkeys. *Salisbury Med Bull.* 1996;87:125-126.

80. Fellows P, Linscott M, Ivins B, et al. Efficacy of a human anthrax vaccine in guinea pigs, rabbits, and rhesus macaques against challenge by *Bacillus anthracis* isolates of diverse geographical origin. *Vaccine.* 2001;20:635.

81. Brachman PS, Gold H, Plotkin SA, Fekety FR, Werrin M, Ingraham NR. Field evaluation of human anthrax vaccine. *Am J Public Health.* 1962;52:632-645.

82. Surveillance for adverse events associated with anthrax vaccination. *MMWR Morb Mortal Wkly Rep.* 2000;49:341-345.

83. Pittman P, Gibbs P, Cannon T, Friedlander A. Anthrax vaccine. *Vaccine.* 2001;20:972-978.

84. Committee to Assess the Safety and Efficacy of the Anthrax Vaccine, Medical Follow-Up Agency. *The Anthrax Vaccine: Is It Safe? Does It Work?* Washington, DC: Institute of Medicine, National Academy Press. March 2002. Available at: http://www.iom.edu/iom/iomhome.nsf/WFiles/Anthrax-8-pager1FINAL/$file/Anthrax-8-pager1FINAL.pdf.

85. Wiesen AR, Littell CT. Relationship between prepregnancy anthrax vaccination and pregnancy and birth outcomes among US Army women. *JAMA.* 2002;287:1556-1560.

86. Turnbull PC. Anthrax vaccines. *Vaccine.* 1991;9:533-539.

87. Statement by the Department of Health and Human Services regarding additional options for preventive treatment for those exposed to inhalational anthrax [news release]. Washington, DC: US Dept of Health and Human Services; December 18, 2001.

88. The Counter Bioterrorism Research Agenda of the National Institute of Allergy and Infectious Diseases for CDC Category A Agents. Washington, DC: National Institute of Allergy and Infectious Diseases; February 2002. Available at: http://www.niaid.nih.gov/dmid/pdf/biotresearchagenda.pdf.

89. Barnes J. Penicillin and *B anthracis. J Pathol Bacteriol.* 1947;194:113-125.

90. Lincoln R, Klein F, Walker J, et al. Successful treatment of monkeys for septicemic anthrax. *Antimicrob Agents and Chemotherapy—1964.* Washington, DC: American Society for Microbiology; 1965:759-763.

91. Odendaal MW, Peterson PM, de Vos V, Botha AD. The antibiotic sensitivity patterns of *Bacillus anthracis* isolated from the Kruger National Park. *Onderstepoort J Vet Res.* 1991;58:17-19.

92. Doganay M, Aydin N. Antimicrobial susceptibility of *Bacillus anthracis. Scand J Infect Dis.* 1991; 23:333-335.

93. Kelly D, Chulay JD, Mikesell P, Friedlander A. Serum concentrations of penicillin, doxycycline, and ciprofloxacin during prolonged therapy in rhesus monkeys. *J Infect Dis.* 1992;166:1184-1187.

94. Stepanov AV, Marinin LI, Pomerantsev AP, Staritsin NA. Development of novel vaccines against anthrax in man. *J Biotechnol.* 1966;44:155-160.

95. Choe C, Bouhaouala S, Brook I, Elliott T, Knudson G. In vitro development of resistance to ofloxacin and doxycycline in *Bacillus anthracis* Sterne. *Antimicrob Agents Chemother.* 2000;44:1766.

96. Investigation of bioterrorism-related anthrax and interim guidelines for exposure management and antimicrobial therapy, October 2001. *MMWR Morb Mortal Wkly Rep.* 2001;50:909-919.

97. Stevens DL, Gibbons AE, Bergstron R, Winn V. The Eagle effect revisited. *J Infect Dis.* 1988;158:23-28.

98. Notice to Readers: Update: Interim Recommendations for Antimicrobial Prophylaxis for Children and Breastfeeding Mothers and Treatment of Children with Anthrax. November 2001. *MMWR Morb Mortal Wkly Rep.* 2001;50:1014-1016.

99. Notice to Readers: Updated Recommendations for Antimicrobial Prophylaxis Among Asymptomatic Pregnant Women After Exposure to *Bacillus Anthracis.* November 2001. *MMWR Morb Mortal Wkly Rep.* 2001;50:960.

100. Interim recommendations for antimicrobial prophylaxis for children and breastfeeding mothers and treatment of children with anthrax. *MMWR Morb Mortal Wkly Rep.* 2001;50:1014-1016.

101. Lightfoot NF, Scott RJ, Turnbull PC. Antimicrobial susceptibility of *Bacillus anthracis. Salisbury Med Bull.* 1990;68:95-98.

102. Perkins WA. Public health implications of airborne infection. *Bacteriol Rev.* 1961;25:347-355.

103. Notice: doxycycline and penicillin G procaine administration for inhalational anthrax (post-exposure). 66 *Federal Register* 55679-55682 (2001).

104. Update: adverse events associated with anthrax prophylaxis among postal employees: New Jersey, New York City, and the District of Columbia metropolitan area, 2001. *MMWR Morb Mortal Wkly Rep.* 2001;50:1051-1054

105. Medical Economics. *Physicians' Desk Reference.* 56th ed. Montvale, NJ: Medical Economics; 2002.

106. American Hospital Formulary Service. *AHFS Drug Information.* Bethesda, Md: American Society of Health System Pharmacists; 1996.

107. American Public Health Association. Anthrax. In: Benson AS, ed. *Control of Communicable Diseases Manual.* Washington, DC: American Public Health Association; 1995:18-22.

108. Kournikakis B, Armour SJ, Boulet CA, Spence M, Parsons B. Risk assessment of anthrax threat letters. Defence Research Establishment Suffield. September 2001. Available at: http://www.dres.dnd.ca/Meetings/FirstResponders/tr01-048_annex.pdf.

109. Use of onsite technologies for rapidly assessing environmental *Bacillus anthracis* contamination on surfaces in buildings. *MMWR Morb Mortal Wkly Rep.* 2001;50:1087.

110. Chinn KS. *Reaerosolization Hazard Assessment for Biological Agent-Contaminated Hardstand Areas.* Life Sciences Division, Dugway Proving Ground, Utah: US Dept of the Army; 1996. Publication DPG/JCP-96/012.

111. Resnick IG, Martin DD, Larsen LD. *Evaluation of Need for Detection of Surface Biological Agent Contamination:* Dugway Proving Ground, Life Sciences Division, US Dept of the Army; 1990:1-35. Publication DPG-FR-90-711.

112. Manchee RJ, Stewart WD. The decontamination of Gruinard Island. *Chem Br.* July 1988:690-691.

113. Hsu SS, Cost of anthrax cleanup on Hill to top $23 million, EPA says. *Washington Post.* March 7, 2002:A7.

114. Altman L. New tests confirm potency of anthrax in Senate office building. *New York Times.* December 11, 2001:B6.

115. Bioterrorism alleging use of anthrax and interim guidelines for management—United States, 1998 . *MMWR Morb Mortal Wkly Rep.* 1999;48:69-74.

116. *Medical Response to Biological Warfare and Terrorism.* Gaithersburg, Md: US Army Medical Research Institute of Infectious Diseases, Centers for Disease Control and Prevention, and US Food and Drug Administration; 1998.

117. Mourez M, Kane R, Mogridge J, et al. Designing a polyvalent inhibitor of anthrax toxin. *Nat Biotechnol.* 2001;19:958-961.

118. Friedlander AM. Microbiology: tackling anthrax. *Nature.* 2001;414:160-161

Smallpox as a Biological Weapon

Donald A. Henderson, MD, MPH; Thomas V. Inglesby, MD; John G. Bartlett, MD; Michael S. Ascher, MD; Edward Eitzen, Jr, MD, MPH; Peter B. Jahrling, PhD; Jerome Hauer, MPH; Marcelle Layton, MD; Joseph McDade, PhD; Michael T. Osterholm, PhD, MPH; Tara O'Toole, MD, MPH; Gerald Parker, PhD, DVM; Trish M. Perl, MD, MSc; Philip K. Russell, MD; Kevin Tonat, DrPH, MPH; for the Working Group on Civilian Biodefense

Reviewed and updated by Donald A. Henderson, MD, MPH; Thomas V. Inglesby, MD; and Tara O'Toole, MD, MPH

This is the second article in a series entitled *Medical and Public Health Management Following the Use of a Biological Weapon: Consensus Statements of the Working Group on Civilian Biodefense.*[1] The working group has identified a limited number of widely known organisms that could cause disease and deaths in sufficient numbers to cripple a city or region. Smallpox is one of the most serious of these diseases.

If used as a biological weapon, smallpox represents a serious threat to civilian populations because of its case-fatality rate of 30% or more among unvaccinated persons and the absence of specific therapy. Although smallpox has long been feared as the most devastating of all infectious diseases,[2] its potential for devastation today is far greater than at any previous time. Routine vaccination throughout the United States ceased more than 25 years ago. In a now highly susceptible, mobile population, smallpox would be able to spread widely and rapidly throughout this country and the world.

Consensus Methods

Members of the working group were selected by the chairman in consultation with principal agency heads in the Department of Health and Human Services (DHHS) and the US Army Medical Research Institute of Infectious Diseases (USAMRIID).

The first author (D.A.H.) conducted a literature search in conjunction with the preparation of another publication on smallpox[2] as well as this article. The literature was reviewed and opinions were sought from experts in the diagnosis and management of smallpox, including members of the working group.

The first draft of the working group's consensus statement was the result of synthesis of information obtained in the evidence-gathering process. Members of the working group were asked to make written comments on the first draft of the document in September 1998. Suggested revisions were incorporated into the second draft of the statement. The working group was convened to review the second draft of the statement on October 30, 1998. Consensus recommendations were made and no significant disagreements existed at the conclusion of this meeting. The third draft incorporated changes suggested at the conference and working group members had an additional opportunity to suggest final revisions. The final statement incorporates all relevant evidence obtained by the literature search in conjunction with final consensus recommendations supported by all working group members. This statement was reviewed and updated by the principal subject-matter authors in December 2001.

This article is intended to provide the scientific foundation and initial framework for the detailed planning needed to prepare for a response to a bioterrorist attack with smallpox. This planning must encompass coordinated systems approaches to bioterrorism, including public policies and consequence management by local and regional public and private institutions. The assessment and recommendations provided herein represent the best professional judgment of the working group at this time based on data and expertise currently available. The conclusions and recommendations need to be regularly reassessed as new information becomes available.

History and Potential as a Bioweapon

Smallpox probably was first used as a biological weapon during the French and Indian Wars (1754-1767) by British forces in North America.[3] Soldiers distributed blankets that had been used by smallpox patients with the intent of initiating outbreaks among American Indians. Epidemics occurred, killing more than 50% of many affected tribes. With Edward Jenner's demonstration in 1796 that an infection caused by cowpox protected against smallpox and the rapid diffusion worldwide of the practice of cowpox inoculation (ie, vaccination),[4] the potential threat of smallpox as a bioweapon was greatly diminished.

A global campaign, begun in 1967 under the aegis of the World Health Organization (WHO), succeeded in eradicating smallpox in 1977.[2] In 1980, the World Health Assembly recommended that all countries cease vaccination.[5] A WHO expert committee recommended that all laboratories destroy their stocks of variola virus or transfer them to 1 of 2 WHO reference laboratories—the Institute of Virus Preparations in Moscow, Russia, or the Centers for Disease Control and Prevention (CDC) in Atlanta, Ga. All countries reported compliance. The WHO committee later recommended that all virus stocks be destroyed in June 1999, and the 1996 World Health Assembly concurred.[6] A number of scientists argued, however, that the existing stocks of variola virus should be retained for a longer period to permit a number of research studies to be undertaken, including those that might lead to a more attenuated smallpox vaccine and to antiviral drugs that could be used in smallpox therapy.[7] The 1999 World Health Assembly agreed that the stocks be temporarily retained up to 2002 and asked that a WHO Advisory

Committee on Variola Virus Research be constituted that, on a continuing basis, could review and approve proposed programs of work. That committee is now meeting regularly. A proposal for the indefinite postponement of virus destruction will be discussed during the 2002 World Health Assembly.

Allegations by Ken Alibek, a former deputy director of the Soviet Union's civilian bioweapons program, have heightened concern that smallpox might be used as a bioweapon. Alibek[8] reported that beginning in 1980, the Soviet government embarked on a successful program to produce the smallpox virus in large quantities and adapt it for use in bombs and intercontinental ballistic missiles; the program had an industrial capacity capable of producing many tons of smallpox virus annually. Furthermore, Alibek reports that Russia even now has a research program that seeks to produce more virulent and contagious recombinant strains. Because financial support for laboratories in Russia has sharply declined in recent years, there are increasing concerns that existing expertise and equipment might fall into non-Russian hands.

The deliberate reintroduction of smallpox as an epidemic disease would be an international crime of unprecedented proportions, but it is now regarded as a possibility. An aerosol release of variola virus would disseminate widely, given the considerable stability of the orthopoxviruses in aerosol form[9] and the likelihood that the infectious dose is very small.[10] Moreover, during the 1960s and 1970s in Europe, when smallpox was imported during the December to April period of high transmission, as many as 10 to 20 second-generation cases were sometimes infected from a single case. Widespread concern and, sometimes, panic occurred, even with outbreaks of fewer than 100 cases, resulting in extensive emergency control measures.[2]

Epidemiology

Smallpox was once worldwide in scope, and before vaccination was practiced, almost everyone eventually contracted the disease. There were 2 principal forms of the disease, variola major and a much milder form, variola minor (or alastrim).[11] Before eradication took place, these forms could be differentiated clinically only when occurring in outbreaks; virological differentiation is now possible.[12] Through the end of the 19th century, variola major predominated throughout the world. However, at the turn of the century, variola minor was first detected in South Africa and later in Florida, from whence it spread across the United States and into Latin America and Europe.[13] Typical variola major epidemics such as those that occurred in Asia resulted in case-fatality rates of 30% or higher among the unvaccinated, whereas variola minor case-fatality rates were customarily 1% or less.[2]

Smallpox usually spread from person to person primarily in droplets expelled from the orophayrnx.[2] Those within 6 to 8 feet of the patient were at greatest risk. However, patients with a cough or with the very severe forms of smallpox could expel the virus in a small particle aerosol, which could remain suspended and spread over a wide area.[10, 14] Historically, the rapidity of smallpox transmission throughout the population was generally slower than for such diseases as

Figure 1. Typical Temperature Chart of Patient With Smallpox Infection

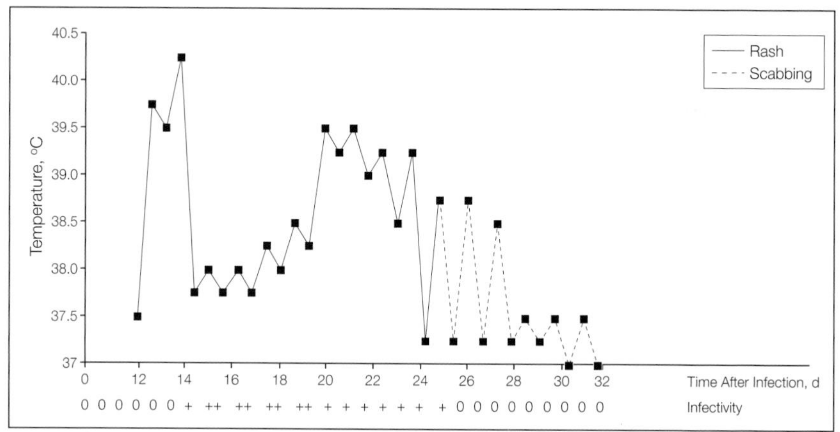

Chart shows approximate time of appearance, evolution of the rash, and magnitude of infectivity relative to the number of days after acquisition of infection.[3, 27, 30]

measles or chickenpox. Patients spread smallpox primarily to household members and friends; large outbreaks in schools, for example, were uncommon. This finding was accounted for in part by the fact that transmission of smallpox virus did not occur until onset of rash. By then, many patients had been confined to bed because of the high fever and malaise of the prodromal illness. Secondary cases were thus usually restricted to those who came into contact with patients, usually in the household or hospital.

Contaminated clothing or bed linens could also spread the virus.[15] There are no known animal or insect reservoirs or vectors.

The seasonal occurrence of smallpox was similar to that of chickenpox and measles—its incidence was highest during winter and early spring.[16] This pattern was consonant with the observation that the duration of survival of orthopoxviruses in the aerosolized form was inversely proportional to both temperature and humidity.[9] Likewise, when imported cases occurred in Europe, large outbreaks sometimes developed during the winter months, rarely during the summer.[17]

The patient was most infectious from onset of rash through the first 7 to 10 days of rash (**Figure 1**).[17, 18] As scabs formed, infectivity waned rapidly. Although the scabs contained large amounts of viable virus, epidemiological and laboratory studies indicate that they were not especially infectious, presumably because the virions were bound tightly in the fibrin matrix.[19]

The age distribution of cases depended primarily on the degree of smallpox susceptibility in the population. In most areas, cases predominated among children because adults were protected by immunity induced by vaccination or previous smallpox infection. In rural areas that had seen little vaccination or smallpox, the age distribution of cases was similar to the age distribution of the population. The age distribution of cases in the United States, should smallpox occur, would include many adults because routine vaccination stopped in 1972 and vaccination immunity among those vaccinated before that time has waned substantially.

Microbiology

Smallpox, a DNA virus, is a member of the genus orthopoxvirus.[20] The orthopoxviruses are among the largest and most complex of all viruses. The virion is characteristically a brick-shaped structure measuring 300 nm by 250 nm by 200 nm. Three other members of this genus (monkeypox, vaccinia, and cowpox) can also infect humans, causing cutaneous lesions, but only smallpox is readily transmitted from person to person.[2] Monkeypox, a zoonotic disease, presently is found only in tropical rain forest areas of central and western Africa and is not readily transmitted among humans. Vaccinia and cowpox seldom spread from person to person.

Pathogenesis and Clinical Presentation

Natural infection occurs following implantation of the virus on the oropharyngeal or respiratory mucosa.[2] The infectious dose is unknown but is believed to be only a few virions.[10] After the migration of virus to and multiplication in regional lymph nodes, an asymptomatic viremia develops on about the third or fourth day, followed by multiplication of virus in the spleen, bone marrow, and lymph nodes. A secondary viremia begins on about the eighth day and is followed by fever and toxemia. The virus, contained in leukocytes, then localizes in small blood vessels of the dermis and beneath the oral and pharyngeal mucosa and subsequently infects adjacent cells. At the end of the 12- to 14-day incubation period (range, 7-17 days), the patient typically experiences high fever, malaise, and prostration with headache and backache.[2] Severe abdominal pain and delirium are sometimes present. A maculopapular rash then appears on the mucosa of the mouth and pharynx, face, and forearms, and spreads to the trunk and legs (**Figure 2**).[2] Within 1 to 2 days, the rash becomes vesicular and, later, pustular. The pustules are characteristically round, tense, and deeply embedded in the dermis; crusts begin to form on about the eighth or ninth day of rash. As the patient recovers, the scabs separate and characteristic pitted scarring gradually develops. The scars are most evident on the face and result from the destruction of sebaceous glands followed by shrinking of granulation tissue and fibrosis.[2]

The lesions that first appear in the mouth and pharynx ulcerate quickly because of the absence of a stratum corneum, releasing large amounts of virus into the saliva.[2] Virus titers in saliva are highest during the first week of illness, corresponding with the period during which patients are most infectious. Vesicular and pustular skin lesions contain abundant virus particles and virus is present in the pharynx, urine, and conjunctival secretions during the acute phase of illness.[21] Although the virus in some instances can be detected in swabs taken from the oropharynx as many as 5 to 6 days before the rash develops,[22] transmission does not occur during this period.

Figure 2. Typical Case of Smallpox Infection in a Child

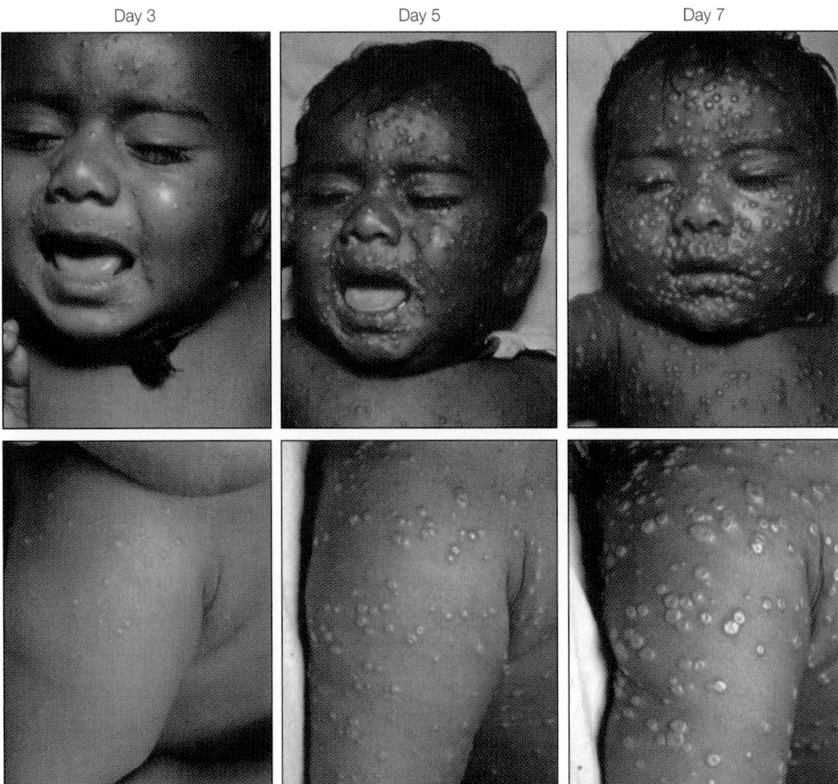

Figure shows the appearance of the rash at days 3, 5, and 7 of evolution. Note that lesions are more dense on the face and extremities than on the trunk and that they are similar in appearance to each other. Lesions may also appear on the palms of the hand. If this were a case of chickenpox, one would expect to see, in any area, macules, papules, pustules, and lesions with scabs (see Figure 3). Reproduced with permission from the World Health Organization.[2]

Except for the lesions in the skin and mucous membranes and reticulum cell hyperplasia, other organs are seldom involved. Secondary bacterial infection is not common, and death, which usually occurs during the second week of illness, most likely results from the toxemia associated with circulating immune complexes and soluble variola antigens.[2] Encephalitis sometimes ensues that is indistinguishable from the acute perivascular demyelination observed as a complication of infection due to vaccinia, measles, or varicella.[23]

Neutralizing antibodies can be detected by the sixth day of rash and remain at high titers for many years.[24] Hemagglutinin-inhibiting antibodies can be detected on about the sixth day of rash, or about 21 days after infection, and complement-fixing antibodies appear approximately 2 days later. Within 5 years, hemagglutinin-inhibiting antibodies decline to low levels and complement-fixing antibodies rarely persist for longer than 6 months.[2]

Although at least 90% of smallpox cases are clinically characteristic and readily diagnosed in endemic areas, 2 other forms of smallpox are difficult to recognize—hemorrhagic and malignant. Hemorrhagic cases are uniformly fatal and occur among all ages and in both sexes, but pregnant women appear to be unusually susceptible. Illness usually begins with a somewhat shorter incubation period and is characterized by a severely prostrating prodromal illness with high fever and head, back, and abdominal pain. Soon thereafter, a dusky erythema develops, followed by petechiae and frank hemorrhages into the skin and mucous membranes. Death usually occurs by the fifth or sixth day after onset of rash,[23] probably as the result of an excessive elaboration of cytokines.[25]

In the frequently fatal malignant form, the abrupt onset and prostrating constitutional symptoms are similar. The confluent lesions develop slowly, never progressing to the pustular stage but remaining soft, flattened, and velvety to the touch. The skin has the appearance of a fine-grained, reddish-colored crepe rubber, sometimes with hemorrhages. If the patient survives, the lesions gradually disappear without forming scabs or, in severe cases, large amounts of epidermis might peel away.[23]

The illness associated with variola minor is generally less severe, with fewer constitutional symptoms and a more sparse rash.[26] A milder form of disease is also seen among those who have residual immunity from previous vaccination. In partially immune persons, the rash tends to be atypical and more scant and the evolution of the lesions more rapid.[15]

There is little information about how individuals with different types of immune deficiency responded to natural smallpox infection. Smallpox was eradicated before human immunodeficiency virus (HIV) was identified and before suitable techniques became available for measuring cell-mediated immunity. However, it is probable that the underlying cause of some cases of malignant and hemorrhagic smallpox was a defective immune response. Vaccination of immune-deficient persons sometimes resulted in a continually spreading primary lesion, persistent viremia, and secondary viral infection of many organs. One such case is documented to have occurred in a vaccinated soldier who had HIV infection.[27]

Diagnosis

The discovery of a single suspected case of smallpox must be treated as an international health emergency and be brought immediately to the attention of national officials through local and state health authorities.

The majority of smallpox cases present with a characteristic rash that is centrifugal in distribution, ie, most dense on the face and extremities. The lesions appear during a 1- to 2-day period and evolve at the same rate. On any given part of the body, they are generally at the same stage of development. In varicella (chickenpox), the disease most frequently confused with smallpox, new lesions

Figure 3. Typical Case of Varicella (Chickenpox) in a Child

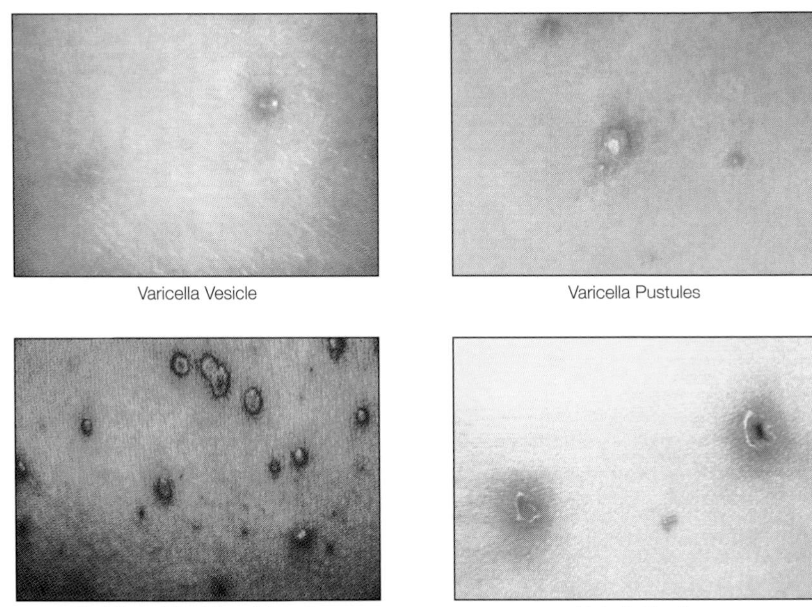

Varicella Vesicle

Varicella Pustules

Umbilicated Pustules of Varicella

Varicella Crusts

Varicella lesions are most dense over the trunk and seldom occur on the palms and soles. The lesions are superficial and, in any area, one will find vesicles, pustules, and scabs, quite unlike smallpox where the lesions are all at approximately the same stage of development. New crops of lesions occur every few days. Reproduced with permission from the Upjohn Collection (DM-24).

appear in crops every few days and lesions at very different stages of maturation (ie, vesicles, pustules, and scabs) are found in adjacent areas of skin (**Figure 3**). Varicella lesions are much more superficial and are almost never found on the palms and soles. The distribution of varicella lesions is centripetal, with a greater concentration of lesions on the trunk than on the face and extremities.

The signs and symptoms of both hemorrhagic and malignant smallpox were such that smallpox was seldom suspected until more typical cases were seen and it was recognized that a smallpox outbreak was in progress. Hemorrhagic cases were most often initially identified as meningococcemia or severe acute leukemia. Malignant cases likewise posed diagnostic problems, most often being mistaken for hemorrhagic chickenpox or prompting surgery because of severe abdominal pain.

Laboratory confirmation of the diagnosis in a smallpox outbreak is important. Specimens should be collected by someone who has recently been vaccinated (or is vaccinated within 1 or 2 days) and who wears gloves and a mask. To obtain vesicular or pustular fluid, it is often necessary to open lesions with the blunt edge of a scalpel. The fluid can then be harvested on a cotton swab. Scabs can be picked off with forceps. Specimens should be deposited in a screw-capped plastic tube that should be sealed with adhesive tape at the juncture of stopper and tube. This tube, in turn, should be enclosed in a second durable, watertight container. State or local health department laboratories should immediately be contacted regarding the shipping of specimens. Laboratory examination requires high-containment (BL-4) facilities and should be undertaken only in designated laboratories with the appropriate training and equipment. Once it is established that the epidemic is caused by smallpox virus, clinically typical cases would not require further laboratory confirmation.

Smallpox infection can be rapidly confirmed in the laboratory by electron microscopic examination of vesicular or pustular fluid or scabs. Although all orthopoxviruses exhibit identically appearing brick-shaped virions, the patient's history and clinical picture readily identify cowpox and vaccinia. Although smallpox and monkeypox virions may be indistinguishable, naturally occurring monkeypox is found only in tropical rain forest areas of Africa. Definitive laboratory identification and characterization of the virus involves growth of the virus in cell culture or on chorioallantoic egg membrane and characterization of strains by use of various biologic assays, including polymerase chain reaction techniques and restriction fragment-length polymorphisms.[28-30] The latter studies can be completed within a few hours.

Preexposure Preventive Vaccination

Before 1972, smallpox vaccination was recommended for all US children at age 1 year. Most states required that each child be vaccinated before school entry. The only other requirement for vaccination was for military recruits and tourists visiting foreign countries. Most countries required that the individual be successfully vaccinated within a 3-year period prior to entering the country. Routine vaccination in the United States stopped in 1972 and since then, few persons younger than 30 years have been vaccinated. Those under 30 years now account for about 45% of the US population.

The immune status of those who were vaccinated more than 30 years ago is not clear. The duration of immunity, based on the experience of naturally exposed susceptible persons, has never been satisfactorily measured. Neutralizing antibodies are thought to reflect levels of protection, although this has not been validated in the field. These antibodies have been shown to decline markedly during a 10- to 20-year period.[24] Thus, a substantial proportion of those who received the recommended single-dose vaccination as children do not have lifelong immunity. However, among a group who had been vaccinated at birth and at ages 8 and 18 years as part of a study, neutralizing antibody levels remained stable during a 30-year period.[31] It is possible, therefore, that those vaccinated successfully on 2 or more occasions may have residual antibody. However, comparatively few persons today have been successfully vaccinated on more than 1 occasion.

It is to be noted that in endemic countries, estimates of vaccine efficacy after primary vaccination have been found to be 90% or higher among adults who were vaccinated only as children.[2] This undoubtedly reflects the fact that inapparent smallpox infections have occurred among vaccinated contacts with a concomitant significant rise in antibody titer.[32] Since naturally occurring smallpox infections result in lifetime immunity, the apparent high level of efficacy of primary vaccination alone, based on experience in endemic areas, is misleading.

At present, the supplies of vaccine worldwide are limited, but actions are being taken to improve the availability of vaccine in case of need. As of late 2001, the United States had an amount of vaccine that, with appropriate dilution, was sufficient to vaccinate 50 million persons. This quantity is based on recently published studies that demonstrated that the US smallpox vaccine currently in reserve (Dryvax, Wyeth Laboratories, Marietta, Pa) could be safely diluted to a 1:5 dilution without reducing the rate of successful vaccination.[33] The smallpox vaccine was produced in the 1970s by growth of vaccinia virus (New York Board of Health strain) on the scarified skin of calves. Production has begun to produce the same strain of vaccinia virus in tissue cell cultures (some in MRC-5 cells and some in Vero cells) with the expectation that a total of 280 million doses of vaccine would be available by late 2002 (D.A.H., oral communication, 2001).

A WHO survey of other countries reveals that, in total, they have in stock between 50 and 100 million doses, not all of which is thought to meet international standards for potency and stability (David Heymann, MD, oral communication, 2001). Several countries have indicated that they expect to augment their vaccine reserves either by production in national laboratories or through purchase.

Because of the small amounts of vaccine available, a preventive vaccination program to protect individuals such as emergency and health care personnel is not an option at this time. When additional supplies of vaccine are procured, a decision to undertake preventive vaccination of some portion of the population will have to weigh the relative risk of vaccination complications against the threat of contracting smallpox.

Before extensive vaccination can be undertaken, adequate supplies of vaccinia immune globulin (VIG) for use in the treatment of progressive vaccinia and severe cutaneous reactions occurring as a complication of vaccination must be available.[34, 35] Such supplies are now being procured for the United States.

Postexposure Therapy

At this time, the best that can be offered to the patient infected with smallpox is supportive therapy plus antibiotics as indicated for treatment of occasional secondary bacterial infections. No antiviral substances have yet proved effective for the treatment of smallpox. Initial reports in the 1960s described the therapeutic benefits of the thiosemicarbazones, cytosine and adenine arabinoside, and rifampicin, but ultimately they proved to be ineffective.[36-38]

Recent studies in tissue culture, mice, and a small number of monkeys have suggested the possibility that cidofovir, a nucleoside analog DNA polymerase inhibitor, might prove useful in preventing smallpox infection if administered within 1 or 2 days after exposure.[38] At this time, there is no evidence to suggest that cidofovir would be effective in the treatment of smallpox once symptoms had appeared. Moreover, the potential utility of this drug would be of limited value in an epidemic, given the fact that it must be administered intravenously and its use is sometimes accompanied by serious renal toxicity.[39]

Postexposure Infection Control

A smallpox outbreak poses difficult public health problems because of the ability of the virus to continue to spread throughout the population unless checked by vaccination and/or isolation of patients and their close contacts.

A clandestine aerosol release of smallpox, even if it infected only 50 to 100 persons to produce the first generation of cases, would rapidly spread in a now highly susceptible population, expanding, with each generation of cases, by a factor of 10 times or more during the winter and spring months when seasonal transmission is highest.[2,10] Between the time of an aerosol release of smallpox virus and diagnosis of the first cases, an interval as long as 2 weeks or more is apt to occur because of the average incubation period of 12 to 14 days and the lapse of several additional days before a rash was sufficiently distinct to suggest the diagnosis of smallpox. By that time, there would be no risk of further environmental exposure from the original aerosol release because the virus is fully inactivated within 2 days. However, close contacts of the first wave of cases would already have been infected and would be incubating the disease.

As soon as the diagnosis of smallpox is made, all individuals in whom smallpox is suspected should be isolated immediately and all household and other face-to-face contacts, as well as their families, should be vaccinated and placed under surveillance.[40] It is important that discretion be used in identifying contacts of patients to ensure, to the extent possible, that vaccination and adequate surveillance measures are focused on those at greatest risk. Specifically, it is recommended that *contacts* be defined as persons who have been in the same household as the infected individual or who have been in face-to-face contact with the patient *after the onset of fever*. Household members of those in face-to-face contact should also be vaccinated. Experience during the smallpox global eradication program showed that patients did not transmit infection until after the prodromal fever had given way to the rash stage of illness.[17,18]An emergency vaccination program is also indicated that would include all health care workers at clinics or hospitals that might receive patients; all other essential disaster response personnel, such as police, firefighters, transit workers, public health staff, and emergency management staff who might come into contact with patients; and mortuary staff who might have to handle bodies. The working group recommends that all such personnel for whom vaccination is not contraindicated should be vaccinated immediately irrespective of prior vaccination status.

Vaccination administered within 4 days of first exposure has been shown to offer some protection against acquiring infection and significant protection against a fatal outcome.[15,41] Those who have been vaccinated at some time in the past will normally exhibit an accelerated immune response to revaccination. Thus, it would be prudent, when possible, to assign those who had been previously vaccinated and just revaccinated to duties involving close patient contact.

Because the widespread dissemination of smallpox virus by aerosol poses a serious threat in hospitals, patients should be isolated in the home or other nonhospital facility whenever possible. Home care for most patients is a reasonable alternative, given the fact that little can be done for a patient other than to offer supportive therapy. Isolation of all contacts of exposed patients would be logistically difficult and, in practice, should not be necessary. Because contacts, even if infected, are not contagious until onset of rash, a practical strategy calls for all contacts to have temperatures checked at least once each day, preferably in the evening. Any increase in temperature higher than 38°C (101°F) during the 17-day period following last exposure to the case would suggest the possible development of smallpox[2] and be cause for isolating the patient immediately, preferably at home, until it could be determined whether the contact had smallpox. All close contacts of the patients should be promptly vaccinated.

Although cooperation by most patients and contacts in observing isolation should be able to be ensured through counseling and persuasion, there may be some for whom forcible quarantine will be required. Some states and cities in the United States, but not all, confer broad discretionary powers on health authorities to ensure the safety of the public's health and, at one time, this included powers to quarantine. Under epidemic circumstances, this could be an important power to have. Thus, each state and city should review its statutes as part of its preparedness activities. (See "Large-Scale Quarantine Following Biological Terrorism in the United States" later in this book.)

During the smallpox epidemics in the 1960s and 1970s in Europe, there was public alarm whenever outbreaks occurred and, sometimes, a demand for mass vaccination over a wide area, even when the vaccination coverage of the population was high.[2] In the United States, where few people now have protective levels of immunity, similar levels of concern must be anticipated. However, until there is an adequate global vaccine supply, the vaccine has to be carefully conserved and a major emphasis placed on the rapid isolation of smallpox patients.

Hospital Epidemiology and Infection Control

Smallpox transmission within hospitals has long been recognized as a serious problem. For this reason, separate hospitals for smallpox patients were used for more than 200 years. Throughout the 1970s, both England and Germany had fully equipped standby hospitals in case smallpox should be imported.[2] Infections acquired in hospitals may occur as the result of droplets spread from patients to staff and visitors in reasonably close contact or by a fine particle aerosol that may spread over a wide area. In 1 such occurrence in Germany, a smallpox patient with a cough, although isolated in a single room, infected persons on 3 floors of a hospital.[10] Persons with the usually fatal hemorrhagic or malignant forms of the disease pose a special problem because they are extremely contagious and often remain undiagnosed until they are near death. A number of outbreaks have occurred in laundry workers who handled linens and blankets used by patients.[15] Thus, the working group recommends that in an outbreak setting, all hospital employees as well as patients in the hospital be vaccinated. For individuals who are immunocompromised or for whom vaccination is otherwise contraindicated, VIG should be provided, if available. If it is not available, a judgment will have to be made regarding the relative risks of acquiring the disease in contrast with the risks associated with vaccination.

In the event of a limited outbreak with few cases, patients should be admitted to the hospital and confined to rooms that are under negative pressure and equipped with high-efficiency particulate air filtration. In larger outbreaks, home isolation and care should be the objective for most patients. However, not all will be able to be so accommodated and, to limit nosocomial infections, authorities should consider the possibility of designating a specific hospital or other suitable facility for smallpox care. All persons isolated as such and those caring for them should be immediately vaccinated. Employees for whom vaccination is contraindicated should be furloughed.

Standard precautions using gloves, gowns, and masks should be observed. All laundry and waste should be placed in biohazard bags and autoclaved before being laundered or incinerated. A special protocol should be developed for decontaminating rooms after they are vacated by patients. (See "Decontamination" later in this chapter.)

Laboratory examination requires high-containment (BL-4) facilities and should be undertaken only in designated laboratories with the appropriate trained personnel and equipment. Specific recommendations for safe specimen transport are described in "Diagnosis," earlier in this chapter.

Protecting against the explosive spread of virus from the hemorrhagic or malignant case is difficult. Such cases occurring during the course of an outbreak may be detected if staff is alert to the possibility that any severe, acute, prostrating illness must be considered smallpox until proven otherwise.

Vaccine Administration and Complications

Smallpox vaccine is currently approved by the US Food and Drug Administration (FDA) for use only in persons in special-risk categories, including laboratory workers directly involved with smallpox or closely related orthopoxviruses. Under epidemic circumstances, widespread vaccination would be indicated, as recommended by the working group.

Vaccination has been successfully and safely administered to persons of all ages, from birth onward.[42] However, there are certain groups for whom elective vaccination has not been recommended because of the risk of complications. Under epidemic circumstances, however, such contraindications will have to be weighed against the grave risks posed by smallpox. If available, VIG can be administered concomitantly with vaccination to minimize the risk of complications in these persons.

Vaccination is normally performed using the bifurcated needle (**Figure 4**). A sterile needle is inserted into an ampule of reconstituted vaccine and, on withdrawal, a droplet of vaccine sufficient for vaccination is held by capillarity between the 2 tines. The needle is held at right angles to the skin; the wrist of the vaccinator rests against the arm. Fifteen perpendicular strokes of the needle are rapidly made in an area of about 5 mm in diameter.[43] The strokes should be

Figure 4. Vaccination With the Bifurcated Needle

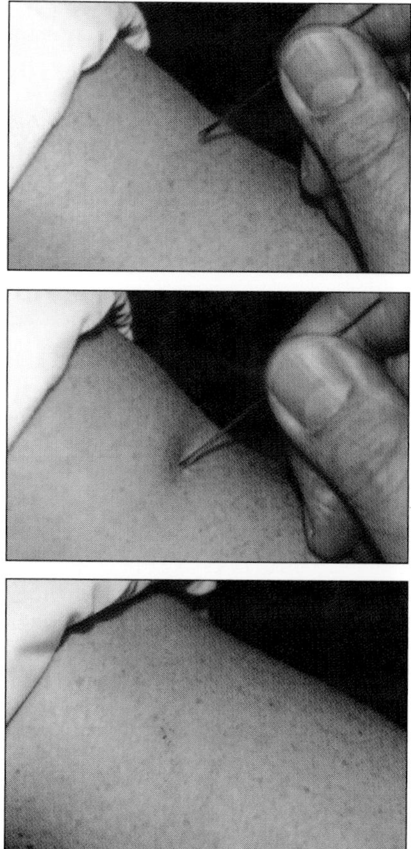

The requisite amount of reconstituted vaccine is held between the prongs of the needle and vaccination is done by multiple punctures; 15 strokes, at right angles to the skin over the deltoid muscle, are rapidly made within an area of about 5 mm in diameter.

sufficiently vigorous so that a trace of blood appears at the vaccination site after 15 to 30 seconds. After vaccination, excess vaccine should be wiped from the site with gauze that should be discarded in a hazardous-waste receptacle. The site should be covered with a loose, nonocclusive bandage to deter the individual from touching the site and perhaps transferring virus to other parts of the body.

After about 3 days, a red papule appears at the vaccination site and becomes vesicular on about the fifth day (**Figure** 5). By the seventh day, it becomes the typical Jennerian pustule, umbilicated, multilocular, containing turbid lymph and surrounded by an erythematous areola that may continue to expand for 3 more days. Regional lymphadenopathy and fever is not uncommon. As many as 70% of children have 1 or more days of temperature higher than 39°C (100°F)

Figure 5. Typical Appearance of an Evolving Primary Vaccination Take

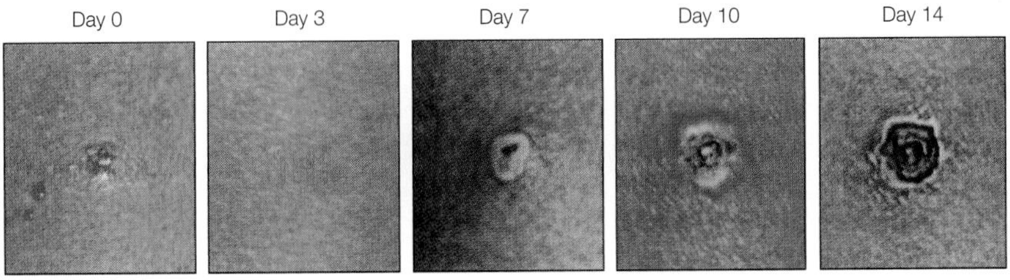

Day 0 | Day 3 | Day 7 | Day 10 | Day 14

Reproduced with permission from the Centers for Disease Control and Prevention.[3]

between days 4 and 14.[44] The pustule gradually dries, leaving a dark crust, which normally falls off after about 3 weeks.

A successful vaccination for those with partial immunity may manifest a gradient of responses. These range from what appears to be a primary take (as described herein) to an accelerated reaction in which there may be little more than a papule surrounded by erythema that reaches a peak between 3 and 7 days. A response that reaches a peak in erythema within 48 hours represents a hypersensitivity reaction and does not signify that growth of the vaccinia virus has occurred.[2] Persons exhibiting such a reaction should be revaccinated.

Complications

The frequency of complications associated with use of the New York Board of Health strain (the strain used throughout the United States and Canada for vaccine) is the lowest for any established vaccinia virus strain, but the risks are not inconsequential.[45, 46] Data on complications gathered by the CDC in 1968 are shown in **Table 1**. Complications occurred most frequently among primary vaccinees.

Postvaccinial Encephalitis. Postvaccinial encephalitis occurred at a rate of 1 case per 300 000 vaccinations and was observed only in primary vaccinees; one fourth of these cases were fatal and several had permanent neurological residua. Between 8 and 15 days after vaccination, encephalitic symptoms developed: fever, headache, vomiting, drowsiness, and, sometimes, spastic paralysis, meningitic signs, coma, and convulsions. Cerebrospinal fluid usually showed a pleocytosis. Recovery was either complete or associated with residual paralysis and other central nervous system symptoms and, sometimes, death. There was no treatment.

Progressive Vaccinia (Vaccinia Gangrenosa). Cases of progressive vaccinia occurred both among primary vaccinees and revaccinees. It was a frequently fatal complication among those with immune deficiency disorders. The vaccinial lesion failed to heal and progressed to involve adjacent skin with necrosis of tissue, spreading to other parts of the skin, to bones, and to viscera. Vaccinia immune globulin was used for this problem.[35, 47] One case in a soldier with acquired immunodeficiency syndrome was successfully treated with VIG and ribavirin.[27]

Table 1. Complications of Smallpox Vaccination in the United States for 1968—Centers for Disease Control and Prevention National Survey*

	Vaccination Status, Age, y			
	Primary Vaccination†	Revaccination	Contacts	Total
Estimated No. of vaccinations	5,594,000	8,574,000	...	14,168,000
No. of Cases				
Postvaccinial encephalitis	16(4)	0	0	16(4)
Progressive vaccinia	5(2)	6(2)	0	11(4)
Eczema vaccinatum	58	8	60(1)	126(1)
Generalized vaccinia	131	10	2	143
Accidental infection	142	7	44	193
Other	66	9	8	83
Total	418(6)	40(2)	114(1)	572(9)

* Data in parentheses indicate number of deaths attributable to vaccination. Ellipses indicate contacts were not vaccinated.

† Data include 31 patients with unknown vaccination status.

Eczema Vaccinatum. A sometimes serious complication, eczema vaccinatum occurred in some vaccinees and contacts with either active or healed eczema. Vaccinial skin lesions extended to cover all or most of the area once or currently afflicted with eczema. Vaccinia immune globulin was therapeutic.[47]

Generalized Vaccinia. A secondary eruption almost always following primary vaccination, generalized vaccinia resulted from blood-borne dissemination of virus. Lesions emerged between 6 and 9 days after vaccination and were either few in number or generalized. This complication was usually self-limited. In severe cases, VIG was indicated.[47]

Inadvertent Inoculation. Transmission to close contacts or autoinoculation to sites such as face, eyelid, mouth, and genitalia sometimes occurred. Most lesions healed without incident, although VIG was useful in some cases of periocular implantation.

Miscellaneous. Many different rashes have been associated with vaccination. Most common are erythema multiforme and variously distributed urticarial, maculopapular, and blotchy erythematous eruptions, which normally clear without therapy.

Groups at Special Risk for Complications

Consensus recommendations for special-risk groups as set forth herein reflect the best clinical and science-based judgment of the working group and do not necessarily correspond to FDA-approved uses.

Five groups of persons are ordinarily considered at special risk of smallpox vaccine complications: (1) persons with eczema or other significant exfoliative skin conditions; (2) patients with leukemia, lymphoma, or generalized malignancy who are receiving therapy with alkylating agents, antimetabolites, radiation, or large doses of corticosteroids; (3) patients with HIV infection; (4) persons with hereditary immune deficiency disorders; and (5) pregnant women. If persons with contraindications have been in close contact with a smallpox patient or the individual is at risk for occupational reasons, VIG, if available, may be given simultaneously with vaccination in a dose of 0.3 mL/kg of body weight to prevent complications. This does not alter vaccine efficacy. If VIG is not available, vaccine administration may still be warranted, given the far higher risk of an adverse outcome from smallpox infection than from vaccination.

VIG Therapy for Complications

Vaccinia immune globulin is valuable in treating patients with progressive vaccinia, eczema vaccinatum, severe generalized vaccinia, and periocular infections resulting from inadvertent inoculation. It is administered intramuscularly in a dose of 0.6 mL/kg of body weight. Because the dose is large (eg, 42 mL for a person weighing 70 kg), the product is given intramuscularly in divided doses over a 24- to 36-hour period and may be repeated, if necessary, after 2 to 3 days if improvement is not occurring.[48] Because the availability of VIG is so limited, its use should be reserved for the most serious cases. Vaccinia immune globulin, as well as vaccinia vaccine, is made available by the CDC through state health departments. Consultative assistance in the diagnosis and management of patients with complications can be obtained through state health departments.

Decontamination

Vaccinia virus, if released as an aerosol and not exposed to UV light, may persist for as long as 24 hours or somewhat longer under favorable conditions.[9] It is believed that variola virus would exhibit similar properties. However, by the time patients had become ill and it had been determined that an aerosol release of smallpox virus had occurred, there would be no viable smallpox virus in the environment. Vaccinia virus, if released as an aerosol, is almost completely destroyed within 6 hours in an atmosphere of high temperature (31°C-33°C) and humidity (80%) (**Table 2**).[9] In cooler temperatures (10°C-11°C) and lower humidity (20%), nearly two thirds of a vaccinia aerosol survives for as long as 24 hours.[9] It is believed that variola would behave similarly.

The occurrence of smallpox infection among personnel who handled laundry from infected patients is well documented[15] and it is believed that virus in such material remains viable for extended periods. Thus, special precautions need to be taken to ensure that all bedding and clothing of smallpox patients is autoclaved or

Table 2. Viability of Vaccinia Virus in Aerosols at Various Intervals After Spraying[9]

		Viable Vaccinia, %*			
Temperature, °C	**Relative Humidity, %**	**1 h**	**4 h**	**6 h**	**23 h**
10.5-11.5	20	82	79	81	66
	50	83	92	77	59
	82-84	79	59	60	27
21.0-23.0	18-19	66	46	45	15
	48-51	86	57	50	12
	82-84	66	24	18	Trace
31.5-33.5	17-19	61	51	33	13
	50	51	26	15	Trace
	80-83	36	5.9	1.2	Trace

* Initial titer of $10^{7.7}$ plaque-forming units per milliliter of McIlvaine buffer, containing 1% dialyzed horse serum.

laundered in hot water to which bleach has been added. Disinfectants that are used for standard hospital infection control, such as hypochlorite and quaternary ammonia, are effective for cleaning surfaces possibly contaminated with virus.

Virus in scabs is more durable. At a temperature of 35°C and 65% relative humidity, the virus has persisted for 3 weeks.[49] At cooler temperatures (26°C), the virus has survived for 8 weeks at high relative humidity and 12 weeks at a relative humidity less than 10%.[49] Dutch investigators demonstrated that it was possible to isolate variola virus from scabs that had been sitting on a shelf for 13 years.[50] It is unlikely, however, that the smallpox virus, bound in the fibrin matrix of a scab, is infectious in humans. This is borne out by studies conducted during the eradication program and by surveillance for cases in newly smallpox-free areas.[2] It was reasoned that if the virus were able to persist in nature and infect humans, there would be cases occurring for which no source could be identified. Cases of this type were not observed. Rather, when cases were found, there were antecedent human cases with whom they had direct contact.

Research

Priority over the near term should be directed to 4 areas of smallpox research: vaccines, immunotherapy, drugs, and diagnostics.

The frequency of vaccine complications is sufficiently great to recommend development, if possible, of a more attenuated vaccine strain that, hopefully, would retain full efficacy. Development of an entirely new, genetically engineered strain would be both costly and time consuming. Moreover, it would be difficult at this time to justify its use in large numbers of human subjects to evaluate safety. There are, however, two candidate attenuated strains that were developed in the

1970s. The first is a Japanese Lister strain–derived vaccine[51] that has been produced in volume in rabbit kidney cell culture and has been given to more than 100 000 persons in Japan. Research showed no severe complications among the first 30 000 vaccinees.[52] The cutaneous responses to vaccination were much less severe and far fewer vaccinees developed fever. More than 95% developed a Jennerian pustule; immunogenicity, as measured by neutralizing antibody, was slightly lower than for nonattenuated strains.

The second strain, called MVA (Modified Vaccine Ankara), was attenuated by German virologists by 572 serial passages of vaccinia in chick embryo fibroblasts.[53] It was intended only for routine use as a pre-immunizing agent, to be followed by vaccination with a conventional vaccine strain. Laboratory studies and limited studies in humans indicated that it was less reactogenic than traditional strains. More experience is now being gained in use of the virus as a recombinant vaccine vehicle, especially for HIV.

Vaccinia immune globulin has been used for the treatment of vaccine complications and for administration with vaccine to those for whom vaccine is otherwise contraindicated. An alternative to VIG would be useful because VIG is cumbersome to administer. Immunotherapy using humanized monoclonal antibodies is an alternative that should be explored. Studies of antiviral agents or drugs, already approved or near approval for marketing for use in other viral diseases, have suggested that 1 or more such products might prove useful.

Finally, a simple, rapid diagnostic test to identify variola virus in the oropharynx during the prodrome or early in the exanthematous phase of illness would be of considerable help in triage of suspected patients during the course of an outbreak and in early application of an antiviral drug should one be developed.

Summary

The specter of resurgent smallpox is ominous, especially given the enormous efforts that have been made to eradicate what has been characterized as the most devastating of all the pestilential diseases. Unfortunately, the threat of an aerosol release of smallpox is real and the potential for a catastrophic scenario is great unless effective control measures can quickly be brought to bear.

Early detection, isolation of infected individuals, surveillance of contacts, and a focused selective vaccination program are the essential items of a control program. Educating health care professionals about the diagnostic features of smallpox should permit early detection; advance regionwide planning for isolation and care of infected individuals in their homes as appropriate and in hospitals when home care is not an option will be critical to deter spread. Ultimately, success in controlling a burgeoning epidemic will depend on the availability of adequate supplies of vaccine and VIG. An adequate stockpile of those commodities would offer a relatively inexpensive safeguard against tragedy.

Ex Officio Participants in the Working Group on Civilian Biodefense: George Curlin, MD, National Institutes of Health, Bethesda, Md; Margaret Hamburg, MD, and William Roub, PhD, Office of Assistant Secretary for Planning and Evaluation, DHHS, Washington, DC; Robert Knouss, MD, Office of Emergency Preparedness, DHHS, Rockville, Md; Marcelle Layton, MD, Office of Communicable Disease, New York City Health Department, New York, NY; and Brian Malkin and Stuart Nightingale, MD, FDA, Rockville, Md.

Funding/Support: Funding for this study primarily was provided by each participant's institution or agency. The Johns Hopkins Center for Civilian Biodefense Studies provided travel funds for 3 members of the group.

Disclaimers: In many cases, the indication and dosages and other information are not consistent with current FDA-approved labeling. The recommendations on the use of drugs and vaccine for uses not approved by the FDA do not represent the official views of the FDA or of any of the federal agencies whose scientists participated in these discussions. Unlabeled uses of the products recommended are noted in the sections of this article in which these products are discussed. Where unlabeled uses are indicated, information used as the basis for the recommendations is discussed.

The views, opinions, assertions, and findings contained herein are those of the authors and should not be construed as official US Department of Defense or US Department of Army positions, policies, or decisions unless so designated by other documentation.

Acknowledgments: The working group wishes to thank Isao Arita, MD, Agency for Cooperation in International Health, Kumamoto, Japan; Joel Bremen, MD, DTPH, Fogarty International Center, Bethesda, Md; Joseph Esposito, PhD, and Brian Mahy, PhD, ScD, CDC, Atlanta, Ga; Frank Fenner, MD, Australian National University, Canberra; and Ralph Henderson, MD, WHO, Geneva, Switzerland.

References

1. Inglesby TV, Henderson DA, Bartlett JG, et al. Anthrax as a biological weapon: medical and public health management. *JAMA.* 1999;281:1735-1745.
2. Fenner F, Henderson DA, Arita I, et al. *Smallpox and Its Eradication.* Geneva, Switzerland: World Health Organization; 1988:1460.
3. Stearn EW, Stearn AE. *The Effect of Smallpox on the Destiny of the Amerindian.* Boston, Mass: Bruce Humphries; 1945.
4. Hopkins DR. *Princes and Peasants.* Chicago, Ill: University of Chicago Press; 1983.
5. World Health Organization. *The Global Eradication of Smallpox: Final Report of the Global Commission for the Certification of Smallpox Eradication.* Geneva, Switzerland: World Health Organization; 1980.
6. Breman JG, Henderson DA. Poxvirus dilemmas: monkeypox, smallpox and biological terrorism. *N Engl J Med.* 1998;339:556-559.
7. World Health Organization. Smallpox eradication: temporary retention of variola virus stocks. *Wkly Epidemiol Rec.* 2001;76:142-145.
8. Alibek K. *Biohazard.* New York, NY: Random House Inc; 1999.
9. Harper GJ. Airborne micro-organisms: survival test with four viruses. *J Hyg.* 1961;59:479-486.
10. Wehrle PF, Posch J, Richter KH, et all. An airborne outbreak of smallpox in a German hospital and its significance with respect to other recent outbreaks in Europe. *Bull World Health Organ.* 1970;43:669-679.
11. Chapin CV, Smith J. Permanency of the mild type of smallpox. *J Prev Med.* 1932;1:1-29.
12. Esposito JJ, Knight JC. Orthopox DNA: a comparison of restriction profiles and maps. *Virology.* 1985;143:230-251.
13. Chapin CV. Variation in the type of infectious disease as shown by the history of smallpox in the United States, 1895-1912. *J Infect Dis.* 1913;13:171-196.
14. Anders W, Sosch J. Die Pockenausbrucke 1961/61 in Nordrhein-Westfalen. *Bundesgesundheitsblatt.* 1962;17:265-269.
15. Dixon CW. *Smallpox.* London, England: J & A Churchill Ltd; 1962:1460.
16. Joarder AK, Tarantola D, Tulloch J. *The Eradication of Smallpox From Bangladesh, New Delhi.* Geneva, Switzerland: WHO Regional Publications; 1980.

17. Mack TM. Smallpox in Europe, 1950-71. *J Infect Dis.* 1972;125:161-169.

18. Mack TM, Thomas DB, Khan MM. Epidemiology of smallpox in West Pakistan, II: determinants of intravillage spread other than acquired immunity. *Am J Epidemiol.* 1972;95:157-168.

19. Rao AR. *Infected Inanimate Objects (Fomites) and Their Role in Transmission of Smallpox.* Geneva, Switzerland: World Health Organization; 1972. WHO/SE/72.40.

20. Fenner F, Wittek R, Dumbell KR. *The Orthopoxviruses.* San Diego, Calif: Academic Press; 1989:432.

21. Sarkar JK, Mitra AC, Mukherjee MK, et al. Virus excretion in smallpox, 1: excretion in the throat, urine and conjuctivae of patients. *Bull World Health Organ.* 1973;48:517-523.

22. Sarkar JK, Mitra AC, Mukherjee MK, et al. Virus excretion in smallpox, 2: excretion in the throat of household contacts. *Bull World Health Organ.* 1973;48:523-527.

23. Rao AR. *Smallpox.* Bombay, India: Kothari Book Depot; 1972.

24. Downie AW, McCarthy K. The antibody response in man following infection with viruses of the pox group, III: antibody response in smallpox. *J Hyg.* 1958;56:479-487.

25. LeDuc JW, Damon I, Meegan JM, et al. Update on smallpox preparedness, 2001. *Emerg Infect Dis,* 2002 (in press).

26. Marsden JP. Variola minor: a personal analysis of 13,686 cases. *Bull Hyg.* 1948;23:735-746.

27. Redfield RR, Wright CD, James WD, et al. Disseminated vaccinia in a military recruit with human immunodeficiency virus (HIV). *N Engl J Med.* 1987;316:673-676.

28. Esposito JJ, Massung RF. Poxvirus infections in humans. In: Murray PR, Baron EJ, Pfaller MA, et al, eds. *Manual of Clinical Microbiology.6th ed.* Washington, DC: American Society of Microbiology; 1995:1131-1138.

29. Knight JC, Massung RF, Esposito JJ. Polymerase chain reaction identification of smallpox virus. In: *PCR: Protocols for Diagnosis of Human and Animal Viral Disease.* Heidelberg, Germany: Springer-Verlag; 1995:297-302.

30. Ropp SL, Knight JC, Massung RF, et al. PCR strategy for identification and differentiation of smallpox and other orthopoxviruses. *J Clin Microbiol.* 1995;33:2069-2076.

31. El-Ad R, Roth Y, Winder A. The persistence of neutralizing antibodies after revaccination against smallpox. *J Infect Dis.* 1990;161:446-448.

32. Heiner GG, Fatima N, Daniel RW, et al. A study of inapparent infection in smallpox. *Am J Epidemiol* 1971; 94:252-268.

33. Frey SE, Couch RB, Tacket CP. Clinical responses to undiluted and diluted smallpox vaccine. *N Engl J Med.* 2002;346(17):1265-1274.

34. Sharp JCM, Fletcher WB. Experience of antivaccinia immunoglobulin in the United Kingdom. *Lancet.* 1973;1:656-659.

35. Kempe CH. Studies on smallpox and complications of smallpox vaccination. *Pediatrics.* 1960;26: 176-189.

36. Koplan J, Monsur KA, Foster SO, et al. Treatment of variola major with adenine arabinoside. *J Infect Dis.* 1975;131:34-39.

37. Monsur KA, Hossain MS, Huq F, et al. Treatment of variola major with cytosine arabinoside. *J Infect Dis.* 1975;131:40-43.

38. Huggins JW, Bray M, Smee DF, et al. Potential antiviral therapeutics for smallpox, monkeypox and other orthopoxvirus infections. Presented at the WHO Advisory Committee on Variola Virus Research. Geneva, Switzerland, 3-6 December 2001.

39. Lalezari JP, Staagg RJ, Kuppermann BD, et al. Intravenous cidofovir for peripheral cytomegalovirus retinitis in patients with AIDS: a randomized, controlled trial. *Ann Intern Med.* 1997;126:257-263.

40. Centers for Disease Control and Prevention. Interim smallpox response plans and guidelines. Draft 21, November 2001. Available at: www.cdc.gov.

41. Dixon CW. Tripolitania, 1946: an epidemiological and clinical study of 500 cases, including trials of penicillin treatment. *J Hyg.* 1948;46:351-377.

42. Centers for Disease Control and Prevention. Vaccinia (smallpox) vaccine recommendations of the immunization practices advisory committee. *MMWR Morb Mortal Wkly Rep.* 2001;50 (RR-10); 1-25.;40(RR-14):445-448.

43. Henderson DA, Arita I, Shafa E. Studies of the bifurcated needle and recommendations for its use. Geneva, Switzerland: World Health Organization; 1972. WHO Smallpox Eradication Paper SE/72.5.

44. McIntosh K, Cherry JD, Benenson AS. Standard percutaneous (smallpox) revaccination of children who received primary percutaneous vaccination. *J Infect Dis.* 1990;161:445-448.

45. Wyeth Smallpox Vaccine [package insert]. Lancaster, Pa: Wyeth Laboratories Inc; 1988.

46. Lane JM, Ruben FL, Neff JM, et al. Complications of smallpox vaccination, 1968: national surveillance in the United States. *N Engl J Med.* 1969;281: 1201-1208.

47. Goldstein VA, Neff JM, Lande JM, Koplan J. Smallpox vaccination reactions, prophylaxis and therapy of complications. *Pediatrics.* 1975;55:342-347.

48. Centers for Disease Control and Prevention. Vaccinia (smallpox) vaccine: recommendations of the Immunization Practices Advisory Committee. *MMWR Morb Mortal Wkly Rep.* 1991;40:1-10.

49. Huq F. Effect of temperature and relative humidity on variola virus in crusts. *Bull World Health Organ.* 1976;54:710-712.

50. Wolff HL, Croon JJ. The survival of smallpox virus (variola minor) in natural circumstances. *Bull World Health Organ.* 1968;38:492-493.

51. Hashizume S, Yoshizawa H, Morita M, et al. Properties of attenuated mutant of vaccinia virus, LC16m8, derived from Lister strain. In: Quinnan GV, ed. *Vaccine Virus as Vectors for Vaccine Antigens.* Amsterdam, the Netherlands: Elsevier Science Publishing; 1985:87-99.

52. Hirayama M. Smallpox vaccination in Japan. In: Fukumi H, ed. *The Vaccination: Theory and Practice* Tokyo: International Medical Foundation of Japan; 1975:113-124.

53. Stickl H, Hochstein-Mintzel V, Mayr A, et al. Stufenimpfung gegen pocken. *Dtsch Med Wockenschr.* 1974; 99:2386-2392.

Plague as a Biological Weapon

Thomas V. Inglesby, MD; David T. Dennis, MD, MPH; Donald A. Henderson, MD, MPH; John G. Bartlett, MD; Michael S. Ascher, MD; Edward Eitzen, MD, MPH; Anne D. Fine, MD; Arthur M. Friedlander, MD, FACP; Jerome Hauer, MPH; John F. Koerner, MPH, CIH; Marcelle Layton, MD; Joseph McDade, PhD; Michael T. Osterholm, PhD, MPH; Tara O'Toole, MD, MPH; Gerald Parker, PhD, DVM; Trish M. Perl, MD, MSc; Philip K. Russell, MD; Monica Schoch-Spana, PhD; Kevin Tonat, DrPH, MPH; for the Working Group on Civilian Biodefense

This is the third article in a series entitled *Medical and Public Health Management Following the Use of a Biological Weapon: Consensus Statements of the Working Group on Civilian Biodefense.*[1,2] The working group has identified a limited number of agents that, if used as weapons, could cause disease and death in sufficient numbers to cripple a city or region. These agents also comprise the top of the list of "Critical Biological Agents" recently developed by the Centers for Disease Control and Prevention (CDC).[3] *Yersinia pestis*, the causative agent of plague, is one of the most serious of these. Given the availability of *Y pestis* around the world, capacity for its mass production and aerosol dissemination, difficulty in preventing such activities, high fatality rate of pneumonic plague, and potential for secondary spread of cases during an epidemic, the potential use of plague as a biological weapon is of great concern.

Consensus Methods

For this article, the working group comprised 25 representatives from major academic medical centers and research, government, military, public health, and emergency management institutions and agencies.

MEDLINE databases were searched from January 1966 to June 1998 using the Medical Subject Headings (MeSH) *plague, Yersinia pestis, biological weapon, biological terrorism, biological warfare,* and *biowarfare.* Review of the bibliographies of the references identified by this search led to subsequent identification of relevant references published prior to 1966. In addition, participants identified other unpublished references and sources in their fields of expertise. Additional MEDLINE searches were conducted through January 2000 during the review and revisions of the statement.

The first draft of the consensus statement was a synthesis of information obtained in the initial formal evidence-gathering process. Members of the working group were asked to make formal written comments on this first draft of the document in September 1998. The document was revised incorporating changes suggested by members of the working group, which was convened to review the second draft of the document on October 30, 1998. Following this meeting and a second meeting of the working group on May 24, 1999, a third draft of the document was completed, reviewed, and revised. Working group members had a final opportunity to review the document and suggest revisions. The final document incorporates all relevant evidence obtained by the literature search in conjunction with consensus recommendations supported by all working group members.

The assessment and recommendations provided herein represent the best professional judgment of the working group based on data and expertise currently available. The conclusions and recommendations need to be regularly reassessed as new information becomes available.

History and Potential as a Bioterrorist Agent

In AD 541, the first recorded plague pandemic began in Egypt and swept across Europe with attributable population losses of between 50% and 60% in North Africa, Europe, and central and southern Asia.[4] The second plague pandemic, also known as the *black death* or *great pestilence*, began in 1346 and eventually killed 20 to 30 million people in Europe, one third of the European population.[5] Plague spread slowly and inexorably from village to village by infected rats and humans or more quickly from country to country by ships. The pandemic lasted more than 130 years and had major political, cultural, and religious ramifications. The third pandemic began in China in 1855, spread to all inhabited continents, and ultimately killed more than 12 million people in India and China alone.[4] Small outbreaks of plague continue to occur throughout the world.[4, 5]

Advances in living conditions, public health, and antibiotic therapy make future pandemics improbable. However, plague outbreaks following use of a biological weapon are a plausible threat. In World War II, a secret branch of the Japanese army, Unit 731, is reported to have dropped plague-infected fleas over populated areas of China, thereby causing outbreaks of plague.[6] In the ensuing years, the biological weapons programs of the United States and the Soviet Union developed techniques to aerosolize plague directly, eliminating dependence on the unpredictable flea vector. In 1970, the World Health Organization (WHO) reported that, in a worst-case scenario, if 50 kg of *Y pestis* were released as an aerosol over a city of 5 million, pneumonic plague could occur in as many as 150,000 persons, 36,000 of whom would be expected to die.[7] The plague bacilli would remain viable as an aerosol for 1 hour for a distance of up to 10 km. Significant numbers of city inhabitants might attempt to flee, further spreading the disease.[7]

While US scientists had not succeeded in making quantities of plague organisms sufficient to use as an effective weapon by the time the US offensive program was terminated in 1970, Soviet scientists were able to manufacture large quantities of the agent suitable for placing into weapons.[8] More than 10 institutes and thousands of scientists were reported to have worked with plague in the former Soviet Union.[8] In contrast, few scientists in the United States study this disease.[9]

There is little published information indicating actions of autonomous groups or individuals seeking to develop plague as a weapon. However, in 1995 in Ohio, a microbiologist with suspect motives was arrested after fraudulently acquiring *Y pestis* by mail.[10] New antiterrorism legislation was introduced in reaction.

Epidemiology

Naturally Occurring Plague

Human plague most commonly occurs when plague-infected fleas bite humans, who then develop bubonic plague. As a prelude to human epidemics, rats frequently die in large numbers, precipitating the movement of the flea population from its natural rat reservoir to humans. Although most persons infected by this route develop bubonic plague, a small minority will develop sepsis with no bubo, a form of plague termed *primary septicemic plague.* Neither bubonic nor septicemic plague spreads directly from person to person. A small percentage of patients with bubonic or septicemic plague develop secondary pneumonic plague and can then spread the disease by respiratory droplet. Persons contracting the disease by this route develop primary pneumonic plague.[11]

Plague remains an enzootic infection of rats, ground squirrels, prairie dogs, and other rodents on every populated continent except Australia.[4] Worldwide, on average in the last 50 years, 1700 cases have been reported annually.[4] In the United States, 390 cases of plague were reported from 1947 to 1996, 84% of which were bubonic, 13% septicemic, and 2% pneumonic. Concomitant case fatality rates were 14%, 22%, and 57%, respectively.[12] Most US cases were in New Mexico, Arizona, Colorado, and California. Of the 15 cases following exposure to domestic cats with plague, 4 were primary pneumonic plague.[13] In the United States, the last case of human-to-human transmission of plague occurred in Los Angeles in 1924.[14, 15]

Although pneumonic plague has rarely been the dominant manifestation of the disease, large outbreaks of pneumonic plague have occurred.[16] In an outbreak in Manchuria in 1910-1911, as many as 60 000 persons developed pneumonic plague; a second large Manchurian pneumonic plague outbreak occurred in 1920-1921.[16, 17] As would be anticipated in the preantibiotic era, nearly 100% of these cases were reported to be fatal.[16, 17] Reports from the Manchurian outbreaks suggested that indoor contacts of affected patients were at higher risk than outdoor contacts and that cold temperature, increased humidity, and crowding contributed to increased spread.[14, 15] In northern India, there was an epidemic of pneumonic plague with 1400 deaths reported at about the same time.[15] While epidemics of pneumonic plague of this scale have not occurred since, smaller epidemics of pneumonic plague have occurred recently. In 1997 in Madagascar, 1 patient with bubonic plague and secondary pneumonic infection transmitted pneumonic plague to 18 persons, 8 of whom died.[18]

Plague Following Use of a Biological Weapon

The epidemiology of plague following its use as a biological weapon would differ substantially from that of naturally occurring infection. Intentional dissemination

Figure 1. Peripheral Blood Smear From Patient With Septicemic Plague

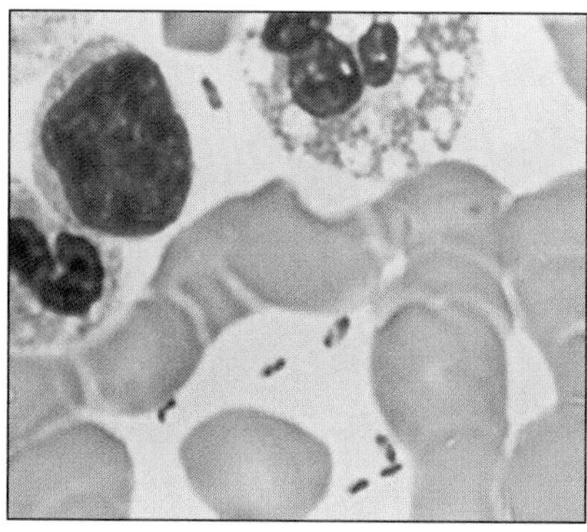

Smear shows characteristic bipolar staining of *Yersinia pestis* bacilli (Wright-Giemsa stain; magnification × 1000). Reproduced with permission from the Centers for Disease Control and Prevention (CDC), Fort Collins, Colo.

of plague would most probably occur via an aerosol of *Y pestis*, a mechanism that has been shown to produce disease in nonhuman primates.[19] A pneumonic plague outbreak would result with symptoms initially resembling those of other severe respiratory illnesses. The size of the outbreak would depend on factors including the quantity of biological agent used, characteristics of the strain, environmental conditions, and methods of aerosolization. Symptoms would begin to occur 1 to 6 days following exposure, and people would die quickly following onset of symptoms.[16] Indications that plague had been artificially disseminated would be the occurrence of cases in locations not known to have enzootic infection, in persons without known risk factors, and in the absence of prior rodent deaths.

Microbiology and Virulence Factors

Y pestis is a nonmotile, gram-negative bacillus, sometimes coccobacillus, that shows bipolar (also termed *safety pin*) staining with Wright, Giemsa, or Wayson stain (**Figure 1**).[20] *Y pestis* is a lactose nonfermenter, urease and indole negative, and a member of the Enterobacteriaceae family.[21] It grows optimally at 28°C on blood agar or MacConkey agar, typically requiring 48 hours for observable growth, but colonies are initially much smaller than other Enterobacteriaceae and may be overlooked. *Y pestis* has a number of virulence factors that enable it to survive in humans by facilitating use of host nutrients, causing damage to host cells, and subverting phagocytosis and other host defense mechanisms.[4,11,21,22]

Pathogenesis and Clinical Manifestations

Naturally Occurring Plague

In most cases of naturally occurring plague, the bite by a plague-infected flea leads to the inoculation of up to thousands of organisms into a patient's skin.

The bacteria migrate through cutaneous lymphatics to regional lymph nodes where they are phagocytosed but resist destruction. They rapidly multiply, causing destruction and necrosis of lymph node architecture with subsequent bacteremia, septicemia, and endotoxemia that can lead quickly to shock, disseminated intravascular coagulation, and coma.[21]

Patients typically develop symptoms of bubonic plague 2 to 8 days after being bitten by an infected flea. There is sudden onset of fever, chills, and weakness and the development of an acutely swollen tender lymph node, or bubo, up to 1 day later.[23] The bubo most typically develops in the groin, axilla, or cervical region (**Figure 2A**) and is often so painful that it prevents patients from moving the affected area of the body. Buboes are 1 to 10 cm in diameter, and the overlying skin is erythematous.[21] They are extremely tender, nonfluctuant, and warm and are often associated with considerable surrounding edema, but seldom lymphangitis. Rarely, buboes become fluctuant and suppurate. In addition, pustules or skin ulcerations may occur at the site of the flea bite in a minority of patients. A small minority of patients infected by fleas develop *Y pestis* septicemia without a discernable bubo, the form of disease termed *primary septicemic plague*.[23] Septicemia can also arise secondary to bubonic plague.[21] Septicemic plague may lead to disseminated intravascular coagulation, necrosis of small vessels, and purpuric skin lesions (**Figure 2B**). Gangrene of acral regions such as the digits and nose may also occur in advanced disease, a process believed responsible for the name *black death* in the second plague pandemic (**Figure 2C**).[21] However, the finding of gangrene would not be expected to be helpful in diagnosing the disease in the early stages of illness when early antibiotic treatment could be lifesaving.

Secondary pneumonic plague develops in a minority of patients with bubonic or primary septicemic plague—approximately 12% of total cases in the United States over the last 50 years.[4] This process, termed *secondary pneumonic plague*, develops via hematogenous spread of plague bacilli to the lungs. Patients commonly have symptoms of severe bronchopneumonia, chest pain, dyspnea, cough, and hemoptysis.[16,21]

Primary pneumonic plague resulting from the inhalation of plague bacilli occurs rarely in the United States.[12] Reports of 2 recent cases of primary pneumonic plague, contracted after handling cats with pneumonic plague, reveal that both patients had pneumonic symptoms as well as prominent gastrointestinal symptoms including nausea, vomiting, abdominal pain, and diarrhea. Diagnosis and treatment were delayed more than 24 hours after symptom onset in both patients, both of whom died.[24,25]

Less common plague syndromes include plague meningitis and plague pharyngitis. Plague meningitis follows the hematogenous seeding of bacilli into the meninges and is associated with fever and meningismus. Plague pharyngitis follows inhalation or ingestion of plague bacilli and is associated with cervical lymphadenopathy.[21]

Figure 2. Patients With Naturally Occurring Plague

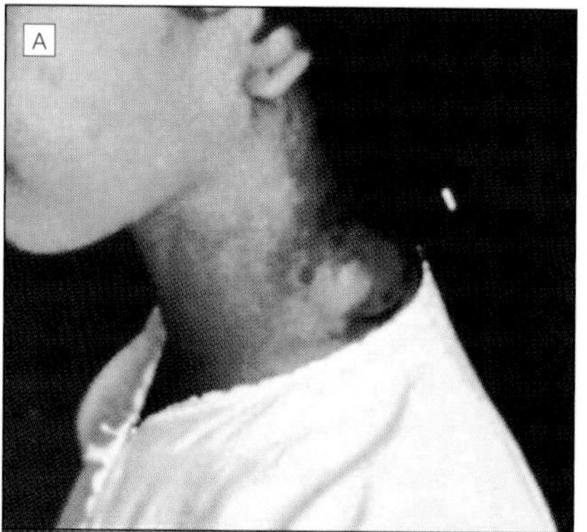

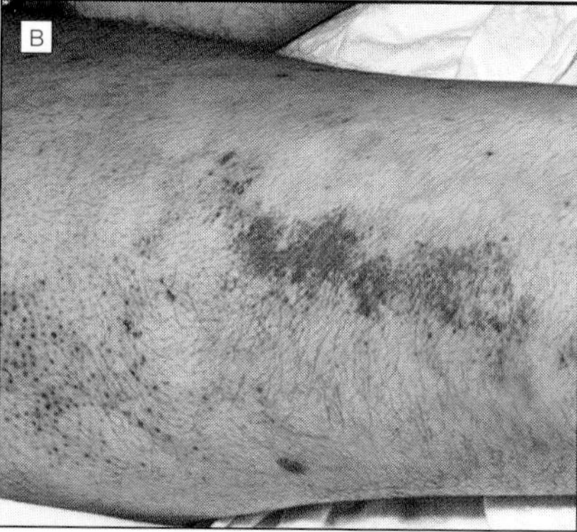

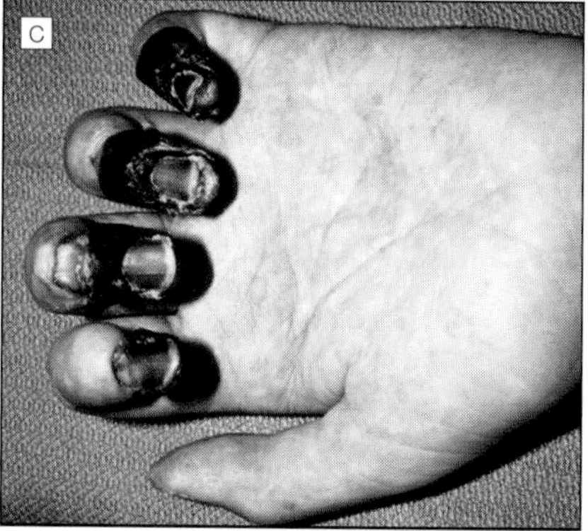

A, Cervical bubo in patient with bubonic plague; B, petechial and ecchymotic bleeding into the skin in patient with septicemic plague; and C, gangrene of the digits during the recovery phase of illness of patient shown in B. In plague following the use of a biological weapon, presence of cervical bubo is rare; purpuric skin lesions and necrotic digits occur only in advanced disease and would not be helpful in diagnosing the disease in the early stages of illness when antibiotic treatment can be lifesaving. Figure A reproduced with permission from the Upjohn collection (DM-24). Figures B and C reproduced with permission from the Centers for Disease Control and Prevention (CDC), Fort Collins, Colo.

Plague Following Use of a Biological Weapon

The pathogenesis and clinical manifestations of plague following a biological attack would be notably different than naturally occurring plague. Inhaled aerosolized *Y pestis* bacilli would cause primary pneumonic plague. The time from exposure to aerosolized plague bacilli until development of first symptoms in humans and nonhuman primates has been found to be 1 to 6 days and most often, 2 to 4 days.[12, 16, 19, 26] The first sign of illness would be expected to be fever with cough and dyspnea, sometimes with the production of bloody, watery, or less commonly, purulent sputum.[16, 19, 27] Prominent gastrointestinal symptoms, including nausea, vomiting, abdominal pain, and diarrhea, might be present.[24, 25]

Figure 3. Chest Radiograph of Patient With Primary Pneumonic Plague

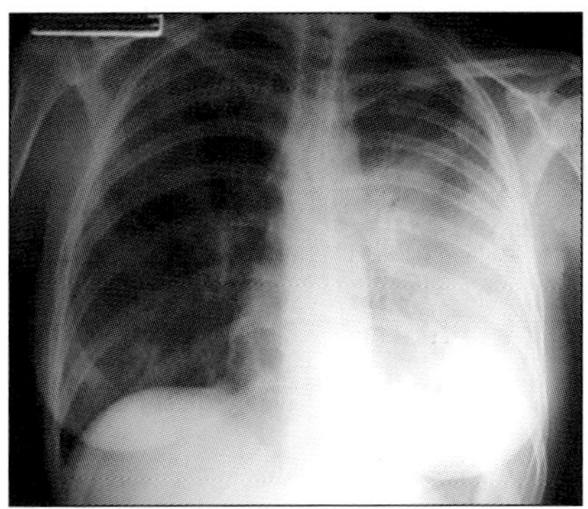

Radiograph shows extensive lobar consolidation in left lower and left middle lung fields. Reproduced with permission from the Centers for Disease Control and Prevention (CDC), Fort Collins, Colo.

The ensuing clinical findings of primary pneumonic plague are similar to those of any severe rapidly progressive pneumonia and are quite similar to those of secondary pneumonic plague. Clinicopathological features may help distinguish primary from secondary pneumonic plague.[11] In contrast to secondary pneumonic plague, features of primary pneumonic plague would include absence of buboes (except, rarely, cervical buboes) and, on pathologic examination, pulmonary disease with areas of profound lobular exudation and bacillary aggregation.[11] Chest radiographic findings are variable but bilateral infiltrates or consolidation are common (**Figure 3**).[22]

Laboratory studies may reveal leukocytosis with toxic granulations, coagulation abnormalities, aminotransferase elevations, azotemia, and other evidence of multiorgan failure. All are nonspecific findings associated with sepsis and systemic inflammatory response syndrome.[11, 21]

The time from respiratory exposure to death in humans is reported to have been between 2 to 6 days in epidemics during the preantibiotic era, with a mean of 2 to 4 days in most epidemics.[16]

Diagnosis

Given the rarity of plague infection and the possibility that early cases are a harbinger of a larger epidemic, the first clinical or laboratory suspicion of plague must lead to immediate notification of the hospital epidemiologist or infection control practitioner, health department, and the local or state health laboratory. Definitive tests can thereby be arranged rapidly through a state reference laboratory or, as necessary, the Diagnostic and Reference Laboratory of the CDC and early interventions instituted.

The early diagnosis of plague requires a high index of suspicion in naturally occurring cases and even more so following the use of a biological weapon.

There are no effective environmental warning systems to detect an aerosol of plague bacilli.[28]

The first indication of a clandestine terrorist attack with plague would most likely be a sudden outbreak of illness presenting as severe pneumonia and sepsis. If there are only small numbers of cases, the possibility of them being plague may be at first overlooked given the clinical similarity to other bacterial or viral pneumonias and that few Western physicians have ever seen a case of pneumonic plague. However, the sudden appearance of a large number of previously healthy patients with fever, cough, shortness of breath, chest pain, and a fulminant course leading to death should immediately suggest the possibility of pneumonic plague or inhalational anthrax.[1] The presence of hemoptysis in this setting would strongly suggest plague (**Table 1**).[22]

There are no widely available, rapid diagnostic tests for plague.[28] Tests that would be used to confirm a suspected diagnosis—antigen detection, IgM enzyme immunoassay, immunostaining, and polymerase chain reactions—are available only at some state health departments, the CDC, and military laboratories.[21] The routinely used passive hemagglutination antibody detection assay is typically only of retrospective value since several days to weeks usually pass after disease onset before antibodies develop.

Microbiologic studies are important in the diagnosis of pneumonic plague. A Gram stain of sputum or blood may reveal gram-negative bacilli or coccobacilli.[4, 21, 29] A Wright, Giemsa, or Wayson stain will often show bipolar staining (Figure 1), and direct fluorescent antibody testing, if available, may be

Table 1. Diagnosis of Pneumonic Plague Infection Following Use of a Biological Weapon

Epidemiology and symptoms	Sudden appearance of many persons with fever, cough, shortness of breath, hemoptysis, and chest pain Gastrointestinal symptoms common (eg, nausea, vomiting, abdominal pain, and diarrhea) Patients have fulminant course and high mortality
Clinical signs	Tachypnea, dyspnea, and cyanosis Pneumonic consolidation on chest examination Sepsis, shock, and organ failure Infrequent presence of cervical bubo (Purpuric skin lesions and necrotic digits only in advanced disease)
Laboratory studies	Sputum, blood, or lymph node aspirate Gram-negative bacilli with bipolar (safety pin) staining on Wright, Giemsa, or Wayson stain Rapid diagnostic tests available only at some health departments, the Centers for Disease Control and Prevention, and military laboratories Pulmonary infiltrates or consolidation on chest radiograph
Pathology	Lobular exudation, bacillary aggregation, and areas of necrosis in pulmonary parenchyma

positive. In the unlikely event that a cervical bubo is present in pneumonic plague, an aspirate (obtained with a 20-gauge needle and a 10-mL syringe containing 1-2 mL of sterile saline for infusing the node) may be cultured and similarly stained (Table 1).[22]

Cultures of sputum, blood, or lymph node aspirate should demonstrate growth approximately 24 to 48 hours after inoculation. Most microbiology laboratories use either automated or semiautomated bacterial identification systems. Some of these systems may misidentify *Y pestis*.[12,30] In laboratories without automated bacterial identification, as many as 6 days may be required for identification, and there is some chance that the diagnosis may be missed entirely. Approaches for biochemical characterization of *Y pestis* are described in detail elsewhere.[20]

If a laboratory using automated or nonautomated techniques is notified that plague is suspected, it should split the culture: 1 culture incubated at 28°C for rapid growth and the second culture incubated at 37°C for identification of the diagnostic capsular (F_1) antigen. Using these methods, up to 72 hours may be required following specimen procurement to make the identification (May Chu, PhD, CDC, Fort Collins, Colo, written communication, April 9, 1999). Antibiotic susceptibility testing should be performed at a reference laboratory because of the lack of standardized susceptibility testing procedures for *Y pestis*. A process establishing criteria and training measures for laboratory diagnosis of this disease is being undertaken jointly by the Association of Public Health Laboratories and the CDC.

Vaccination

The US-licensed formaldehyde-killed whole bacilli vaccine was discontinued by its manufacturers in 1999 and is no longer available. Plans for future licensure and production are unclear. This killed vaccine demonstrated efficacy in preventing or ameliorating bubonic disease, but it does not prevent or ameliorate the development of primary pneumonic plague.[19,31] It was used in special circumstances for individuals deemed to be at high risk of developing plague, such as military personnel working in plague endemic areas, microbiologists working with *Y pestis* in the laboratory, or researchers working with plague-infected rats or fleas. Research is ongoing in the pursuit of a vaccine that protects against primary pneumonic plague.[22,32]

Therapy

Recommendations for the use of antibiotics following a plague biological weapon exposure are conditioned by the lack of published trials in treating plague in humans, limited number of studies in animals, and possible requirement to treat large numbers of persons. A number of possible therapeutic regimens for treating plague have yet to be adequately studied or submitted for approval to the Food and Drug Administration (FDA). For these reasons, the working group offers consensus recommendations based on the best available evidence. The recommendations do not necessarily represent uses currently approved by the FDA or an official position on the part of any of the federal agencies whose scientists participated in these discussions. Recommendations will need to be revised as further relevant information becomes available.

In the United States during the last 50 years, 4 of the 7 reported primary pneumonic plague patients died.[12] Fatality rates depend on various factors including time to initiation of antibiotics, access to advanced supportive care, and the dose of inhaled bacilli. The fatality rate of patients with pneumonic plague when treatment is delayed more than 24 hours after symptom onset is extremely high.[14, 24, 25, 33]

Historically, the preferred treatment for plague infection has been streptomycin, an FDA-approved treatment for plague.[21, 34, 35] Administered early during the disease, streptomycin has reduced overall plague mortality to the 5% to 14% range.[12, 21, 34] However, streptomycin is infrequently used in the United States and only modest supplies are available.[35] Gentamicin is not FDA approved for the treatment of plague but has been used successfully[36-39] and is recommended as an acceptable alternative by experts.[23, 40] In 1 case series, 8 patients with plague were treated with gentamicin with morbidity or mortality equivalent to that of patients treated with streptomycin (Lucy Boulanger, MD, Indian Health Services, Crown Point, NM, written communication, July 20, 1999). In vitro studies and an in vivo study in mice show equal or improved activity of gentamicin against many strains of *Y pestis* when compared with streptomycin.[41, 42] In addition, gentamicin is widely available, inexpensive, and can be given once daily.[35]

Tetracycline and doxycycline also have been used in the treatment and prophylaxis of plague; both are FDA approved for these purposes. In vitro studies have shown that *Y pestis* susceptibility to tetracycline[43] and doxycycline[41, 44] is equivalent to that of the aminoglycosides. In another investigation, 13% of *Y pestis* strains in Madagascar were found to have some in vitro resistance to tetracycline.[45] Experimental murine models of *Y pestis* infection have yielded data that are difficult to extrapolate to humans. Some mouse studies have shown doxycycline to be a highly efficacious treatment of infection[44, 46] or prophylaxis[47] against naturally occurring plague strains. Experimental murine infection with F_1-deficient variants of *Y pestis* have shown decreased efficacy of doxycycline,[47, 48] but only 1 human case of F_1-deficient plague infection has been reported.[49] Russell and colleagues[50] reported poor efficacy of doxycycline against plague-infected mice, but the dosing schedules used in this experiment would have failed to maintain drug levels above the minimum inhibitory concentration due to the short half-life of doxycycline in mice. In another study, doxycycline failed to prevent death in mice intraperitoneally infected with 29 to 290 000 times the median lethal inocula of *Y pestis*.[51]

There are no controlled clinical trials comparing either tetracycline or doxycycline to aminoglycoside in the treatment of plague, but anecdotal case series and a number of medical authorities support use of this class of antimicrobials for prophylaxis and for therapy in the event that streptomycin or gentamicin cannot be administered[23, 27, 38-40, 52-54] Based on evidence from in vitro studies, animal studies, and uncontrolled human data, the working group recommends that the tetracycline class of antibiotics be used to treat pneumonic plague if aminoglycoside therapy cannot be administered. This might be the case in a mass casualty scenario when parenteral therapy was either unavailable or impractical. Doxycycline would be considered pharmacologically superior to other antibiotics in the tetracycline class for this indication, because it is well absorbed without food interactions, is well distributed with good tissue penetration, and has a long half-life.[35]

The fluoroquinolone family of antimicrobials has demonstrated efficacy in animal studies. Ciprofloxacin has been demonstrated to be at least as efficacious as aminoglycosides and tetracyclines in studies of mice with experimentally induced pneumonic plague.[44, 50, 51] In vitro studies also suggest equivalent or greater activity of ciprofloxacin, levofloxacin, and ofloxacin against *Y pestis* when compared with aminoglycosides or tetracyclines.[41, 55] However, there have been no trials of fluoroquinolones in human plague, and they are not FDA approved for this indication.

Chloramphenicol has been used to treat plague infection and has been recommended for treatment of plague meningitis because of its ability to cross the blood-brain barrier.[21, 34] However, human clinical trials demonstrating the superiority of chloramphenicol in the therapy of classic plague infection or plague meningitis have not been performed. It has been associated with dose-dependent hematologic abnormalities and with rare idiosyncratic fatal aplastic anemia.[35]

A number of different sulfonamides have been used successfully in the treatment of human plague infection: sulfathiazole,[56] sulfadiazine, sulfamerazine, and trimethoprim-sulfamethoxazole.[57, 58] The 1970 WHO analysis reported that sulfadiazine reduced mortality for bubonic plague but was ineffective against pneumonic plague and was less effective than tetracycline overall.[59] In a study comparing trimethoprim-sulfamethoxazole with streptomycin, patients treated with trimethoprim-sulfamethoxazole had a longer median duration of fever and a higher incidence of complications.[58] Authorities have generally considered trimethoprim-sulfamethoxazole a second-tier choice.[21, 23, 34] Some have recommended sulfonamides only in the setting of pediatric prophylaxis.[22] No sulfonamides have been FDA approved for the treatment of plague.

Antimicrobials that have been shown to have poor or only modest efficacy in animal studies have included rifampin, aztreonam, ceftazidime, cefotetan, and cefazolin; these antibiotics should not be used.[42]

Antibiotic resistance patterns must also be considered in making treatment recommendations. Naturally occurring antibiotic resistance to the tetracycline class of drugs has occurred rarely.[4] Recently, a plasmid-mediated multidrug-resistant strain was isolated in Madagascar.[60] A report published by Russian scientists cited quinolone-resistant *Y pestis*.[61] There have been assertions that Russian scientists have engineered multidrug-resistant strains of *Y pestis*,[8] although there is as yet no scientific publication confirming this.

Recommendations for Antibiotic Therapy

The working group treatment recommendations are based on literature reports on treatment of human disease, reports of studies in animal models, reports on in vitro susceptibility testing, and antibiotic safety. Should antibiotic susceptibility testing reveal resistance, proper antibiotic substitution would need to be made.

In a contained casualty setting, a situation in which a modest number of patients require treatment, the working group recommends parenteral antibiotic therapy (**Table 2**). Preferred parenteral forms of the antimicrobials streptomycin or gentamicin are recommended. However, in a mass casualty setting, intravenous or intramuscular therapy may not be possible for reasons of patient care logistics and/or exhaustion of equipment and antibiotic supplies, and parenteral therapy will need to be supplanted by oral therapy. In a mass casualty setting, the working group recommends oral therapy, preferably with doxycycline (or tetracycline) or ciprofloxacin (**Table 3**).

Patients with pneumonic plague will require substantial advanced medical supportive care in addition to antimicrobial therapy. Complications of gram-negative sepsis would be expected, including adult respiratory distress syndrome, disseminated intravascular coagulation, shock, and multiorgan failure.[23]

Once it was known or strongly suspected that pneumonic plague cases were occurring, anyone with fever or cough in the presumed area of exposure should be immediately treated with antimicrobials for presumptive pneumonic plague. Delaying therapy until confirmatory testing is performed would greatly decrease survival.[59] Clinical deterioration of patients despite early initiation of empiric therapy could signal antimicrobial resistance and should be promptly evaluated.

Management of Special Groups

Consensus recommendations for special groups as set forth in the following reflect the clinical and evidence-based judgments of the working group and do not necessarily correspond to FDA-approved use, indications, or labeling.

Children. The treatment of choice for plague in children has been streptomycin or gentamicin.[21,40] If aminoglycosides are not available or cannot be used, recommendations for alternative antimicrobial treatment with efficacy against plague are conditioned by balancing risks associated with treatment against those posed by pneumonic plague. Children aged 8 years and older can be safely treated with tetracycline antibiotics.[35,40] However, in children younger than 8 years, tetracycline antibiotics may cause discolored teeth, and rare instances of retarded skeletal growth have been reported in infants.[35] Chloramphenicol is considered safe in children except for children younger than 2 years who are at risk of "gray baby syndrome."[35,40] Some concern exists that fluoroquinolone use in children may cause arthropathy,[35] although fluoroquinolones have been used to treat serious infections in children.[64] No comparative studies assessing efficacy or safety of alternative treatment strategies for plague in children has or can be performed.

Given these considerations, the working group recommends that children in the contained casualty setting receive streptomycin or gentamicin (Table 2). In a mass casualty setting or for postexposure prophylaxis, we recommend that doxycycline be used. Alternatives are listed for both settings (Table 3). The working group assessment is that the potential benefits of these antimicrobials in the treating of pneumonic plague infection substantially outweigh the risks.

Table 2. Working Group Recommendations for Treatment of Patients With Pneumonic Plague in the Contained Casualty Settings*

Patient Category	Recommended Therapy
	Contained Casualty Setting
Adults	Preferred choices Streptomycin, 1 g IM twice daily Gentamicin, 5 mg/kg IM or IV once daily or 2 mg/kg loading dose followed by 1.7 mg/kg IM or IV 3 times daily† Alternative choices Doxycycline, 100 mg IV twice daily or 200 mg IV once daily Ciprofloxacin, 400 mg IV twice daily‡ Chloramphenicol, 25 mg/kg IV 4 times daily§
Children‖	Preferred choices Streptomycin, 15 mg/kg IM twice daily (maximum daily dose, 2 g) Gentamicin, 2.5 mg/kg IM or IV 3 times daily† Alternative choices Doxycycline, If ≥45 kg, give adult dosage If <45 kg, give 2.2 mg/kg IV twice daily (maximum, 200 mg/d) Ciprofloxacin, 15 mg/kg IV twice daily‡ Chloramphenicol, 25 mg/kg IV 4 times daily§
Pregnant women¶	Preferred choice Gentamicin, 5 mg/kg IM or IV once daily or 2 mg/kg loading dose followed by 1.7 mg/kg IM or IV 3 times daily† Alternative choices Doxycycline, 100 mg IV twice daily or 200 mg IV once daily Ciprofloxacin, 400 mg IV twice daily‡

* These are consensus recommendations of the Working Group on Civilian Biodefense and are not necessarily approved by the Food and Drug Administration. See "Therapy" earlier in this chapter for explanations. One antimicrobial agent should be selected. Therapy should be continued for 10 days. Oral therapy should be substituted when patient's condition improves. IM indicates intramuscularly; IV, intravenously.

† Aminoglycosides must be adjusted according to renal function. Evidence suggests that gentamicin, 5 mg/kg IM or IV once daily, would be efficacious in children, although this is not yet widely accepted in clinical practice. Neonates up to 1 week of age and premature infants should receive gentamicin, 2.5 mg/kg IV twice daily.

‡ Other fluoroquinolones can be substituted at doses appropriate for age. Ciprofloxacin dosage should not exceed 1 g/d in children.

§ Concentration should be maintained between 5 and 20 μg/mL. Concentrations greater than 25 μg/mL can cause reversible bone marrow suppression.[35, 62]

‖ Refer to "Management of Special Groups" for details. In children, ciprofloxacin dose should not exceed 1 g/d, chloramphenicol should not exceed 4 g/d. Children younger than 2 years should not receive chloramphenicol.

¶ Refer to "Management of Special Groups" for details and for discussion of breast-feeding women. In neonates, gentamicin loading dose of 4 mg/kg should be given initially.[63]

Table 3. Working Group Recommendations for Treatment of Patients With Pneumonic Plague in Mass Casualty Settings and for Postexposure Prophylaxis*

Patient Category	Recommended Therapy
	Mass Casualty Setting and Postexposure Prophylaxis
Adults	Preferred choices Doxycycline, 100 mg orally twice daily[†] Ciprofloxacin, 500 mg orally twice daily[‡] Alternative choice Chloramphenicol, 25 mg/kg orally 4 times daily[§,#]
Children[‖]	Preferred choices Doxycycline, If ≥45 kg, give adult dosage If <45 kg, then give 2.2 mg/kg orally twice daily Ciprofloxacin, 20 mg/kg orally twice daily[‡] Alternative choice Chloramphenicol, 25 mg/kg orally 4 times daily[§,#]
Pregnant women[¶]	Preferred choices Doxycycline, 100 mg orally twice daily† Ciprofloxacin, 500 mg orally twice daily Alternative choice Chloramphenicol, 25 mg/kg orally 4 times daily[§,#]

* These are consensus recommendations of the Working Group on Civilian Biodefense and are not necessarily approved by the Food and Drug Administration. See "Therapy" earlier in this chapter for explanations. One antimicrobial agent should be selected. Therapy should be continued for 10 days. Duration of treatment of plague in mass casualty setting is 10 days. Duration of postexposure prophylaxis to prevent plague infection is 7 days.

† Tetracycline could be substituted for doxycycline.

‡ Other fluoroquinolones can be substituted at doses appropriate for age. Ciprofloxacin dosage should not exceed 1 g/d in children.

§ Concentration should be maintained between 5 and 20 µg/mL. Concentrations greater than 25 µg/mL can cause reversible bone marrow suppression.[35, 62]

‖ Refer to "Management of Special Groups" for details. In children, ciprofloxacin dose should not exceed 1 g/d, chloramphenicol should not exceed 4 g/d. Children younger than 2 years should not receive chloramphenicol.

¶ Refer to "Management of Special Groups" for details and for discussion of breast-feeding women. In neonates, gentamicin loading dose of 4 mg/kg should be given initially.[63]

Children younger than 2 years should not receive chloramphenicol. Oral formulation available only outside the United States.

Pregnant Women. It has been recommended that aminoglycosides be avoided in pregnancy unless severe illness warrants,[35,65] but there is no more efficacious treatment for pneumonic plague. Therefore, the working group recommendsthat pregnant women in the contained casualty setting receive gentamicin (Table 2). Since streptomycin has been associated with rare reports of irreversible deafness in children following fetal exposure, this medication should be avoided if possible.[35]

The tetracycline class of antibiotics has been associated with fetal toxicity including retarded skeletal growth,[35] although a large case-control study of doxycycline use in pregnancy showed no significant increase in teratogenic risk to the fetus.[66] Liver toxicity has been reported in pregnant women following large doses of intravenous tetracycline (no longer sold in the United States), but it has also been reported following oral administration of tetracycline to nonpregnant individuals.[35] Balancing the risks of pneumonic plague infection with those associated with doxycycline use in pregnancy, the working group recommends that doxycycline be used to treat pregnant women with pneumonic plague if gentamicin is not available.

Of the oral antibiotics historically used to treat plague, only trimethoprim-sulfamethoxazole has a category C pregnancy classification[65]; however, many experts do not recommend trimethoprim-sulfamethoxazole for treatment of pneumonic plague. Therefore, the working group recommends that pregnant women receive oral doxycycline for mass casualty treatment or postexposure prophylaxis. If the patient is unable to take doxycycline or the medication is unavailable, ciprofloxacin or other fluoroquinolones would be recommended in the mass casualty setting (Table 3).

The working group recommendation for treatment of breast-feeding women is to provide the mother and infant with the same antibiotic based on what is most safe and effective for the infant: gentamicin in the contained casualty setting and doxycycline in the mass casualty setting. Fluoroquinolones would be the recommended alternative.

Immunosuppressed Persons. The antibiotic treatment or postexposure prophylaxis for pneumonic plague among those who are immunosuppressed has not been studied in human or animal models of pneumonic plague infection. Therefore, the consensus recommendation is to administer antibiotics according to the guidelines developed for immunocompetent adults and children.

Postexposure Prophylaxis Recommendations

The working group recommends that in a community experiencing a pneumonic plague epidemic, all persons developing a temperature of 38.5°C or higher or new cough should promptly begin parenteral antibiotic treatment. If the resources required to administer parenteral antibiotics are unavailable, oral antibiotics should be used according to the mass casualty recommendations (Table 3). For infants in this setting, tachypnea would also be an additional indication for immediate treatment.[29] Special measures would need to be initiated for treatment or prophylaxis of those who are either unaware of the outbreak or require special assistance, such as the homeless or mentally handicapped persons. Continuing surveillance of patients would be needed to identify individuals and communities at risk requiring postexposure prophylaxis.

Asymptomatic persons having household, hospital, or other close contact with persons with untreated pneumonic plague should receive postexposure antibiotic prophylaxis for 7 days[29] and watch for fever and cough. Close contact is defined as contact with a patient at less than 2 meters.[16, 31] Tetracycline, doxycycline, sulfonamides, and chloramphenicol have each been used or recommended as postexposure prophylaxis in this setting.[16, 22, 29, 31, 59] Fluoroquinolones could also be used based on studies in mice.[51]

The working group recommends the use of doxycycline as the first choice antibiotic for postexposure prophylaxis; other recommended antibiotics are noted (Table 3). Contacts who develop fever or cough while receiving prophylaxis should seek prompt medical attention and begin antibiotic treatment as described in Table 2.

Infection Control

Previous public health guidelines have advised strict isolation for all close contacts of patients with pneumonic plague who refuse prophylaxis.[29] In the modern setting, however, pneumonic plague has not spread widely or rapidly in a community,[4, 14, 24] and therefore isolation of close contacts refusing antibiotic prophylaxis is not recommended by the working group. Instead, persons refusing prophylaxis should be carefully watched for the development of fever or cough during the first 7 days after exposure and treated immediately should either occur.

Modern experience with person-to-person spread of pneumonic plague is limited; few data are available to make specific recommendations regarding appropriate infection control measures. The available evidence indicates that person-to-person transmission of pneumonic plague occurs via respiratory droplets; transmission by droplet nuclei has not been demonstrated.[14, 15, 16, 17] In large pneumonic plague epidemics earlier this century, pneumonic plague transmission was prevented in close contacts by wearing masks.[14, 16, 17] Commensurate with this, existing national infection control guidelines recommend the use of disposable surgical masks to prevent the transmission of pneumonic plague.[29, 67]

Given the available evidence, the working group recommends that, in addition to beginning antibiotic prophylaxis, persons living or working in close contact with patients with confirmed or suspect pneumonic plague that have had less than 48 hours of antimicrobial treatment should follow respiratory droplet precautions and wear a surgical mask. Further, the working group recommends avoidance of unnecessary close contact with patients with pneumonic plague until at least 48 hours of antibiotic therapy and clinical improvement has taken place. Other standard respiratory droplet precautions (gown, gloves, and eye protection) should be used as well.[29, 31]

The patient should remain isolated during the first 48 hours of antibiotic therapy and until clinical improvement occurs.[29, 31, 59] If large numbers of patients make individual isolation impossible, patients with pneumonic plague may be cohorted while undergoing antibiotic therapy. Patients being transported should also wear surgical masks. Hospital rooms of patients with pneumonic plague should receive terminal cleaning in a manner consistent with standard precautions, and clothing or linens contaminated with body fluids of patients infected with plague should be disinfected as per hospital protocol.[29]

Microbiology laboratory personnel should be alerted when *Y pestis* is suspected. Four laboratory-acquired cases of plague have been reported in the United States.[68] Simple clinical materials and cultures should be processed in biosafety level 2 conditions.[31, 69] Only during activities involving high potential for aerosol or droplet production (eg, centrifuging, grinding, vigorous shaking, and animal studies) are biosafety level 3 conditions necessary.[69]

Bodies of patients who have died following infection with plague should be handled with routine strict precautions.[29] Contact with the remains should be limited to trained personnel, and the safety precautions for transporting corpses for burial should be the same as those when transporting ill patients.[70] Aerosol-generating procedures, such as bone-sawing associated with surgery or postmortem examinations, would be associated with special risks of transmission and are not recommended. If such aerosol-generating procedures are necessary, then high-efficiency particulate air filtered masks and negative-pressure rooms should be used as would be customary in cases in which contagious biological aerosols, such as *Mycobacterium tuberculosis*, are deemed a possible risk.[71]

Environmental Decontamination

There is no evidence to suggest that residual plague bacilli pose an environmental threat to the population following the dissolution of the primary aerosol. There is no spore form in the *Y pestis* life cycle, so it is far more susceptible to environmental conditions than sporulating bacteria such as *Bacillus anthracis*. Moreover, *Y pestis* is very sensitive to the action of sunlight and heating and does not survive long outside the host.[72] Although some reports suggest that the bacterium may survive in the soil for some time,[72] there is no evidence to suggest environmental risk to humans in this setting and thus no need for environmental decontamination of an area exposed to an aerosol of plague. In the WHO analysis, in a worst-case scenario, a plague aerosol was estimated to be effective and infectious for as long as 1 hour.[7] In the setting of a clandestine release of plague bacilli, the aerosol would have dissipated long before the first case of pneumonic plague occurred.

Additional Research

Improving the medical and public health response to an outbreak of plague following the use of a biological weapon will require additional knowledge of the organism, its genetics, and pathogenesis. In addition, improved rapid diagnostic and standard laboratory microbiology techniques are necessary. An improved understanding of prophylactic and therapeutic antibiotic regimens would be of benefit in defining optimal antibiotic strategy.

Ex officio participants in the Working Group on Civilian Biodefense: George Counts, MD, National Institutes of Health; Margaret Hamburg, MD, Assistant Secretary for Planning and Evaluation; Robert Knouss, MD, Office of Emergency Preparedness; Brian Malkin, Food and Drug Administration; Stuart Nightingale, MD, Food and Drug Administration; and William Raub, PhD, Office of Assistant Secretary for Planning and Evaluation, Department of Health and Human Services.

Funding/Support: Funding for the development of this working group document was primarily provided by each representative's individual institution or agency; the Johns Hopkins Center for Civilian Biodefense Studies provided travel funds for 5 members of the group (Drs Ascher, Fine, Layton, and Osterholm and Mr Hauer).

Acknowledgments: We thank Christopher Davis, OBE, MD, PhD, ORAQ Consultancy, Marlborough, England; Edward B. Hayes, MD, Centers for Disease Control and Prevention (CDC), Atlanta, Ga; May Chu, PhD, CDC, Fort Collins, Colo; Timothy Townsend, MD, Johns Hopkins University, Baltimore, Md; Jane Wong, MS, California Department of Health, Berkeley; and Paul A. Pham, PharmD, Johns Hopkins University, for their review of the manuscript and Molly D'Esopo for administrative support.

References

1. Inglesby TV, Henderson DA, Bartlett JG, et al. Anthrax as a biological weapon: medical and public health management. *JAMA.* 1999;281: 1735-1745.
2. Henderson DA, Inglesby TV, Bartlett JG, et al. Smallpox as a biological weapon: medical and public health management. *JAMA.* 1999;281: 2127-2137.
3. Centers for Disease Control and Prevention. *Critical Biological Agents for Public Health Preparedness: Summary of Selection Process and Recommendations.* October 16, 1999. Unpublished report.
4. Perry RD, Fetherston JD. *Yersinia pestis*—etiologic agent of plague. *Clin Microbiol Rev.* 1997;10:35-66.
5. Slack P. The black death past and present. *Trans R Soc Trop Med Hyg.* 1989;83:461-463.
6. Harris SH. *Factories of Death.* New York, NY: Routledge; 1994:78, 96.
7. *Health Aspects of Chemical and Biological Weapons.* Geneva, Switzerland: World Health Organization; 1970:98-109.
8. Alibek K, Handelman S. *Biohazard.* New York, NY: Random House; 1999.
9. Hughes J. *Nation's Public Health Infrastructure Regarding Epidemics and Bioterrorism* [congressional testimony]. Washington, DC: Appropriations Committee, US Senate; June 2, 1998.
10. Carus WS. *Bioterrorism and Biocrimes: The Illicit Use of Biological Agents in the 20th Century.* Washington, DC: Center for Counterproliferation Research, National Defense University; 1998.
11. Dennis D, Meier F. Plague. In: Horsburgh CR, Nelson AM, eds. *Pathology of Emerging Infections.* Washington, DC: ASM Press; 1997:21-47.
12. Centers for Disease Control and Prevention. Fatal human plague—Arizona and Colorado, 1996. *MMWR Morb Mortal Wkly Rep.* 1997;46:617-620. Cited in *JAMA* 1997;278:380-382.
13. Centers for Disease Control and Prevention. Human plague—United States, 1993-1994. *MMWR Morb Mortal Wkly Rep.* 1994;43:242-246.
14. Meyer K. Pneumonic plague. *Bacteriol Rev.* 1961;25:249-261.
15. Kellogg WH. An epidemic of pneumonic plague. *Am J Public Health.* 1920;10:599-605.
16. Wu L-T. *A Treatise on Pneumonic Plague.* Geneva, Switzerland: League of Nations Health Organization; 1926.
17. Chernin E. Richard Pearson Strong and the Manchurian epidemic of pneumonic plague, 1910-1911. *J Hist Med Allied Sci.* 1989;44:296-319.
18. Ratsitorahina M, Chanteau S, Rahalison L, Ratisofasoamanana L, Boisier P. Epidemiological and diagnostic aspects of the outbreak of pneumonic plague in Madagascar. *Lancet.* 2000;355: 111-113.

19. Speck RS, Wolochow H. Studies on the experimental epidemiology of respiratory infections: experimental pneumonic plague in *Macaccus rhesus*. *J Infect Dis*. 1957;100:58-69.

20. Aleksic S, Bockemuhl J. *Yersinia* and other Enterobacteriaceae. In: Murray P, ed. *Manual of Clinical Microbiology*. Washington, DC: American Society for Microbiology; 1999:483-496.

21. Butler T. *Yersinia* species (including plague). In: Mandell GL, Bennett JE, Dolin R, eds. *Principles and Practice of Infectious Diseases*. New York, NY: Churchill Livingstone; 1995:2070-2078.

22. McGovern TW, Friedlander A. Plague. In: Zajtchuk R, Bellamy RF, eds. *Medical Aspects of Chemical and Biological Warfare*. Bethesda, Md: Office of the Surgeon General; 1997:479-502.

23. Campbell GL, Dennis DT. Plague and other *Yersinia* infections. In: Fauci AS, Braunwald E, Isselbacher KJ, et al, eds. *Harrison's Principles of Internal Medicine*. New York, NY: McGraw-Hill; 1998:975-983.

24. Centers for Disease Control and Prevention. Pneumonic plague—Arizona. *MMWR Morb Mortal Wkly Rep*. 1992;41:737-739.

25. Werner SB, Weidmer CE, Nelson BC, Nygaard GS, Goethals RM, Poland JD. Primary plague pneumonia contracted from a domestic cat in South Lake Tahoe, California. *JAMA*. 1984;251:929-931.

26. Finegold MJ, Petery JJ, Berendt RF, Adams HR. Studies on the pathogenesis of plague. *J Infect Dis*. 1968;53:99-114.

27. Poland JD, Dennis DT. Plague. In: Evans AS, Brachman PS, eds. *Bacterial Infections of Humans: Epidemiology and Control*. New York, NY: Plenum Medical Book Co; 1998:545-558.

28. Institute of Medicine National Research Council. Detection and measurement of biological agents. In: *Chemical and Biological Terrorism: Research and Development to Improve Civilian Medical Response*. Washington, DC: National Academy Press; 1999:95.

29. American Public Health Association. Plague. In: Benenson AS, ed. *Control of Communicable Diseases Manual*. Washington, DC: American Public Health Association; 1995:353-358.

30. Wilmoth BA, Chu MC, Quan TC.Identification of *Yersinia pestis* by BBL crystal enteric/nonfermenter identification system. *J Clin Microbiol*. 1996;34:2829-2830.

31. Centers for Disease Control and Prevention. Prevention of plague: recommendations of the Advisory Committee on Immunization Practice (ACIP). *MMWR Morb Mortal Wkly Rep*. 1996;45(RR-14):1-15.

32. Titball RW, Eley S, Williamson ED, Dennis DT. Plague. In: Plotkin S, Mortimer EA, eds. *Vaccines*. Philadelphia, Pa: WB Saunders; 1999:734-742.

33. McCrumb FR, Mercier S, Robic J, et al. Chloramphenicol and terramycin in the treatment of pneumonic plague. *Am J Med*. 1953;14:284-293.

34. Barnes AM, Quan TJ. Plague. In: Gorbach SL, Bartlett JG, Blacklow NR, eds. *Infectious Diseases*. Philadelphia, Pa: WB Saunders Co; 1992: 1285-1291.

35. American Hospital Formulary Service. *AHFS Drug Information*. Bethesda, Md: American Society of Health System Pharmacists; 2000.

36. Wong TW. Plague in a pregnant patient. *Trop Doct*. 1986;16:187-188.

37. Lewiecki EM. Primary plague septicemia. *Rocky Mt Med J*. 1978;75:201-202.

38. Welty TK, Grabman J, Kompare E, et al. Nineteen cases of plague in Arizona. *West J Med*. 1985;142:641-646.

39. Crook LD, Tempest B. Plague: a clinical review of 27 cases. *Arch Intern Med*. 1992;152:1253-1256.

40. Committee on Infectious Diseases. Plague. In: Peter G, ed. *1997 Redbook*. Elk Grove Village, Ill: American Academy of Pediatrics; 1997:408-410.

41. Smith MD, Vinh SX, Hoa NT, Wain J, Thung D, White NJ. In vitro antimicrobial susceptibilities of strains of *Yersinia pestis*. *Antimicrob Agents Chemother*. 1995;39:2153-2154.

42. Byrne WR, Welkos SL, Pitt ML, et al. Antibiotic treatment of experimental pneumonic plague in mice. *Antimicrob Agents Chemother*. 1998;42: 675-681.

43. Lyamuya EF, Nyanda P, Mohammedali H, Mhalu FS. Laboratory studies on *Yersinia pestis* during the 1991 outbreak of plague in Lushoto, Tanzania. *J Trop Med Hyg*. 1992;95:335-338.

44. Bonacorsi SP, Scavizzi MR, Guiyoule A, Amouroux JH, Carniel E. Assessment of a fluoroquinolone, three ß-lactams, two aminoglycosides, and a cycline in the treatment of murine *Yersinia pestis* infection. *Antimicrob Agents Chemother*. 1994;38:481-486.

45. Rasoamanana B, Coulanges P, Michel P, Rasolofonirina N. Sensitivity of *Yersinia pestis* to antibiotics: 277 strains isolated in Madagascar between 1926 and 1989. *Arch Inst Pasteur Madagascar.* 1989;56:37-53.

46. Makarovskaia LN, Shcherbaniuk AI, Ryzhkova VV, Sorokina TB. Effectiveness of doxycycline in experimental plague. *Antibiot Khimioter.* 1993;38:48-50.

47. Samokhodkina ED, Ryzhko IV, Shcherbaniuk AI, Kasatkina IV, Tsuraeva RI, Zhigalova TA. Doxycycline in the prevention of experimental plague induced by plague microbe variants. *Antibiot Khimioter.* 1992;37:26-28.

48. Ryzhko IV, Samokhodkina ED, Tsuraeva RI, Shcherbaniuk AI, Tsetskhladze NS. Characteristics of etiotropic therapy of plague infection induced by atypical strains of F_1-phenotype plague microbe. *Antibiot Khimioter.* 1998;43:24-28.

49. Davis KJ, Fritz DL, Pitt ML, Welkos SL, Worsham PL, Friedlander A. Pathology of experimental pneumonic plague produced by fraction-1 positive and fraction-1 negative *Yersinia pestis* in African green monkeys. *Arch Pathol Lab Med.* 1996;120:156-163.

50. Russell P, Eley SM, Green M, et al. Efficacy of doxycycline and ciprofloxacin against experimental *Yersinia pestis* infection. *J Antimicrob Chemother.* 1998;41:301-305.

51. Russell P, Eley SM, Bell DL, Manchee RJ, Titball RW. Doxycycline or ciprofloxacin prophylaxis and therapy against experimental *Y. pestis* infection in mice. *J Antimicrob Chemother.* 1996;37:769-774.

52. Butler T. Plague. In: Strickland GT, ed. *Tropical Medicine.* Philadelphia, Pa: WB Saunders Co; 1991:408-416.

53. *Expert Committee on Plague.* Geneva, Switzerland: World Health Organization; 1959. Technical Report Series 165.

54. Burkle FM. Plague as seen in South Vietnamese children. *Clin Pediatr.* 1973;12:291-298.

55. Frean JA, Arntzen L, Capper T, Bryskier A, Klugman KP. In vitro activities of 14 antibiotics against 100 human isolates of *Yersinia pestis* from a southern African plague focus. *Antimicrob Agents Chemother.* 1996;40:2646-2647.

56. Brygoo ER, Gonon M. Une epidemie de peste pulmonaire dans le nor-est de Madagascar. *Bull Soc Pathol Exot.* 1958;51:47-66.

57. Nguyen VI, Nguyen DH, Pham VD, Nguyen VL. Peste bubonique et septicemique traitée avec succes par du trimethoprime-sulfamethoxazole. *Bull Soc Pathol Exot.* 1972;769-779.

58. Butler TJ, Levin J, Linh NN, Chau DM, Adickman M, Arnold K. *Yersinia pestis* infection in Vietnam. *J Infect Dis.* 1976;133:493-499.

59. *WHO Expert Committee on Plague: Third Report.* Geneva, Switzerland: World Health Organization; 1970:1-25. Technical Report Series 447.

60. Galimand M, Guiyoule A, Gerbaud G, et al. Multidrug resistance in *Yersinia pestis* mediated by a transferable plasmid. *N Engl J Med.* 1997;337:677-680.

61. Ryzhko IV, Shcherbaniuk AI, Samokhodkina ED, et al. Virulence of rifampicin and quinolone resistant mutants of strains of plague microbe with Fra+ and Fra– phenotypes. *Antibiot Khimioter.* 1994;39:32-36.

62. Scott JL, Finegold SM, Belkin GA, et al. A controlled double blind study of the hematologic toxicity of chloramphenicol. *N Engl J Med.* 1965;272:113-142.

63. Watterberg KL, Kelly HW, Angelus P, Backstrom C. The need for a loading dose of gentamicin in neonates. *Ther Drug Monit.* 1989;11:16-20.

64. Consensus Report of the International Society of Chemotherapy Commission: use of fluoroquinolones in pediatrics. *Pediatr Infect Dis J.* 1995;14:1-9.

65. Sakala E. *Obstetrics and Gynecology.* Baltimore, Md: Williams & Wilkins; 1997:945.

66. Cziel A, Rockenbauer M. Teratogenic study of doxycycline. *Obstet Gynecol.* 1997;89:524-528.

67. Garner JS. Guidelines for isolation precautions in hospitals: Hospital Infection Control Practices Advisory Committee. *Infect Control Hosp Epidemiol.* 1996;17:53-80.

68. Burmeister RW, Tigertt WD, Overholt EL. Laboratory-acquired pneumonic plague. *Ann Intern Med.* 1962;56:789-800.

69. Morse S, McDade J. Recommendations for working with pathogenic bacteria. *Methods Enzymol.* 1994;235:1-26.

70. *Safety Measures for Use in Outbreaks in Communicable Disease Outbreaks.* Geneva, Switzerland: World Health Organization; 1986.

71. Gershon RR, Vlahov D, Cejudo JA, et al. Tuberculosis risk in funeral home employees. *J Occup Environ Med.* 1998;40:497-503.

72. Freeman BA. *Yersinia*; *Pasturella*; *Francisella*; *Actinobacillus.* In: *Textbook of Microbiology.* Philadelphia, Pa: WB Saunders Co; 1985:513-530.

Botulinum Toxin as a Biological Weapon

Stephen S. Arnon, MD; Robert Schechter, MD; Thomas V. Inglesby, MD; Donald A. Henderson, MD, MPH; John G. Bartlett, MD; Michael S. Ascher, MD; Edward Eitzen, Jr, MD, MPH; Anne D. Fine, MD; Jerome Hauer, MPH; Marcelle Layton, MD; Scott Lillibridge, MD; Michael T. Osterholm, PhD, MPH; Tara O'Toole, MD, MPH; Gerald Parker, PhD, DVM; Trish M. Perl, MD, MSc; Philip K. Russell, MD; David L. Swerdlow, MD; Kevin Tonat, DrPH, MPH; for the Working Group on Civilian Biodefense

Updated addendum, incorporating comments and revisions from the Working Group on Civilian Biodefense, written by Stephen S. Arnon, MD, and Robert Schechter, MD

This is the fourth article in a series entitled *Medical and Public Health Management Following the Use of a Biological Weapon: Consensus Statements of the Working Group on Civilian Biodefense.*[1-3] This article is the only one in the series to feature a biological toxin rather than a replicating agent. Botulinum toxin poses a major bioweapon threat because of its extreme potency and lethality; its ease of production, transport, and misuse; and the need for prolonged intensive care among affected persons.[4,5] An outbreak of botulism constitutes a medical emergency that requires prompt provision of botulinum antitoxin and, often, mechanical ventilation, and it constitutes a public health emergency that requires immediate intervention to prevent additional cases. Timely recognition of a botulism outbreak begins with the astute clinician who quickly notifies public health officials.

Botulinum toxin is the most poisonous substance known.[6,7] A single gram of crystalline toxin, evenly dispersed and inhaled, would kill more than 1 million people, although technical factors would make such dissemination difficult. The basis of the phenomenal potency of botulinum toxin is enzymatic; the toxin is a zinc proteinase that cleaves 1 or more of the fusion proteins by which neuronal vesicles release acetylcholine into the neuromuscular junction.[8]

It is regrettable that botulinum toxin still needs to be considered as a bioweapon at the historic moment when it has become the first microbial toxin to become licensed for treatment of human disease. In the United States, botulinum toxin is currently licensed for treatment of cervical torticollis, strabismus, and blepharospasm associated with dystonia. It is also used "off label" for a variety of more prevalent conditions that include migraine headache, chronic low back pain, stroke, traumatic brain injury, cerebral palsy, achalasia, and various dystonias.[9-13]

Consensus Methods

For this article, the working group included 23 representatives from academic, government, and private institutions with expertise in public health, emergency management, and clinical medicine. The first 2 authors (S.S.A. and R.S.) conducted a literature search on use of botulinum toxin as a bioweapon. The OLDMEDLINE and MEDLINE databases were queried for all articles published between January 1960 and March 1999 that contained words referring to biological warfare (*bioterrorism*, *biowarfare*, *terrorism*, *war*, *warfare*, and *weapon*) in combination with terms related to *Clostridium botulinum* (*bacillus*, *botulin*, *botulinal*, *botulinum*, *botulinus*, *botulism*, *clostridia*, *clostridial*, and *Clostridium*). The articles identified in the databases were fully reviewed. In addition, published and unpublished articles, books, monographs, and special reports in the primary authors' collections were reviewed. Additional MEDLINE searches were conducted through April 2000 during the review and revisions of the consensus statement.

The first draft of the consensus statement was a synthesis of information obtained in the formal evidence-gathering process. Members of the working group provided written and oral comments about the first draft at their meeting in May 1999. Working group members then reviewed subsequent drafts and suggested additional revisions. The final statement incorporates all relevant evidence obtained in the literature search in conjunction with final consensus recommendations supported by all working group members. An updated addendum was written by Drs Schecter and Arnon that incorporates comments and revisions from the Working Group on Civilian Biodefense in January 2002.

The assessment and recommendations provided herein represent the best professional judgment of the working group based on currently available data and expertise. These conclusions and recommendations should be regularly reassessed as new information becomes available.

History of Current Threat

Terrorists have already attempted to use botulinum toxin as a bioweapon. Aerosols were dispersed at multiple sites in downtown Tokyo, Japan, and at US military installations in Japan on at least 3 occasions between 1990 and 1995 by the Japanese cult Aum Shinrikō. These attacks failed, apparently because of faulty microbiological technique, deficient aerosol-generating equipment, or internal sabotage. The perpetrators obtained their *C botulinum* from soil that they had collected in northern Japan.[14, 15]

Development and use of botulinum toxin as a possible bioweapon began at least 60 years ago.[16, 17] The head of the Japanese biological warfare group (Unit 731) admitted to feeding cultures of *C botulinum* to prisoners with lethal effect during that country's occupation of Manchuria, which began in the 1930s.[18] The US biological weapons program first produced botulinum toxin during World War II. Because of concerns that Germany had weaponized botulinum toxin, more than 1 million doses of botulinum toxoid vaccine were made for Allied troops preparing to invade Normandy on D-Day.[19, 20] The US biological weapons program was ended in 1969-1970 by executive orders of Richard M. Nixon, then president. Research pertaining to biowarfare use of botulinum toxin took place in other countries as well.[21]

Although the 1972 Biological and Toxin Weapons Convention prohibited offensive research and production of biological weapons, signatories Iraq and the Soviet Union subsequently produced botulinum toxin for use as a weapon.[22, 23] Botulinum toxin was 1 of several agents tested at the Soviet site Aralsk-7 on Vozrozhdeniye Island in the Aral Sea.[23, 24] A former senior scientist of the Russian civilian bioweapons program reported that the Soviets had attempted splicing the botulinum toxin gene from *C botulinum* into other bacteria.[25] With the economic difficulties in Russia after the demise of the Soviet Union, some of the thousands of scientists formerly employed by its bioweapons program have been recruited by nations attempting to develop biological weapons.[25, 26] Four of the countries listed by the US government as "state sponsors of terrorism" (Iran, Iraq, North Korea, and Syria)[27] have developed, or are believed to be developing, botulinum toxin as a weapon.[28, 29]

After the 1991 Persian Gulf War, Iraq admitted to the United Nations inspection team to having produced 19 000 L of concentrated botulinum toxin, of which approximately 10 000 L were loaded into military weapons.[22, 30] These 19 000 L of concentrated toxin are not fully accounted for and constitute approximately 3 times the amount needed to kill the entire current human population by inhalation. In 1990, Iraq deployed specially designed missiles with a 600-km range; 13 of these were filled with botulinum toxin, 10 with aflatoxin, and 2 with anthrax spores. Iraq also deployed special 400-lb (180-kg) bombs for immediate use; 100 bombs contained botulinum toxin, 50 contained anthrax spores, and 7 contained aflatoxin.[22, 30] It is noteworthy that Iraq chose to weaponize more botulinum toxin than any other of its known biological agents.

Some contemporary analyses discount the potential of botulinum toxin as a bioweapon because of constraints in concentrating and stabilizing the toxin for aerosol dissemination. However, these analyses pertain to military uses of botulinum toxin to immobilize an opponent (William C. Patrick, unpublished data, 1998). In contrast, deliberate release of botulinum toxin in a civilian population would be able to cause substantial disruption and distress. For example, it is estimated that a point-source aerosol release of botulinum toxin could incapacitate or kill 10% of persons within 0.5 km downwind (William C. Patrick, unpublished data, 1998). An assessment of the economic impact of an aerosolized botulinum toxin attack on a civilian population in Canada was recently published. (See addendum at end of this chapter for details.) In addition, terrorist use of botulinum toxin might be manifested as deliberate contamination of food. Misuse of toxin in this manner could produce either a large botulism outbreak from a single meal or episodic, widely separated outbreaks.[31] In the United States, the Centers for Disease Control and Prevention (CDC) maintains a well-established surveillance system for human botulism based on clinician reporting that would promptly detect such events.[32]

Microbiology and Virulence Factors

Clostridium botulinum is a spore-forming, obligate anaerobe whose natural habitat is soil, from which it can be isolated without undue difficulty. The species *C botulinum* consists of 4 genetically diverse groups that would not otherwise be designated as a single species except for their common characteristic of producing botulinum toxin.[33,34] Botulinum toxin exists in 7 distinct antigenic types that have been assigned the letters A through G. The toxin types are defined by their absence of cross-neutralization (eg, anti-A antitoxin does not neutralize toxin types B-G). The toxin types also serve as convenient epidemiological markers. In addition to *C botulinum*, unique strains of *Clostridium baratii* and *Clostridium butyricum* have the capacity to produce botulinum toxin.[35-37] Botulinum toxin is a simple dichain polypeptide that consists of a 100-kd "heavy" chain joined by a single disulfide bond to a 50-kd "light" chain; its 3-dimensional structure was recently resolved to 3.3 A.[38] The toxin's light chain is a Zn^{++}-containing endopeptidase that blocks acetylcholine-containing vesicles from fusing with the terminal membrane of the motor neuron, resulting in flaccid muscle paralysis (**Figure 1**).[8]

The lethal dose of botulinum toxin for humans is not known but can be estimated from primate studies. By extrapolation, the lethal amounts of crystalline type A toxin for a 70-kg human would be approximately 0.09 to 0.15 μg intravenously or intramuscularly, 0.70 to 0.90 μg inhalationally, and 70 μg orally.[10,39-41] Therapeutic botulinum toxin represents an impractical bioterrorist weapon because a vial of the type A preparation currently licensed in the United States contains only about 0.3% of the estimated human lethal inhalational dose and 0.005% of the estimated lethal oral dose.

Pathogenesis and Clinical Manifestations

Three forms of naturally occurring human botulism exist: foodborne, wound, and intestinal (infant and adult). Fewer than 200 cases of all forms of botulism are reported annually in the United States.[42] All forms of botulism result from absorption of botulinum toxin into the circulation from either a mucosal surface (gut, lung) or a wound. Botulinum toxin does not penetrate intact skin. Wound botulism and intestinal botulism are infectious diseases that result from production of botulinum toxin by *C botulinum* either in devitalized (ie, anaerobic) tissue[43] or in the intestinal lumen,[37] respectively. Neither would result from bioterrorist use of botulinum toxin.

A fourth, man-made form that results from aerosolized botulinum toxin is inhalational botulism. This mode of transmission has been demonstrated experimentally in primates,[39] has been attempted by bioterrorists,[14,15] and has been the intended outcome of at least 1 country's specially designed missiles and artillery shells.[22,30] Inhalational botulism has occurred accidentally in humans. A brief report from West Germany in 1962 described 3 veterinary personnel who were exposed to reaerosolized botulinum toxin while disposing of rabbits and guinea pigs whose fur was coated with aerosolized type A botulinum toxin. Type A botulinum toxin was detected in serum samples from all 3 affected individuals.[21]

Figure 1. Mechanism of Action of Botulinum Toxin

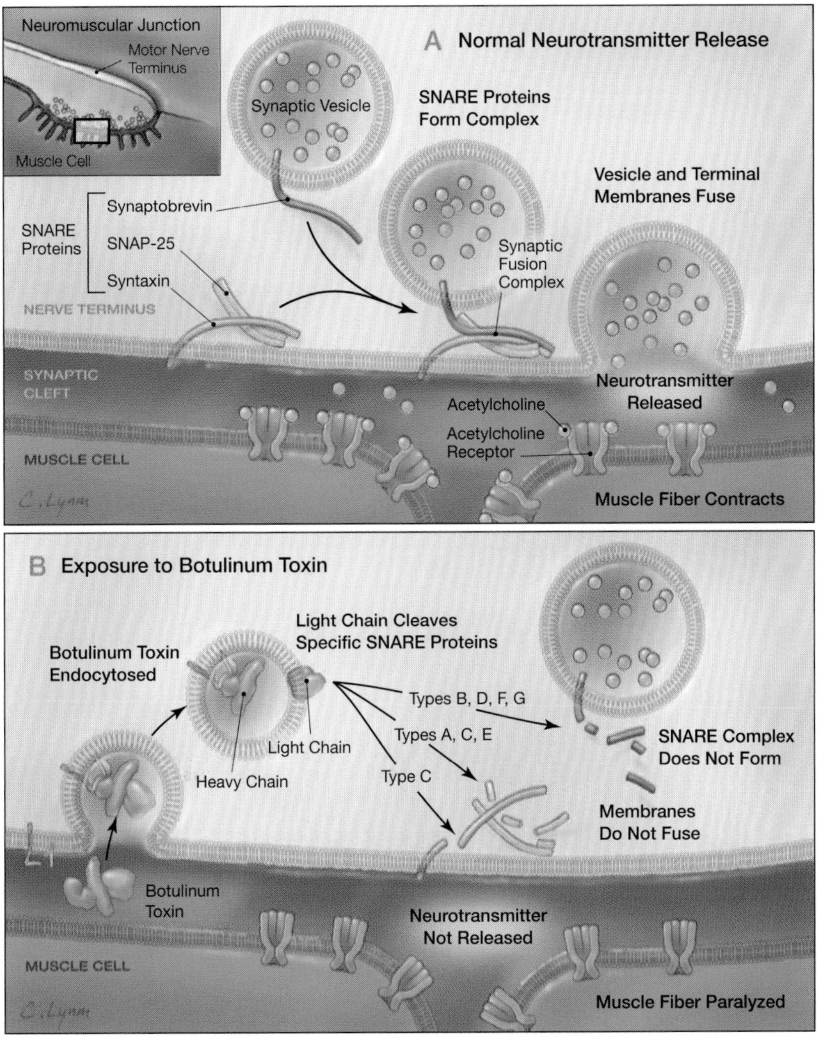

A, Release of acetylcholine at the neuromuscular junction is mediated by the assembly of a synaptic fusion complex that allows the membrane of the synaptic vesicle containing acetylcholine to fuse with the neuronal cell membrane. The synaptic fusion complex is a set of SNARE proteins, which include synaptobrevin, SNAP-25, and syntaxin. After membrane fusion, acetylcholine is released into the synaptic cleft and then bound by receptors on the muscle cell.

B, Botulinum toxin binds to the neuronal cell membrane at the nerve terminus and enters the neuron by endocytosis. The light chain of botulinum toxin cleaves specific sites on the SNARE proteins, preventing complete assembly of the synaptic fusion complex and thereby blocking acetylcholine release. Botulinum toxins types B, D, F, and G cleave synaptobrevin; types A, C, and E cleave SNAP-25; and type C cleaves syntaxin. Without acetylcholine release, the muscle is unable to contract.

SNARE indicates soluble NSF-attachment protein receptor; NSF, N-ethylmaleimide-sensitive fusion protein; and SNAP-25, synaptosomal-associated protein of 25 kd.

Figure 2. Seventeen-Year-Old Patient With Mild Botulism

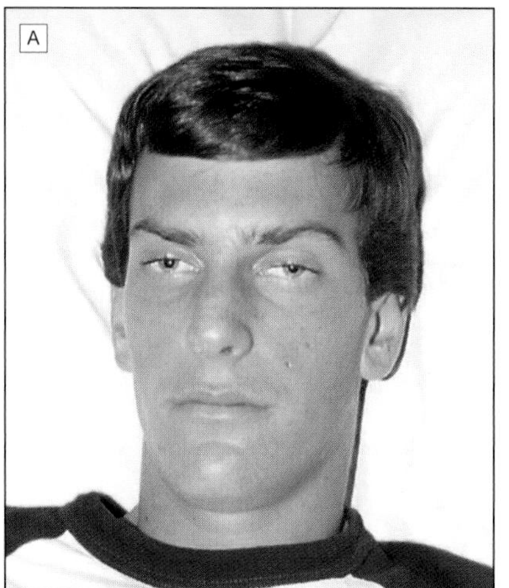

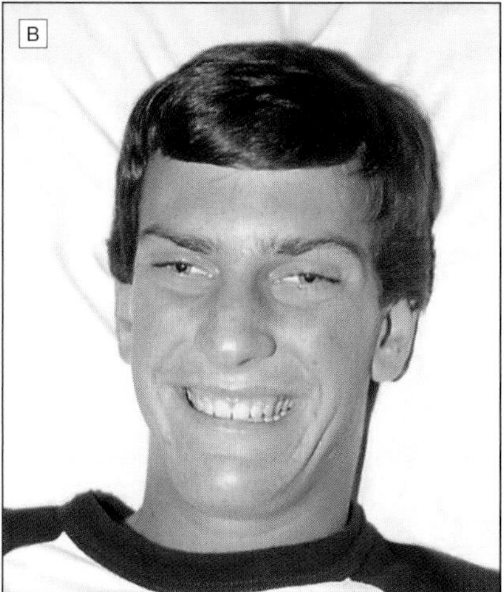

A, Patient at rest. Note bilateral mild ptosis, dilated pupils, disconjugate gaze, and symmetric facial muscles. B, Patient was requested to perform his maximum smile. Note absent periorbital smile creases, ptosis, disconjugate gaze, dilated pupils, and minimally asymmetric smile. As an indication of the extreme potency of botulinum toxin, the patient had 40×10^{-12}g/mL of type A botulinum toxin in his serum (ie, 1.25 mouse units/mL) when these photographs were taken.

Once botulinum toxin is absorbed, the bloodstream carries it to peripheral cholinergic synapses, principally, the neuromuscular junction, where it binds irreversibly. The toxin is then internalized and enzymatically blocks acetylcholine release (Figure 1). Accordingly, all forms of human botulism display virtually identical neurologic signs. However, the neurologic signs in naturally occurring foodborne botulism may be preceded by abdominal cramps, nausea, vomiting, or diarrhea.[44] These gastrointestinal symptoms are thought to be caused by other bacterial metabolites also present in the food[33] and may not occur if purified botulinum toxin is intentionally placed in foods or aerosols.

Botulism is an acute, afebrile, symmetric, descending flaccid paralysis that always begins in bulbar musculature. It is not possible to have botulism without having multiple cranial nerve palsies. Disease manifestations are similar regardless of botulinum toxin type. However, the extent and pace of paralysis may vary considerably among patients. Some patients may be mildly affected (**Figure 2**), while others may be so paralyzed that they appear comatose and require months of ventilatory support. The rapidity of onset and the severity of paralysis depend on the amount of toxin absorbed into the circulation. Recovery results from new motor axon twigs that sprout to reinnervate paralyzed muscle fibers, a process that, in adults, may take weeks or months to complete.[45,46]

Patients with botulism typically present with difficulty seeing, speaking, and/or swallowing (**Table 1** and **Table 2**). Prominent neurologic findings in all forms of botulism include ptosis, diplopia, blurred vision, often enlarged or sluggishly

Table 1. Symptoms and Signs of Foodborne Botulism, Types A and B*

	Cases, %
Symptoms	
Fatigue	77
Dizziness	51
Double vision	91
Blurred vision	65
Dysphagia	96
Dry mouth	93
Dysarthria	84
Sore throat	54
Dyspnea	60
Constipation	73
Nausea	64
Vomiting	59
Abdominal cramps	42
Diarrhea	19
Arm weakness	73
Leg weakness	69
Paresthesia	14
Signs	
Alert mental status	90
Ptosis	73
Gaze paralysis	65
Pupils dilated or fixed	44
Nystagmus	22
Facial palsy	63
Diminished gag reflex	65
Tongue weakness	58
Arm weakness	75
Leg weakness	69
Hyporeflexia or areflexia	40
Ataxia	17

*Data are from outbreaks of botulism reported in the United States in 1973-1974. The number of patients with available data varied from 35 to 55. Adapted from Hughes et al[44] with permission.

reactive pupils, dysarthria, dysphonia, and dysphagia.[5, 44, 47, 48] The mouth may appear dry and the pharynx injected because of peripheral parasympathetic cholinergic blockade. Sensory changes are not observed except for infrequent circumoral and peripheral paresthesias from hyperventilation as a patient becomes frightened by onset of paralysis.

Table 2. Symptoms and Signs of Inhalational Botulism in Order of Onset

Humans (n = 3)[21]	Monkeys (n = 9)[39*]
Third day after exposure	12–18 hours after exposure
Mucus in throat	Mild muscular weakness
Difficulty swallowing solid food	Intermittent ptosis
Dizziness	Disconjugate gaze
Fourth day after exposure	Followed by
Difficulty moving eyes	Severe weakness of postural neck muscles
Mild pupillary dilation and nystagmus	Occasional mouth breathing
Indistinct speech	Serous nasal discharge
Unsteady gait	Salivation, dysphagia
Extreme weakness	Mouth breathing
	Rales
	Anorexia
	Severe generalized weakness
	Lateral recumbency
	Second to fourth day after exposure
	Death in some animals

*After exposure to 4 to 7 monkey median lethal doses of botulinum toxin. The time to onset and pace of paralysis were dose-dependent. Adapted from Middlebrook and Franz[48] with permission.

As paralysis extends beyond bulbar musculature, loss of head control, hypotonia, and generalized weakness become prominent. Dysphagia and loss of the protective gag reflex may require intubation and, usually, mechanical ventilation. Deep tendon reflexes may be present initially but diminish or disappear in the ensuing days, and constipation may occur. In untreated persons, death results from airway obstruction (pharyngeal and upper airway muscle paralysis) and inadequate tidal volume (diaphragmatic and accessory respiratory muscle paralysis).

Because botulism is an intoxication, patients remain afebrile unless they also have acquired a secondary infection (eg, aspiration pneumonia). The toxin does not penetrate brain parenchyma, so patients are not confused or obtunded. However, they often appear lethargic and have communication difficulties because of bulbar palsies (Figure 2). Botulism may be recognized by its classic triad: (1) symmetric, descending flaccid paralysis with prominent bulbar palsies in (2) an afebrile patient with (3) a clear sensorium. The prominent bulbar palsies can be summarized in part as "4 Ds": diplopia, dysarthria, dysphonia, and dysphagia.

Epidemiology

Early recognition of outbreaks of botulism, whether natural or intentional, depends on heightened clinical suspicion. Aerosol dissemination may not be difficult to recognize because a large number of cases will share a common temporal and geographical exposure and will lack a common dietary exposure. However, identification of the common exposure site initially may be difficult because of the mobility of persons exposed during the incubation period. Botulism and botulinum toxin are not contagious and cannot be transmitted from person to person. In contrast, a microbe intentionally modified to produce botulinum toxin might be contagious. See also addendum on unusual modes of dissemination at end of this chapter.

No instances of waterborne botulism have ever been reported.[42, 49, 50] Although the potency of botulinum toxin has led to speculation that it might be used to contaminate a municipal water supply, this scenario is unlikely for at least 2 reasons.[51] First, botulinum toxin is rapidly inactivated by standard potable water treatments (eg, chlorination, aeration).[52] Second, because of the slow turnover time of large-capacity reservoirs, a comparably large (and technically difficult to produce and deliver) inoculum of botulinum toxin would be needed.[53] In contrast with treated water, botulinum toxin may be stable for several days in untreated water or beverages.[52, 54] Hence, such items should be investigated in a botulism outbreak if no other vehicle for toxin can be identified.

If food were deliberately used as a vehicle for the toxin, the outbreak would need to be distinguished from naturally occurring foodborne botulism. During the past 20 years, the epidemiology of foodborne botulism has expanded beyond its traditional association with home-preserved foods and now includes nonpreserved foods and public eating places,[47] features that could make terrorist use of botulinum toxin more difficult to detect. Characteristics of outbreaks of botulism include

Incubation Period

The rapidity of onset and severity of botulism depend on the rate and amount of toxin absorption. Symptoms of foodborne botulism may begin as early as 2 hours or as long as 8 days after ingestion of toxin.[55, 56] Typically, cases present 12 to 72 hours after the implicated meal. In 1 large foodborne outbreak, new cases presented during the ensuing 3 days at a fairly even rate before decreasing (**Figure 3**).[57] The time to onset of inhalational botulism cannot be stated with certainty because so few cases are known. Monkeys showed signs of botulism 12 to 80 hours after aerosol exposure to 4 to 7 multiples of the monkey median lethal dose.[39] The 3 known human cases of inhalational botulism had onset of symptoms approximately 72 hours after exposure to an unknown but probably small amount of reaerosolized toxin.[21]

Age and Sex

Persons of all ages are potentially susceptible to botulism. There are no sex differences in susceptibility.

Agent and Vehicles

Botulinum toxin in solution is colorless, odorless, and, as far as is known, tasteless. The toxin is readily inactivated by heat (≥85°C for 5 minutes).[33, 34, 52] Thus, foodborne botulism is always transmitted by foods that are not heated, or not heated thoroughly, before eating. Almost every type of food has been associated

Figure 3. Fifty-nine Cases of Botulism, by Interval Between Eating at a Restaurant and Onset of First Neurologic Symptom—Michigan, 1977

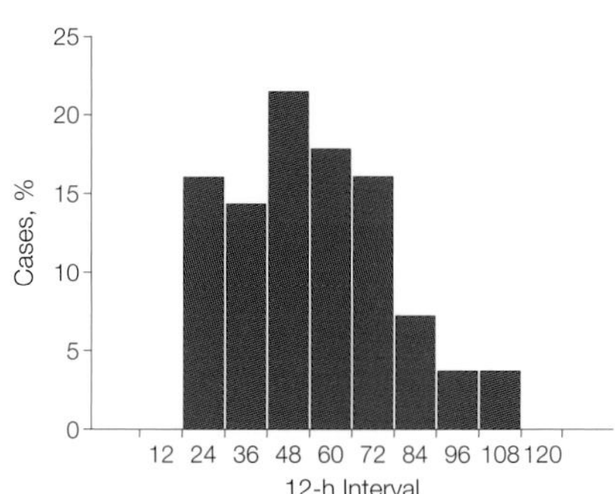

Reproduced from Terranova et al[57] with permission of Oxford University Press.

with outbreaks of botulism, but the most commonly implicated foods in the United States are vegetables, particularly "low-acid" (ie, higher pH) vegetables such as beans, peppers, carrots, and corn.[42, 50, 58]

A novel epidemiological development is the occurrence of foodborne botulism after eating various nonpreserved foods in restaurants or delicatessens. Foil-wrapped baked potatoes are now known to be capable of causing restaurant-associated foodborne botulism[59] when held at room temperature after baking and then served plain,[60] as potato salad,[61, 62] or as a Mediterranean-style dip.[59] Other outbreaks that originated in restaurants resulted from contaminated condiments such as sautéed onions,[63] garlic in oil,[64] and commercial cheese sauce.[65] Additional examples of notable commercial foods that have caused botulism outbreaks include inadequately eviscerated fish,[66] yogurt,[67] cream cheese,[68] and jarred peanuts.[69]

Incidence and Outbreak Size

Naturally occurring foodborne botulism is a rare disease. Approximately 9 outbreaks of foodborne botulism and a median of 24 cases occur annually in the United States.[42, 47] The mean outbreak size has remained constant over the years at approximately 2.5 cases per outbreak. The largest outbreak of foodborne botulism in the United States in the last 100 years occurred in Michigan in 1977; 59 cases resulted from eating home-preserved jalapeño peppers at a restaurant.[57] However, only 45 of the 59 patients had clinically evident weakness and hypotonia.

Toxin Types

Of the 135 foodborne outbreaks in the 16 years from 1980 to 1996 in the United States, the toxin types represented were type A, 54.1%; type B, 14.8%; type E, 26.7%; type F, 1.5%; and unknown, 3.0%.[42] Type F foodborne outbreaks are rare in the United States; a 1962 outbreak resulted from homemade venison jerky,[70] while other type F cases actually may have had intestinal botulism.[71] Toxin types

Box 1. Features of an Outbreak That Would Suggest a Deliberate Release of Botulinum Toxin

Outbreak of a large number of cases of acute flaccid paralysis with prominent bulbar palsies

Outbreak with an unusual botulinum toxin type (ie, type C, D, F, or G, or type E toxin not acquired from an aquatic food)

Outbreak with a common geographic factor among cases (eg, airport, work location) but without a common dietary exposure (ie, features suggestive of an aerosol attack)

Multiple simultaneous outbreaks with no common source

Note: A careful travel and activity history, as well as dietary history, should be taken in any suspected botulism outbreak. Patients should also be asked if they know of other persons with similar symptoms.

C and D cause botulism in wildlife and domestic animals but have not caused human foodborne disease. However, humans are thought to be susceptible to these toxin types because they have caused botulism in primates when ingested.[72-74] Toxin type G is produced by a bacterial species discovered in South American soil in 1969 that has never caused recognized foodborne botulism.[75] Aerosol challenge studies in monkeys have established the susceptibility of primates to inhaled botulinum toxin types C, D, and G.[48]

Distribution

Although outbreaks of foodborne botulism have occurred in almost all states, more than half (53.8%) of the US outbreaks have occurred in just 5 western states (California, Washington, Oregon, Colorado, and Alaska). East of the Mississippi River, 60% of the foodborne outbreaks have resulted from type B toxin, while west of the Mississippi River, 85% have resulted from type A toxin. In the 46 years between 1950 and 1996, 20 states, mainly in the eastern United States, did not report any type A botulism outbreaks, while 24 states, mostly in the western United States, did not report any type B outbreaks.[42] In Canada and Alaska, most foodborne outbreaks resulted from type E toxin associated with native Inuit and Eskimo foods.[50, 76]

Bioterrorism Considerations

Any outbreak of botulism should bring to mind the possibility of bioterrorism, but certain features would be particularly suggestive (**Box 1**). The availability and speed of air transportation mandate that a careful travel and activity history, as well as a careful dietary history, be taken. Patients should also be asked whether they know of other persons with similar symptoms. Absence of a common dietary exposure among temporally clustered patients should suggest the possibility of inhalational botulism.

Box 2. Who Clinicians Caring for Patients With Suspected Botulism Should Immediately Contact

1. Hospital epidemiologist or infection control practitioner
   and
2. Local and state health departments

Consult your local telephone operator, the telephone directory under "government listings," or the Internet at www.cdc.gov/other.htm#states or http://www.astho.org/state.html.

If the local and state health departments are unavailable, contact the Centers for Disease Control and Prevention: (404) 639-2206; (404) 639-2888 [after hours].

Diagnosis and Differential Diagnosis

Clinical diagnosis of botulism is confirmed by specialized laboratory testing that often requires days to complete. Routine laboratory test results are usually unremarkable. Therefore, clinical diagnosis is the foundation for early recognition of and response to a bioterrorist attack with botulinum toxin.

Any case of suspected botulism represents a potential public health emergency because of the possibility that a contaminated food remains available to others or that botulinum toxin has been deliberately released. In these settings, prompt intervention by civil authorities is needed to prevent additional cases. Consequently, clinicians caring for patients with suspected botulism should notify their local public health department and hospital epidemiologist immediately to coordinate shipment of therapeutic antitoxin, laboratory diagnostic testing, and epidemiological investigation (**Box 2**). In most jurisdictions of the United States, botulism suspected on clinical grounds alone by law must be reported immediately by telephone to local public health authorities. The attending clinician needs to be both prompt and persistent in accomplishing this notification.

Differential Diagnosis

Botulism is frequently misdiagnosed, most often as a polyradiculoneuropathy (Guillain-Barré or Miller-Fisher syndrome), myasthenia gravis, or a disease of the central nervous system (**Table 3**). In the United States, botulism is more likely than Guillain-Barré syndrome, intoxication, or poliomyelitis to cause a cluster of cases of acute flaccid paralysis. Botulism differs from other flaccid paralyses in its prominent cranial nerve palsies disproportionate to milder weakness and hypotonia below the neck, in its symmetry, and in its absence of sensory nerve damage.

A large, unintentional outbreak of foodborne botulism caused by a restaurant condiment in Canada provides a cautionary lesson about the potential difficulties in recognizing a covert, intentional contamination of food.[64] During a 6-week period in which the condiment was served, 28 persons in 2 countries became ill, but all were misdiagnosed (Table 3). The 28 were identified retrospectively only after correct diagnoses in a mother and her 2 daughters who had returned to their

Table 3. Selected Mimics and Misdiagnoses of Botulism*

Conditions	Features That Distinguish Condition From Botulism
Common Misdiagnoses	
Guillain-Barré syndrome† and its variants, especially Miller-Fisher syndrome	History of antecedent infection; paresthesias; often ascending paralysis; early areflexia; eventual CSF protein increase; EMG findings
Myasthenia gravis†	Recurrent paralysis; EMG findings; sustained response to anticholinesterase
Stroke†	Paralysis often asymmetric; abnormal CNS image
Intoxication with depressants (eg, acute ethanol intoxication), organophosphates, carbon monoxide, or nerve gas	History of exposure; excessive drug levels detected in body fluids
Lambert-Eaton syndrome	Increased strength with sustained contraction; evidence of lung carcinoma; EMG findings similar to botulism
Tick paralysis	Paresthesias; ascending paralysis; tick attached to skin
Other Misdiagnoses	
Poliomyelitis	Antecedent febrile illness; asymmetric paralysis; CSF pleocytosis
CNS infections, especially of the brainstem	Mental status changes; CSF and EEG abnormalities
CNS tumor	Paralysis often asymmetric; abnormal CNS image
Streptococcal pharyngitis (pharyngeal erythema can occur in botulism)	Absence of bulbar palsies; positive rapid antigen test result or throat
Psychiatric illness†	Normal EMG in conversion paralysis
Viral syndrome†	Absence of bulbar palsies and flaccid paralysis
Inflammatory myopathy†	Elevated creatine kinase levels
Diabetic complications†	Sensory neuropathy; few cranial nerve palsies
Hyperemesis gravidarum†	Absence of bulbar palsies and acute flaccid paralysis
Hypothyroidism†	Abnormal thyroid function test results
Laryngeal trauma†	Absence of flaccid paralysis; dysphonia without bulbar palsies
Overexertion†	Absence of bulbar palsies and acute flaccid paralysis

* CSF indicates cerebrospinal fluid; EMG, electromyogram; CNS, central nervous system; and EEG, electroencephalogram.

† Misdiagnoses made in a large outbreak of botulism.[64]

home more than 2000 miles away from the restaurant. Four (14%) of the cases had been misdiagnosed as having psychiatric disease, including "factitious" symptoms. It is possible that hysterical paralysis might occur as a conversion reaction in the anxiety that would follow a deliberate release of botulinum toxin.

Diagnostic Testing

At present, laboratory diagnostic testing for botulism in the United States is available only at the CDC and approximately 20 state and municipal public health laboratories.[42] The laboratory should be consulted prospectively about specimen collection and processing. Samples used in diagnosis of botulism include serum (≥30 mL of blood in "tiger"-top or red-top tubes from adults, less from children), stool, gastric aspirate, and, if available, vomitus and suspect foods. Serum samples must be obtained before therapy with antitoxin, which nullifies the diagnostic mouse bioassay. An enema may be required to obtain an adequate fecal sample if the patient is constipated. Sterile water should be used for this procedure because saline enema solution can confound the mouse bioassay. Gastric aspirates and, perhaps, stool may be useful for detecting inhaled aerosolized botulinum toxin released in a bioterrorist attack.[77] A list of the patient's medications should accompany the diagnostic samples because anticholinesterases, such as pyridostigmine bromide, and other medicines that are toxic to mice can be dialyzed from samples before testing. All samples should be kept refrigerated after collection.

The standard laboratory diagnostic test for clinical specimens and foods is the mouse bioassay,[42] in which type-specific antitoxin protects mice against any botulinum toxin present in the sample. The mouse bioassay can detect as little as 0.03 ng of botulinum toxin[10] and usually yields results in 1 to 2 days (range, 6-96 hours). Fecal and gastric specimens also are cultured anaerobically, with results typically available in 7 to 10 days (range, 5-21 days). Toxin production by culture isolates is confirmed by the mouse bioassay.

An electromyogram with repetitive nerve stimulation at 20 to 50 Hz can sometimes distinguish between causes of acute flaccid paralysis.[78,79] The characteristic electromyographic findings of botulism include normal nerve conduction velocity; normal sensory nerve function; a pattern of brief, small-amplitude motor potentials; and, most distinctively, an incremental response (facilitation) to repetitive stimulation often seen only at 50 Hz. Immediate access to electrophysiological studies may be difficult to obtain in an outbreak of botulism.

Additional diagnostic procedures may be useful in rapidly excluding botulism as the cause of paralysis (Table 3). Cerebrospinal fluid (CSF) is unchanged in botulism but is abnormal in many central nervous system diseases. Although the CSF protein level eventually is elevated in Guillain-Barré syndrome, it may be normal early in illness. Imaging of the brain, spine, and chest may reveal hemorrhage, inflammation, or neoplasm. A test dose of edrophonium chloride briefly reverses paralytic symptoms in many patients with myasthenia gravis and, reportedly, in some with botulism.[64] A close inspection of the skin, especially the scalp, may reveal an attached tick that is causing paralysis.[80] Other tests that require days for results include stool culture for *Campylobacter jejuni* as a precipitant of Guillain-Barré syndrome and assays for the autoantibodies that cause myasthenia gravis, Lambert-Eaton syndrome, and Guillain-Barré syndrome.

Foods suspected of being contaminated should be refrigerated until retrieval by public health personnel. The US Food and Drug Administration and the US Department of Agriculture can assist other public health laboratories with testing of suspect foods by using methods similar to those applied to clinical samples.

Therapy

The mortality and sequelae associated with botulism have diminished with contemporary therapy. In the United States, the percentage of persons who died of foodborne botulism decreased from 25% during 1950-1959 to 6% during 1990-1996, with a similar reduction for each botulinum toxin type.[42] Despite this increase in survival, the paralysis of botulism can persist for weeks to months with concurrent requirements for fluid and nutritional support, assisted ventilation, and treatment of complications.

Therapy for botulism consists of supportive care and passive immunization with equine antitoxin. Optimal use of botulinum antitoxin requires early suspicion of botulism. Timely administration of passive neutralizing antibody will minimize subsequent nerve damage and severity of disease but will not reverse existent paralysis.[81, 82] Antitoxin should be given to patients with neurologic signs of botulism as soon as possible after clinical diagnosis.[47] Treatment should not be delayed for microbiological testing. Antitoxin may be withheld at the time of diagnosis if it is certain that the patient is improving from maximal paralysis.

In the United States, botulinum antitoxin is available from the CDC via state and local health departments (Box 2). The components of the formerly licensed trivalent antitoxin that contained neutralizing antibodies against botulinum toxin types A, B, and E (the most common causes of human botulism) have been reformulated into a licensed bivalent (AB) product and an investigational monovalent anti-E product. (See the addendum at end of this chapter.) If another toxin type was intentionally disseminated, patients could potentially be treated with an investigational heptavalent (ABCDEFG) antitoxin held by the US Army.[83] However, the time required for correct toxin typing and subsequent administration of heptavalent antitoxin would decrease the utility of this product in an outbreak.

Since the dose and safety precautions for equine botulinum antitoxin have changed over time, clinicians should review the package insert with public health authorities before using antitoxin. At present, the dose of licensed botulinum antitoxin is a single 10-mL vial per patient, diluted 1:10 in 0.9% saline solution, administered by slow intravenous infusion. One vial provides between 5500 and 8500 IU of each type-specific antitoxin. The amount of neutralizing antibody in both the licensed and the investigational equine antitoxins far exceeds the highest serum toxin levels found in foodborne botulism patients, and additional doses are usually not required. If a patient has been exposed to an unnaturally large amount of botulinum toxin as a biological weapon, the adequacy of neutralization by antitoxin can be confirmed by retesting serum for toxin after treatment.

There are few published data on the safety of botulinum antitoxins. From 1967 to 1977, when the recommended dose was larger than today, approximately 9% of recipients of equine botulinum antitoxin in the United States displayed urticaria, serum sickness, or other reactions suggestive of hypersensitivity.[84] Anaphylaxis occurred within 10 minutes of receiving antitoxin in 2% of recipients. When the US Army's investigational heptavalent antitoxin was given to 50 individuals in a large Egyptian outbreak of type E foodborne botulism in 1991, 1 recipient (2%) displayed serum sickness, and 9 (18%) had mild reactions.[83] To screen for hypersensitivity, patients are given small challenge doses of equine antitoxin before receiving a full dose. Patients responding to challenge with a substantial wheal and flare may be desensitized over 3 to 4 hours before additional antitoxin is given. During the infusion of antitoxin, diphenhydramine and epinephrine should be on hand for rapid administration in case of adverse reaction. Although both equine antitoxins have been partially despeciated by enzymatic cleavage of the allogenic F_c region, each contains a small residual of intact antibody that may sensitize recipients to additional doses. Botulism patients require supportive care that often includes feeding by enteral tube or parenteral nutrition, intensive care, mechanical ventilation, and treatment of secondary infections. Patients with suspected botulism should be closely monitored for impending respiratory failure. In nonventilated infants with botulism, a reverse Trendelenburg positioning with cervical vertebral support has been helpful, but applicability of this positioning to adults with botulism remains untested. This tilted, flat-body positioning with neck support may improve ventilation by reducing entry of oral secretions into the airway and by suspending more of the weight of the abdominal viscera from the diaphragm, thereby improving respiratory excursion (**Figure 4**). In contrast, placing a botulism patient in a supine or semirecumbent position (trunk flexed 45° at the waist) may impede respiratory excursion and airway clearance, especially if the patient is obese. The desired angle of the reverse Trendelenburg position is 20° to 25°.

Botulism patients should be assessed for adequacy of gag and cough reflexes, control of oropharyngeal secretions, oxygen saturation, vital capacity, and inspiratory force. Airway obstruction or aspiration usually precedes hypoventilation in botulism. When respiratory function deteriorates, controlled, anticipatory intubation is indicated. The proportion of patients with botulism who require mechanical ventilation has varied from 20% in a foodborne outbreak[64] to more than 60% in infant botulism.[85] In a large outbreak of botulism, the need for mechanical ventilators, critical care beds, and skilled personnel might quickly exceed local capacity and persist for weeks or months. Development of a reserve stockpile of mechanical ventilators in the United States is under way[86] and will require a complement of staff trained in their use.

Antibiotics have no known direct effect on botulinum toxin. However, secondary infections acquired during botulism often require antibiotic therapy.

Figure 4. Preferred Positioning of Nonventilated Botulism Patients

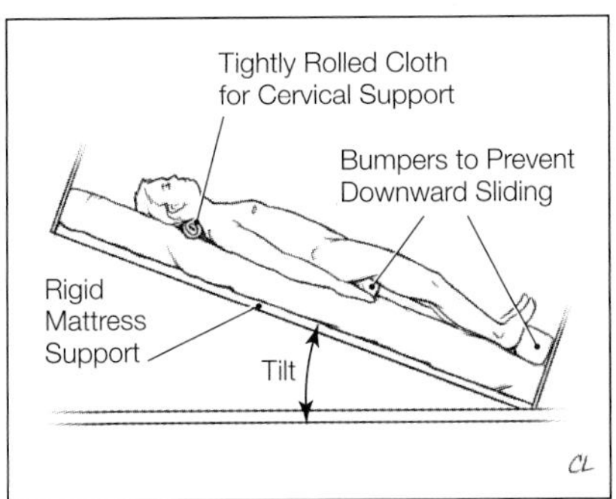

Note flat, rigid mattress tilted at 20°, tightly rolled cloth to support cervical vertebrae, and bumpers to prevent downward sliding. Use of this position may postpone or avoid the need for mechanical ventilation in mildly affected patients because of improved respiratory mechanics and airway protection.

Aminoglycoside antibiotics and clindamycin are contraindicated because of their ability to exacerbate neuromuscular blockade.[87, 88] Standard treatments for detoxification, such as activated charcoal,[89] may be given before antitoxin becomes available, but there are no data regarding their effectiveness in human botulism.

Special Populations

Based on limited information, there is no indication that treatment of children, pregnant women, and immunocompromised persons with botulism should differ from standard therapy. Despite the risks of immediate hypersensitivity and sensitization to equine proteins, both children[43, 90] and pregnant women[91, 92] have received equine antitoxin without apparent short-term adverse effects. The risks to fetuses of exposure to equine antitoxin are unknown. Treatment with human-derived neutralizing antibody would decrease the risk of allergic reactions posed by equine botulinum antitoxin, but use of the investigational product, Botulism Immune Globulin Intravenous (Human) (California Department of Health Services, Berkeley) is limited to suspected cases of infant botulism.[82, 93]

Prophylaxis

Botulism can be prevented by the presence of neutralizing antibody in the bloodstream. Immediate immunity can be provided by passive administration of equine botulinum antitoxin or specific human hyperimmune globulin, while endogenous immunity can be induced by immunization with botulinum toxoid. Use of antitoxin for postexposure prophylaxis is limited by its scarcity and its reactogenicity. Because of the risks of equine antitoxin therapy, it is less certain how best to care for persons who may have been exposed to botulinum toxin but who are not yet ill. In a small study of primates exposed to aerosolized toxin in which supportive care was not provided, all 7 monkeys given antitoxin after exposure but before the appearance of neurologic signs survived, while 2 of 4 monkeys treated with antitoxin only after the appearance of neurologic signs died.[39] Moreover, all monkeys infused with neutralizing antibody before exposure to toxin displayed no signs of botulism. In a balance between avoiding the potential adverse effects of equine antitoxin and needing to rapidly neutralize toxin, it is current practice in foodborne botulism outbreaks to closely monitor persons who may have been exposed to botulinum toxin and to treat them promptly with antitoxin at the first signs of illness.[47] To facilitate distribution of scarce antitoxin following the intentional use of botulinum toxin, asymptomatic persons who are believed to have been exposed should remain under close medical observation and, if feasible, near critical care services.

In the United States, an investigational pentavalent (ABCDE) botulinum toxoid is distributed by the CDC for laboratory workers at high risk of exposure to botulinum toxin and by the military for protection of troops against attack.[94] A recombinant vaccine is also in development.[95] The pentavalent toxoid has been used for more than 30 years to immunize more than 3000 laboratory workers in many countries. Immunization of the population with botulinum toxoid could in theory eliminate the hazard posed by botulinum toxins A through E. However, mass immunization is neither feasible nor desirable for reasons that include scarcity of the toxoid, rarity of natural disease, and elimination of the potential therapeutic benefits of medicinal botulinum toxin. Accordingly, preexposure immunization currently is neither recommended for nor available to the general population. Botulinum toxoid induces immunity over several months and, so, is ineffective as postexposure prophylaxis.

Decontamination

Despite its extreme potency, botulinum toxin is easily destroyed. Heating to an internal temperature of 85°C for at least 5 minutes will detoxify contaminated food or drink.[52] All foods suspected of contamination should be promptly removed from potential consumers and submitted to public health authorities for testing.

Persistence of aerosolized botulinum toxin at a site of deliberate release is determined by atmospheric conditions and the particle size of the aerosol. Extremes of temperature and humidity will degrade the toxin, while fine aerosols will eventually dissipate into the atmosphere. Depending on the weather, aerosolized toxin has been estimated to decay at between less than 1% to 4% per minute.[96] At a decay rate of 1% per minute, substantial inactivation (≥13 logs) of toxin occurs by 2 days after aerosolization.

Recognition of a covert release of finely aerosolized botulinum toxin would probably occur too late to prevent additional exposures. When exposure is anticipated, some protection may be conferred by covering the mouth and nose with clothing such as an undershirt, shirt, scarf, or handkerchief.[97] In contrast with mucosal surfaces, intact skin is impermeable to botulinum toxin.

After exposure to botulinum toxin, clothing and skin should be washed with soap and water.[98] Contaminated objects or surfaces should be cleaned with 0.1% hypochlorite bleach solution if they cannot be avoided for the hours to days required for natural degradation.[33, 52, 98]

Infection Control

Medical personnel caring for patients with suspected botulism should use standard precautions. Patients with suspected botulism do not need to be isolated, but those with flaccid paralysis from suspected meningitis require droplet precautions.

Research Needs

Additional research in diagnosis and treatment of botulism is required to minimize its threat as a weapon. Rapid diagnostic and toxin typing techniques currently under development would be useful for recognizing and responding to a bioterrorist attack. Although polymerase chain reaction assays can detect the botulinum toxin gene,[99] they are unable, as yet, to determine whether the toxin gene is expressed and whether the expressed protein is indeed toxic. Assays that exploit the enzymatic activity of botulinum toxin have the potential to supplant the mouse bioassay as the standard for diagnosis.[100] Detection of botulinum toxin in aerosols by enzyme-linked immunosorbent assay[101] is a component of the US military's Biological Integrated Detection System for rapid recognition of biological agents in the battlefield.[17]

The distribution of botulinum antitoxin to local hospitals from regional depots takes several hours. In contrast, standard detoxification techniques can be applied immediately. Studies are needed to assess whether activated charcoal and osmotic catharsis can prevent gastrointestinal tract absorption or reduce circulating levels of botulinum toxin. Enteral detoxification may be less useful in inhalational botulism than in foodborne disease.

The competing needs for immunity to weaponized botulinum toxin and for susceptibility to medicinal botulinum toxin could be reconciled by supplying human antibody that neutralizes toxin. With a half-life of approximately 1 month,[102] human antibody would provide immediate immunity for long periods and would avoid the reactogenicity of equine products. Existing in vitro technologies could produce the stockpiles of fully human antibody necessary both to deter terrorist attacks and to avoid the rationing of antitoxin that currently would be required in a large outbreak of botulism.[103-106] A single small injection of oligoclonal human antibodies could, in theory, provide protection against toxins A through G for many months. Until such a product becomes available, the possibilities for reducing the population's vulnerability to the intentional misuse of botulinum toxin remain limited.

Addendum

Since publication of the original statement, information pertinent to the following topics has appeared:

1. Production of monoclonal antibodies that neutralize botulinum toxin.
Two recent publications describe potent recombinant human and murine monoclonal antibodies that neutralize type A botulinum toxin, which were made by using phage display technology. A combination of three human-compatible monoclonal antibodies that bind to heavy-chain epitopes neutralized 4×10^5 mouse LD_{50}s of toxin (Marks JD et al, submitted for publication). In a separate investigation a single murine antibody that bound to a heavy-chain epitope neutralized 10^4 mouse LD_{50}s, while another single murine antibody that bound to a light-chain epitope neutralized 10^3 mouse LD_{50}s.[107] The development of these recombinant antibodies establishes the "proof of concept" needed to make a supply of high-potency, fully human heptavalent (A-G) botulinum antitoxin sufficient to defend both civilian and military populations.[108] However, before beginning large-scale production of a recombinant human heptavalent antitoxin, the most efficacious neutralizing epitopes on both toxin heavy and light chains need to be established.

2. Changes in the availability of licensed equine botulinum antitoxin.
The use of equine antitoxin to treat the common types of human botulism has become more complicated because of a change in its formulation. The components of the former trivalent (ABE) licensed antitoxin mixture have been reformulated into a licensed bivalent (AB) product and an investigational monovalent anti-E product. Efforts to license the anti-E antitoxin are under way. Both antitoxin products may be given to cases when type E botulinum toxin is suspected but test results are pending. The US government also maintains limited stocks of an investigational equine heptavalent (A-G) antitoxin product for use in emergency situations.

3. Economic impact of an aerosolized botulinum toxin attack on a civilian population in Canada.
The cost of such an attack on a suburban population with aerosolized botulinum toxin was conservatively calculated to be \$8.6 billion (Canadian) per 100 000 persons exposed[109]. This figure computes to \$86 000 (Canadian) per person exposed, or equivalently, to \$57 000 (US) per person exposed and \$114 000 per person ill. The model that produced these figures used the following assumptions: 100 000 persons were exposed for 2 hours, half of whom became paralyzed. The case-fatality ratio was 60% in patients who could not be provided with both antitoxin and mechanical ventilation and was 30% in patients who could be provided with both. At 48 hours a supply of ventilators and antitoxin adequate for all patients surviving to that point had become available.[109] Although the case-fatality ratios used in this analysis are higher than recent US experience,[108] their use probably resulted in a lower overall cost estimate because fewer patients would have survived to need prolonged mechanical ventilation and intensive care hospitalization.

4. Unusual modes of dissemination.

The transmission of weaponized anthrax spores via letters in the US postal system in September and October 2001 demonstrates that terrorists may utilize unconventional methods or vehicles to spread a bioweapon such as botulinum toxin. In addition, more than one agent may be released at the same time or in the same vehicle. This possibility underscores the need for new rapid diagnostic assays. When confronted with epidemiologically or clinically perplexing situations, medical and public health personnel should consider atypical routes and vehicles of dissemination of one or more bioweapon agents.

Ex Officio Participants in the Working Group on Civilian Biodefense: George Counts, MD, National Institutes of Health; Margaret Hamburg, MD, and Stuart Nightingale, MD, Office of Assistant Secretary for Planning and Evaluation; Robert Knouss, MD, Office of Emergency Preparedness; and Brian Malkin, US Food and Drug Administration.

Funding/Support: Funding for this study primarily was provided by each participant's institution or agency. The Johns Hopkins Center for Civilian Biodefense Studies provided travel funds for 6 members of the group.

Disclaimers: In some instances, the indications, dosages, and other information in this article are not consistent with current approved labeling by the US Food and Drug Administration (FDA). The recommendations on use of drugs and vaccine for uses not approved by the FDA do not represent the official views of the FDA nor of any of the federal agencies whose scientists participated in these discussions. Unlabeled uses of the products recommended are noted in the sections of this article in which these products are discussed. Where unlabeled uses are indicated, information used as the basis for the recommendation is discussed.

The views, opinions, assertions, and findings contained herein are those of the authors and should not be construed as official US Department of Defense or US Department of Army positions, policies, or decisions unless so designated by other documentation.

Acknowledgments: The working group wishes to thank Christopher Davis, OBE, MD, PhD, for his participation in the consensus process; David Franz, DVM, PhD, for helpful information; Ellen Doyle, MPH, for epidemiological assistance; the reference librarians at the School of Public Health, University of California, Berkeley, for many years of superb help; and Molly D'Esopo, for administrative support.

References

1. Inglesby TV, Henderson DA, Bartlett JG, et al, for the Working Group on Civilian Biodefense. Anthrax as a biological weapon: medical and public health management. *JAMA.* 1999;281:1735-1745.
2. Henderson DA, Inglesby TV, Bartlett JG, et al, for the Working Group on Civilian Biodefense. Smallpox as a biological weapon: medical and public health management. *JAMA.* 1999;281:2127-2137.
3. Inglesby TV, Henderson DA, Bartlett JG, et al, for the Working Group on Civilian Biodefense. Plague as a biological weapon: medical and public health management. *JAMA.* 2000;283:2281-2290.
4. Biological and chemical terrorism: strategic plan for preparedness and response: recommendations of the CDC Strategic Planning Workgroup. *MMWR Morb Mortal Wkly Rep.* 2000;49(RR-4):1-14.

5. Franz DR, Jahrling PB, Friedlander AM, et al. Clinical recognition and management of patients exposed to biological warfare agents. *JAMA.* 1997;278:399-411.

6. Gill MD. Bacterial toxins: a table of lethal amounts. *Microbiol Rev.* 1982;46:86-94.

7. National Institute of Occupational Safety and Health. *Registry of Toxic Effects of Chemical Substances (R-TECS).* Cincinnati, Ohio: National Institute of Occupational Safety and Health; 1996.

8. Montecucco C, ed. Clostridial neurotoxins: the molecular pathogenesis of tetanus and botulism. *Curr Top Microbiol Immunol.* 1995;195:1-278.

9. Scott AB. Botulinum toxin injection into extraocular muscles as an alternative to strabismus surgery. *J Pediatr Ophthalmol Strabismus.* 1980;17:21-25.

10. Schantz EJ, Johnson EA. Properties and use of botulinum toxin and other microbial neurotoxins in medicine. *Microbiol Rev.* 1992;56:80-99.

11. Jankovic J, Hallet M, eds. *Therapy With Botulinum Toxin.* New York, NY: Marcel Dekker Inc; 1994.

12. Silberstein S, Mathew N, Saper J, Jenkins S, for the Botox Migraine Clinical Research Group. Botulinum toxin type A as a migraine preventive treatment. *Headache.* 2000;40:445-450.

13. Foster L, Clapp L, Erickson M, Jabbari B. Botulinum toxin A and mechanical low back pain [abstract]. *Neurology.* 2000;54(suppl 3):A178.

14. Tucker JB, ed. *Toxic Terror: Assessing the Terrorist Use of Chemical and Biological Weapons.* Cambridge, Mass: MIT Press; 2000.

15. WuDunn S, Miller J, Broad WJ. How Japan germ terror alerted world. *New York Times.* May 26, 1998:A1, A10.

16. Geissler E, Moon JE, eds. *Biological and Toxin Weapons: Research, Development and Use From the Middle Ages to 1945.* New York, NY: Oxford University Press; 1999. Sipri Chemical & Biological Warfare Studies No. 18.

17. Smart JK. History of chemical and biological warfare: an American perspective. In: Sidell FR, Takafuji ET, Franz DR, eds. *Medical Aspects of Chemical and Biological Warfare.* Washington, DC: Office of the Surgeon General; 1997:9-86. *Textbook of Military Medicine*; part I, vol 3.

18. Hill EV. Botulism. In: *Summary Report on B. W. Investigations.* Memorandum to Alden C. Waitt, Chief Chemical Corps, United States Army, December 12, 1947; tab D. Archived at the US Library of Congress.

19. Cochrane RC. *History of the Chemical Warfare Service in World War II (1 July 1940-15 August 1945).* Historical Section, Plans, Training and Intelligence Division, Office of Chief, Chemical Corps, United States Army; November 1947. *Biological Warfare Research in the United States*; vol II. Archived at the US Army Medical Research Institute of Infectious Diseases, Fort Detrick, Md.

20. Bryden J. *Deadly Allies: Canada's Secret War, 1937-1947.* Toronto, Ontario: McClelland & Stewart; 1989.

21. Holzer VE. Botulism from inhalation [in German]. *Med Klin.* 1962;57:1735-1738.

22. United Nations Security Council. *Tenth Report of the Executive Chairman of the Special Commission Established by the Secretary-General Pursuant to Paragraph 9(b)(I) of Security Council Resolution 687 (1991), and Paragraph 3 of Resolution 699 (1991) on the Activities of the Special Commission.* New York, NY: United Nations Security Council; 1995. S/1995/1038.

23. Bozheyeva G, Kunakbayev Y, Yeleukenov D. *Former Soviet Biological Weapons Facilities in Kazakhstan: Past, Present and Future.* Monterey, Calif: Center for Nonproliferation Studies, Monterey Institute of International Studies; June 1999:1-20. Occasional paper No. 1.

24. Miller J. At bleak Asian site, killer germs survive. *New York Times.* June 2, 1999:A1, A10.

25. Alibek K, Handleman S. *Biohazard.* New York, NY: Random House; 1999.

26. Smithson AE. *Toxic Archipelago: Preventing Proliferation From the Former Soviet Chemical and Biological Weapons Complexes.* Washington, DC: The Henry L. Stimson Center; December 1999:7-21. Report No. 32. Available at: http://www.stimson.org/pubs.cfm?ID=27.

27. United States Department of State. *Patterns of Global Terrorism 1999.* Washington, DC: US Dept of State; April 2000. Department of State publication 10687. Available at: http://www.state.gov/www/global/terrorism/1999report/1999index.html.

28. Cordesman AH. *Weapons of Mass Destruction in the Gulf and Greater Middle East: Force Trends, Strategy, Tactics and Damage Effects.* Washington, DC: Center for Strategic and International Studies; November 9, 1998:18-52.

29. Bermudez JS. *The Armed Forces of North Korea.* London, England: IB Tauris; 2001.

30. Zilinskas RA. Iraq's biological weapons: the past as future? *JAMA.* 1997;278:418-424.

31. Hooper RR. The covert use of chemical and biological warfare against United States strategic forces. *Mil Med.* 1983;148:901-902.

32. Shapiro RL, Hatheway C, Becher J, Swerdlow DL. Botulism surveillance and emergency response: a public health strategy for a global challenge. *JAMA.* 1997;278:433-435.

33. Smith LDS. *Botulism: The Organism, Its Toxins, the Disease.* Springfield, Ill: Charles C. Thomas Publisher; 1977.

34. Hatheway CL, Johnson EA. *Clostridium*: the spore-bearing anaerobes. In: Collier L, Balows A, Sussman M, eds. *Topley & Wilson's Microbiology and Microbial Infections.* 9th ed. New York, NY: Oxford University Press; 1998:731-782.

35. Hall JD, McCroskey LM, Pincomb BJ, Hatheway CL. Isolation of an organism resembling *Clostridium baratii* which produces type F botulinal toxin from an infant with botulism. *J Clin Microbiol.* 1985;21:654-655.

36. Aureli P, Fenicia L, Pasolini B, Gianfranceschi M, McCroskey LM, Hatheway CL. Two cases of type E infant botulism caused by neurotoxigenic *Clostridium butyricum* in Italy. *J Infect Dis.* 1986;154: 207-211.

37. Arnon SS. Botulism as an intestinal toxemia. In: Blaser MJ, Smith PD, Ravdin JI, Greenberg HB, Guerrant RL, eds. *Infections of the Gastrointestinal Tract.* New York, NY: Raven Press; 1995:257-271.

38. Lacy DB, Tepp W, Cohen AC, DasGupta BR, Stevens RC. Crystal structure of botulinum neurotoxin type A and implications for toxicity. *Nat Struct Biol.* 1998;5:898-902.

39. Franz DR, Pitt LM, Clayton MA, Hanes MA, Rose KJ. Efficacy of prophylactic and therapeutic administration of antitoxin for inhalation botulism. In: DasGupta BR, ed. *Botulinum and Tetanus Neurotoxins: Neurotransmission and Biomedical Aspects.* New York, NY: Plenum Press; 1993:473-476.

40. Herrero BA, Ecklung AE, Streett CS, Ford DF, King JK. Experimental botulism in monkeys: a clinical pathological study. *Exp Mol Pathol.* 1967;6:84-95.

41. Scott AB, Suzuki D. Systemic toxicity of botulinum toxin by intramuscular injection in the monkey. *Mov Disord.* 1988;3:333-335.

42. Centers for Disease Control and Prevention. *Botulism in the United States 1899-1996: Handbook for Epidemiologists, Clinicians, and Laboratory Workers.* Atlanta, Ga: Centers for Disease Control and Prevention; 1998. Available at: http://www.cdc.gov/ncidod/dbmd/diseaseinfo/botulism.pdf.

43. Weber JT, Goodpasture HC, Alexander H, Werner SB, Hatheway CL, Tauxe RV. Wound botulism in a patient with a tooth abscess: case report and literature review. *Clin Infect Dis.* 1993;16:635-639.

44. Hughes JM, Blumenthal JR, Merson MH, Lombard GL, Dowell VR Jr, Gangarosa EJ. Clinical features of types A and B food-borne botulism. *Ann Intern Med.* 1981;95:442-445.

45. Duchen LW. Motor nerve growth induced by botulinum toxin as a regenerative phenomenon. *Proc R Soc Med.* 1972;65:196-197.

46. Mann JM, Martin S, Hoffman R, Marrazzo S. Patient recovery from type A botulism: morbidity assessment following a large outbreak. *Am J Public Health.* 1981;71:266-269.

47. Shapiro RL, Hatheway C, Swerdlow DL. Botulism in the United States: a clinical and epidemiologic review. *Ann Intern Med.* 1998;129:221-228.

48. Middlebrook JL, Franz DR. Botulinum toxins. In: Sidell FR, Takafuji ET, Franz DR, eds. *Medical Aspects of Chemical and Biological Warfare.* Washington, DC: Office of the Surgeon General; 1997: 643-654. *Textbook of Military Medicine*; part I, vol 3.

49. Gangarosa EJ, Donadio JA, Armstrong RW, Meyer KF, Brachman PH, Dowell VR. Botulism in the United States, 1899-1969. *Am J Epidemiol.* 1971;93:93-101.

50. Hauschild AH. Epidemiology of human foodborne botulism. In: Hauschild AH , Dodds KL, eds. *Clostridium botulinum: Ecology and Control in Foods.* New York, NY: Marcel Dekker Inc; 1993:69-104.

51. Wannemacher RW Jr, Dinterman RE, Thompson WL, Schmidt MO, Burrows WD. Treatment for removal of biotoxins from drinking water. Frederick, Md: US Army Biomedical Research and Development Command; September 1993. Technical Report 9120.

52. Siegel LS. Destruction of botulinum toxin in food and water. In: Hauschild AH, Dodds KL, eds. *Clostridium botulinum: Ecology and Control in Foods.* New York, NY: Marcel Dekker Inc; 1993:323-341.

53. Burrows WD, Renner SE. Biological warfare agents as threats to potable water. *Environ Health Perspect.* 1999;107:975-984.

54. Kazdobina IS. Stability of botulin toxins in solutions and beverages [in Russian with English abstract]. *Gig Sanit.* January-February 1995:9-12.

55. Koenig MG, Drutz D, Mushlin AI, Schaffer W, Rogers DE. Type B botulism in man. *Am J Med.* 1967;42:208-219.

56. Geiger JC, Dickson EC, Meyer KF. *The Epidemiology of Botulism.* Washington, DC: US Government Printing Office; 1922. Public Health Bulletin 127.

57. Terranova W, Breman JG, Locey RP, Speck S. Botulism type B: epidemiological aspects of an extensive outbreak. *Am J Epidemiol.* 1978;108:150-156.

58. Meyer KF, Eddie B. *Sixty-Five Years of Human Botulism in the United States and Canada: Epidemiology and Tabulations of Reported Cases 1899 Through 1964.* San Francisco, Calif: G. W. Hooper Foundation and University of California San Francisco; 1965.

59. Angulo FJ, Getz J, Taylor JP, et al. A large outbreak of botulism: the hazardous baked potato. *J Infect Dis.* 1998;178:172-177.

60. MacDonald KL, Cohen ML, Blake PA. The changing epidemiology of adult botulism in the United States. *Am J Epidemiol.* 1986;124:794-799.

61. Mann JM, Hatheway CL, Gardiner TM. Laboratory diagnosis in a large outbreak of type A botulism: confirmation of the value of coproexamination. *Am J Epidemiol.* 1982;115:598-695.

62. Seals JE, Snyder JD, Kedell TA, Restaurant-associated type A botulism: transmission by potato salad. *Am J Epidemiol.* 1981;113:436-444.

63. MacDonald KL, Spengler RF, Hatheway CL, Hargrett NT, Cohen ML. Type A botulism from sauteed onions: clinical and epidemiological observations. *JAMA.* 1985;253:1275-1278.

64. St Louis ME, Peck SH, Bowering D et al. Botulism from chopped garlic: delayed recognition of a major outbreak. *Ann Intern Med.* 1988;108:363-368.

65. Townes JM, Cieslak PR, Hatheway CL, An outbreak of type A botulism associated with a commercial cheese sauce. *Ann Intern Med.* 1996;125:558-563.

66. Telzak EE, Bell EP, Kautter DA. An international outbreak of type E botulism due to uneviscerated fish. *J Infect Dis.* 1990;161:340-342.

67. O'Mahony M, Mitchell E, Gilbert RJ, et al. An outbreak of foodborne botulism associated with contaminated hazelnut yoghurt. *Epidemiol Infect.* 1990;104:389-395.

68. Aureli P, Franciosa G, Pourshaban M. Foodborne botulism in Italy. *Lancet.* 1996;348:1594.

69. Chou JH, Hwant PH, Malison MD. An outbreak of type A foodborne botulism in Taiwan due to commercially preserved peanuts. *Int J Epidemiol.* 1988;17:899-902.

70. Midura TF, Nygaard GS, Wood RM, Bodily HL. *Clostridium botulinum* type F: isolation from venison jerky. *Appl Microbiol.* 1972;24:165-167.

71. McCroskey LM, Hatheway CL, Woodruff BA, Greenberg JA, Jurgenson P. Type F botulism due to neurotoxigenic *Clostridium baratii* from an unknown source in an adult. *J Clin Microbiol.* 1991;29:2618-2620.

72. Gunnison JB, Meyer KF. Susceptibility of monkeys, goats and small animals to oral administration of botulinum toxin types B, C and D. *J Infect Dis.* 1930;46:335-340.

73. Dolman CE, Murakami L. *Clostridium botulinum* type F with recent observations on other types. *J Infect Dis.* 1961;109:107-128.

74. Smart JL, Roberts TA, McCullagh KG, Lucke VM, Pearson H. An outbreak of type C botulism in captive monkeys. *Vet Rec.* 1980;107:445-446.

75. Giménez DF, Ciccarelli AS. Another type of *Clostridium botulinum. Zentralbl Bakteriol [Orig].* 1970;215:221-224.

76. Beller M, Gessner B, Wainwright R, Barrett DH. *Botulism in Alaska: A Guide for Physicians and Health Care Providers.* Anchorage: State of Alaska, Dept of Health and Social Services, Division of Public Health, Section of Epidemiology; 1993.

77. Woodruff BA, Griffin PM, McCroskey LM, et al. Clinical and laboratory comparison of botulism from toxin types A, B, and E in the United States, 1975-1988. *J Infect Dis.* 1992;166:1281-1286.

78. Maselli RA, Bakshi N, American Association of Electrodiagnostic Medicine case report 16: botulism. *Muscle Nerve.* 2000;23:1137-1144.

79. Cherington M. Clinical spectrum of botulism. *Muscle Nerve.* 1998;21:701-710.

80. Felz MW, Smith CD, Swift TR. A six-year-old girl with tick paralysis. *N Engl J Med.* 2000;342:90-94.

81. Tacket CO, Shandera WX, Mann JM, Hargrett NT, Blake PA. Equine antitoxin use and other factors that predict outcome in type A foodborne botulism. *Am J Med.* 1984;76:794-798.

82. Arnon SS. Infant botulism. In: Feigin RD, Cherry JD, eds. *Textbook of Pediatric Infectious Diseases.* 4th ed. Philadelphia, Pa: WB Saunders Co; 1998: 1570-1577.

83. Hibbs RG, Weber JT, Corwin A, et al. Experience with the use of an investigational $F(ab')_2$ heptavalent botulism immune globulin of equine origin during an outbreak of type E botulism in Egypt. *Clin Infect Dis.* 1996;23:337-340.

84. Black RE, Gunn RA. Hypersensitivity reactions associated with botulinal antitoxin. *Am J Med.* 1980;69:567-570.

85. Schreiner MS, Field E, Ruddy R. Infant botulism: a review of 12 years' experience at the Children's Hospital of Philadelphia. *Pediatrics.* 1991;87: 159-165.

86. Kahn AS, Morse S, Lillibridge S. Public-health preparedness for biological terrorism in the USA. *Lancet.* 2000;356:1179-1182.

87. Santos JI, Swensen P, Glasgow LA. Potentiation of *Clostridium botulinum* toxin by aminoglycoside antibiotics: clinical and laboratory observations. *Pediatrics.* 1981;68:50-54.

88. Schulze J, Toepfer M, Schroff KC, et al. Clindamycin and nicotinic neuromuscular transmission. *Lancet.* 1999;354:1792-1793.

89. Olson KR ed. *Poisoning and Drug Overdose.* 3rd ed. Stamford, Conn: Appleton & Lange; 1999.

90. Keller MA, Miller VH, Berkowitz CD, Yoshimori RN. Wound botulism in pediatrics. *Am J Dis Child.* 1982;136:320-322.

91. Robin L, Herman D, Redett R. Botulism in a pregnant woman. *N Engl J Med.* 1996;335:823-824.

92. St Clair EH, DiLiberti JH, O'Brien ML. Observations of an infant born to a mother with botulism. *J Pediatr.* 1975;87:658.

93. Arnon SS. Clinical trial of human botulism immune globulin. In: DasGupta BR, ed. *Botulinum and Tetanus Neurotoxins: Neurotransmission and Biomedical Aspects.* New York, NY: Plenum Press; 1993:477-482.

94. Siegel LS. Human immune response to botulinum pentavalent (ABCDE) toxoid determined by a neutralization test and by an enzyme-linked immunosorbent assay. *J Clin Microbiol.* 1988;26: 2351-2356.

95. Byrne MP, Smith LA. Development of vaccines for prevention of botulism. *Biochimie.* 2000;82: 955-966.

96. Dorsey EL, Beebe M, Johns EE. Responses of air-borne *Clostridium botulinum* toxin to certain atmospheric stresses. Frederick, Md: US Army Biological Laboratories; October 1964. Technical Memorandum 62.

97. Wiener SL. Strategies for the prevention of a successful biological warfare aerosol attack. *Mil Med.* 1996;161:251-256.

98. Franz DR. *Defense Against Toxin Weapons.* Fort Detrick, Md: US Army Medical Research Institute of Infectious Diseases; 1997.

99. Franciosa G, Ferreira JL, Hatheway CL. Detection of type A, B, and E botulism neurotoxin genes in *Clostridium botulinum* and other *Clostridium* species by PCR: evidence of unexpressed type B toxin genes in type A toxigenic organisms. *J Clin Microbiol.* 1994;32:1911-1917.

100. Wictome M, Newton K, Jameson K, et al. Development of an in vitro bioassay for *Clostridium botulinum* type B neurotoxin in foods that is more sensitive than the mouse bioassay. *Appl Environ Microbiol.* 1999;65:3787-3792.

101. Dezfulian M, Bartlett JG. Detection of *Clostridium botulinum* type A toxin by enzyme-linked immunosorbent assay with antibodies produced in immunologically tolerant animals. *J Clin Microbiol.* 1984;19:645-648.

102. Sarvas H, Seppala I, Kurikka S, Siegberg R, Makela O. Half-life of the maternal IgG1 allotype in infants. *J Clin Immunol.* 1993;13:145-151.

103. Amersdorfer P, Marks JD. Phage libraries for generation of anti-botulinum scFv antibodies. *Methods Mol Biol.* 2000;145:219-240.

104. Green LL, Hardy MC, Maynard-Currie CE, et al. Antigen-specific human monoclonal antibodies from mice engineered with human Ig heavy and light chain YACs. *Nat Genet.* 1994;7:13-21.

105. Bavari S, Pless DD, Torres ER, Lebeda FJ, Olson MA. Identifying the principal protective antigenic determinants of type A botulinum neurotoxin. *Vaccine.* 1998;16:1850-1856.

106. Marks C, Marks JD. Phage libraries: a new route to clinically useful antibodies. *N Engl J Med.* 1996;335:730-733.

107. Wu H-C, Yeh C-T, Huang Y-L, Tarn L-J, Lung C-C. Characterization of neutralizing antibodies and identification of neutralizing epitope mimics on the *Clostridium botulinum* neurotoxin type A. *Appl Environ Microbiol.* 2001;67:3201-3207.

108. Arnon SS, Schechter R, Inglesby TV et al. Botulinum toxin as a bioweapon: medical and public health management. *JAMA.* 2001;285:1059-1070.

109. St. John R, Finlay B, Blair C. Bioterrorism in Canada: an economic assessment of prevention and postattack response. *Can J Infect Dis.* 2001;12:275-284.

Tularemia as a Biological Weapon

David T. Dennis, MD, MPH; Thomas V. Inglesby, MD; Donald A. Henderson, MD, MPH; John G. Bartlett, MD; Michael S. Ascher, MD, FACLP; Edward Eitzen, Jr, MD, MPH; Anne D. Fine, MD; Arthur M. Friedlander, MD; Jerome Hauer, MPH; Marcelle Layton, MD; Scott Lillibridge, MD; Joseph McDade, PhD; Michael T. Osterholm, PhD, MPH; Tara O'Toole, MD, MPH; Gerald Parker, PhD, DVM; Trish M. Perl, MD, MSc; Philip K. Russell, MD; Kevin Tonat, DrPH, MPH; for the Working Group on Civilian Biodefense

Reviewed and updated by David T. Dennis for the Working Group on Civilian Biodefense

I know of no other infection of animals communicable to man that can be acquired from sources so numerous and so diverse. In short, one can but feel that the status of tularemia, both as a disease in nature and of man, is one of potentiality. —*R.R. Parker*[1]

Tularemia, a bacterial zoonosis, is the subject of this fifth article in a series providing recommendations for medical and public health management following use of various agents as biological weapons of terrorism.[2-5] The causative agent of tularemia, *Francisella tularensis*, is one of the most infectious pathogenic bacteria known, requiring inoculation or inhalation of as few as 10 organisms to cause disease.[6,7] Humans become incidentally infected through diverse environmental exposures and can develop severe and sometimes fatal illness but do not transmit infection to others. The Working Group on Civilian Biodefense considers *F tularensis* to be a dangerous potential biological weapon because of its extreme infectivity, ease of dissemination, and substantial capacity to cause illness and death.[8-11]

Consensus Methods

For this article, the working group comprised 25 representatives from academic medical centers, civilian and military governmental agencies, and other public health and emergency management institutions. This group followed a specified process in developing a consensus statement. MEDLINE databases from January 1966 to October 2000 were searched using the Medical Subject Headings *Francisella tularensis*, *Pasteurella tularensis*, *biological weapon*, *biological terrorism*, *bioterrorism*, *biological warfare*, and *biowarfare*. Review of the bibliographies of these references led to identification of relevant materials published prior to 1966. In addition, participants identified other published and unpublished references and sources for review.

The first draft of the consensus statement was a synthesis of information obtained in the formal evidence-gathering process. Members of the working group were asked to make written comments on this first draft in May 1999. Subsequent revised drafts were reviewed and edited until full consensus of the working group was achieved.

History and Potential as a Biological Weapon

Tularemia was first described as a plague-like disease of rodents in 1911 and, shortly thereafter, was recognized as a potentially severe and fatal illness in humans.[12] Tularemia's epidemic potential became apparent in the 1930s and 1940s, when large waterborne outbreaks occurred in Europe and the Soviet Union[13-15] and epizootic-associated cases occurred in the United States.[16, 17] As well, *F tularensis* quickly gained notoriety as a virulent laboratory hazard.[18, 19] Public health concerns impelled substantial early investigations into tularemia's ecology, microbiology, pathogenicity, and prevention.[19-22]

Francisella tularensis has long been considered a potential biological weapon. It was one of a number of agents studied at Japanese germ warfare research units operating in Manchuria between 1932 and 1945[23]; it was also examined for military purposes in the West. A former Soviet Union biological weapons scientist, Ken Alibeck, has suggested that tularemia outbreaks affecting tens of thousands of Soviet and German soldiers on the eastern European front during World War II may have been the result of intentional use.[24] Following the war, there were continuing military studies of tularemia. In the 1950s and 1960s, the US military developed weapons that would disseminate *F tularensis* aerosols[10]; concurrently, it conducted research to better understand the pathophysiology of tularemia and to develop vaccines and antibiotic prophylaxis and treatment regimens. In some studies, volunteers were infected with *F tularensis* by direct aerosol delivery systems and by exposures in an aerosol chamber.[10] A live attenuated vaccine was developed that partially protected against respiratory and intracutaneous challenges with the virulent SCHU S-4 strain of *F tularensis*,[6, 7] and various regimens of streptomycin, tetracyclines, and chloramphenicol were found to be effective in prophylaxis and treatment.[25-27] By the late 1960s, *F tularensis* was one of several biological weapons stockpiled by the US military.[10] According to Alibeck, a large parallel effort by the Soviet Union continued into the early 1990s and resulted in weapons production of *F tularensis* strains engineered to be resistant to antibiotics and vaccines.[24]

In 1969, a World Health Organization expert committee estimated that an aerosol dispersal of 50 kg of virulent *F tularensis* over a metropolitan area with 5 million inhabitants would result in 250 000 incapacitating casualties, including 19 000 deaths.[28] Illness would be expected to persist for several weeks and disease relapses to occur during the ensuing weeks or months. It was assumed that vaccinated individuals would be only partially protected against an aerosol exposure. Referring to this model, the Centers for Disease Control and Prevention (CDC) examined the expected economic impact of bioterrorist attacks and estimated the total base costs to society of an *F tularensis* aerosol attack to be $5.4 billion for every 100 000 persons exposed.[9]

The United States terminated its biological weapons development program by executive order in 1970 and, by 1973, had destroyed its entire biological arsenal.[10] Since then, the US Army Medical Research Institute of Infectious Diseases has been responsible for defensive medical research on *F tularensis* and other potential biological warfare agents to better protect the US military, including protocols on decontamination, prophylaxis, clinical recognition, laboratory diagnosis, and medical management.[29] The CDC operates a national program for bioterrorism preparedness and response that incorporates a broad range of public health partnerships.[30, 31]

Epidemiology

Geographic Distribution and Human Exposures

Tularemia occurs throughout much of North America and Eurasia.[15, 21, 22, 32] In the United States, human cases have been reported from every state except Hawaii; however, most cases occur in south-central and western states (especially Missouri, Arkansas, Oklahoma, South Dakota, and Montana).[33-35] In Eurasia, the disease is also widely endemic, although the greatest numbers of human cases are reported from northern and central Europe, especially Scandinavian countries and those of the former Soviet Union.[36, 37] Tularemia is almost entirely a rural disease, although urban and suburban exposures occasionally do occur.[38-41]

Throughout its range, *F tularensis* is found in widely diverse animal hosts and habitats and can be recovered from contaminated water, soil, and vegetation.[15, 20-22, 32] A variety of small mammals, including voles, mice, water rats, squirrels, rabbits, and hares, are natural reservoirs of infection. They acquire infection through bites by ticks, flies, and mosquitoes, and by contact with contaminated environments. Although enzootic cycles of *F tularensis* typically occur without notice, epizootics with sometimes extensive die-offs of animal hosts may herald outbreaks of tularemia in humans.[16, 22, 42, 43] Humans become infected with *F tularensis* by various modes, including bites by infective arthropods,[42, 44-47] handling infectious animal tissues or fluids,[17, 48, 49] direct contact with or ingestion of contaminated water, food, or soil,[13, 20, 40, 50, 51] and inhalation of infective aerosols.[43, 52-56] Persons of all ages and both sexes appear to be equally susceptible to tularemia. Certain activities, such as hunting, trapping, butchering, and farming, are most likely to expose adult men. Laboratory workers are especially vulnerable to infection, either by accidentally inoculating themselves or by inhaling aerosolized organisms.[18, 22, 56-58] Ordinary exposures during examination of an open culture plate can cause infection. Although *F tularensis* is highly infectious and pathogenic, its transmission from person to person has not been documented.

Incidence

The worldwide incidence of tularemia is not known, and the disease is probably greatly underrecognized and underreported. In the United States, reported cases have dropped sharply from several thousand per year prior to 1950 to less than

200 per year in the 1990s.[33-35] Between 1985 and 1992, 1409 cases and 20 deaths were reported in the United States, for a mean of 171 cases per year and a case-fatality rate of 1.4%.[34] Persons in all age groups were affected, but most were children younger than 10 years and adults aged 50 years or older. Of 1298 cases for which information on sex was available, 942 (72.6%) occurred in males, and males outnumbered females in all age groups. Most cases occur in June through September, when arthropod-borne transmission is most common.[17, 35, 59] Cases in winter usually occur among hunters and trappers who handle infected animal carcasses.[17, 35, 48] In the United States, cases are mostly sporadic or occur in small clusters[34, 35, 49]; in Eurasia, waterborne, arthropod-borne, and airborne outbreaks involving hundreds of persons have been reported.[40, 43, 44, 51, 53-55]

Natural Occurrences of Inhalational Tularemia

The largest recorded airborne tularemia outbreak occurred in 1966-1967 in an extensive farming area of Sweden.[43] This outbreak involved more than 600 patients infected with strains of the milder European biovar of *F tularensis* (*F tularensis* biovar palaearctica [type B]), most of whom acquired infection while doing farm work that created contaminated aerosols. Case exposures and disease onsets occurred during a period of months but peaked during the winter, when rodent-infested hay was being sorted and moved from field storage sites to barns. Among 140 serologically confirmed cases thought to have been infected by inhalation, most had typical acute symptoms of fever, fatigue, chills, headache, and malaise; only 14 (10%) of confirmed patients had symptoms of pneumonia, such as dyspnea and chest pains. Patients generally responded well to tetracycline, and no deaths were reported. Inhalational tularemia in the United States has involved only single cases or small clusters of cases, variously resulting from laboratory exposures,[18, 56, 57] disturbance of contaminated animal carcasses,[38, 39, 41] and suspected infective environmental aerosols.[41, 52] Cases of inhalational tularemia in the United States are thought to be due mostly to the more virulent *F tularensis* biovar tularensis (type A) and usually follow an acute and severe course, with prominent pneumonitis. Some cases, however, have radiographic evidence of pleuropneumonia with minimal or absent respiratory signs on physical examination.[39, 41, 52]

Although airborne *F tularensis* would be expected to principally cause primary pleuropneumonic infection, some exposures might contaminate the eye, resulting in ocular tularemia; penetrate broken skin, resulting in ulceroglandular or glandular disease; or cause oropharyngeal disease with cervical lymphadenitis. In the aforementioned Swedish outbreak, conjunctivitis was reported in 26% of 140 confirmed cases and an infected ulcer of the skin was reported in nearly 12%; pharyngitis was reported in 31% and oral ulcers in about 9% of the cases; and 32% of these patients had various exanthemas, such as erythema multiforme and erythema nodosum.[43] Tularemia outbreaks arising from similar agricultural exposures have been reported from Finland,[53] mostly presenting with general constitutional symptoms rather than specific manifestations of pneumonia; enlargement of hilar nodes was the principal radiographic finding in these cases.[54]

Inhalational Tularemia Following Use as a Biological Weapon

Although *F tularensis* could be used as a weapon in a number of ways, the working group believes that an aerosol release would have the greatest adverse medical and public health consequences. Release in a densely populated area would be expected to result in an abrupt onset of large numbers of cases of acute, nonspecific febrile illness beginning 3 to 5 days later (incubation range, 1-14 days), with pleuropneumonitis developing in a significant proportion of cases during the ensuing days and weeks. Public health authorities would most likely become aware of an outbreak of unusual respiratory disease in its early stages, but this could be difficult to distinguish from a natural outbreak of community-acquired infection, especially influenza or various atypical pneumonias. The abrupt onset of large numbers of acutely ill persons, the rapid progression in a relatively high proportion of cases from upper respiratory symptoms and bronchitis to life-threatening pleuropneumonitis and systemic infection affecting, among others, young, previously healthy adults and children should, however, quickly alert medical professionals and public health authorities to a critical and unexpected public health event and to bioterrorism as a possible cause (**Table 1**). Until the etiology became clear, clinicians would need to work closely with epidemiologists and diagnostic laboratories to differentiate the illness from various community-acquired pneumonias and to determine if it could have resulted from use of one of several potential bioterrorism weapons agents, such as those causing tularemia, plague, anthrax, or Q fever.[2, 4, 29]

In general, tularemia would be expected to have a slower progression of illness and a lower case-fatality rate than either inhalational plague or anthrax. (See "Anthrax as a Biological Weapon" and "Plague as a Biological Weapon" earlier in this book.) Plague would most likely progress very rapidly to severe pneumonia, with copious watery or purulent sputum production, hemoptysis, respiratory insufficiency, sepsis, and shock.[4] Inhalational anthrax would be differentiated by its characteristic radiological findings of prominent symmetric mediastinal widening and absence of bronchopneumonia.[2] As well, anthrax patients would be expected to develop fulminating, toxic, and fatal illness despite antibiotic treatment.[29] Milder forms of inhalational tularemia could be clinically indistinguishable from Q fever; establishing a diagnosis of either would be problematic without reference laboratory testing. Presumptive laboratory diagnoses of plague or anthrax would be expected to be made relatively quickly, although microbiological confirmation could take days. Isolation and identification of *F tularensis* using routine laboratory procedures could take several weeks.

Once a substantial cluster of cases of inhalational tularemia had been identified, epidemiological findings should suggest a bioterrorist event. The abrupt onset and single peak of cases would implicate a point-source exposure without secondary transmission. Among exposed persons, attack rates would likely be similar across sex and age groups, and risk would be related to degree of exposure to the point source (Table 1). An outbreak of inhalational tularemia in an urban setting should trigger a high level of suspicion of an intentional event, since all reported inhalational tularemia outbreaks have occurred in rural areas.

Table 1. Diagnosis of Inhalational Tularemia Following Use of a Biological Weapon

Clinical Findings
Sudden onset of acute febrile illness, progressing in some patients to pharyngitis, bronchiolitis, pneumonitis, pleuritis, hilar lymphadenitis.
Complications of overwhelming untreated infection may lead to sepsis and inflammatory response syndrome.
Epidemiology
Point-source outbreak pattern; likely urban, nonagricultural setting.
Unexpected, severe respiratory illness in otherwise healthy persons.
Risk related to degree of exposure with no differences in susceptibility by age or sex.
Microbiology
Small, gram-negative coccobacilli in direct stain of respiratory secretions.
Sputum, tracheobronchial secretions, and blood should be cultured using cysteine-enriched medium.
Antimicrobial susceptibility of isolates should be determined. Direct fluorescent antibody stain is first-line, rapid identification procedure at reference laboratories. Polymerase chain reaction and antigen detection procedures may also provide rapid identification.
Microagglutination assay can detect serum antibodies beginning 10 days after illness onset.
Virulence testing and molecular genetic characterizations are performed at specialized laboratories.
Pathology
Histological findings of acute suppurative necrosis followed by granulomatous reactions.
Target organs include lungs, lymph nodes, spleen, liver, and kidney.
Radiology
Peribronchial infiltrates leading to bronchopneumonia in 1 or more lobes, often accompanied by pleural effusion and enlarged hilar nodes. Signs may be absent or minimal, with only 1 or several small, discrete pulmonary infiltrates, or scattered granulomatous lesions of lung parenchyma or pleura.

Microbiology and Virulence Factors

Francisella tularensis is a small, nonmotile, aerobic, gram-negative coccobacillus. It has a thin lipopolysaccharide-containing envelope and is a hardy non–spore-forming organism that survives for weeks at low temperatures in water, moist soil, hay, straw, and decaying animal carcasses.[21,22,60,61] *Francisella tularensis* has been divided into 2 major subspecies (biovars) by virulence testing, biochemical reactions, and epidemiological features.[62] *Francisella tularensis* biovar tularensis (type A) may be highly virulent in humans and animals, produces acid from glycerol, demonstrates citrulline ureidase activity, and is the most common biovar isolated in North America.[22,60]

Francisella tularensis biovar palaearctica (type B) is relatively avirulent, does not produce acid from glycerol, and does not demonstrate citrulline ureidase activity. In Europe and Asia, all human tularemia is thought to be caused by the milder type B strains, although recent studies there have identified naturally occurring *F tularensis* related to *F tularensis* biovar tularensis.[63, 64] A few rapidly growing strains of *F tularensis* have been recovered from the blood of immunocompromised patients not showing seroreactivity to *F tularensis*.[65]

Transformed plasmids have been engineered to express chloramphenicol and tetracycline resistance in *F tularensis*.[66] Virulent, streptomycin-resistant *F tularensis* strains have been examined in biowarfare agent studies both in the United States and the Soviet Union.[24, 27, 56] Although *F tularensis* virulence factors are poorly understood and characterized,[67, 68] it is possible that strain virulence could be enhanced through laboratory manipulation.

Pathogenesis and Clinical Manifestations

Pathogenesis

Francisella tularensis can infect humans through the skin, mucous membranes, gastrointestinal tract, and lungs. It is a facultative intracellular bacterium that multiplies within macrophages.[68, 69] The major target organs are the lymph nodes, lungs and pleura, spleen, liver, and kidney.[19, 20, 49, 70-72] Untreated, bacilli inoculated into skin or mucous membranes multiply, spread to the regional lymph nodes and further multiply, and may then disseminate to organs throughout the body. Bacteremia may be common in the early phase of infection. The initial tissue reaction to infection is a focal, intensely suppurative necrosis consisting largely of accumulations of polymorphonuclear leukocytes, followed by invasion of macrophages, epithelioid cells, and lymphocytes. Suppurative lesions become granulomatous, and histopathological examination of the granulomas shows a central necrotic, sometimes caseating zone surrounded by a layer of epithelioid cells, multinucleated giant cells, and fibroblasts in a radial arrangement, typical of other granulomatous conditions, such as tuberculosis and sarcoidosis.[20, 70, 71]

Monkeys that inhaled the virulent SCHU S-4 strain of *F tularensis* (type A) developed acute bronchiolitis within 24 hours of exposure to 1-μm particles and within 48 hours of exposure to 8-μm particles.[73] By 72 hours following challenge, inflammation was present in peribronchial tissues and alveolar septa. Bronchopneumonia was most pronounced in animals exposed to the smaller particles and was characterized by tracheobronchial lymph node enlargement and reddish, firm, 0.2- to 0.5-cm-diameter discrete inflammatory lesions scattered throughout the lungs. In the absence of treatment, the disease progressed to pneumonic consolidation and organization, granuloma formation, and eventual chronic interstitial fibrosis.

Humans with inhalational exposures also develop hemorrhagic inflammation of the airways early in the course of illness, which may progress to bronchopneumonia.[54] Histopathological examination of affected lungs shows alveolar spaces filled with an exudate of mononuclear cells. Pleuritis with adhesions and effusion and hilar lymphadenopathy are common radiological and pathological findings.[70, 72]

Clinical Manifestations

The primary clinical forms of tularemia vary in severity and presentation according to virulence of the infecting organism, dose, and site of inoculum. Primary disease presentations include ulceroglandular, glandular, oculoglandular, oropharyngeal, pneumonic, typhoidal, and septic forms.[19, 20, 49, 70, 72, 74, 75] The term *typhoidal tularemia* has been used to describe illness in tularemia patients with systemic infections manifesting as fever and other constitutional signs without cutaneous or mucosal membrane lesions or regional lymphadenitis. Sometimes, these patients present with prominent gastrointestinal manifestations, such as diarrhea and pain. Confusion is created when *typhoidal tularemia* is used to describe the illness in patients infected by inhalation, especially when there are signs of pleuropneumonic disease; this usage can be misleading and has been discouraged.[54, 75]

The onset of tularemia is usually abrupt, with fever (38°C-40°C), headache, chills and rigors, generalized body aches (often prominent in the low back), coryza, and sore throat. A pulse-temperature dissociation has been noted in as many as 42% of patients.[49] A dry or slightly productive cough and substernal pain or tightness frequently occur with or without objective signs of pneumonia, such as purulent sputum, dyspnea, tachypnea, pleuritic pain, or hemoptysis.[7, 19, 26, 70, 74] Nausea, vomiting, and diarrhea sometimes occur. Sweats, fever and chills, progressive weakness, malaise, anorexia, and weight loss characterize the continuing illness. Studies of volunteers have shown that *F tularensis* aerosol exposures can incapacitate some persons in the first 1 or 2 days of illness, and significant impairment in performing tasks can continue for days after antibiotic treatment is begun.[76] In untreated tularemia, symptoms often persist for several weeks and, sometimes, for months, usually with progressive debility. Any form of tularemia may be complicated by hematogenous spread, resulting in secondary pleuropneumonia, sepsis, and, rarely, meningitis.[74, 77]

Prior to the advent of antibiotics, the overall mortality from infections with the more severe type A strains was in the range of 5% to 15%, and fatality rates as high as 30% to 60% were reported for untreated pneumonic and severe systemic forms of disease.[72, 78] Currently, the overall case-fatality rate of reported cases in the United States is less than 2%.[34, 49] Type B infections are rarely fatal.

Ulceroglandular tularemia is the most readily recognized and common form of the naturally occurring disease. It results from the cutaneous inoculation of *F tularensis*, either by a bite of an infective arthropod, or by a direct contact exposure with contaminated material. In the usual sequence of events, inoculation is followed within 1 or 2 days by the appearance of a tender erythematous papule, which enlarges over the next 48 hours to a diameter of 1 to 2 cm, becoming an indurated, tender, vesiculated lesion. Over the next several days the lesion ulcerates; the ulcer most often has a punched-out appearance with a necrotic granulomatous base and is surrounded by an indurated, raised, and erythematous margin. An eschar may cover the ulcer (**Figure 1**). Malaise, fever, generalized aches, and other systemic manifestations usually begin within 3 days of the appearance of the skin

Figure 1. Tularemia Ulcer at Site of Inoculation of *Francisella tularensis*, Thought to Result from the Bite of an Infective Deer Fly.

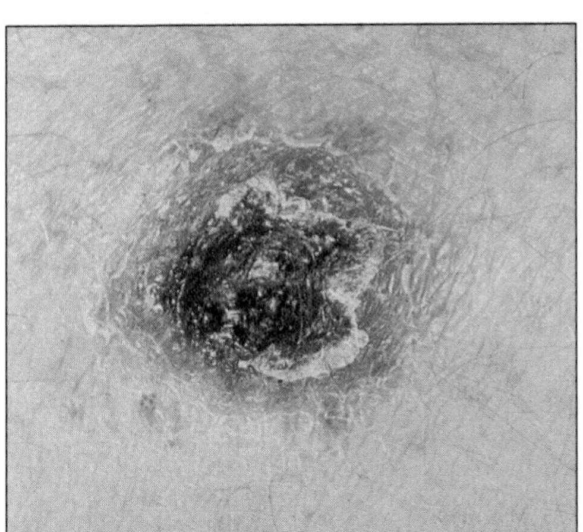

The lesion is approximately 2 cm in diameter and demonstrates a margin that is typically raised, indurated, erythematous, and irregular-shaped and is covered by an eshar. This stage of development would be expected a week or more after the infective exposure. Reproduced with permission from the Centers for Disease Control and Prevention (CDC), Fort Collins, Colo.

lesion, and are typically accompanied by the development of one or more painful, tender, and swollen lymph nodes in the afferent lymphatic chain draining the site of inoculation. If the patient is untreated, tularemic ulcers and associated lymphadenopathy may persist for weeks or months; lymph nodes may rupture and drain purulent material through sinus tracts to the skin. *Francisella tularensis* may be cultured from scrapings of the ulcer, from aspirates of an involved node, or from sinus discharges.

In oculoglandular tularemia, which follows direct contamination of the eye, ulceration occurs on the conjunctiva, accompanied by pronounced chemosis, vasculitis, and regional lymphadenitis. Glandular tularemia is characterized by lymphadenopathy without an ulcer.

Oropharyngeal tularemia is acquired by drinking contaminated water, ingesting contaminated food, and, sometimes, by inhaling contaminated droplets or aerosols.[14, 20, 36, 43, 50, 51, 79] Affected persons may develop stomatitis but more commonly develop exudative pharyngitis or tonsillitis, sometimes with ulceration. Pronounced cervical or retropharyngeal lymphadenopathy may occur (**Figure 2**).[74, 79]

Tularemia pneumonia can be the direct result of inhaling contaminated aerosols or be secondary to hematogenous spread from a distal site. An aerosol release of *F tularensis* would be expected to result in acute illness with signs and symptoms of 1 or more of pharyngitis, bronchiolitis, pleuropneumonitis, and hilar lymphadenitis, accompanied by various manifestations of systemic illness. Inhalational exposures, however, commonly result in an initial clinical picture

Figure 2. Cervical Lymphadenitis in a Patient With Pharyngeal Tularemia

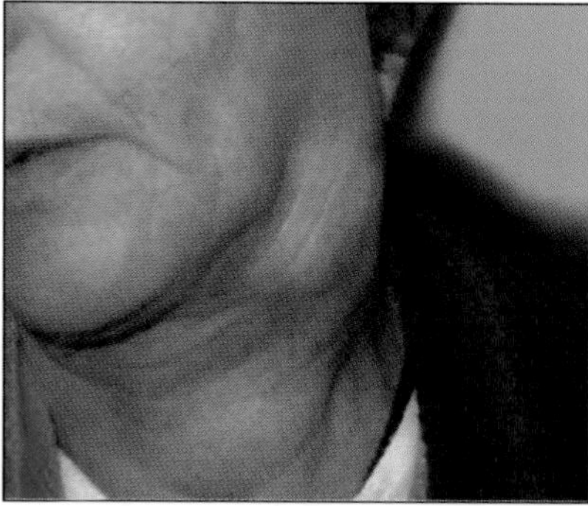

Patient has marked swelling and fluctuant suppuration of several anterior cervical nodes. Infection was acquired by ingestion of contaminated food or water. Reproduced with permission from the World Health Organization.

Figure 3. Chest Radiograph of a Patient With Pulmonary Tularemia

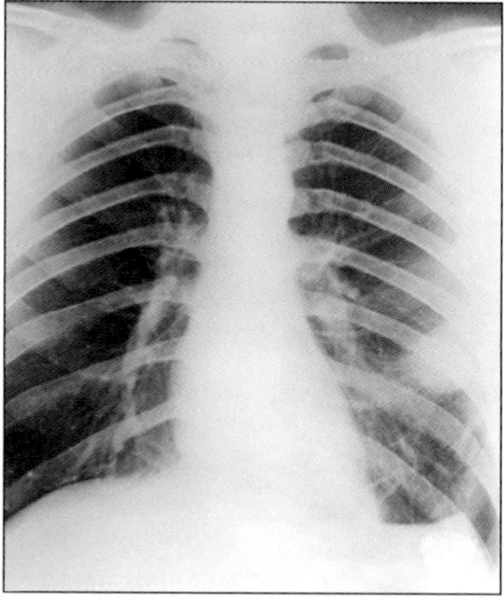

Infiltrates in left lower lung, tenting of diaphragm, probably caused by pleural effusion, and enlargement of left hilum. Figure courtesy Armed Forces Institute of Pathology.

of systemic illness without prominent signs of respiratory disease.[7, 43, 53, 56] The earliest pulmonary radiographic findings of inhalational tularemia may be peribronchial infiltrates, typically advancing to bronchopneumonia in 1 or more lobes, and often accompanied by pleural effusions and hilar lymphadenopathy (**Figure 3**).[72, 75] Signs may, however, be minimal or absent, and some patients will show only 1 or several small, discrete pulmonary infiltrates or scattered granulomatous lesions of lung parenchyma or pleura. Although volunteers challenged with aerosols of virulent *F tularensis* (type A) regularly developed systemic symptoms of acute illness 3 to 5 days following exposure, only 25% to 50% of participants had radiological evidence of pneumonia in the early stages of infection.[7,26] On the other hand, pulmonary infection can sometimes rapidly progress to severe pneumonia, respiratory failure, and death.[72,80] Lung abscesses occur infrequently.[75]

Typhoidal tularemia is used to describe systemic illness in the absence of signs indicating either site of inoculation or anatomic localization of infection. This should be differentiated from inhalational tularemia with pleuropneumonic disease.[54,75]

Tularemia sepsis is potentially severe and fatal. As in typhoidal tularemia, nonspecific findings of fever, abdominal pain, diarrhea, and vomiting may be prominent early in the course of illness. The patient typically appears toxic and may develop confusion and coma. Unless treated promptly, septic shock and other complications of systemic inflammatory response syndrome may ensue, including disseminated intravascular coagulation and bleeding, acute respiratory distress syndrome, and organ failure.[80]

Diagnosis

Inhalational tularemia in humans occurs infrequently, resulting in a low index of diagnostic suspicion among clinicians and laboratorians. Since rapid diagnostic testing for tularemia is not widely available, the first indication of intentional tularemia might follow recognition by public health authorities of a clustering of acute, severe respiratory illness with unusual epidemiological features (Table 1). Suspicion of tularemia might be triggered in alert clinicians encountering patients with findings of atypical pneumonia, pleuritis, and hilar lymphadenopathy. Identification of *F tularensis* in clinical specimens may be missed or delayed for days or weeks when procedures for routine microbiological screening of bacterial pathogens are followed, and it is unlikely that a serendipitous laboratory identification would be the sentinel event that alerted authorities to a major bioterrorism action.

Physicians who suspect inhalational tularemia should promptly collect specimens of respiratory secretions and blood and alert the laboratory to the need for special diagnostic and safety procedures. *Francisella tularensis* may be identified by direct examination of secretions, exudates, or biopsy specimens using direct fluorescent antibody or immunohistochemical stains.[81-83] By light microscopy, the organism is characterized by its small size (0.2 µm × 0.2-0.7 µm), pleomorphism, and faint staining. It does not show the bipolar staining characteristics of *Yersinia pestis*,[4] the agent of plague, and is easily distinguished from the large gram-positive rods characteristic of vegetative forms of *Bacillus anthracis* (**Figure 4**).[2] Microscopic demonstration of *F tularensis* using fluorescent-labeled antibodies is a rapid diagnostic procedure performed in designated reference laboratories in the Laboratory Response Network; test results can be made available within several hours of receiving the appropriate specimens if the laboratory is

Figure 4. Gram Stain Smears of the Agents of Anthrax (*Bacillus anthracis*), Plague (*Yersinia pestis*), and Tularemia (*Francisella tularensis*), Demonstrating Comparative Morphology, Size, and Staining Characteristics

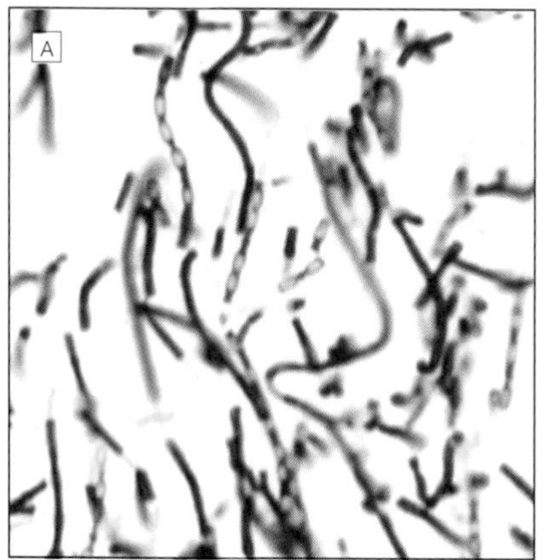

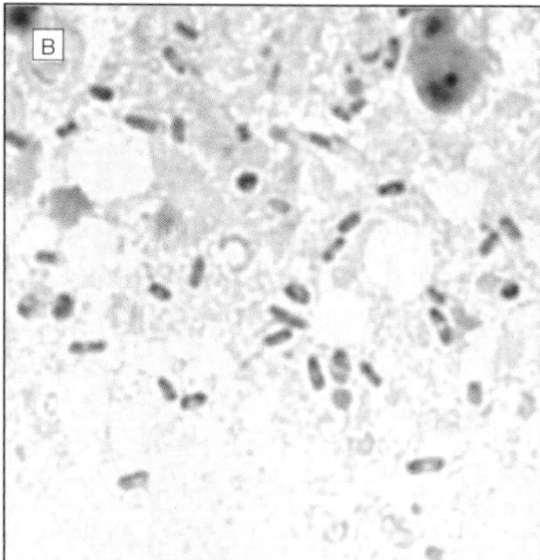

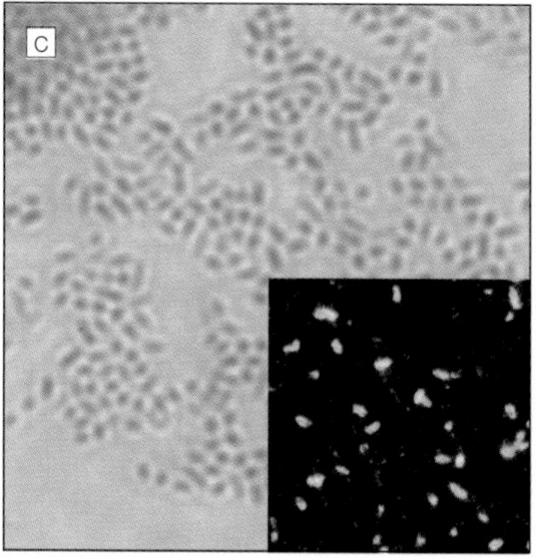

A, *B anthracis* is a large (0.5-1.2 μm × 2.5-10.0 μm), chain-forming, gram-positive rod that sporulates under certain conditions (Gram stain of organism from culture; original magnification × 250); B, *Y pestis* is a gram-negative, plump, non–spore-forming, bipolar-staining bacillus that is approximately 0.5-0.8 μm × 1-3 μm (Gram stain of smear from infected tissue; original magnification × 250); C, *F tularensis* is a small (0.2 μm × 0.2-0.7 μm), pleomorphic, poorly staining, gram-negative coccobacillus (Gram stain of organism from culture; original magnification × 500) (inset, direct immunofluorescence of smear of *F tularensis*; original magnification × 400. Figures A and B reproduced with permission from Sherif Zaki, MD, PhD, Centers for Disease Control and Prevention (CDC); Figure C courtesy Armed Forces Institute of Pathology.

alerted and prepared. Suspicion of inhalational tularemia must be promptly reported to local or state public health authorities so timely epidemiological and environmental investigations can be made (**Box 1**).

Box 1. Who Clinicians Caring for Patients With Suspected Tularemia Should Immediately Contact

1. Hospital epidemiologist or infection control practitioner

   and

2. Local or state health departments

Consult your local telephone operator, the telephone directory under "governmental listings," or the Internet at www.cdc.gov/other.htm#states or www.astho.org/state.html.

If the local and state health departments are unavailable, contact the Centers for Disease Control and Prevention at (970) 221-6400 or www.cdc.gov/ncidod/dvbid/dvbid.htm.

Growth of *F tularensis* in culture is the definitive means of confirming the diagnosis of tularemia.[60, 81] *Francisella tularensis* can be grown from pharyngeal washings, sputum specimens, and even fasting gastric aspirates in a high proportion of patients with inhalational tularemia.[56] It is only occasionally isolated from the blood. *Francisella tularensis* grows best in cysteine-enriched broth and thioglycollate broth and on cysteine heart blood agar, buffered charcoal-yeast agar, and chocolate agar. Selective agar (such as chocolate agar selective for *Neisseria gonorrheae* isolation) may be useful when culturing materials from nonsterile sites, such as sputum. Inoculated media should be incubated at 37°C. Although growth may be visible as early as 24 to 48 hours after inoculation, growth may be delayed and cultures should be held for at least 10 days before discarding. Under ideal conditions, bacterial colonies on cysteine-enriched agar are typically 1 mm in diameter after 24 to 48 hours of incubation and 3 to 5 mm in diameter by 96 hours.[60, 81] On cysteine heart agar, *F tularensis* colonies are characteristically opalescent and do not discolor the medium (**Figure 5**).

Antigen detection assays, polymerase chain reaction, enzyme-linked immunoassays, immunoblotting, pulsed-field gel electrophoresis, and other specialized techniques may be used to identify *F tularensis* and to characterize strains.[84-87] These procedures are usually performed only in research and reference laboratories, however. In laboratories where advanced methods are established, results of antigen detection and polymerase chain reaction analyses can be obtained within several hours of receipt of isolates. Typically, serum antibody titers do not attain diagnostic levels until 10 or more days after onset of illness, and serology would provide minimal useful information for managing an outbreak. Serological confirmation of cases, however, may be of value for forensic or epidemiological purposes. Most laboratories use tube agglutination or microagglutination tests that detect combined immunoglobulin M and immunoglobulin G.[84, 85] A 4-fold change in titer between acute and convalescent serum specimens, a single titer of at least 1:160 for tube agglutination or 1:128 for microagglutination is diagnostic for *F tularensis* infection. Information on reference diagnostic

Figure 5. ***Francisella tularensis*** **Growth at 72 Hours After Inoculation**

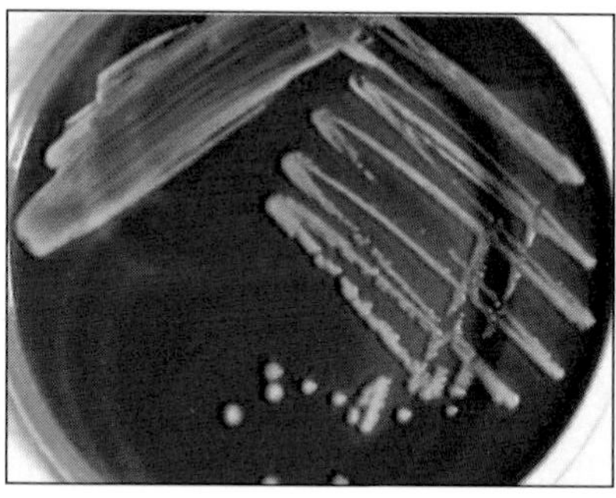

These *F tularensis* colonies show characteristic opalescence on cysteine heart agar with sheep blood (cultured at 37°C for 72 hours). Reproduced with permission from the Centers for Disease Control and Prevention (CDC), Fort Collins, Colo.

testing and shipping/handling of specimens can be obtained from state public health laboratories and from the Division of Vector-Borne Infectious Diseases, CDC, Fort Collins, Colo.

Vaccination

Beginning in the 1930s, the Soviet Union used a live attenuated vaccine to immunize tens of millions of persons living in tularemia-endemic areas.[88] In the United States, a live attenuated vaccine derived from the avirulent live vaccine strain has been used to protect laboratorians routinely working with *F tularensis*; until recently, this vaccine was available as an investigational new drug.[89] It is currently under review by the US Food and Drug Administration (FDA), and its future availability is undetermined.

In a retrospective study of civilians working with *F tularensis* at a US Army research facility, the incidence of accidental acute inhalational tularemia among laboratorians declined from 5.70 cases per 1000 person-years of risk at a time when a killed vaccine was in use to 0.27 cases per 1000 person-years of risk after introduction of the live vaccine.[58] Although the incidence of ulceroglandular disease remained unchanged in the 2 periods, signs and symptoms were considered milder among those who received the live vaccine. In volunteer studies, the live attenuated vaccine did not protect all recipients against aerosol challenges with virulent *F tularensis*.[7,26]

Correlates of protective immunity appear about 2 weeks following natural infection or vaccination. Given the short incubation period of tularemia and incomplete protection of current vaccines against inhalational tularemia, vaccination is not recommended for postexposure prophylaxis. The working group recommends use of the live vaccine strain only for laboratory personnel routinely working with *F tularensis*.

Treatment

Contained Casualty Situation

Adults. In a contained casualty situation in which logistics permit individual medical management, the working group recommends parenteral antimicrobial therapy for tularemia (**Table 2**). Streptomycin is the drug of choice.[49, 74, 90, 91] Gentamicin, which is more widely available and may be used intravenously, is an acceptable alternative.[49, 74, 90-93] Treatment with aminoglycosides should be continued for 10 days. Tetracyclines and chloramphenicol are also used to treat tularemia[49, 74, 90]; however, relapses and primary treatment failures occur at a higher rate with these bacteriostatic agents than with aminoglycosides, and they should be given for at least 14 days to reduce chance of relapse.[27, 74, 90] Fluoroquinolones, which have intracellular activity, are promising candidates for treating tularemia. Ciprofloxacin, which is not labeled for use in tularemia, has been shown to be active against *F tularensis* in vitro[94] and in animals[95] and has been used to successfully treat tularemia in both adults and children.[90, 94, 96, 97] Treatment with ciprofloxacin should be continued for 10 days. In persons beginning treatment with parenteral doxycycline, ciprofloxacin, or chloramphenicol, therapy can be switched to oral antibiotic administration when clinically indicated. Very limited experiences in treating tularemia patients with ß-lactam and macrolide antibiotics have been reported, and treatment failures have occurred.[98] Use of ß-lactam and macrolide antibiotics in treating tularemia is neither FDA-approved nor recommended by the working group.

Children. In children, streptomycin or gentamicin is recommended by the working group as first-line treatment in a contained casualty situation (Table 2). Doxycycline, ciprofloxacin (≤1 g/d), and chloramphenicol can be used as alternatives to aminoglycosides. Fluoroquinolones have been reported to cause cartilage damage in immature animals and are not FDA-approved for use in children. However, short courses of these agents have not been associated with arthropathy in pediatric patients, and the potential risks of their use must be weighed against their benefits in treating serious infections.[96, 99, 100]

Mass Casualty Situation

Doxycycline and ciprofloxacin, administered orally, are the preferred choices for treatment in the mass casualty setting, for both adults and children (**Table 3**). The ciprofloxacin dosage for children should not exceed 1 g/d. In a mass casualty situation, the working group believes the benefits to children from short courses of doxycycline or fluoroquinolones (Table 3) outweigh the risks of their use.

Since it is unknown whether drug-resistant organisms might be used in a bioterrorist event, antimicrobial susceptibility testing of isolates should be conducted quickly and treatments altered according to test results and clinical responses.

Antibiotics for treating patients infected with tularemia in a bioterrorism scenario are included in a national pharmaceutical stockpile maintained by the CDC,

Table 2. **Working Group Consensus Recommendations for Treatment of Patients With Tularemia in a Contained Casualty Setting***

Contained Casualty Recommended Therapy	
Adults	
Preferred choices	
	Streptomycin, 1 g IM twice daily
	Gentamicin, 5 mg/kg IM or IV once daily†
Alternative choices	
	Doxycycline, 100 mg IV twice daily
	Chloramphenicol, 15 mg/kg IV 4 times daily†
	Ciprofloxacin, 400 mg IV twice daily†
Children	
Preferred choices	
	Streptomycin, 15 mg/kg IM twice daily (should not exceed 2 g/d)
	Gentamicin, 2.5 mg/kg IM or IV 3 times daily†
Alternative choices	
	Doxycycline; if weight ≥45 kg, 100 mg IV twice daily; if weight <45 kg, give 2.2 mg/kg IV twice daily
	Chloramphenicol, 15 mg/kg IV 4 times daily†
	Ciprofloxacin, 15 mg/kg IV twice daily‡
Pregnant Women	
Preferred choices	
	Gentamicin, 5 mg/kg IM or IV once daily†
	Streptomycin, 1 g IM twice daily
Alternative choices	
	Doxycycline, 100 mg IV twice daily
	Ciprofloxacin, 400 mg IV twice daily†

*Treatment with streptomycin, gentamicin, or ciprofloxacin should be continued for 10 days; treatment with doxycycline or chloramphenicol should be continued for 14 to 21 days. Persons beginning treatment with intramuscular (IM) or intravenous (IV) doxycycline, ciprofloxacin, or chloramphenicol can switch to oral antibiotic administration when clinically indicated.

†Not a US Food and Drug Administration–approved use.

‡Ciprofloxacin dosage should not exceed 1 g/d in children.

as are ventilators and other emergency equipment needed to respond to situations of large numbers of critically ill persons that strip local and state resources.[30]

Management of Special Groups

Pregnant Women. In a contained casualty situation, short courses of gentamicin are likely to pose a low risk to fetuses when used to treat tularemia in pregnant women (Table 2). Rare cases of fetal nerve deafness and renal damage have been reported with other aminoglycosides but have not been reported with gentamicin. The benefits of gentamicin in treating pregnant women with tularemia

Table 3. Working Group Consensus Recommendations for Treatment of Patients With Tularemia in a Mass Casualty Setting and for Postexposure Prophylaxis*

Mass Casualty Recommended Therapy	
Adults	
Preferred choices	
	Doxycycline, 100 mg orally twice daily
	Ciprofloxacin, 500 mg orally twice daily†
Children	
Preferred choices	
	Doxycycline; if ≥45 kg, give 100 mg orally twice daily; if <45 kg, give 2.2 mg/kg orally twice daily
	Ciprofloxacin, 15 mg/kg orally twice daily‡
Pregnant Women	
Preferred choices	
	Ciprofloxacin, 500 mg orally twice daily†
	Doxycycline, 100 mg orally twice daily

*One antibiotic, appropriate for patient age, should be chosen from among alternatives. The duration of all recommended therapies in Table 3 is 14 days.

†Not a US Food and Drug Administration–approved use.

‡Ciprofloxacin dosage should not exceed 1 g/d in children.

are expected to outweigh any potential risk to fetuses. In a mass casualty situation, oral ciprofloxacin is considered the best alternative to gentamicin for pregnant women (Table 3).

Immunosuppressed Persons. There is scant experience in treating tularemia in immunocompromised patients. However, considering the greater occurrence in immunocompetent patients of tularemia relapses and treatment failures following use of bacteriostatic antimicrobial agents compared with aminoglycosides, streptomycin or gentamicin should be used when possible to treat patients with known immune dysfunction in either contained casualty or mass casualty situations (Tables 2 and 3).

Postexposure Antibiotic Recommendations

Persons beginning treatment with streptomycin, gentamicin, doxycycline, or ciprofloxacin in the incubation period of tularemia and continuing treatment daily for 14 days might be protected against symptomatic infection. In studies of aerosol challenge with infective doses of the virulent SCHU S-4 strain of *F tularensis*, each of 8 volunteers given oral dosages of tetracycline, 1 g/d for 28 days, and each of 8 volunteers given tetracycline, 2 g/d for 14 days, were fully protected when treatment was begun 24 hours following challenge.[27] Two of 10 volunteers given tetracycline, 1 g/d for only 5 days, developed symptomatic tularemia after antibiotic treatment was stopped.

In the unlikely event that authorities quickly become aware that an *F tularensis* biological weapon has been used and are able to identify and reach exposed persons during the early incubation period, the working group recommends that exposed persons be prophylactically treated with 14 days of oral doxycycline or ciprofloxacin (Table 3). In a circumstance in which the weapon attack has been covert and the event is discovered only after persons start to become ill, persons potentially exposed should be instructed to begin a fever watch. Persons who develop an otherwise unexplained fever or flu-like illness within 14 days of presumed exposure should begin treatment as outlined in Table 2 and Table 3.

In the laboratory, persons who have had potentially infective exposures to *F tularensis* should be administered oral postexposure antibiotic prophylaxis if the risk of infection is high (eg, spill, centrifuge accident, or needlestick). If the risk is low, exposed persons can be placed on a fever watch and treated if they develop symptoms.

Postexposure prophylactic antibiotic treatment of close contacts of tularemia patients is not recommended since human-to-human transmission of *F tularensis* is not known to occur.

Infection Control

Isolation is not recommended for tularemia patients, given the lack of human-to-human transmission. In hospitals, standard precautions[101] are recommended by the working group for treatment of patients with tularemia.

Microbiology laboratory personnel should be alerted when tularemia is clinically suspected. Routine diagnostic procedures can be performed in biological safety level 2 (BSL-2) conditions. Examination of cultures in which *F tularensis* is suspected should be carried out in a biological safety cabinet. Manipulation of cultures and other activities involving infectious materials with a potential for aerosol or droplet production (centrifuging, grinding, vigorous shaking, growing cultures in volume, animal studies) require BSL-3 conditions.[102] When *F tularensis* is presumptively identified in a routine BSL-2 clinical laboratory (level A), specimens should be forwarded to a BSL-3 laboratory (level B) (eg, a state public health laboratory) for confirmation of agent and other studies, such as antimicrobial susceptibility testing.[11] Bodies of patients who die of tularemia should be handled using standard precautions. Autopsy procedures likely to cause aerosols, such as bone sawing, should be avoided. Clothing or linens contaminated with body fluids of patients infected with *F tularensis* should be disinfected per standard precaution protocols.[101]

Environmental Decontamination and Protection

Under natural conditions, *F tularensis* may survive for extended periods in a cold, moist environment. The working group lacks information on survival of intentionally dispersed particles but would expect a short half-life due to desiccation, solar radiation, oxidation and other environmental factors, and a very limited risk from secondary dispersal. In circumstances of a laboratory spill or intentional use in which authorities are concerned about an environmental risk (eg, inanimate surfaces wet with material thought to contain *F tularensis)*, decontamination can be achieved by spraying the suspected contaminant with a 10% bleach solution (1 part household bleach and 9 parts water). After 10 minutes, a 70% solution of alcohol can be used to further clean the area and reduce the corrosive action of the bleach. Soap water can be used to flush away less hazardous contaminations. Persons with direct exposure to powder or liquid aerosols containing *F tularensis* should wash body surfaces and clothing with soap water. Standard levels of chlorine in municipal water sources should protect against waterborne infection.[60] Following an urban release, the risk to humans of acquiring tularemia from infected animals or arthropod bites is considered minimal and could be reduced by educating the public on simple avoidance of sick or dead animals and on personal protective measures against biting arthropods.

Additional Research

Simple, rapid, and reliable diagnostic tests that could be used to identify persons infected with *F tularensis* in the mass exposure setting need to be developed. Further methods should be designed to rapidly define the molecular genetic characteristics of organisms, especially as they may relate to engineered attributes, such as enhanced virulence and resistance to antimicrobial agents or normally lethal environmental conditions. Complete sequencing and analysis of the genome of natural strains of *F tularensis* would provide an archival base for understanding genetic variants, functions of genes, and mechanisms of action useful in developing means to protect against *F tularensis.* Research is also needed to develop accurate and reliable procedures to rapidly detect *F tularensis* in environmental samples.

New technologies should be explored for developing active (eg, DNA-based) or passive (eg, monoclonal antibody–based) vaccines for rapid preexposure or postexposure protection.

Acknowledgments: We thank May C. Chu, PhD, CDC, for assistance with laboratory diagnostic aspects of tularemia, and Edward B. Hayes, MD, CDC, for assistance with clinical and epidemiological aspects of tularemia.

Ex Officio Participants in the Working Group on Civilian Biodefense: George Counts, MD, CDC; Margaret Hamburg, MD, former assistant secretary for planning and evaluation, Department of Health and Human Services (DHHS); Robert Knouss, MD, Office of Emergency Preparedness, DHHS; Brian Malkin, Esq, formerly with the FDA; and Stuart Nightingale, MD, Office of the Assistant Secretary for Planning and Evaluation, DHHS.

Funding/Support: Funding for this study primarily was provided by each participant's institution or agency. The Johns Hopkins Center for Civilian Biodefense Studies provided travel funds for 5 of the group.

Disclaimers: In some instances, the indications, dosages, and other information in this article are not consistent with current approved labeling by the US Food and Drug Administration (FDA). The recommendations on use of drugs and vaccine for uses not approved by the FDA do not represent the official views of the FDA nor of any of the federal agencies whose scientists participated in these discussions. Unlabeled uses of the products recommended are noted in the sections of this article in which these products are discussed. Where unlabeled uses are indicated, information used as the basis for the recommendation is discussed.

The views, opinions, assertions, and findings contained herein are those of the authors and should not be construed as official US Department of Defense or US Department of Army positions, policies, or decisions unless so designated by other documentation.

References

1. Parker RR. Recent studies of tick-borne diseases made at the United States Public Health Service Laboratory at Hamilton, Montana. In: Proceedings of the Fifth Pacific Congress; 1934:3367-3374.
2. Inglesby TV, Henderson DA, Bartlett JG, et al, for the Working Group on Civilian Biodefense. Anthrax as a biological weapon: medical and public health management. *JAMA*. 1999;281:1735-1745.
3. Henderson DA, Inglesby TV, Bartlett JG, et al, for the Working Group on Civilain Biodefense. Smallpox as a biological weapon: medical and public health management. *JAMA*. 1999;281:2127-2137.
4. Inglesby TV, Dennis DT, Henderson DA, et al, for the Working Group on Civilian Biodefense. Plague as a biological weapon: medical and public health management. *JAMA*. 2000;283:2281-2290.
5. Arnon SA, Schecter R, Inglesby TV, et al, for the Working Group on Civilian Biodefense. Botulinum toxin as a biological weapon: medical and public health management. *JAMA*. 2001;285:1059-1070.
6. Saslaw S, Eigelsbach HT, Wilson HE, Prior JA, Carhart S. Tularemia vaccine study, I: intracutaneous challenge. *Arch Intern Med*. 1961;107: 121-133.
7. Saslaw S, Eigelsbach HT, Prior JA, Wilson HE, Carhart S. Tularemia vaccine study, II: respiratory challenge. *Arch Intern Med*.1961;107:134-146.
8. World Health Organization. *Health Aspects of Chemical and Biological Weapons*. Geneva, Switzerland: World Health Organization; 1970: 75-76.
9. Kaufmann AF, Meltzer MI, Schmid GP. The economic impact of a bioterrorist attack: are prevention and post-attack intervention programs justifiable? *Emerg Infect Dis*. 1997;3:83-94.
10. Christopher GW, Cieslak TJ, Pavlin JA, Eitzen EM. Biological warfare: a historical perspective. *JAMA*. 1997;278:412-417.
11. Centers for Disease Control and Prevention. Biological and chemical terrorism: strategic plan for preparedness and response: recommendations of the CDC Strategic Planning Workgroup. *MMWR Morb Mortal Wkly Rep*. 2000;49(RR-4):1-14.
12. Francis E. Tularemia. *JAMA*. 1925;84:1243-1250.
13. Karpoff SP, Antononoff NI. The spread of tularemia through water as a new factor in its epidemiology. *J Bacteriol*. 1936;32:243-258.
14. Silchenko VS. Epidemiological and clinical features of tularemia caused by waterborne infection. *Zh Mikrobiol Epidemiol Immunobiol*. 1957;28:788-795.
15. Gelman AC. The ecology of tularemia. In: May JM, ed. *Studies in Disease Ecology*. New York, NY: Hafner Publishing Co; 1961:89-108.
16. Jellison WL, Kohls GM. *Tularemia in Sheep and Sheep Industry Workers in Western United States*. Washington, DC: US Public Health Service; 1955:1-17. Public health monograph 28.
17. Francis E. Sources of infection and seasonal incidence of tularemia in man. *Public Health Rep*. 1937;52:103-113.
18. Lake GC, Francis E. Six cases of tularemia occurring in laboratory workers. *Public Health Rep*. 1922;37:392-413.
19. Simpson WM. Tularemia (Francis' disease). *Ann Intern Med*. 1928;1:1007-1059.
20. Francis E. A summary of present knowledge of tularemia. *Medicine*. 1928;7:411-432.
21. Hopla CE. The ecology of tularemia. *Adv Vet Sci Comp Med*. 1974;18:25-53.
22. Jellison WL. *Tularemia in North America*. Missoula: University of Montana; 1974:1-276.
23. Harris S. Japanese biological warfare research on humans: a case study of microbiology and ethics. *Ann N Y Acad Sci*. 1992;666:21-52.
24. Alibek K. *Biohazard*. New York, NY: Random House; 1999:29-38.
25. McCrumb FR Jr, Snyder MJ, Woodward TE. Studies on human infection with *Pasteurella tularensis* : comparison of streptomycin and chloramphenicol in the prophylaxis of clinical disease. *Trans Assoc Am Physicians*. 1957;70:74-80.
26. McCrumb FR Jr. Aerosol infection in man with *Pasteurella tularensis*. *Bacteriol Rev*. 1961;25:262-267.

27. Sawyer WD, Dangerfield HG, Hogge AL, Crozier D. Antibiotic prophylaxis and therapy of airborne tularemia. *Bacteriol Rev.* 1966;30:542-548.

28. *Health Aspects of Chemical and Biological Weapons.* Geneva, Switzerland: World Health Organization; 1970:105-107.

29. Franz DR, Jahrling PB, Friedlander AM, et al. Clinical recognition and management of patients exposed to biological warfare agents. *JAMA.* 1997;278:399-411.

30. Khan AS, Morse S, Lillibridge S. Public health preparedness for biological terrorism in the USA. *Lancet.* 2000;356:1179-1182.

31. Tucker JB. National health and medical services response to incidents of chemical and biological terrorism. *JAMA.* 1997;278:362-368.

32. Hopla CE, Hopla AK. Tularemia. In: Beran GW, Steele JH, eds. *Handbook of Zoonoses.* 2nd ed. Boca Raton, Fla: CRC Press; 1994:113-126.

33. Centers for Disease Control and Prevention. Summary of notifiable diseases, United States, 1997. *MMWR Morb Mortal Wkly Rep.* 1998;46: ii-vii, 3-87.

34. Dennis DT. Tularemia. In: Wallace RB, ed. *Maxcy-Rosenau-Last Public Health and Preventive Medicine.* 14th ed. Stamford, Conn: Appleton & Lange; 1998:354-357.

35. Boyce JM. Recent trends in the epidemiology of tularemia in the United States. *J Infect Dis.* 1975;131:197-199.

36. Tärnvik A, Sandström G, Sjöstedt A. Epidemiological analysis of tularemia in Sweden 1931-1993. *FEMS Immunol Med Microbiol.* 1996;13: 201-204.

37. Pollitzer R. *History and Incidence of Tularemia in the Soviet Union: A Review.* Bronx, NY: Institute for Contemporary Russian Studies, Fordham University; 1967:1-103.

38. Halsted CC, Klasinghe P. Tularemia pneumonia in urban children. *Pediatrics.* 1978;61:660-662.

39. Martone WJ, Marshall LW, Kaufmann AF, Hobbs JH, Levy ME. Tularemia pneumonia in Washington, DC: a report of three cases with possible common-source exposures. *JAMA.* 1979;242:2315-2317.

40. Rogutsky SV, Khramtsov MM, Avchinikov AV, et al. Epidemiological investigation of an outbreak of tularemia in the Smolensk region. *Zh Mikrobiol (Moscow).* 1997;2:33-37.

41. McCarthy VP, Murphy MD. Lawnmower tularemia. *Pediatr Infect Dis J.* 1990;9:298-299.

42. Klock LE, Olsen PF, Fukushima T. Tularemia epidemic associated with the deerfly. *JAMA.* 1973;226:149-152.

43. Dahlstrand S, Ringertz O, Zetterberg B. Airborne tularemia in Sweden. *Scand J Infect Dis.* 1971;3: 7-16.

44. Christenson B. An outbreak of tularemia in the northern part of central Sweden. *Scand J Infect Dis.* 1984;16:285-290.

45. Warring WB, Ruffin JS. A tick-borne epidemic of tularemia. *N Engl J Med.* 1946;234:137-140.

46. Ohara Y, Sato T, Homma M. Arthropod-borne tularemia in Japan: clinical analysis of 1,374 cases observed between 1924 and 1996. *J Med Entomol.* 1998;35:471-473.

47. Markowitz LE, Hynes NA, de la Cruz P, et al. Tick-borne tularemia: an outbreak of lymphadenopathy in children. *JAMA.* 1985;254:2922-2925.

48. Young LS, Bicknell DS, Archer BG, et al. Tularemia epidemic, Vermont, 1968: forty-seven cases linked to contact with muskrats. *N Engl J Med.* 1969;280:1253-1260.

49. Evans ME, Gregory DW, Schaffner W, McGee ZA. Tularemia: a 30-year experience with 88 cases. *Medicine (Baltimore).* 1985;64:251-269.

50. Jellison WL, Epler DC, Kuhns E, Kohls GM. Tularemia in man from a domestic rural water supply. *Public Health Rep.* 1950;65:1219-1226.

51. Mignani E, Palmieri F, Fontana M, Marigo S. Italian epidemic of waterborne tularaemia. *Lancet.* 1988;2:1423.

52. Teutsch SM, Martone WJ, Brink EW, et al. Pneumonic tularemia on Martha's Vineyard. *N Engl J Med.* 1979;301:826-828.

53. Syrjälä H, Kujala P, Myllylä V, Salminen A. Airborne transmission of tularemia in farmers. *Scand J Infect Dis.* 1985;17:371-375.

54. Syrjälä H, Sutinen S, Jokinen K, Nieminen P, Tuuponen T, Salminen A. Bronchial changes in airborne tularemia. *J Laryngol Otol.* 1986;100: 1169-1176.

55. Puntigam F. Erkrakungen an torakalen formen der tularämia bei arbeitnehmern in Zuckerfabriken. *Z Hyg.* 1960;147:162-168.

56. Overholt EL, Tigertt WD, Kadull PJ, et al. An analysis of forty-two cases of laboratory-acquired tularemia. *Am J Med.* 1961;30:785-806.

57. Pike RM. Laboratory-associated infections: summary and analysis of 3921 cases. *Health Lab Sci.* 1976;13:105-114.

58. Burke DS. Immunization against tularemia: analysis of the effectiveness of live *Francisella tularensis* vaccine in prevention of laboratory-acquired tularemia. *J Infect Dis.* 1977;135:55-60.

59. Centers for Disease Control and Prevention. Summary of notifiable diseases, United States, 1994. *MMWR Morb Mortal Wkly Rep.* 1994;43:1-80.

60. Bell JF. Tularemia. In: Steele JH, ed. *CRC Handbook Series in Zoonoses.* Vol 2. Boca Raton, Fla: CRC Press; 1980:161-193.

61. Pomanskaia LA. The survival times of the organisms of tularaemia on grain and straw. *J Microbiol Epidemiol Immunobiol.* 1957;28:597-603.

62. Wong JD, Shapiro DS. *Francisella.* In : Murray PR, ed. *Manual of Clinical Microbiology.* 7th ed. Washington, DC: ASM Press; 1999:647-651.

63. Johansson A, Ibrahim A, Goransson I, et al. Evaluation of PCR-based methods for discrimination of *Francisella* species and subspecies and development of a specific PCR that distinguishes the two major subspecies of *Francisella tularensis. J Clin Microbiol.* 2000;38:4180-4185.

64. Gurycova D. First isolation of *Francisella tularensis* subspecies tularensis in Europe. *Eur J Epidemiol.* 1998;14:797-802.

65. Clarridge JE III, Raich TJ, Sjösted A, et al. Characterization of two unusual clinically significant *Francisella* strains. *J Clin Microbiol.* 1996;34:1995-2000.

66. Pavlov VM, Mokrievich AN, Volkovoy K.Cryptic plasmid pFNL10 from *Francisella novicida* -like F6168: the base of plasmid vectors for *Francisella tularensis. FEMS Immunol Med Microbiol.* 1996;13:253-256.

67. Sandström G, Sjöstedt A, Johansson T, Kuoppa K, Williams JC. Immunogenicity and toxicity of lipopolysaccharide from *Francisella tularensis* LVS. *FEMS Microbiol Immunol.* 1992;5:201-210.

68. Tärnvik A. Nature of protective immunity to *Francisella tularensis. Rev Infect Dis.* 1989;11:440-451.

69. Fortier AH, Green SJ, Polsinelli T, et al. Life and death of an intracellular pathogen: *Francisella tularensis* and the macrophage. *Immunol Ser.* 1994;60:349-361.

70. Pullen RL, Stuart BM. Tularemia: analysis of 225 cases. *JAMA.* 1945;129:495-500.

71. Lillie RD, Francis EI. The pathology of tularaemia in man (*Homo sapiens*). In: *The Pathology of Tularaemia.* Washington, DC: US Government Printing Office; 1937:1-81. National Institutes of Health Bulletin No. 167.

72. Stuart BM, Pullen RL. Tularemic pneumonia: review of American literature and report of 15 additional cases. *Am J Med Sci.* 1945;210:223-236.

73. White JD, Rooney JR, Prickett PA, Derrenbacher EH, Beard CW, Griffith WR. Pathogenesis of experimental respiratory tularemia in monkeys. *J Infect Dis.* 1964;114:277-283.

74. Cross JT, Penn RL. *Francisella tularensis* (tularemia). In: Mandell GL, et al, eds. *Principles and Practice of Infectious Diseases.* Philadelphia, Pa: Churchill Livingstone; 2000:2393-2402.

75. Avery FW, Barnett TB. Pulmonary tularemia: a report of five cases and consideration of pathogenesis and terminology. *Am Rev Respir Dis.* 1967;95:584-591.

76. Alluisi EA, Beisel WR, Bartonelli PJ, Coates GD. Behavioral effects of tularaemia and sandfly fever in man. *J Infect Dis.* 1973;128:710-717.

77. Stuart BM, Pullen RL. Tularemic meningitis: review of the literature and report of a case with postmortem observations. *Arch Intern Med.* 1945;76:163-166.

78. American Public Health Association. Tularemia. In: Chin J, ed. *Control of Communicable Diseases Manual.* Washington, DC: American Public Health Association; 2000:532-535.

79. Amoss HL, Sprunt DH. Tularemia: review of literature of cases contracted by ingestion of rabbit and the report of additional cases with a necropsy. *JAMA.* 1936;106:1078-1080.

80. Sunderrajan EV, Hutton J, Marienfeld D. Adult respiratory distress syndrome secondary to tularemia pneumonia. *Arch Intern Med.* 1985;145:1435-1437.

81. Centers for Disease Control and Prevention. Basic laboratory protocols for the presumptive identification of *Francisella tularensis.* Available at: http://www.bt.cdc.gov/Agent/Tularemia/tularemia20010417.pdf. Accessed April 20, 2001.

82. White JD, McGavran MH. Identification of *Pasteurella tularensis* by immunofluorescence. *JAMA.* 1965;194:294-296.

83. Guarner J, Greer PW, Bartlett J, Chu MC, Shieh WJ, Zaki SR. Immunohistochemical detection of *Francisella tularensis* in formalin-fixed paraffin-embedded tissue. *Appl Immunohistochem Mol Morphol.* 1999;7:122-126.

84. Syrjälä H, Koskela P, Ripatti T, Salminen A, Herva E. Agglutination and ELISA methods in the diagnosis of tularemia in different clinical forms and severities of the disease. *J Infect Dis.* 1986;153:142-145.

85. Bevanger L, Macland JA, Naess AI. Agglutinins and antibodies to *Francisella tularensis* outer membrane antigens in the early diagnosis of disease during an outbreak of tularemia. *J Clin Microbiol.* 1988;26:433-437.

86. Grunow R, Splettstoesser W, McDonald S, et al. Detection of *Francisella tularensis* in biological specimens using a capture enzyme-linked immunosorbent assay, an immunochromatographic handheld assay, and a PCR. *Clin Diagn Lab Immunol.* 2000;7:86-90.

87. Higgins JA, Hubalek Z, Halouzka J, et al. Detection of Francisella tularensis in infected mammals and vectors using a proble-based polymerase chain reaction. *Am J Trop Med Hyg.* 2000;62:310-318.

88. Sjöstedt A, Tärnvik A, Sandström G. *Francisella tularensis* : host-parasite interaction. *FEMS Immunol Med Microbiol.* 1996;13:181-184.

89. French GR, Plotkin SA. Miscellaneous limited-use vaccines. In: Plotkin S, Mortimer EA, eds. *Vaccine.* Philadelphia, Pa: WB Saunders; 1999:728-733.

90. Enderlin G, Morales L, Jacobs RF, Cross TJ. Streptomycin and alternative agents for the treatment of tularemia: review of the literature. *Clin Infect Dis.* 1994;19:42-47.

91. Jacobs RF, Narain JP. Tularemia in children. *Pediatr Infect Dis.* 1983;2:487-491.

92. Mason WL, Eigelsbach HT, Little SF, et al. Treatment of tularemia, including pulmonary tularemia, with gentamicin. *Am Rev Respir Dis.* 1980;121:39-45.

93. Cross JT, Schutze GE, Jacobs RF. Treatment of tularemia with gentamicin in pediatric patients. *Pediatr Infect Dis J.* 1995;14:151-152.

94. Syrjälä H, Schildt R, Räisäinen S. In vitro susceptibility of *Francisella tularensis* to fluoroquinolones and treatment of tularemia with norfloxacin and ciprofloxacin. *Eur J Clin Microbiol Infect Dis.* 1991;10:68-70.

95. Russell P, Eley SM, Fulop MJ, Bell DL, Titball RW. The efficacy of ciprofloxacin and doxycycline against tularemia. *J Antimicrob Chemother.* 1998;41:461-465.

96. Limaye AP, Hooper CJ. Treatment of tularemia with fluoroquinolones: two cases and review. *Clin Infect Dis.* 1999;29:922-924.

97. Johansson A, Berglund L, Gothefors L, et al. Ciprofloxacin for treatment of tularemia in children. *Pediatr Infect Dis J.* 2000;19:449-453.

98. Cross JT, Jacobs RF. Tularemia: treatment failures with outpatient use of ceftriaxone. *Clin Infect Dis.* 1993;17:976-980.

99. Quinolones. In: *AHFS Drug Information 1999.* Bethesda, Md: American Society of Health-System Pharmacists; 1999:670-684.

100. American Academy of Pediatrics. Antimicrobials and related therapy. In: Peter G, ed. *Red Book 2000: Report of the Committee on Infectious Diseases.* 25th ed. Elk Grove Village, Ill: American Academy of Pediatrics; 2000:645-646.

101. Garner JS. Guideline for isolation precautions in hospitals. *Infect Control Hosp Epidemiol.* 1996;17:53-80.

102. US Department of Health and Human Services. Laboratory biosafety level criteria. In: Richmond JY, McKinney RW, eds. *Biosafety in Microbiological and Biomedical Laboratories.* 4th ed. Washington, DC: Dept of Health and Human Services; 1999: 17-52.

Hemorrhagic Fever Viruses as Biological Weapons

Luciana Borio, MD; Thomas V. Inglesby, MD; C. J. Peters, MD; Alan L. Schmaljohn, PhD; James M. Hughes, MD; Peter B. Jahrling, PhD; Thomas Ksiazek, DVM, PhD; Karl M. Johnson, MD; Andrea Meyerhoff, MD; Tara O'Toole, MD, MPH; Michael S. Ascher, MD, FACP; John G. Bartlett, MD; Joel G. Breman, MD, DTPH; Edward Eitzen, Jr, MD, MPH; Margaret A. Hamburg, MD; Jerome Hauer, MPH; Donald A. Henderson, MD, MPH; Richard T. Johnson, MD; Gigi Kwik, PhD; Marcelle Layton, MD; Scott Lillibridge, MD; Gary J. Nabel, MD, PhD; Michael T. Osterholm, PhD, MPH; Trish M. Perl, MD, MSc; Philip K. Russell, MD; Kevin Tonat, DrPH, MPH; for the Working Group on Civilian Biodefense

Hemorrhagic fever viruses (HFVs) are the subject of the sixth article in a series on medical and public health management of civilian populations following use of biological weapons.[1-5] Historically, the term *viral hemorrhagic fever* (VHF) has referred to a clinical illness associated with fever and a bleeding diathesis caused by a virus belonging to 1 of 4 distinct families: Filoviridae, Arenaviridae, Bunyaviridae, and Flaviviridae (**Table 1**).

The HFVs are transmitted to humans via contact with infected animal reservoirs or arthropod vectors (the natural reservoirs and vectors of the Ebola and Marburg viruses are unknown). The mode of transmission, clinical course, and mortality of these illnesses vary with the specific virus, but each is capable of causing a hemorrhagic fever syndrome. Clinical and epidemiological data are limited; outbreaks are sporadic and unanticipated, and there are few case series or clinical trials involving human subjects.

The Working Group on Civilian Biodefense previously established a list of key features that characterize biological agents that pose particularly serious risks if used as biological weapons against civilian populations: (1) high morbidity and mortality; (2) potential for person-to-person transmission, with a commensurate ability to cause large outbreaks; (3) low infective dose and highly infectious by aerosol dissemination; (4) effective therapy or vaccine unavailable or available only in limited supply; (5) potential to cause public and health care worker anxiety; (6) availability of pathogen or toxin; (7) feasibility of large-scale production; (8) environmental stability; and (9) prior research and development as a biological weapon. Some HFVs exhibit a significant number of these key characteristics and pose serious risk as biological weapons, including Ebola and Marburg viruses

Table 1. Hemorrhagic Fever Viruses*

Family	Genus	Virus	Disease	Vector in Nature	Geographic Distribution
Filoviridae	Filovirus	**Ebola**†	Ebola hemorrhagic fever	Unknown	Africa
		Marburg	Marburg hemorrhagic fever	Unknown	Africa
Arenaviridae	Arenavirus	**Lassa**	Lassa fever	Rodent	West Africa
		New World Arenaviridae‡	New World hemorrhagic fever	Rodent	Americas
Bunyaviridae	Nairovirus	Crimean-Congo hemorrhagic fever	Crimean-Congo hemorrhagic fever	Tick	Africa, central Asia, eastern Europe, Middle East
	Phlebovirus	**Rift Valley fever**	Rift Valley fever	Mosquito	Africa, Saudi Arabia, Yemen
	Hantavirus	Agents of hemorrhagic fever with renal syndrome	Hemorrhagic fever with renal syndrome	Rodent	Asia, Balkans, Europe, Eurasia§
Flaviviridae	Flavivirus	Dengue	Dengue fever, hemorrhagic fever, Dengue and Dengue shock syndrome	Mosquito	Asia, Africa, Pacific, Americas
		Yellow fever	Yellow fever	Mosquito	Africa, tropical Americas
		Omsk hemorrhagic fever	Omsk hemorrhagic fever	Tick	Central Asia
		Kyasanur Forest disease	Kyasanur Forest disease	Tick	India

* Bold indicates hemorrhagic fever viruses that pose serious risk as biological weapons (addressed in this consensus statement).

† There are 4 subtypes of Ebola: Zaire, Sudan, Ivory Coast, and Reston.

‡ The New World Arenaviridae include Machupo, the cause of Bolivian hemorrhagic fever; Junin, the cause of Argentine hemorrhagic fever; Guanarito, the cause of Venezuelan hemorrhagic fever; and Sabia, the cause of Brazilian hemorrhagic fever. An additional arenavirus has been isolated following 3 fatal cases of hemorrhagic fever in California, 1999-2000.[6]

§ Additionally, the agents of hantavirus pulmonary syndrome have been isolated in North America.

(Filoviridae), Lassa fever and New World arenaviruses (Arenaviridae), Rift Valley fever (Bunyaviridae), and yellow fever, Omsk hemorrhagic fever, and Kyasanur Forest disease (Flaviviridae).

Several viruses that can cause VHF will not be considered further in this analysis. Dengue is excluded because it is not transmissible by small-particle aerosol,[7] and primary dengue causes VHF only rarely. Crimean-Congo hemorrhagic fever (CCHF) and the agents of hemorrhagic fever with renal syndrome (HFRS) also have been excluded after much deliberation. Although these pathogens can cause VHF and may be transmissible by aerosol dissemination, the Working Group noted that technical difficulties (ie, barriers to large-scale production) currently preclude their development as mass casualty weapons. Crimean-Congo hemorrhagic fever and the agents of HFRS do not readily replicate to high concentrations in cell cultures, a prerequisite for weaponization of an infectious organism. However, CCHF, the agents of HFRS, and dengue may carry great morbidity and mortality in naturally occurring outbreaks. In particular, CCHF may be transmitted from person to person, has a high case-fatality rate, and is endemic in central Asia and southern Africa. We acknowledge that technical difficulties may be overcome with advances in technology and science, and these excluded viruses may become a greater threat in the future. Other sources provide information on the viruses not addressed herein.[8-12]

The consequences of an unannounced aerosol attack with an HFV are the primary focus of this analysis. A variety of attack scenarios with these agents are possible. This analysis does not attempt to forecast the most likely but focuses on perhaps the most serious scenario. Understanding and planning for a covert aerosol attack with HFVs will improve preparedness for other scenarios as well.

Consensus Methods

The working group for this article was composed of 26 professionals from academic medical centers, public health, military services, governmental agencies, and emergency management institutions. MEDLINE databases were searched from January 1966 to January 2002 for the Medical Subject Headings *viral hemorrhagic fever*, *Ebola*, *Marburg*, *Lassa*, *arenavirus*, *Junin*, *Guanarito*, *Machupo*, *Sabia*, *CCHF*, *Rift Valley fever*, *hantavirus*, *dengue*, *yellow fever*, *Omsk hemorrhagic fever*, *Kyasanur Forest disease*, *biological weapons*, *biological terrorism*, *biological warfare*, and *biowarfare*. The references were reviewed and relevant materials published prior to 1966 were identified. The working group also identified other published and unpublished references for review.

A first draft resulted from the synthesis of information obtained during the evidence-gathering process. Members of the working group were convened to discuss the first draft of the formulated guidelines on January 10, 2002. Subsequently, a second draft was produced incorporating comments and judgments of the working group. They reviewed the second draft and submitted comments, which were incorporated into a third and final draft of the document.

History and Potential as Biological Weapons

Hemorrhagic fever viruses have been weaponized by the former Soviet Union, Russia, and the United States.[13-15] There are reports that yellow fever may have been weaponized by North Korea.[14] The former Soviet Union and Russia produced large quantities of Marburg, Ebola, Lassa, and New World arenaviruses (specifically, Junin and Machupo) until 1992.[13,15] Soviet Union researchers quantified the aerosol infectivity of Marburg virus for monkeys, determining that no more than a few virions are required to cause infection.[16] Yellow fever and Rift Valley fever viruses were developed as weapons by the US offensive biological weapons program prior to its termination in 1969.[14] The Japanese terrorist cult Aum Shinrikyo unsuccessfully attempted to obtain Ebola virus as part of an effort to create biological weapons.[17]

Several studies have demonstrated successful infection of nonhuman primates by aerosol preparations of Ebola,[18] Marburg,[19] Lassa,[20] and New World arenaviruses.[21] Arguments asserting that the absence of effective antiviral therapy and vaccines would make these viruses too dangerous to develop as weapons are not supported by the historical record.

In 1999, the Centers for Disease Control and Prevention (CDC) classified the HFVs as category A bioweapon agents, based on the potential to cause widespread illness and death, ease of dissemination or person-to-person transmission, potential for major public health impact, and requirement of special action for public health preparedness.[22]

Epidemiology of Disease Transmission

In nature, HFVs reside in animal hosts or arthropod vectors. The natural reservoir of filoviruses is unknown. Humans are infected incidentally, acquiring the disease by the bite of an infected arthropod, via aerosol generated from infected rodent excreta, or by direct contact with infected animal carcasses.[23] With the exception of Rift Valley fever and the diseases caused by flaviviruses (yellow fever, Omsk hemorrhagic fever, and Kyasanur Forest disease), which are not transmissible from person to person, infected humans can spread the disease to close contacts, which may result in community outbreaks and nosocomial infections. Limited knowledge exists about transmission because outbreaks of these diseases are sporadic and unpredicted and often occur in areas without adequate medical and public health infrastructure. Outbreaks are usually well under way or have subsided by the time data gathering begins. The risks associated with various modes of transmission are not well defined because most persons who acquire these infections have a history of multiple contacts by multiple modes. Infections acquired percutaneously are associated with the shortest incubation period and highest mortality. Person-to-person airborne transmission by way of small-droplet nuclei appears to be rare but cannot be ruled out.

Filoviridae: Ebola and Marburg

Since 1967, when the first outbreak of VHF caused by Marburg virus occurred in Germany and Yugoslavia, there have been 18 reports of human outbreaks of VHF secondary to Ebola or Marburg viruses, resulting in approximately 1500 cases to date.[24] Most have occurred in Africa. Epidemiological investigation indicates that most cases occurred after direct contact with blood, secretions, or tissues of infected patients or nonhuman primates.

Several cases have followed needlestick injuries. During the 1976 Ebola epidemic in Zaire (now Democratic Republic of the Congo), 85 (26.7%) of 318 cases occurred in individuals who had received an injection, and every case of disease acquired by contaminated syringes resulted in death.[25] Mortality was substantially higher when the disease was acquired percutaneously. Evidence suggests that percutaneous exposure to very low inocula can result in infection.[26]

Filoviruses can also be transmitted by mucosal exposure. Experiments in nonhuman primates have documented transmission of infection after direct administration of Marburg virus into the mouths and noses of experimental animals[27] and after direct administration of Ebola virus into the mouths or conjunctiva[28] of experimental animals. Human infections might occur through contact of contaminated fingers with oral mucosa or conjunctiva,[29] but direct evidence is lacking.

Copious numbers of Ebola viral particles found in human skin and lumina of sweat glands have raised concern that disease transmission may occur from touching an infected patient or corpse.[30] In the 1995 Ebola outbreak in Kikwit, Democratic Republic of the Congo, several persons preparing bodies for burial acquired the infection.[31-33] According to local custom, burial practices may involve washing the body and cutting the hair and nails of the corpse.[34] However, a study using guinea pigs was unable to document Marburg virus transmission through intact skin, while infection through skin lesions did occur.[35]

A few cases of disease transmission by uncertain mechanisms described in 2 recent Ebola outbreaks,[36, 37] and findings from animal studies[16, 18, 38] and 1 outbreak of Ebola in nonhuman primates,[39] raise concern about the potential for person-to-person airborne transmission by way of small-droplet nuclei. However, to date, Ebola epidemics in Africa were ultimately controlled and ended without use of specific airborne precautions. (HICPAC's definitions of standard, contact, droplet, and airborne precautions are at www.cdc.gov/ncidod/hip/isolat/isopart2.htm.)

Airborne transmission of Marburg virus was not observed in the 1967 outbreak in Germany and Yugoslavia following the importation of infected African green monkeys from eastern Africa.[40] In 1975, only 1 of 35 health care workers who cared for 2 patients with Marburg disease in South Africa without any barrier precautions became ill.[41] In 1979, an outbreak of Ebola in southern Sudan infected 34 people. Although direct physical contact could not be established in 2 instances, 29 cases resulted from direct physical contact with an infected person and there were no cases of illness among 103 persons who were exposed to cases in confined spaces without any physical contact.[42] In 1994, only 1 of 70 contacts of a patient with Ebola acquired the disease despite lack of airborne precautions.[43] In 1996, none of the 300 contacts of 2 patients with Ebola acquired the disease[44] despite involvement in numerous hazardous procedures prior to the patients' diagnosis, protected only by standard blood and bodily fluid precautions.

In 1995, 316 people became ill with Ebola in the Democratic Republic of the Congo; 25% of the cases involved health care workers. When barrier precautions were instituted, only 3 health care workers became infected. One was nonadherent to barrier precautions, the second had a needlestick injury, and it is speculated that the third, who always used protective equipment, became infected after touching her eyes with a contaminated glove.[45] None of the 78 household members who did not have direct physical contact with an infected person developed disease.[31] However, in this outbreak, the only risk factor identified for 5 patients was visiting an infected patient in the absence of physical contact. These few cases led researchers to conclude that airborne transmission could not be ruled out[37] but seemed to be, at most, a minor mode of transmission.

In 2000, 224 people died in Uganda during an Ebola outbreak.[37] Fourteen (64%) of 22 medical personnel were infected after institution of isolation wards and infection control measures,[37] including donning gowns, gloves, shoe covers, standard surgical masks, and either goggles or eye glasses.[46] It is not clear whether lack of adherence to guidelines contributed to nosocomial cases in this outbreak, but airborne transmission could not be ruled out.

Although Marburg virus has been isolated from healthy-appearing infected monkeys several days before clinical signs appear,[27] no transmission has been observed in this stage.[40] In humans, transmission of Ebola during the incubation period does not appear to be common.[31] Transmissibility of Ebola increases with the duration of disease, and direct physical contact with an ill person during the late phase of clinical illness confers an additional risk.[31] There has been only 1 reported case, during the outbreak in Zaire in 1976, in which the only possible source of infection was contact with an unconfirmed case hours before the patient developed symptoms.[25] The preponderance of evidence suggests that transmission of Ebola and Marburg virus rarely, if ever, occurs before the onset of signs and symptoms.

In several studies after the 1995 Kikwit outbreak, Ebola was detected in the seminal fluid of convalescing patients by reverse transcriptase polymerase chain reaction (RT-PCR) up to 101 days after disease onset,[47,48] and virus was isolated 82 days after disease onset in the seminal fluid of 1 patient.[48] Marburg has been isolated 83 days after disease onset from the seminal fluid of a patient who may have sexually transmitted the disease to his spouse.[40]

Arenaviridae: Lassa Fever and New World Arenaviruses

In nature, arenaviruses are transmitted to humans via inhalation of aerosols present in rodent urine and feces,[49] by ingestion of food contaminated with rodent excreta, or by direct contact of rodent excreta with abraded skin and mucous membranes.[50] Like filoviruses, person-to-person transmission of the arenaviruses occurs predominantly by direct contact with infectious blood and bodily fluids. A number of nosocomial outbreaks of Lassa fever[51-53] and of New World arenaviruses[54] have occurred via this mechanism. As with filoviruses, person-to-person airborne transmission has been suspected in a few instances.

In 1969, during a nosocomial outbreak in Nigeria, an index patient with severe pulmonary involvement caused 16 secondary cases in persons who shared the same hospital ward with her. Airborne transmission was believed to have contributed to this outbreak, as there were no tertiary cases of Lassa fever in the hospital, despite the admission of Lassa fever–infected patients to other hospital wards.[51] However, there is no definitive evidence of airborne transmission and the exact mechanisms of disease transmission during that outbreak remain unknown. Conversely, in the case of 1 Lassa fever–infected individual who traveled from Sierra Leone to the United States, no cases were detected in 522 contacts, even prior to initiating additional barrier precautions beyond standard precautions.[55] In another instance, in which an infected individual originated in Nigeria and traveled to St Thomas in the US Virgin Islands, none of the 159 people who had direct contact with the patient developed clinical or serological evidence of infection, even though they attended to the patient, without barrier precautions, during a 5-day period before the diagnosis.[56]

Airborne transmission of Bolivian hemorrhagic fever has been implicated after a student became infected after watching a nursing instructor demonstrate the changing of bed linens of an infected patient, although the student did not touch the patient or any objects in the room and kept a distance of greater than 6 ft from the patient.[54] Conversely, approximately 80 involved health care workers who did not use airborne precautions remained healthy. Definitive evidence of person-to-person airborne transmission is lacking but, in these rare instances, there have been no plausible alternative explanations.

There have been no reports documenting transmission of arenaviruses by infected persons during the incubation period.[54, 57] However, Lassa fever virus can be detected in semen up to 3 months after acute infection[58] and in urine 32 days after disease onset,[59] and Argentine hemorrhagic fever has been transmitted to spouses of convalescent patients 7 to 22 days after onset of illness.[60]

Bunyaviridae: Rift Valley Fever

Humans acquire Rift Valley fever from the bite of an infected mosquito, direct contact with infected animal tissues, or aerosolization of virus from infected animal carcasses.[61] Ingestion of contaminated raw animal milk has been implicated epidemiologically.[62] Despite high levels of viremia and isolation of low titers of virus from throat washings, there are no reported cases of person-to-person transmission of Rift Valley fever.[62] However, laboratory technicians are at risk of acquiring the disease by inhalation of infectious aerosols generated from specimens.[61, 63]

If Rift Valley fever were used as a biological weapon, susceptible domestic livestock (sheep, cattle, buffalo, and goats) could also be infected. Infected livestock develop high levels of viremia, sufficient to infect susceptible mosquito vectors and lead to establishment of the disease in the environment[61] and large epizootic epidemics, as occurred in Egypt in 1977[64] and the Arabian peninsula in 2000.[65] Several genera of mosquitoes (eg, *Aedes*, *Anopheles*, and *Culex*) in the United States have the capacity to act as vectors of Rift Valley fever.[66, 67]

Flaviviridae: Yellow Fever, Omsk Hemorrhagic Fever, and Kyasanur Forest Disease

Humans acquire yellow fever virus from the bite of an infected mosquito[68] and acquire Omsk hemorrhagic fever and Kyasanur Forest disease viruses from the bite of an infected tick.[69] There are no reported cases of person-to-person transmission or nosocomial spread of flaviviruses. Infection of laboratory personnel via inhalation of aerosols during cultivation of these viruses has been reported.[69, 70] As with Rift Valley fever, there is a theoretical risk of flaviviruses becoming established in an environment following infection of susceptible arthropod vectors.

Microbiology and Pathogenesis

All of the HFVs are small RNA viruses with lipid envelopes. Specific microbiological characteristics of these viruses are listed in **Table 2.**

Information regarding the pathogenesis of these agents following infection in humans is incomplete. Most data have been derived from clinical observations and experimentally induced disease in nonhuman primates. Interpretation of data derived from animal studies may be confounded by a series of factors, such as the species of the animal, the route of inoculation, and the virus dose.[40]

All of the viruses of concern may lead to thrombocytopenia, and data suggest that platelet dysfunction is present in Ebola, Lassa fever, and Argentine hemorrhagic fever.[72] Reduced levels of coagulation factors may be secondary to hepatic dysfunction and/or disseminated intravascular coagulation and are most prominent in Rift Valley fever and yellow fever.[72] In addition, Ebola and Marburg viruses may lead to a hemorrhagic diathesis through direct damage of cells involved in hemostasis (such as platelets and endothelial cells) and/or indirectly through immunological and inflammatory pathways.[72]

Filoviruses are extremely virulent in nonhuman primates and humans.[73] Necrosis of visceral organs (such as liver, spleen, and kidneys) has been associated with both direct viral-induced cellular damage and impairment of the microcirculation. Filoviruses are cytotoxic to cells. In general, inflammatory infiltration is absent in the affected visceral organs.[74] Even when viral titers in the lungs of monkeys are elevated, the virus is not apparent in the alveoli or airways, occurring primarily in the vascular structures.[28] All experimentally infected monkeys develop disseminated intravascular coagulation. Ebola, but not Marburg virus, makes a secreted form of its glycoprotein that has been suggested to have a role in virulence.[73] Endothelial cells support Marburg virus replication, and their destruction may contribute to the associated hemorrhagic diathesis and shock.[75]

Infection with arenaviruses is initiated in nasopharyngeal mucosa.[76] Arenaviruses produce carrier states in rodents, their natural hosts, and viral multiplication is not associated with extensive cell damage. In vitro infections with Arenaviridae show that virus spreads throughout a variety of different cellular monolayers, with little or absent cytopathic effects[77]; hence, it is believed that these viruses may exert their effects (at least in part) by inducing the secretion of inflammatory mediators from macrophages. Following experimental infection of nonhuman primates with

Table 2. Microbiology of Hemorrhagic Fever Viruses[71]

Family	Diameter, nm	Morphology	Presence of Envelope	Genome		
				Size, kbp	Nature*	Configuration*
Filoviridae	80	Bacilliform (filamentous)	Yes	19	Single-strand RNA (–)	Nonsegmented (1 – segment)
Arenaviridae	110-130	Spherical	Yes	11	Single-strand RNA (±)	2 ± Segments
Bunyaviridae	80-120	Spherical	Yes	11-19	Single-strand RNA (–)	3 – Segments
Flaviviridae	40-50	Isometric	Yes	10-12	Single-strand RNA (+)	Nonsegmented (1 + segment)

* Minus sign indicates negative-strand genome; plus sign, positive-strand genome; and plus/minus sign, ambisense genome.

arenaviruses, virtually all tissues become infected, with little histologic evidence of damage.[78] Hemorrhage following arenavirus infection appears to be associated with the presence of a circulating inhibitor of platelet aggregation and thrombocytopenia. However, disseminated intravascular coagulation does not appear to be a central pathogenic mechanism.[79] Lassa fever appears to be terminated by a cellular, not humoral, immune response,[77] whereas in New World arenaviruses, recovery is preceded by cellular and humoral immune responses.[80]

In contrast with arenaviruses, Rift Valley fever virus leads to destruction of infected cells.[77] The hemostatic derangements in Rift Valley fever are poorly understood, and a combination of vasculitis and hepatic necrosis has been postulated.[81,82] Interferon alfa given shortly before or after experimental infection with Rift Valley fever virus has been shown to protect rhesus monkeys from viremia and hepatocellular damage.[83] Clinical recovery is associated with appearance of neutralizing antibodies, and passive immunization prevented development of viremia in nonhuman primates inoculated with the virus.[83]

Like Rift Valley fever, yellow fever virus leads to destruction of infected cells. Hepatocyte infection and degeneration is a late event in the course of infection,[84] associated with virtually no inflammation.[68] Neutralizing antibodies correlate with clearance of viremia, and paradoxically, with the second phase of illness, when patients may develop hemorrhage and shock.[68]

Little is known about the pathogenesis of Omsk hemorrhagic fever and Kyasanur Forest disease viruses. Findings from postmortem examinations of 3 individuals who died of Kyasanur Forest disease showed degeneration of the larger visceral organs (especially liver and spleen) and hemorrhagic pneumonia.[85]

Clinical Manifestations

Information on the clinical manifestations of these diseases is derived from naturally occurring outbreaks. Although data derived from experimentally infected animals do not support marked differences in the clinical presentation according to route of exposure (parenteral vs aerosol),[18, 21] it is not possible to be certain that the same manifestations would follow bioweapons attacks on humans.

There are a variety of potential clinical manifestations following infection with these viruses, and not all patients develop the classic VHF syndrome. Clinical manifestations are nonspecific and may include fever, myalgias, rash, and encephalitis. The propensity to cause the classic VHF syndrome also differs among agents. Therefore, in the event of a bioterrorist attack with one of these agents, infected patients may have a variety of clinical presentations, complicating early detection and management. It may not be possible to differentiate among these diseases on clinical grounds alone, although a number of specific clinical features may be useful clues to diagnosis (**Table 3**).

The overall incubation period for HFVs ranges from 2 to 21 days. Patients initially exhibit a nonspecific prodrome, which typically lasts less than 1 week. Symptoms typically include high fever, headache, malaise, arthralgias, myalgias, nausea, abdominal pain, and nonbloody diarrhea. Filoviruses, Rift Valley fever,

Table 3. Clinical Characteristics of Hemorrhagic Fever Viruses Noted in Past Case Series or Outbreaks

Virus	Distinctive Clinical Features	Person-to-Person Transmission	Incubation Period, d	Mortality, %	Treatment
Ebola[25, 42-44, 47, 86, 99]	High fever and severe prostration. A diffuse maculopapular rash may occur by day 5 of illness. Bleeding and disseminated intravascular coagulation are common.	Yes	2-21	50-90*	Supportive
Marburg[40, 41, 87, 102]	High fever, myalgias. Nonpruritic maculopapular rash of the face, neck, trunk, and arms may develop. Bleeding and disseminated intravascular coagulation are common.	Yes	2-14	23-70†	Supportive
Lassa fever[52, 88-91, 100, 101, 110]	Gradual onset of fever, nausea, abdominal pain, severe sore throat, cough, conjunctivitis, ulceration of buccal mucosa, exudative pharyngitis, and cervical lymphadenopathy. Late signs include severe swelling of head and neck; pleural and pericardial effusions. Hemorrhagic complications less common.	Yes	5-16	15-20	Ribavirin, supportive

Virus	Distinctive Clinical Features	Person-to-Person Trans-mission	Incubation Period, d	Mortality, %	Treatment
New World arenaviruses [54, 92, 128]	Gradual onset of fever, myalgias, nausea, abdominal pain, conjunctivitis, flushing of face and trunk, and generalized lymphadenopathy. May develop petechiae, bleeding, and central nervous system dysfunction (tremors of the tongue and upper extremities, myoclonic movements, dysarthria, and generalized seizures).	Yes	7-14	15-30	Ribavirin, supportive
Rift Valley fever[61, 93-96]	Fever, headache, retro-orbital pain, photophobia, and jaundice. Less than 1% develop hemorrhagic fever or encephalitis. Retinitis affects approximately 10%, which may occur at time of acute febrile illness or up to 4 weeks later.	No	2-6	<1	Ribavirin, supportive
Yellow fever [68, 97]	Fever, myalgias, facial flushing, and conjunctival injection. Patients either recover or enter a short remission followed by fever, relative bradycardia, jaundice, renal failure, and hemorrhagic complications.	No	3-6	20	Supportive
Omsk hemorrhagic fever[69‡]	Fever, cough, conjunctivitis, papulovesicular eruption on the soft palate, marked hyperemia of the face and trunk (but no rash), generalized lymphadenopathy, and splenomegaly. Some patients may develop pneumonia and central nervous system dysfunction.	No	2-9	0.5-10	Supportive
Kyasanur Forest disease[69, 98]	Similar to Omsk but biphasic illness: first phase lasts 6-11 days and is followed by an afebrile period of 9-21 days. Up to 50% of patients relapse and develop meningoencephalitis.	No	2-9	3-10	Supportive

* Reported Ebola data are for Sudan (50%) and Zaire (90%) subtypes. The Ivory Coast subtype has an indeterminate case-fatality rate, as there has been a single nonfatal human case. The Reston subtype causes subclinical infection in humans.

† Mortality ranges from 23% in the 1967 outbreak in Germany to 70% in the largest outbreak of 1999 in the Democratic Republic of the Congo.

‡ Also Sergey Netesov, MD, written communication, February 27, 2002.

and flaviviruses are characterized by an abrupt onset, while arenaviruses have a more insidious onset.[40, 54, 61, 68, 69, 99, 100]

Early signs typically include fever, hypotension, relative bradycardia, tachypnea, conjunctivitis, and pharyngitis. Most diseases are associated with cutaneous flushing or a rash (**Figure 1** and **Figure 2**), but the specific characteristics of the rash vary with each disease (Table 3). Later, patients may show signs of progressive hemorrhagic diathesis, such as petechiae, mucous membrane, and conjunctival hemorrhage (**Figure 3**); hematuria; hematemesis; and melena. Disseminated intravascular coagulation and circulatory shock may ensue. Central nervous system dysfunction may be present and manifested by delirium, convulsions, cerebellar signs, or coma and imparts a poor prognosis.

The differential diagnosis includes a variety of viral and bacterial diseases: influenza, viral hepatitis, staphylococcal or gram-negative sepsis, toxic shock syndrome, meningococcemia, salmonellosis and shigellosis, rickettsial diseases (such as Rocky Mountain spotted fever), leptospirosis, borreliosis, psittacosis, dengue, hantavirus pulmonary syndrome, malaria, trypanosomiasis, septicemic plague, rubella, measles, and hemorrhagic smallpox. Noninfectious processes associated with bleeding diathesis that should be included in the differential diagnosis include idiopathic or thrombotic thrombocytopenic purpura, hemolytic uremic syndrome, acute leukemia, and collagen-vascular diseases.

Laboratory abnormalities include leukopenia (except in some cases of Lassa fever, in which leukocytosis occurs), anemia or hemoconcentration, thrombocytopenia, and elevated liver enzymes. Jaundice is typical in Rift Valley fever and yellow fever.[61, 68] In addition, coagulation abnormalities may include prolonged bleeding time, prothrombin time, and activated partial thromboplastin time; elevated fibrin degradation products; and decreased fibrinogen. Urinalysis may reveal proteinuria and hematuria, and patients may develop oliguria and azotemia.[26, 40, 54, 61, 68, 100, 101]

Convalescence may be prolonged and complicated by weakness, fatigue, anorexia, cachexia, alopecia, and arthralgias.[43, 45] Reported clinical sequelae include hearing or vision loss, impaired motor coordination, transverse myelitis, uveitis, pericarditis, orchitis, parotitis, and pancreatitis.[36, 40, 52, 54, 61, 102]

The case-fatality rate varies markedly among these agents, ranging from as low as 0.5% for Omsk hemorrhagic fever[69] to as high as 90% for Ebola (subtype Zaire).[33] Death is typically preceded by hemorrhagic diathesis, shock, and multiorgan system failure 1 to 2 weeks following onset of symptoms.

Diagnosis

A high index of suspicion will be required to diagnose VHF among persons exposed to a covert bioterrorist attack. In naturally occurring cases, patients are likely to have risk factors such as travel to Africa or Asia, handling of animal carcasses, contact with sick animals or people, or arthropod bites within 21 days of onset of symptoms. No such risk factors would be associated with a bioterrorist attack. The variable clinical presentation of these diseases presents

Figure 1. Maculopapular Rash in Marburg Disease

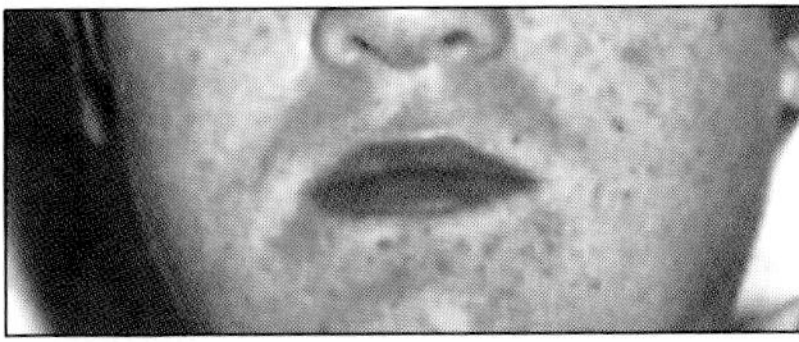

A nonpruritic maculopapular rash (resembling the rash of measles) may occur in up to 50% of patients infected with the Ebola or Marburg viruses within the first week of illness. The rash is more common in light-colored skin and desquamates on resolution. Reproduced with permission from Thieme (Martini GA, Knauff HG, Schmidt HA, et al. A hitherto unknown infectious disease contracted from monkeys. *Ger Med Mon.* 1968;13:457-470).

Figure 2. Erythematous Rash in Bolivian Hemorrhagic Fever

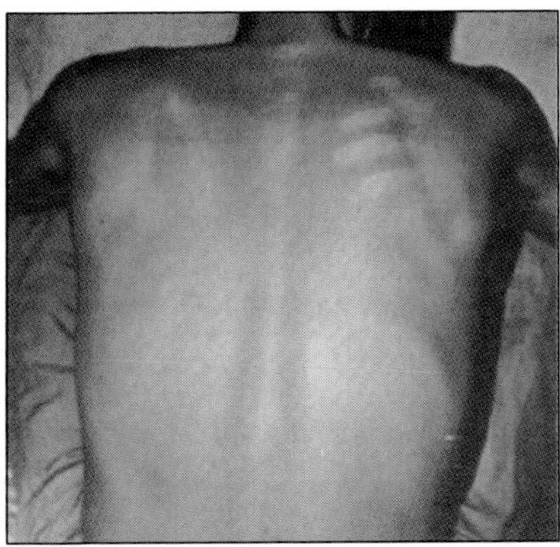

This macular, flushed, erythematous rash that blanches with pressure may be associated with infections caused by arenaviruses. The rash most commonly involves the face and thorax and may desquamate on convalescence. Reproduced with permission from Current Science/Current Medicine (Peters CJ, Zaki SR, Rollin PE. Viral hemorrhagic fevers. In: Fekety R, vol ed. *Atlas of Infectious Diseases, Volume VIII.* Philadelphia, Pa: Churchill Livingstone; 1997:10.1-10.26).

Figure 3. Ocular Manifestations in Bolivian Hemorrhagic Fever

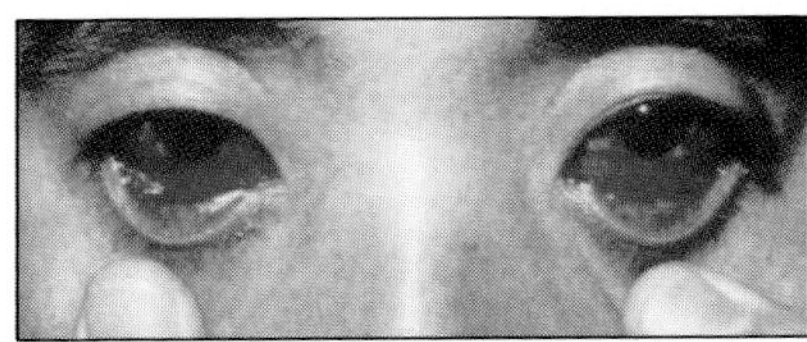

Ocular manifestations associated with hemorrhagic fever viruses range from conjunctival injection to subconjunctival hemorrhage, as seen in this patient. Reproduced with permission from Current Science/Current Medicine (Peters CJ, Zaki SR, Rollin PE. Viral hemorrhagic fevers. In: Fekety R, vol ed. *Atlas of Infectious Diseases, Volume VIII.* Philadelphia, Pa: Churchill Livingstone; 1997:10.1-10.26).

a major diagnostic challenge. Clinical microbiology and public health laboratories are not currently equipped to make a rapid diagnosis of any of these viruses, and clinical specimens would need to be sent to the CDC or the US Army Medical Research Institute of Infectious Diseases (USAMRIID; Frederick, Md), the only 2 level D laboratories in the Laboratory Response Network. There are future plans to decentralize the process required for the laboratory confirmation of these viruses by equipping selected US public health laboratories in the Laboratory Response Network with standard diagnostic reagents. This would likely expedite laboratory confirmation of suspected cases in the event of an outbreak (M.S.A., written communication, February 26, 2002).

All suspected cases of HFV disease should be immediately reported to local and/or state health departments (**Box 1**), who would then notify the CDC. The World Health Organization has developed surveillance standards for acute VHF syndrome with the aim of early detection of naturally occurring outbreaks and notification of cases, even before identification of the causal agent.[103] This includes prompt reporting to public health authorities of any patient with acute onset of fever of less than 3 weeks' duration who is severely ill, has no known predisposing host factors for hemorrhagic manifestations, and has any 2 of the following: hemorrhagic or purpuric rash, epistaxis, hematemesis, hemoptysis, blood in stool, or other hemorrhagic symptom. This broad definition may be useful in the early period following a confirmed bioterrorist-related case of VHF as well. Public health authorities may develop more specific case definitions after the etiologic agent is identified.

Public health authorities, in consultation with the CDC, should provide assistance and detailed instructions to clinical laboratories and to clinicians for processing and transport of laboratory specimens required for diagnosis of these agents. (See "Packaging Protocols for Biological Agents/Diseases" at www.bt.cdc.gov/Agent/VHF/VHF.asp.)

Methods of diagnosis at specialized laboratories include antigen detection by antigen-capture enzyme-linked immunosorbent assay (ELISA), IgM antibody detection by antibody-capture ELISA, RT-PCR, and viral isolation. Antigen detection (by ELISA) and RT-PCR are the most useful diagnostic techniques in the acute clinical setting. Viral isolation is of limited value because it requires a biosafety level 4 (BSL-4) laboratory. (A full description of BSL-4 criteria is available at www.cdc.gov/od/ohs/biosfty/bmbl4/bmbl4s3.htm.) There are only 2 BSL-4 facilities in the United States, located at the CDC and the USAMRIID, with in-depth diagnostic capability. Either the presence of IgM or a 4-fold rise in titer of IgG antibody between acute- and convalescent-phase serum samples are diagnostic of these viral illnesses, but antibody-capture ELISA is of limited value in early diagnosis because antibodies to these viruses usually do not appear until onset of recovery, approximately at the second week of illness. The CDC requires approximately 1 working day (with prior notification of arrival) to offer a preliminary laboratory diagnosis following receipt of patient specimens.

The diagnosis of VHF should be based initially on clinical criteria and judgment, with laboratory testing used to confirm or exclude this clinical diagnosis.

Box 1. Key Medical and Public Health Interventions After Identification of Suspected Index Case of Viral Hemorrhagic Fever (VHF)

Identification

Identify suspected index case using these clinical criteria*: temperature ≥101°F (38.3°C) of <3 weeks' duration; severe illness, and no predisposing factors for hemorrhagic manifestations; and at least 2 of the following hemorrhagic symptoms: hemorrhagic or purple rash, epistaxis, hematemesis, hemoptysis, blood in stools, other, and no established alternative diagnosis.

Reporting

1. Report immediately to local and/or state health department.
2. Report immediately to infection control professional and laboratory personnel.

Treatment

1. Initiate supportive and ribavirin therapy (see Table 4) immediately while diagnostic confirmation is pending.
2. If infection with arenavirus or bunyavirus is confirmed, continue 10-day course of ribavirin.
3. If infection with filovirus or flavivirus is confirmed, or if the diagnosis of VHF is excluded or an alternative diagnosis is established, discontinue ribavirin.

Infection Control Measures

1. Initiate VHF-specific barrier precautions.
2. Initiate airborne precautions, with negative air-pressure rooms if resources are available.

Public Health Measures

1. Confirm or exclude diagnosis via Laboratory Response Network.
2. Designated public health authority begins epidemiologic investigation.
3. Identify close and high-risk contacts and place under medical surveillance for 21 days from day of suspected/known exposure.
4. If contact does not have temperature ≥101°F (38.3°C) or signs or symptoms of VHF by the end of 21 days, discontinue medical surveillance.
5. If contact has temperature ≥101°F (38.3°C) or signs or symptoms consistent with VHF, initiate diagnostic workup and treatment, infection control, and public health interventions described for index case.

* Criteria are adapted from the World Health Organization's surveillance standards for acute hemorrhagic fever syndrome.[103]

Laboratory testing will require time and, in the event of a large attack, may be delayed or perhaps not possible given current laboratory capacities.

Treatment

The mainstay of treatment of VHF is supportive, with careful maintenance of fluid and electrolyte balance, circulatory volume, and blood pressure. Because in some cases intravenous fluids have not reversed hypotension and may have contributed to pulmonary edema,[104] consideration should be given to early vasopressor support with hemodynamic monitoring. Mechanical ventilation, renal dialysis, and antiseizure therapy may be required. Intramuscular injections, aspirin, nonsteroidal anti-inflammatory drugs, and anticoagulant therapies are contraindicated. Steroids are not indicated.[9]

Drug Therapy

There are no antiviral drugs approved by the US Food and Drug Administration (FDA) for treatment of HFVs. Ribavirin, a nucleoside analog, has some in vitro and in vivo activity against Arenaviridae and Bunyaviridae (including CCHF) but no utility against Filoviridae or Flaviviridae. Oral ribavirin, in combination with interferon alfa, is FDA-approved for treatment of chronic hepatitis C virus infection. Intravenous ribavirin is of limited availability in the United States. It is produced by ICN Pharmaceuticals Inc (Costa Mesa, Calif) for compassionate use under an investigational new drug (IND) application. Although a risk of human teratogenicity has not been demonstrated for ribavirin, its pharmacologic action and its teratogenicity and embryolethality in several animal species raise concern that such a risk may exist with maternal therapy during pregnancy. Therefore, ribavirin is classified as a pregnancy category X drug, and is contraindicated in pregnancy.[105] The primary adverse effect caused by ribavirin is a dose-related, reversible, hemolytic anemia. However, a range of cardiac and pulmonary events associated with anemia occurred in approximately 10% of patients treated with combination ribavirin-interferon therapy for hepatitis C.[105]

Small trials have shown that ribavirin may reduce mortality after infection with Lassa fever[106] and select New World arenaviruses.[57, 107] Ribavirin does not penetrate the brain well; therefore, it is not expected to be particularly effective against the neurological effects of these pathogens.[57, 108] Intravenous ribavirin given within the first 6 days of fever to patients with Lassa fever who had high levels of viremia decreased mortality from 76% to 9%.[107] A controlled trial of 18 patients with Argentine hemorrhagic fever resulted in 12.5% mortality in treated patients compared with 40% in untreated patients.[108]

Recommendations for drug therapy by the working group are not approved by the FDA for any of these indications and should always be administered under an IND protocol. In a mass casualty situation, these requirements may need to be modified to permit timely administration of the drug. In addition, treatment of other suspected possible causes, such as bacterial sepsis, should not be withheld while awaiting confirmation or exclusion of the diagnosis of VHF.

In a contained casualty situation (in which a modest number of patients require therapy), the working group recommends that an intravenous regimen of ribavirin be given as described in **Table 4**, in accordance with CDC's recommendations for treating patients with suspected VHF of unknown cause, pending identification of the agent.[109] A similar dose has been used in the treatment of Lassa fever.[106]

In a mass casualty situation (in which the number of persons requiring therapy is sufficiently high that delivery of intravenous therapy is no longer possible),

Table 4. Recommendations for Ribavirin Therapy in Patients With Clinically Evident Viral Hemorrhagic Fever of Unknown Etiology or Secondary to Arenaviruses or Bunyaviruses*

	Contained Casualty Setting	Mass Casualty Setting†
Adults	Loading dose of 30 mg/kg intravenously (IV) (maximum, 2 g) once, followed by 16 mg/kg IV (maximum, 1 g per dose) every 6 hours for 4 days, followed by 8 mg/kg IV (maximum, 500 mg per dose) every 8 hours for 6 days	Loading dose of 2000 mg orally once, followed by 1200 mg/d orally in 2 divided doses (if weight >75 kg), or 1000 mg/d orally in 2 doses (400 mg in AM and 600 mg in PM) (if weight ≤75 kg) for 10 days‡
Pregnant women§	Same as for adults	Same as for adults
Children	Same as for adults, dosed according to weight	Loading dose of 30 mg/kg orally once, followed by 15 mg/kg per day orally in 2 divided doses for 10 days

* Recommendations are not approved by the US Food and Drug Administration for any of these indications and should always be administered under an investigational new drug protocol. However, in a mass casualty setting, these requirements may need to be modified to permit timely administration of the drug.

† The threshold number of cases at which parenteral therapy becomes impossible depends on a variety of factors, including local health care resources.

‡ Although a similar dosage (1000 mg/d in 3 divided doses) has been used in a small number of patients with Lassa fever,[106] this regimen would be impractical because the current formulation of oral ribavirin in the United States consists of 200-mg capsules, and ribavirin capsules may not be broken open.

§ Refer to the section in text on treatment of pregnant women for details.

an oral regimen of ribavirin as described in Table 4 is recommended. This dose is currently licensed for treatment of chronic hepatitis C infection in the United States.[105] Although it is substantially lower than that in the intravenous regimen, a similar dose has been used to treat a few patients with Lassa fever,[106] and there are no available studies on tolerability or efficacy of higher doses of oral ribavirin.

Ribavirin is contraindicated in pregnancy. However, in the context of infection with VHF of unknown cause or secondary to an arenavirus or Rift Valley fever, the working group believes that the benefits appear likely to outweigh any fetal risk of ribavirin therapy, and ribavirin is therefore recommended. The associated mortality of VHF tends to be higher in pregnancy.[110]

The use of oral or intravenous ribavirin is not approved by the FDA for children, and proper doses have not been established. Only aerosolized ribavirin has been approved by the FDA for children, to treat respiratory syncytial virus infection. However, in the context of infection with VHF of unknown cause or secondary to an arenavirus or Rift Valley fever, the working group believes that the benefits likely outweigh the risks of ribavirin therapy, and it is therefore recommended as described in Table 4. Similar doses have been used to treat children with adenovirus pneumonia[111] and hepatitis C[112] and were well tolerated. Ribavirin capsules may not be broken open and are only available in 200-mg doses. However, Schering-Plough Corp (Kenilworth, NJ) produces a pediatric syrup formulation (which is not commercially available) for use under an IND application.

For infections caused by filoviruses or flaviviruses, the working group recommends supportive medical care only. Ribavirin has been shown to have no clinical utility against these groups of viruses.

Passive Immunization

Studies and case reports evaluating convalescent plasma as therapy (or prophylaxis) of the diseases caused by HFVs have yielded mixed results depending on the disease, with some reports suggesting clinical utility[26, 80, 82, 101, 113-117] and other studies showing no benefit.[52, 106, 118] Passive immunization has also been associated with enhanced viral replication in experimentally infected animals.[119] The logistics of collection, testing, and storing immune convalescent plasma are formidable. In the United States, the paucity of survivors of these diseases and the lack of a national program that collects and stores HFV immune plasma preclude its use in the initial response to a bioterrorist attack. Development of methods to manufacture monoclonal antibodies and recent advances in selecting highly effective human-derived or humanized products may provide new approaches to therapy in the future.

Postexposure Prophylaxis

Effective prophylaxis following exposure to an HFV is hampered by the absence of licensed or effective vaccines and antiviral medications. The working group does not recommend preemptive administration of ribavirin in the absence of signs of infection to persons with known or suspected exposures to the HFVs. Ribavirin has no utility against filoviruses or flaviviruses. For arenaviruses, there is limited experimental evidence that postexposure prophylaxis with ribavirin will delay onset of disease but not prevent it.[120, 121] Furthermore, the effectiveness of ribavirin as postexposure prophylaxis for arenaviruses or Rift Valley fever virus has never been studied in humans. While 1995 CDC guidelines recommend ribavirin to high-risk contacts of patients with Lassa fever,[109] a review and possible revision of these recommendations is to be shortly undertaken (J.M.H., oral communication, January 10, 2002). However, public health professionals suggest that stratification of risk groups into high-risk and close contacts may facilitate counseling and outbreak investigation. High-risk contacts are those who have had mucous membrane contact with a patient (such as during kissing or sexual intercourse) or have had a percutaneous injury involving contact with the patient's secretions, excretions, or blood. Close contacts are those who live with, shake hands with, hug, process laboratory specimens from, or care for a patient with clinical evidence of VHF prior to initiation of appropriate precautions.

Persons considered potentially exposed to HFVs in a bioterrorist attack and all known high-risk and close contacts of patients diagnosed with VHF should be placed under medical surveillance. All such individuals should be instructed to record their temperatures twice daily and report any temperature of 101°F

(38.3°C) or higher (or any symptom noted in Table 3) to a clinician, hospital epidemiologist, or public health authority designated with surveillance. Surveillance should be continued for 21 days after the person's deemed potential exposure or last contact with the ill patient.

If a temperature of 101°F (38.3°C) or higher develops, ribavirin therapy should be initiated promptly as presumptive treatment of VHF, as described in Table 4, unless an alternative diagnosis is established or the etiologic agent is known to be a filovirus or a flavivirus. In the case of close and high-risk contacts of patients diagnosed with Rift Valley fever or a flavivirus, only those who process laboratory specimens from a patient prior to initiation of appropriate precautions require medical surveillance, as these specific viruses are not transmitted from person to person but may be transmitted in the laboratory setting.

Vaccine

With the exception of yellow fever live attenuated 17D vaccine, which is highly effective when administered to travelers to endemic areas,[68] there is no licensed vaccine for any of the HFVs. The yellow fever vaccine is produced in limited supply, and world stocks are not sufficient to meet a surge.[122] This vaccine would not be useful in preventing disease if given in the postexposure setting because yellow fever has a short incubation period of 3 to 6 days, and neutralizing antibodies take longer to appear following vaccination.[68]

Infection Control

Given the lack of licensed or effective therapies and vaccines against the HFVs, efforts to prevent transmission of infection must rely on the meticulous implementation of and compliance with strict infection control measures. Filoviruses and arenaviruses are highly infectious after direct contact with infected blood and bodily secretions. A suspected case of VHF must be immediately reported to the hospital epidemiologist (or infection control professional) and to the local or state health department. The epidemiologist (or infection control professional) should, in turn, notify the clinical laboratory (so that additional precautions are put in place) as well as other clinicians and public health authorities.

Isolation Precautions

Direct contact with infected blood and bodily fluids has accounted for the majority of person-to-person transmission of filoviruses and arenaviruses. Therefore, we recommend that in the case of any patient with suspected or documented VHF, VHF-specific barrier precautions should be implemented immediately (**Box 2**). These precautions do not reflect HICPAC's isolation guidelines terminology and are defined here as strict hand hygiene plus use of double gloves, impermeable gowns, face shields, eye protection, and leg and shoe coverings (given the copious amounts of infected material, such as vomitus and liquid stool, that may be present in the environment).

Person-to-person airborne transmission of HFVs appears to be a rare event but cannot be conclusively excluded. Given the inability to completely exclude this

Box 2. Recommendations for Protective Measures Against Nosocomial Transmission of Hemorrhagic Fever Viruses

- Strict adherence to hand hygiene: Health care workers should clean their hands prior to donning personal protective equipment for patient contact. After patient contact, health care workers should remove gown, leg and shoe coverings, and gloves and immediately clean their hands. Hands should be clean prior to the removal of facial protective equipment (ie, personal respirators, face shields, and goggles) to minimize exposure of mucous membranes with potentially contaminated hands, and once again after the removal of all personal protective equipment.
- Double gloves
- Impermeable gowns
- N-95 masks or powered air-purifying respirators, and a negative air-pressure isolation room with 6-12 air changes per hour, as required by the Healthcare Infection Control Practices Advisory Committee standards for airborne precautions*
- Leg and shoe coverings
- Face shields†
- Goggles for eye protection†
- Restricted access of nonessential staff and visitors to patient's room
- Dedicated medical equipment, such as stethoscopes, glucose monitors, and, if available, point-of-care analyzers
- Environmental disinfection with an Environmental Protection Agency–registered hospital disinfectant or a 1:100 dilution of household bleach
- If there are multiple patients with viral hemorrhagic fever in one health care facility, they should be cared for in the same part of the hospital to minimize exposures to other patients and health care workers

* These resources may not be possible in many health care facilities or in a mass casualty situation. In this case, all other measures should be taken and would, in combination, be expected to substantially diminish the risk of nosocomial spread.

† Face shields and eye protection may be already incorporated in certain personal protective equipment, such as powered air-purifying respirators.

potential, the lack of preventive vaccines, and, in the case of filoviruses, the lack of effective drug therapy, we recommend that, in addition to VHF-specific barrier precautions, airborne precautions also be instituted. Airborne precautions entail the use of a high-efficiency particulate respirator for any person entering the room and, as required by HICPAC standards,[123] the patient should be placed in a room with negative air pressure, 6 to 12 air changes per hour, air exhausted directly to the outdoors or passage through a high-efficiency particulate air (HEPA) filter before recirculation, and doors kept closed. There are many circumstances in which the use of negative air-pressure rooms may not be possible, including mass casualty situations. In such conditions, all other infection control measures should be taken (ie, VHF-specific barrier precautions and a HEPA respirator for any person entering the room), which would, in combination, substantially reduce the risk of nosocomial transmission. Available evidence suggests that in the great preponderance of historical cases, these measures were sufficient to prevent transmission of disease to health care workers, family members, and other patients. Nonessential staff and visitors should have restricted access to patients' rooms. If there are multiple patients with VHF in a health care facility, they should be cared for in the same part of the hospital to minimize exposure to other persons.

All persons, including health care workers and laboratory personnel who have had a close or high-risk contact with a patient infected with a filovirus or an arenavirus within 21 days of the patient's onset of symptoms, prior to the institution of appropriate infection control precautions, should be placed under medical surveillance and managed as described in the section on postexposure prophylaxis. Laboratory personnel who have processed laboratory specimens from a patient with any HFVs (including Rift Valley fever and the flaviviruses) within 21 days of the patient's onset of symptoms, prior to the institution of appropriate infection control precautions, should also be placed under medical surveillance.

Because some of these viruses may remain present in bodily fluids for long periods following clinical recovery, convalescent patients continue to pose a risk of disease transmission.[40, 60] Therefore, patients convalescing from a filoviral or an arenaviral infection should refrain from sexual activity for 3 months after clinical recovery.

Personal Protective Equipment

Powered air-purifying respirators (PAPRs) are theoretically more efficacious than N-95 disposable masks in providing respiratory protection from small-particle aerosols, mostly due to issues related to proper fitting of the masks.[124] However, no data exist to support higher efficacy of PAPRs over N-95 masks in preventing airborne transmission of infection in the health care setting.[125] PAPRs are more expensive ($300–$600 vs less than $1 for disposable N-95 masks), are bulky, require maintenance, and impair voice communication to a higher degree than disposable N-95 masks.[126] One study has shown that PAPRs are associated with a higher incidence of needlestick injuries.[127] Disadvantages of the N-95 masks include the difficulty in ensuring a reliable face-mask seal with each use and impossibility of effective use by bearded individuals. The theoretical advantage of PAPRs over N-95 masks may be offset by the danger of increased needlestick or sharp injuries to those using PAPRs in these settings. The N-95 masks (in combination with face shields and goggles) are likely equivalent in protection to PAPRs in the health care setting.

Therefore, we recommend that clinicians caring for patients with a VHF use either N-95 masks or PAPRs, depending on their familiarity with one or the other, the suitability for the individual, and availability at a given institution. Some experts have advocated that PAPRs be used during cough-inducing procedures (ie, endotracheal intubations, bronchoscopies), autopsies, and centrifugation or pipetting of laboratory specimens. While there are no data to support this recommendation, we would concur as long as the health care workers are familiar with the use of PAPRs and are not subjecting themselves to the risk of inadvertent needlestick injury.

Laboratory Testing

The HFVs described herein (including Rift Valley fever and the flaviviruses) are highly infectious in the laboratory setting and may be transmitted to laboratory personnel via small-particle aerosols. The risk is especially high during aerosol-generating procedures, such as centrifugation. To minimize the possibility of small-particle aerosol generation, all laboratory staff must be alerted to any suspected diagnosis of VHF. Designated laboratory workers should receive training in handling specimens from any suspected VHF patients in advance of such an event. Laboratory workers should wear personal protective equipment that ensures VHF-specific barrier and airborne precautions (Box 2). All specimens should be handled, at a minimum, in a class 2 biological safety cabinet following BSL-3 practices.[127] (A detailed description of class 2 biological safety cabinets is available at www.cdc.gov/od/ohs/biosfty/bmbl4/b4aa.htm, and a detailed description of BSL-3 practices is available at www.cdc.gov/od/ohs/biosfty/bmbl4/bmbl4s3.htm.) Most clinical facilities are not equipped with a BSL-3 laboratory. Virus isolation should only be attempted in a BSL-4 laboratory.

Potential hazards associated with handling of clinical specimens from patients infected with an HFV pose great problems in hospital facilities. Laboratory tests should be limited to critical diagnostic tests. If adequate resources are available, point-of-care analyzers for routine laboratory analysis of infected patients should be used. Point-of-care analyzers are small, portable devices that may be used at the bedside, require only a few drops of fresh whole blood, display test results in a few minutes, limit the exposure of laboratory personnel to infectious clinical specimens, do not disrupt the clinical laboratory routine, and do not contaminate clinical laboratory equipment.

If point-of-care analyzers are not available, clinical specimens need to be processed in a clinical laboratory. Precautions that parallel those of a US hospital's successful efforts to care for a patient infected with a New World arenavirus should be followed.[128] Laboratory specimens should be clearly identified, double bagged, and hand carried to the laboratory at prescheduled times, preferably prior to equipment maintenance to enable decontamination of instruments after testing. Specimens should never be transported in pneumatic tube systems. Only dedicated, trained laboratory personnel should process clinical specimens from patients with VHF, wearing protective equipment to ensure airborne and VHF-specific barrier precautions. Serum should be pretreated with the detergent Triton X-100 (10 μL of 10% Triton X-100 per 1 mL of serum for 1 hour). Pretreatment with Triton X-100 may reduce the titers of these enveloped viruses, but efficacy has not been tested.[109] Pretreatment with Triton X-100 does not significantly alter serum electrolytes, urea nitrogen, creatinine, and glucose or liver function test results.[128] Additional guidelines for the transport, processing, and disposal have been described by Armstrong et al.[128]

Postmortem Practices

In the event of an outbreak of VHF, special provisions will be required for burial practices. Contact with cadavers has been implicated as a source of transmission in the Kikwit Ebola outbreak of 1995[36] and in Uganda in 2000.[37] We recommend that trained personnel, using the same infection control precautions as those used to transport ill patients, handle the bodies of patients who die of VHF. Autopsies should be performed only by specially trained persons using VHF-specific barrier precautions and HEPA-filtered respirators (N-95 masks or PAPRs) and negative air-pressure rooms, as would be customary in cases in which contagious biological aerosols, such as *Mycobacterium tuberculosis*, are deemed a possible risk.[129] We recommend prompt burial or cremation of the deceased, with minimal handling. Specifically, no embalming should be done. Surgery or postmortem examinations are associated with increased risks of transmission and should be done only when absolutely indicated and after consultation with experts.

Environmental Decontamination

Linen handlers and workers involved in environmental decontamination should wear personal protective equipment that ensures VHF-specific barrier precautions (Box 2). We recommend that contaminated linens be placed in double bags and washed without sorting in a normal hot water cycle with bleach. Alternatively, they may be autoclaved or incinerated.[109] Detailed instructions on handling and disinfection of contaminated linens are available from the CDC.[109] Environmental surfaces in patients' rooms and contaminated medical equipment should be disinfected with an Environmental Protection Agency–registered hospital disinfectant or a 1:100 dilution of household bleach.[109]

It has been suggested that excreta should be disinfected with 0.6% sodium hypochlorite before disposal.[130] Although a theoretical concern remains that the disposal of contaminated human excreta may contaminate sewage systems, the working group does not recommend the addition of disinfectants to human excreta prior to disposal. Disinfectants are not effective in sterilizing solid waste, the indiscriminate addition of hypochlorite may damage septic tanks, and these viruses are not likely to survive standard sewage treatment in the United States.

In general, in their natural state, these lipid-enveloped viruses are not environmentally stable and are not expected to persist in the environment for prolonged periods.[7] Decisions regarding the need for and methods of decontamination following an attack with an HFV should be made following expert analysis of the contaminated environment and the weapons used in the attack, in consultation with experts in environmental remediation.

Ongoing Research and Proposed Agenda

Mechanisms of disease transmission in human outbreaks of HFVs are still poorly understood. Clarification of the role of airborne transmission is vital. Rapid diagnostic methods need to be developed for all of the HFVs, including those that have been excluded from this article and made available to selected state health departments for the expedient diagnosis of suspected cases. Methods to safely handle potentially infected specimens in a clinical laboratory should be developed.

The diagnostic and therapeutic armamentarium urgently needs to be augmented. There also is an urgent need to develop vaccines and drug therapy. A live attenuated vaccine against Argentine hemorrhagic fever (candid No. 1) developed at the USAMRIID[131] is available as an IND. This vaccine has been shown to be safe and effective in protecting agricultural workers in South America[132] and may provide cross-protection against Bolivian hemorrhagic fever.[9] There are 2 vaccines against Rift Valley fever also available as INDs. One is formalin inactivated and appears to be safe and effective when administered to laboratory workers. However, it is available only in limited supply, and the manufacturing capacity for producing additional vaccine no longer exists in the United States.[133, 134] Lastly, a formalin-inactivated Kyasanur Forest disease vaccine exists and has been shown to be protective in field trials in India.[135] There are several promising vaccines in development for prevention of filoviruses and Lassa fever, some in nonhuman primate models.[136-139] Passive immunization strategies using recombinant human monoclonal antibodies should be pursued, given the potential benefit of passive immunization in a series of reports.[80, 114, 116, 117, 140] Research with these agents is hampered by the requirement of conducting experiments in BSL-4 laboratories. More BSL-4 laboratories would expand research opportunities.

Ribavirin is the only potentially effective drug available for selected HFVs because it is approved by the FDA for another indication. However, it is not effective against all of the HFVs and it is not widely available. The supply of ribavirin should be rapidly augmented, and studies to demonstrate its efficacy and safety against selected HFVs should be conducted to support an FDA approval for those indications. We also recommend the addition of intravenous and oral formulations of ribavirin to the US National Pharmaceutical Stockpile (a repository of antibiotics, chemical antidotes, and other medical supplies managed by the CDC that may be emergently sent to the site of a disaster anywhere in the United States). New antiviral therapies should be pursued for the treatment of all HFVs, including those excluded from this article. The effects of any developed therapy in pediatric populations should also be evaluated.

Disclaimer: The views, opinions, assertions, and findings contained herein are those of the authors and should not be construed as official US Department of Health and Human Services, US Department of Defense, or US Department of Army positions, policies, or decisions unless so designated by other documentation. The recommendations on the use of drugs for uses not approved by the FDA do not represent the official views of the FDA or of any of the federal agencies whose scientists participated in these discussions. Unlabeled uses of the products recommended are noted in the sections of this article in which these products are discussed. Where unlabeled uses are indicated, information used as the basis for the recommendation is discussed.

Acknowledgments: We thank those who generously provided invaluable assistance in the preparation of this article: Julie Gerberding, MD, MPH; Jim LeDuc, PhD; Steve Ostroff, MD; Duane Gubler, ScD; Denise Cardo, MD; Lynn Steele, MS, CDC; Anthony Suffredini, MD, National Institutes of Health; Elin Gursky, ScD, Paul Pham, PharmD, Johns Hopkins University; Lauren Iacono-Connors, PhD, Karen Midthun, MD; Joanne Holmes, MBA; Jerry Weir, PhD; Kathleen Uhl, MD; Diane Kennedy, RPh, MPH; Dianne Murphy, MD; Harry Haverkos, MD; Brad Leissa, MD, Sandra Folkendt; Lewis Markoff, MD; and Karen Oliver, MSN, FDA.

References

1. Inglesby TV, Henderson DA, Bartlett JG, et al, for the Working Group on Civilian Biodefense. Anthrax as a biological weapon. *JAMA.* 1999;281: 1735-1745.
2. Henderson DA, Inglesby TV, Bartlett JG, et al, for the Working Group on Civilian Biodefense. Smallpox as a biological weapon. *JAMA.* 1999;281: 2127-2137.
3. Inglesby TV, Dennis DT, Henderson DA, et al, for the Working Group on Civilian Biodefense. Plague as a biological weapon. *JAMA.* 2000;283: 2281-2290.
4. Arnon SS, Schechter R, Inglesby TV, et al, for the Working Group on Civilian Biodefense. Botulinum toxin as a biological weapon. *JAMA.* 2001;285: 1059-1070.
5. Dennis DT, Inglesby TV, Henderson DA, et al, for the Working Group on Civilian Biodefense. Tularemia as a biological weapon. *JAMA.* 2001;285: 2763-2773.
6. Fatal illnesses associated with a new world arenavirus—California, 1999-2000. *MMWR Morb Mortal Wkly Rep.* 2000;49:709-711.
7. Peters CJ, Jahrling PB, Khan AS. Patients infected with high-hazard viruses. *Arch Virol Suppl.* 1996;11:141-168.
8. Solomon T, Mallewa M. Dengue and other emerging flaviviruses. *J Infect.* 2001;42:104-115.
9. Jahrling P. Viral hemorrhagic fevers. In: *Textbook of Military Medicine.* Vol 1. Falls Church, Va: Office of the Surgeon General; 1989.
10. Mandell GL, Douglas RG, Bennett JE, Dolin R. *Mandell, Douglas, and Bennett's Principles and Practice of Infectious Diseases.* 5th ed. Philadelphia, Pa: Churchill Livingstone; 2000.
11. Swanepoel R, Shepherd AJ, Leman PA, et al. Epidemiologic and clinical features of Crimean-Congo hemorrhagic fever in southern Africa. *Am J Trop Med Hyg.* 1987;3:120-132.
12. Peters CJ, Simpson GL, Levy H. Spectrum of hantavirus infection: hemorrhagic fever with renal syndrome and hantavirus pulmonary syndrome. *Annu Rev Med.* 1999;50:531-545.
13. Alibek K, Handelman S. *Biohazard: The Chilling True Story of the Largest Covert Biological Weapons Program in the World, Told From the Inside by the Man Who Ran It.* New York, NY: Random House; 1999.
14. Center for Nonproliferation Studies. Chemical and biological weapons: possession and programs past and present. November 2000. Available at: http://cns.miis.edu/research/cbw/possess.htm. Accessed January 10, 2002.
15. Miller J, Engelberg S, Broad WJ. *Germs: Biological Weapons and America's Secret War.* Waterville, Me: GK Hall; 2002.
16. Bazhutin NB, Belanov EF, Spiridonov VA, et al. The effect of the methods for producing an experimental Marburg virus infection on the characteristics of the course of the disease in green monkeys [in Russian]. *Vopr Virusol.* 1992;37: 153-156.
17. *Global Proliferation of Weapons of Mass Destruction: Hearings Before the Permanent Subcommittee on Investigations of the Committee on Governmental Affairs, United States Senate,* 104th Cong, 1st-2nd Sess (1996).
18. Johnson E, Jaax N, White J, Jahrling P. Lethal experimental infections of rhesus monkeys by aerosolized Ebola virus. *Int J Exp Pathol.* 1995;76:227-236.
19. Lub M, Sergeev AN, P'Iankov OV, P'Iankova OG, Petrishchenko VA, Kotliarov LA. Certain pathogenetic characteristics of a disease in monkeys infected with the Marburg virus by an airborne route [in Russian]. *Vopr Virusol.* 1995;40:158-161.
20. Stephenson EH, Larson EW, Dominik JW. Effect of environmental factors on aerosol-induced Lassa virus infection. *J Med Virol.* 1984;14:295-303.
21. Kenyon RH, McKee KT Jr, Zack PM, et al. Aerosol infection of rhesus macaques with Junin virus. *Intervirology.* 1992;33:23-31.
22. Centers for Disease Control and Prevention. Category A agents. Available at: http://www.bt.cdc.gov/Agent/Agentlist.asp. Accessed January 10, 2002.
23. LeDuc JW. Epidemiology of hemorrhagic fever viruses. *Rev Infect Dis.* 1989;11(suppl 4):S730-S735.
24. Schou S, Hansen AK. Marburg and Ebola virus infections in laboratory nonhuman primates: a literature review. *Comp Med.* 2000;50:108-123.
25. Ebola haemorrhagic fever in Zaire, 1976. *Bull World Health Organ.* 1978;56:271-293.
26. Emond RT, Evans B, Bowen ET, Lloyd G. A case of Ebola virus infection. *BMJ.* 1977;2:541-544.

27. Simpson DI. Marburg agent disease. *Trans R Soc Trop Med Hyg.* 1969;63:303-309. Cited by: Schou S, Hansen AK. Marburg and Ebola virus infections in laboratory nonhuman primates. *Comp Med.* 2000;50:2108-2123.

28. Jaax NK, Davis KJ, Geisbert TJ, et al. Lethal experimental infection of rhesus monkeys with Ebola-Zaire (Mayinga) virus by the oral and conjunctival route of exposure. *Arch Pathol Lab Med.* 1996;120:140-155.

29. Colebunders R, Borchert M. Ebola haemorrhagic fever—a review. *J Infect.* 2000;40:16-20.

30. Zaki SR, Shieh WJ, Greer PW, et al. A novel immunohistochemical assay for the detection of Ebola virus in skin. *J Infect Dis.* 1999;179(suppl 1):S36-S47.

31. Dowell SF, Mukunu R, Ksiazek TG, Khan AS, Rollin PE, Peters CJ. Transmission of Ebola hemorrhagic fever: a study of risk factors in family members, Kikwit, Democratic Republic of the Congo, 1995. *J Infect Dis.* 1999;179(suppl 1):S87-S91.

32. Khan AS, Tshioko FK, Heymann DL, et al. The reemergence of Ebola hemorrhagic fever, Democratic Republic of the Congo, 1995. *J Infect Dis.* 1999;179(suppl 1):S76-S86.

33. Muyembe-Tamfum JJ, Kipasa M, Kiyungu C, Colebunders R. Ebola outbreak in Kikwit, Democratic Republic of the Congo: discovery and control measures. *J Infect Dis.* 1999;179(suppl 1):S259-S262.

34. Butler JC, Kilmarx PH, Jernigan DB, Ostroff SM. Perspectives in fatal epidemics. *Infect Dis Clin North Am.* 1996;10:917-937.

35. Shu HL, Siegert R, Slenczka W. The pathogenesis and epidemiology of the "Marburg-virus" infection. *Ger Med Mon.* 1969;14:7-10.Cited by: Schou S, Hansen AK. Marburg and Ebola virus infections in laboratory nonhuman primates. *Comp Med.* 2000;50:2108-2123.

36. Roels TH, Bloom AS, Buffington J, et al. Ebola hemorrhagic fever, Kikwit, Democratic Republic of the Congo, 1995: risk factors for patients without a reported exposure. *J Infect Dis.* 1999;179(suppl 1):S92-S97.

37. Outbreak of Ebola hemorrhagic fever, Uganda, August 2000–January 2001. *MMWR Morb Mortal Wkly Rep.* 2001;50:73-77.

38. Jaax N, Jahrling P, Geisbert T, et al. Transmission of Ebola virus (Zaire strain) to uninfected control monkeys in a biocontainment laboratory. *Lancet.* 1995;346:1669-1671.

39. Dalgard DW, Hardy RJ, Pearson SL, et al. Combined simian hemorrhagic fever and Ebola virus infection in cynomolgus monkeys. *Lab Anim Sci.* 1992;42:152-157.

40. Slenczka WG. The Marburg virus outbreak of 1967 and subsequent episodes. *Curr Top Microbiol Immunol.* 1999;235:49-75.

41. Gear JS, Cassel GA, Gear AJ, et al. Outbreak of Marburg virus disease in Johannesburg. *BMJ.* 1975;4:489-493.

42. Baron RC, McCormick JB, Zubeir OA. Ebola virus disease in southern Sudan. *Bull World Health Organ.* 1983;61:997-1003.

43. Formenty P, Hatz C, Le Guenno B, Stoll A, Rogenmoser P, Widmer A. Human infection due to Ebola virus, subtype Cote d'Ivoire. *J Infect Dis.* 1999;179(suppl 1):S48-S53.

44. Richards GA, Murphy S, Jobson R, et al. Unexpected Ebola virus in a tertiary setting. *Crit Care Med.* 2000;28:240-244.

45. Guimard Y, Bwaka MA, Colebunders R, et al. Organization of patient care during the Ebola hemorrhagic fever epidemic in Kikwit, Democratic Republic of the Congo, 1995. *J Infect Dis.* 1999;179(suppl 1):S268-S273.

46. Centers for Disease Control and Prevention and World Health Organization. Infection control for viral hemorrhagic fevers in the African health care setting. Atlanta, Ga: Centers for Disease Control and Prevention. Available at: http://www.cdc.gov/ncidod/dvrd/spb/mnpages/vhfmanual.htm. Accessed January 10, 2002.

47. Rowe AK, Bertolli J, Khan AS, et al. Clinical, virologic, and immunologic follow-up of convalescent Ebola hemorrhagic fever patients and their household contacts, Kikwit, Democratic Republic of the Congo. *J Infect Dis.* 1999;179(suppl 1):S28-S35.

48. Rodriguez LL, De Roo A, Guimard Y, et al. Persistence and genetic stability of Ebola virus during the outbreak in Kikwit, Democratic Republic of the Congo, 1995. *J Infect Dis.* 1999;179(suppl 1):S170-S176.

49. Johnson KM, Mackenzie RB, Webb PA, Kuns ML. Chronic infection of rodents by Machupo virus. *Science.* 1965;150:1618-1619.

50. Johnson KM, Kuns ML, Mackenzie RB, Webb PA, Yunker CE. Isolation of Machupo virus from wild rodent Calomys callosus. *Am J Trop Med Hyg.* 1966;15:103-106.

51. Carey DE, Kemp GE, White HA, et al. Lassa fever: epidemiological aspects of the 1970 epidemic, Jos, Nigeria. *Trans R Soc Trop Med Hyg.* 1972;66:402-408.

52. White HA. Lassa fever: a study of 23 hospital cases. *Trans R Soc Trop Med Hyg.* 1972;66: 390-401.

53. Monath TP, Mertens PE, Patton R, et al. A hospital epidemic of Lassa fever in Zorzor, Liberia, March-April 1972. *Am J Trop Med Hyg.* 1973;22:773-779.

54. Peters CJ, Kuehne RW, Mercado RR, Le Bow RH, Spertzel RO, Webb PA. Hemorrhagic fever in Cochabamba, Bolivia, 1971. *Am J Epidemiol.* 1974;99:425-433.

55. Zweighaft RM, Fraser DW, Hattwick MA, et al. Lassa fever: response to an imported case. *N Engl J Med.* 1977;297:803-807.

56. Cooper CB, Gransden WR, Webster M, et al. A case of Lassa fever: experience at St Thomas's Hospital. *BMJ.* 1982;285:1003-1005.

57. Kilgore PE, Ksiazek TG, Rollin PE, et al. Treatment of Bolivian hemorrhagic fever with intravenous ribavirin. *Clin Infect Dis.* 1997;24:718-722.

58. World Health Organization. Fact sheet 179: Lassa fever. April 2000. Available at: http://www.who.int/inf-fs/en/fact179.html. Accessed January 10, 2002.

59. Buckley SM, Casals J. Lassa fever, a new virus disease of man from West Africa, III: isolation and characterization of the virus. *Am J Trop Med Hyg.* 1970;19:680-691.

60. Briggiler AM, Enria DA, Feuillade MR, Maiztegui JI. Contagio interhumano e infeccion clinical con virus Junin en matrimonios residentes en el area endemica de fiebre hemorragica Argentina. *Medicina (B Aires).* 1987;47:565.

61. Swanapoel R, Coetzer JA. Rift Valley fever. In: *Infectious Diseases of Livestock With Special Reference to Southern Africa.* Vol 1. New York, NY: Oxford University Press; 1994.

62. Jouan A, Coulibaly I, Adam F, et al. Analytical study of a Rift Valley fever epidemic. *Res Virol.* 1989;140: 175-186.

63. Smithburn KC, Mahaffy AF, Haddow AJ, Kitchen SF, Smith JF. Rift Valley fever: accidental infections among laboratory workers. *J Immunol.* 1949;62: 213-227.

64. Meegan JM. The Rift Valley fever epizootic in Egypt 1977-78, I: description of the epizootic and virological studies. *Trans R Soc Trop Med Hyg.* 1979;73: 618-623.

65. Shawky S. Rift Valley fever. *Saudi Med J.* 2000;21: 1109-1115.

66. Turell MJ, Kay BH. Susceptibility of selected strains of Australian mosquitoes (*Diptera: Culicidae*) to Rift Valley fever virus. *J Med Entomol.* 1998;35:132-135.

67. Gargan TP II, Clark GG, Dohm DJ, Turell MJ, Bailey CL. Vector potential of selected North American mosquito species for Rift Valley fever virus. *Am J Trop Med Hyg.* 1988;38:440-446.

68. Monath TP. Yellow fever: an update. *Lancet Infect Dis.* 2001;1:11-20.

69. Cunha BA. *Tickborne Infectious Diseases: Diagnosis and Management.* New York, NY: Marcel Dekker; 2000.

70. Banerjee K, Gupta NP, Goverdhan MK. Viral infections in laboratory personnel. *Indian J Med Res.* 1979;69:363-373.

71. International Committee on Taxonomy of Viruses. *Seventh Report of the International Committee on Taxonomy of Viruses.* San Diego, Calif: Academic Press; 2000.

72. Chen JP, Cosgriff TM. Hemorrhagic fever virus-induced changes in hemostasis and vascular biology. *Blood Coagul Fibrinolysis.* 2000;11:461-483.

73. Feldmann H, Volchkov VE, Volchkova VA, Klenk HD. The glycoproteins of Marburg and Ebola virus and their potential roles in pathogenesis. *Arch Virol Suppl.* 1999;15:159-169.

74. Ryabchikova EI, Kolesnikova LV, Luchko SV. An analysis of features of pathogenesis in 2 animal models of Ebola virus infection. *J Infect Dis.* 1999;179(suppl 1):S199-S202.

75. Schnittler HJ, Mahner F, Drenckhahn D, Klenk HD, Feldmann H. Replication of Marburg virus in human endothelial cells. *J Clin Invest.* 1993;91:1301-1309.

76. Samoilovich SR, Carballal G, Weissenbacher MC. Protection against a pathogenic strain of Junin virus by mucosal infection with an attenuated strain. *Am J Trop Med Hyg.* 1983;32:825-828.

77. Peters CJ, Liu CT, Anderson GW, Morrill JC Jr, Jahrling PB. Pathogenesis of viral hemorrhagic fevers. *Rev Infect Dis.* 1989;11(suppl 4): S743-S749.

78. Jahrling PB, Hesse RA, Eddy GA, Johnson KM, Callis RT, Stephen EL. Lassa virus infection of rhesus monkeys. *J Infect Dis.* 1980;141: 580-589.

79. Cummins D, Molinas FC, Lerer G, Maiztegui JI, Faint R, Machin SJ. A plasma inhibitor of platelet aggregation in patients with Argentine hemorrhagic fever. *Am J Trop Med Hyg.* 1990;42:470-475.

80. Enria DA, Briggiler AM, Fernandez NJ, Levis SC, Maiztegui JI. Importance of dose of neutralising antibodies in treatment of Argentine haemorrhagic fever with immune plasma. *Lancet.* 1984;2: 255-256.

81. Cosgriff TM, Morrill JC, Jennings GB, et al. Hemostatic derangement produced by Rift Valley fever virus in rhesus monkeys. *Rev Infect Dis.* 1989; 11(suppl 4):S807-S814.

82. Peters CJ, Jones D, Trotter R, et al. Experimental Rift Valley fever in rhesus macaques. *Arch Virol.* 1988;99:31-44.

83. Morrill JC, Jennings GB, Cosgriff TM, Gibbs PH, Peters CJ. Prevention of Rift Valley fever in rhesus monkeys with interferon-alpha. *Rev Infect Dis.* 1989;11(suppl 4):S815-S825.

84. Monath TP, Brinker KR, Chandler FW, Kemp GE, Cropp CB. Pathophysiologic correlations in a rhesus monkey model of yellow fever with special observations on the acute necrosis of B cell areas of lymphoid tissues. *Am J Trop Med Hyg.* 1981;30: 431-443.

85. Iyer CG, Laxmana Rao R, Work TH, Narasimha Murthy DP. Pathological findings in 3 fatal human cases of Kyasanur Forest disease. *Indian J Med Sci.* 1959;13:1011-1022. Cited by: Pavri K. Clinical, clinicopathologic, and hematologic features of Kyasanur Forest disease. *Rev Infect Dis.* 1989; 11(suppl 4):S854-S859.

86. Ebola haemorrhagic fever in Sudan, 1976. *Bull World Health Organ.* 1978;56:247-270.

87. Smith DH, Johnson BK, Isaacson M, et al. Marburg-virus disease in Kenya. *Lancet.* 1982;1: 816-820.

88. Monson MH, Frame JD, Jahrling PB, Alexander K. Endemic Lassa fever in Liberia, I: clinical and epidemiological aspects at Curran Lutheran Hospital, Zorzor, Liberia. *Trans R Soc Trop Med Hyg.* 1984;78:549-553.

89. Keane E, Gilles HM. Lassa fever in Panguma Hospital, Sierra Leone, 1973-6. *BMJ.* 1977;1: 1399-1402.

90. Mertens PE, Patton R, Baum JJ, Monath TP. Clinical presentation of Lassa fever cases during the hospital epidemic at Zorzor, Liberia, March-April 1972. *Am J Trop Med Hyg.* 1973;22:780-784.

91. McCormick JB, King IJ, Webb PA, et al. A case-control study of the clinical diagnosis and course of Lassa fever. *J Infect Dis.* 1987;155:445-455.

92. Re-emergence of Bolivian hemorrhagic fever. *Epidemiol Bull.* 1994;15:4-5.

93. Gear JH. Haemorrhagic fevers of Africa: an account of 2 recent outbreaks. *J S Afr Vet Assoc.* 1977;48:5-8. As cited in: Gear JH. Clinical aspects of African viral hemorrhagic fevers. *Rev Infect Dis.* 1989;11(suppl 4):S777-S782.

94. Abd el-Rahim IH, Abd el-Hakim U, Hussein M. An epizootic of Rift Valley fever in Egypt in 1997. *Rev Sci Tech.* 1999;18:741-748.

95. Laughlin LW, Meegan JM, Strausbaugh LJ, Morens DM, Watten RH. Epidemic Rift Valley fever in Egypt. *Trans R Soc Trop Med Hyg.* 1979;73:630-633.

96. Strausbaugh LJ, Laughlin LW, Meegan JM, Watten RH. Clinical studies on Rift Valley fever, I: acute febrile and hemorrhagic-like diseases. *J Egypt Public Health Assoc.* 1978;53:181-182.

97. Craven RB. Flaviviruses. In: *Textbook of Human Virology.* 2nd ed. St Louis, Mo: Mosby–Year Book Medical; 1991.

98. Adhikari Prabha MR, Prabhu MG, Raghuveer CV, Bai M, Mala MA. Clinical study of 100 cases of Kyasanur Forest disease with clinicopathological correlation. *Indian J Med Sci.* 1993;47:124-130.

99. Bwaka MA, Bonnet MJ, Calain P, et al. Ebola hemorrhagic fever in Kikwit, Democratic Republic of the Congo: clinical observations in 103 patients. *J Infect Dis.* 1999;179(suppl 1):S1-S7.

100. Frame JD, Baldwin JM Jr, Gocke DJ, Troup JM. Lassa fever, a new virus disease of man from West Africa, I: clinical description and pathological findings. *Am J Trop Med Hyg.* 1970;19:670-676.

101. Monath TP, Maher M, Casals J, Kissling RE, Cacciapuoti A. Lassa fever in the Eastern Province of Sierra Leone, 1970-1972, II: clinical observations and virological studies on selected hospital cases. *Am J Trop Med Hyg.* 1974;23:1140-1149.

102. Kuming BS, Kokoris N. Uveal involvement in Marburg virus disease. *Br J Ophthalmol.* 1977;61: 265-266.

103. World Health Organization. Acute haemorrhagic fever syndrome. Available at: http://www.who.int/emc-documents/surveillance/docs/whocdscsrisr992.html/41Acute%20haemorrhagic%20fever%20syndrome .htm. Accessed February 10, 2002.

104. Franz DR, Jahrling PB, Friedlander AM, et al. Clinical recognition and management of patients exposed to biological warfare agents. *JAMA.* 1997;278:399-411.

105. Rebetol product information. Available at: http://www.hepatitisinnovations.com/pro/rebetol/rebetol_pi.html. Accessed January 10, 2002.

106. McCormick JB, King IJ, Webb PA, et al. Lassa fever: effective therapy with ribavirin. *N Engl J Med.* 1986;314:20-26.

107. Enria DA, Maiztegui JI. Antiviral treatment of Argentine hemorrhagic fever. *Antiviral Res.* 1994;23: 23-31.

108. Huggins JW. Prospects for treatment of viral hemorrhagic fevers with ribavirin, a broad-spectrum antiviral drug. *Rev Infect Dis.* 1989;11(suppl 4): S750-S761.

109. Update: management of patients with suspected viral hemorrhagic fever—United States. *MMWR Morb Mortal Wkly Rep.* 1995;44:475-479.

110. Frame JD. Clinical features of Lassa fever in Liberia. *Rev Infect Dis.* 1989;11(suppl 4):S783-S789.

111. Shetty AK, Gans HA, So S, Millan MT, Arvin AM, Gutierrez KM. Intravenous ribavirin therapy for adenovirus pneumonia. *Pediatr Pulmonol.* 2000; 29:69-73.

112. Kelly DA, Bunn, SK, Apelian D, et al. Safety, efficacy, and pharmacokinetics of interferon alfa-2b plus ribavirin in children with chronic hepatitis C. *Hepatology.* 2001;342A:abstract 680.

113. Mupapa K, Massamba M, Kibadi K, et al. Treatment of Ebola hemorrhagic fever with blood transfusions from convalescent patients. *J Infect Dis.* 1999;179(suppl 1):S18-S23.

114. Stille W, Bohle E, Helm E, van Rey W, Siede W. On an infectious disease transmitted by *Cercopithecus aethiops* ("green monkey disease") [in German]. *Dtsch Med Wochenschr.* 1968;93:572-582. Cited by: Slenczka WG. The Marburg virus outbreak of 1967 and subsequent episodes. *Curr Top Microbiol Immunol.* 1999;235:49-75.

115. Leifer E, Gocke DJ, Bourne H. Lassa fever, a new virus disease of man from West Africa, II: report of a laboratory-acquired infection treated with plasma from a person recently recovered from the disease. *Am J Trop Med Hyg.* 1970;19:677-679.

116. Frame JD, Verbrugge GP, Gill RG, Pinneo L. The use of Lassa fever convalescent plasma in Nigeria. *Trans R Soc Trop Med Hyg.* 1984;78:319-324.

117. Maiztegui JI, Fernandez NJ, de Damilano AJ. Efficacy of immune plasma in treatment of Argentine haemorrhagic fever and association between treatment and a late neurological syndrome. *Lancet.* 1979;2:1216-1217.

118. Clayton AJ. Lassa immune serum. *Bull World Health Organ.* 1977;55:435-439.

119. Halstead SB. In vivo enhancement of dengue virus infection in rhesus monkeys by passively transferred antibody. *J Infect Dis.* 1979;140:527-533.

120. Kenyon RH, Canonico PG, Green DE, Peters CJ. Effect of ribavirin and tributylribavirin on argentine hemorrhagic fever (Junin virus) in guinea pigs. *Antimicrob Agents Chemother.* 1986;29: 521-523.

121. Seiler P, Senn BM, Klenerman P, Kalinke U, Hengartner H, Zinkernagel RM. Additive effect of neutralizing antibody and antiviral drug treatment in preventing virus escape and persistence. *J Virol.* 2000;74:5896-5901.

122. Nathan N, Barry M, Van Herp M, Zeller H. Shortage of vaccines during a yellow fever outbreak in Guinea. *Lancet.* 2001;358:2129-2130.

123. Garner JS. Guideline for isolation precautions in hospitals. *Infect Control Hosp Epidemiol.* 1996;17:53-80.

124. National Institute for Occupational Safety and Health. *NIOSH Guide to the Selection and Use of Particulate Respirators.* Cincinnati, Ohio: National Institute for Occupational Safety and Health; January 1996. Publication 96-101.

125. Fennelly KP. Personal respiratory protection against Mycobacterium tuberculosis. *Clin Chest Med.* 1997;18:1-17.

126. Eck EK, Vannier A. The effect of high-efficiency particulate air respirator design on occupational health. *Infect Control Hosp Epidemiol.* 1997;18: 122-127.

127. Richmond JY, McKinney RW. *Biosafety in Microbiological and Biomedical Laboratories.* 4th ed. Washington, DC: US Government Printing Office; 1999.

128. Armstrong LR, Dembry LM, Rainey PM, et al. Management of Sabia virus-infected patients in a US hospital. *Infect Control Hosp Epidemiol.* 1999; 20:176-182.

129. Gershon RR, Vlahov D, Escamilla-Cejudo JA, et al. Tuberculosis risk in funeral home employees. *J Occup Environ Med.* 1998;40:497-503.

130. Management of patients with suspected viral hemorrhagic fever. *MMWR Morb Mortal Wkly Rep.* 1988;37(suppl 3):1-16.

131. McKee KT Jr, Oro JG, Kuehne AI, Spisso JA, Mahlandt BG. Candid No. 1 Argentine hemorrhagic fever vaccine protects against lethal Junin virus challenge in rhesus macaques. *Intervirology.* 1992;34:154-163.

132. Maiztegui JI, McKee KT Jr, Barrera Oro JG, et al. Protective efficacy of a live attenuated vaccine against Argentine hemorrhagic fever. *J Infect Dis.* 1998;177:277-283.

133. Niklasson B, Peters CJ, Bengtsson E, Norrby E. Rift Valley fever virus vaccine trial. *Vaccine.* 1985;3:123-127.

134. Pittman PR, Liu CT, Cannon TL, et al. Immunogenicity of an inactivated Rift Valley fever vaccine in humans. *Vaccine.* 1999;18:181-189.

135. Dandawate CN, Desai GB, Achar TR, Banerjee K. Field evaluation of formalin inactivated Kyasanur Forest disease virus tissue culture vaccine in 3 districts of Karnataka state. *Indian J Med Res.* 1994;99:152-158.

136. Sullivan NJ, Sanchez A, Rollin PE, Yang ZY, Nabel GJ. Development of a preventive vaccine for Ebola virus infection in primates. *Nature.* 2000;408:605-609.

137. Vanderzanden L, Bray M, Fuller D, et al. DNA vaccines expressing either the GP or NP genes of Ebola virus protect mice from lethal challenge. *Virology.* 1998;246:134-144.

138. Hevey M, Negley D, Pushko P, Smith J, Schmaljohn A. Marburg virus vaccines based upon alphavirus replicons protect guinea pigs and nonhuman primates. *Virology.* 1998;251:28-37.

139. Fisher-Hoch SP, Hutwagner L, Brown B, McCormick JB. Effective vaccine for Lassa fever. *J Virol.* 2000;74:6777-6783.

140. Gupta M, Mahanty S, Bray M, Ahmed R, Rollin PE. Passive transfer of antibodies protects immunocompetent and immunodeficient mice against lethal Ebola virus infection without complete inhibition of viral replication. *J Virol.* 2001;75:4649-4654.

Large-Scale Quarantine Following Biological Terrorism in the United States

Scientific Examination, Logistic and Legal Limits, and Possible Consequences

Joseph Barbera, MD; Anthony Macintyre, MD; Larry Gostin, JD, PhD; Thomas V. Inglesby, MD; Tara O'Toole, MD; Craig DeAtley, PA-C; Kevin Tonat, DrPH, MPH; Marcelle Layton, MD

During the past few years, the US government has grown increasingly concerned about the threat that biological terrorism poses to the civilian population.[1-3] A number of events have occurred that have raised awareness about the potential threat of bioterrorism. These include the suspected attempt to disseminate anthrax by Aum Shinrikyo in Japan,[4] widespread occurrence of bioterrorist hoaxes,[5] and revelations about the bioweapons programs in the former Soviet Union[6] and Iraq.[7] Most recently, the anthrax-related deaths, illnesses, and exposures in the United States have generated even more concern.[8,9] It is now generally acknowledged that a large-scale bioterrorist attack is plausible and could conceivably generate large numbers of seriously ill exposed individuals, potentially overwhelming local or regional health care systems.[10-12] In the event of a large bioterrorist attack with a communicable disease, the potential for person-to-person transmission of the disease would create serious health care and emergency management problems at the local and federal levels.

Throughout history, medical and public health personnel have contended with epidemics and, in the process, evolved procedures to lessen morbidity and mortality. Historically, quarantine was a recognized public health tool used to manage some infectious disease outbreaks, from the plague epidemic in the 13th century to the influenza epidemics of the 20th century. During the past century in the United States, professional medical and public health familiarity with the practice of quarantine has faded. A review of the medical literature found no large-scale human quarantine implemented within US borders during the past 8 decades.[13] Despite this lack of modern operational experience, local, state, and federal incident managers commonly propose or have called for quarantine in the early or advanced stages of bioterrorism exercises.[14] Management of some incidents that later proved to be hoaxes included the quarantine of large numbers of people for periods of hours while the purported biological weapon was analyzed.[4, 15] A striking example of the inclination to resort to quarantine was demonstrated during a recent federally sponsored national terrorism exercise, TOPOFF 2000.[16, 17] During the biological terrorism component of this drill, a national, large-scale geographic quarantine was imposed in response to a growing pneumonic plague epidemic caused by the intentional release of aerosolized *Yersinia pestis*, the bacteria that causes plague. An array of significant political, practical, and ethical problems became apparent when quarantine was imposed.

Given the rising concerns about the threat of bioterrorism and the concomitant renewed consideration of quarantine as a possible public health response to epidemics, it is important that the implications of quarantine in the modern context be carefully analyzed.

Quarantine vs Isolation

One of the first challenges to address is the lack of a precise definition of *quarantine*. In the historical context, quarantine was defined as detention and enforced segregation of persons suspected to be carrying a contagious disease. Travelers or voyagers were sometimes subjected to quarantine before they were permitted to enter a country or town and mix with inhabitants. The term *quarantine* is derived from the Italian *quarante*, which refers to the 40-day sequestration imposed on arriving merchant ships during plague outbreaks of the 13th century.[18]

In the modern era, the meaning of the term *quarantine* has become less clear. The *Oxford English Dictionary* defines *quarantine* as "a period of isolation imposed on a person, animal or thing that might otherwise spread a contagious disease."[19] Unfortunately, during modern bioterrorism response exercises, this term has been used broadly and confusingly to include a variety of public health disease containment measures, including travel limitations, restrictions on public gatherings, and isolation of sick individuals to prevent disease spread. The authors believe it is most appropriate to use *quarantine* to refer to compulsory physical separation, including restriction of movement, of populations or groups of healthy people who have been potentially exposed to a contagious disease, or to efforts to segregate these persons within specified geographic areas. For clarity in this chapter, this action is termed *large-scale quarantine* to differentiate it from incidents of exposure by only a few persons. To avoid confusion, we do not use the terms *quarantine* and *isolation* interchangeably. We use the term *isolation* to denote the separation and confinement of individuals known or suspected (via signs, symptoms, or laboratory criteria) to be infected with a contagious disease to prevent them from transmitting disease to others.[20, 21] It is operationally important that medical and public health emergency managers use accurate terminology.

Legislative Framework for Disease Containment

The moral authority for human quarantine is historically based on the concept of the public health contract.[22] Under the public health contract, individuals agree to forgo certain rights and liberties, if necessary, to prevent a significant risk to other persons. Civil rights and liberties are subject to limitation because each person gains the benefits of living in a healthier and safer society.[23]

The statutory authority for the imposition of quarantine in the United States originated at a local level during the colonial period. Massachusetts established state quarantine powers in the first comprehensive state public health statute in 1797.[24,25] At approximately the same time (1796), a federal statute authorized the president to assist in state quarantines.[26] The act was later replaced by a federal inspection system for maritime quarantines.[27] Thereafter, the federal government became more active in regulating the practice of quarantine, and a 19th-century conflict between federal and state quarantine powers resulted. In the ensuing federalism debate, the states maintained that they had authority pursuant to police power.[28-30] The federal government maintained that its preeminent authority was derived from regulatory powers over interstate commerce. Today, states are primarily responsible for the exercise of public health powers. However, if the exercise of quarantine clearly would affect interstate commerce, the federal government may claim that its authority is supreme.[31,32] Following is a brief summary of which institutions or levels of government have statutory authority to apply quarantine in distinct contexts.

Local Outbreaks in the United States

When an infectious disease is confined to a specific locale, the authority for quarantine usually rests with local or state public health officials. The authority is generally relinquished to the state when the event affects more than a single community or has the potential to spread across jurisdictional boundaries within the state. The individuality of each state authority has led to a widely divergent group of regulations providing for the use of quarantine.[33] Few local and state jurisdictions, however, have established specific policies and procedures to assist officials in deciding whether an individual event merits imposition of quarantine.[34]

Interstate and National Outbreaks

The federal government has the authority to enact quarantine when presented with the risk of transmission of infectious disease across state lines.[35] Legislation stipulates that this is an executive decision to be made by the president. Once the decision has been made, the Centers for Disease Control and Prevention (CDC) is the federal agency authorized to manage federal quarantine actions.[36] The implementation apparatus for such an order could involve federal assets from other agencies, such as the Department of Defense or the Federal Emergency Management Agency, deploying in support of federal, state, or local authorities.[37] The federal government may also assert supremacy in managing specific intrastate incidents if so requested by that state's authorities or if it is believed that local efforts are inadequate.[35,38] Other legal venues for federal action may exist but have not been well delineated.[39]

Foreign Outbreaks and US Border Control

For travelers seeking to enter the United States, the CDC has the authority to enact quarantine. At the turn of the 20th century, the Marine Hospital Service (forerunner to the modern US Public Health Service) established this federal power.[40] The authority was later delegated to the CDC's Division of Global Migration and Quarantine, currently consisting of 43 employees in the field and 30 at department headquarters in Atlanta, Ga.[41] In areas where Division of Global Migration and Quarantine personnel are not stationed, Immigration and Naturalization Service and US Customs Service personnel are trained to recognize travelers with potential illness of public health significance. While rarely used, detention of arriving individuals, including US citizens, is authorized to prevent the entry of specified communicable diseases into the United States. Using definitions delineated in this article, the detention of arriving passengers with visible signs of illness would be termed *isolation*.[42]

Currently, federal law authorizes cooperative efforts between the federal government and the states related to planning, training, and prevention of disease epidemics and other health emergencies.[43] Despite this, lines of authority between federal and state/local jurisdictions have not been sufficiently tested to ensure that all essential parties have clear understanding of the boundaries and interface between these potentially conflicting authorities. In a large-scale or rapidly evolving natural or deliberate biological incident, confusion and conflict in this public health authority may result. This issue was demonstrated in the TOPOFF exercise.[16,17]

Extensive reviews of the legal basis for quarantine actions have been published elsewhere and will not be reviewed in detail here.[21,44,45] Perhaps the most important understanding that can be extracted from these reviews is that though legal powers exist to quarantine in many contexts, the imposition of quarantine would likely be challenged in the courts using modern interpretations of civil liberties provided by the US Constitution.

Additionally, courts have suggested that, in the event of a quarantine, detainees would have to be provided with reasonable amenities to reduce harm (eg, adequate shelter and medical care). Ultimately, extensive quarantines would likely cause the judicial system to become a slow and deliberate arbitrator between the conflicting ideals of public health and individual civil liberties. The CDC and many states are currently in the process of reexamining the legal authority for public health actions, including quarantine.[46,47]

Historical Illustrations of Adverse Consequences of Quarantine

United States history has demonstrated that quarantine actions themselves may cause harm. Large-scale quarantine today can be expected to create similar problems, perhaps to a greater degree. Three historical events in the United States provide examples of the unintended consequences of quarantine implementation.

Increased Risk of Disease Transmission in the Quarantined Population

One of the most controversial US quarantines was imposed by the New York City Port Authority in 1892 on ships traveling from Europe, where a cholera outbreak had occurred.[48] Cholera had been detected among immigrants, and the subsequent public health response included quarantining passengers aboard arriving vessels. Passengers of lower socioeconomic standing were clearly subjected to separate, more severe conditions than wealthy passengers. Authorities sequestered these impoverished immigrants below deck without sanitary provisions during the confinement. Cholera spread disproportionately among the poor on board the vessels and resulted in at least 58 deaths on one ship alone.[48]

Mistrust in Government Recommendations Led to Violence

The municipality of Muncie, Indiana, was confronted with an outbreak of smallpox in 1893.[49] Public health officials had great difficult convincing citizens that intrusive public health actions were necessary, in part because the diagnosis of smallpox was repeatedly challenged. Many infected citizens were isolated under home detention and their presumably uninfected family members were quarantined with them. Entire neighborhoods were quarantined by patrolling armed guards; violators were incarcerated. Mandatory vaccination was instituted. Violence broke out as some civilians resisted the public health impositions, and several public officials were shot. Public health officials ultimately concluded that their quarantine actions had been "an utter failure" as the public had repeatedly defied their quarantine efforts.[49]

Ethnic Bias Adversely Altered Public Health Decision Making

A quarantine was instituted in the Chinese neighborhood of San Francisco, California, in 1900, after plague was diagnosed in several inhabitants.[50] The boundaries for the quarantine were arbitrarily established such that only Chinese households and businesses were included. This resulted in severe economic damage to the once-thriving Chinese business community. A federal court found the quarantine unconstitutional on grounds that it was unfair—health authorities acted with an "evil eye and an unequal hand."[51]

Key Considerations in Quarantine Decisions

In most infectious disease outbreak scenarios, there are alternatives to large-scale quarantine that may be more medically defensible, more likely to effectively contain the spread of disease, less challenging to implement, and less likely to generate unintended adverse consequences. Decisions to invoke quarantine, therefore, should be made only after careful consideration of 3 major questions examined within the specific context of a particular outbreak: (1) Do public health and medical analyses warrant the imposition of large-scale quarantine? (2) Are the implementation and maintenance of large-scale quarantine feasible? and (3) Do the potential benefits of large-scale quarantine outweigh the possible adverse consequences?

1. Do Public Health and Medical Analyses Warrant the Imposition of Large-Scale Quarantine?

Decision-makers must consider whether large-scale quarantine implementation at the time of discovery of disease outbreak has a reasonable scientific chance of substantially diminishing the spread of disease. There is no valid public health or scientific justification for any type of quarantine in the setting of disease outbreaks with low or no person-to-person transmission, such as anthrax. Despite this, quarantine has been invoked in anthrax bioterrorism hoaxes in recent years.[4, 15] Among the many diseases that are termed contagious (ie, capable of being spread by contact with sick persons), only a limited number could pose a serious risk of widespread person-to-person transmission. Of these contagious diseases with potential for widespread person-to-person transmission, only a limited number confer sufficient risk of serious illness or death to justify consideration of the sequestration of large groups or geographic areas. In addition to the agent characteristics, available treatment and prophylaxis options also create the context for the decision process. Public health responses must be accurately tailored to meet the specific risks and resource needs imposed by individual agents.

There are imaginable contexts in which a large-scale smallpox outbreak would generate reasonable considerations for quarantine. But even in the setting of a bioterrorist attack with smallpox, the long incubation period (10-17 days) almost ensures that some persons who were infected in the attack will have traveled great distances from the site of exposure before the disease is recognized or quarantine could be implemented. Subsequent issues with quarantine will remain problematic.

2. Are the Implementation and Maintenance of Large-Scale Quarantine Feasible?

If medical and public health principles lead to a judgment that quarantine is an effective and necessary action to stop the spread of a dangerous disease outbreak, the next set of issues that should be considered involves the logistics of actually establishing the large-scale quarantine. These issues are applicable to local, state, and federal decision-makers.

Is There a Plausible Way to Determine Who Should Be Quarantined? Are there practically available criteria for defining and identifying a group or a geographic area that is at higher risk of transmitting a dangerous disease? As noted, depending on the disease-specific incubation period and due to the mobility of modern society, it is probable that a population exposed to a biological weapon will have dispersed well beyond any easily definable geographic boundaries before the infection becomes manifest and any disease containment measures can be initiated. Even within a specific locale, it will be initially impossible to clearly define persons who have been exposed and, therefore, at risk of spreading the disease. A quarantine of a neighborhood would potentially miss exposed individuals, but a large-scale quarantine of a municipality could include many with no significant risk of disease. Currently proposed or functional health surveillance systems have not yet demonstrated adequate proficiency in rapid disease distribution analysis.[52, 53]

Are Resources Available to Enforce the Confinement? The human and material resources that would be required to enforce the confinement of large groups of persons, perhaps against their will, would likely be substantial, even in a modest-sized quarantine action. The behavioral reaction of law enforcement or military personnel charged with enforcing quarantine should also be considered. It is possible that fear of personal exposure or public reaction to enforcement actions may compromise police willingness to enforce compliance.

Can the Quarantined Group Be Confined for the Duration During Which They Could Transmit the Disease? Quarantine will not be over quickly. The period during which confined persons could develop disease might be days or weeks, depending on the specific infectious agent. Development of illness among detainees could prolong the confinement of those remaining healthy. Resources and political resolve must be sufficient to sustain a quarantine of at least days, and probably weeks. Furthermore, the multiple needs of detainees must be addressed in a systematic and competent fashion. During previous events, the courts have required that those quarantined be detained in safe and hygienic locations.[44] Adequate food and other necessities must be provided. Competent medical care for those detained is an ethical and possibly constitutional requirement.[21] Transferring supplies across quarantine lines can be difficult, as can recruiting qualified medical personnel to enter quarantined areas. The shortage of trained medical persons to adequately care for quarantine detainees should be anticipated and was clearly demonstrated during the influenza epidemic of 1918.[13, 54]

Given the presumption that biological terrorism would impose multiple competing demands for human and material resources within the affected region, decision-makers must weigh the costs and benefits of devoting available assets to the maintenance of quarantine.

3. Do the Potential Benefits of Large-Scale Quarantine Outweigh the Possible Adverse Consequences?

If valid public health and medical principles lead to a judgment that quarantine is an effective and necessary action to stop the spread of a dangerous disease outbreak, and it is established that a quarantine could logistically be put into place, the possible unintended adverse consequences of a quarantine action must then be carefully considered.

What Are the Health Risks to Those Quarantined? As noted herein, there are US historical examples in which persons with clear evidence of infection with a contagious disease have been quarantined together with persons with no evidence of infection.[48, 49] It is now beyond dispute that such measures would be unethical today, but a recent event illustrates that this ethical principle might still be disregarded or misunderstood.[55] A passenger returning to the United States was noted to be ill and vomiting on an airline flight, and the passenger's consequent subconjunctival hemorrhages were initially mistaken to be a sign of a coagulopathic infection. On arrival at a major US airport, the plane was diverted and quarantined by airport authorities with all passengers on board, including the potential index case. They were released after an hour-long period of investigation, when public health authorities arrived and concluded that there was no dangerous contagion. Had this been an actual contagious disease, quarantined passengers may have been subjected to an increased risk by continued confinement on the parked aircraft with the ill person. At a minimum, passengers should have been allowed to disembark and remain in an area separate from the index case while this person was being evaluated.

What Are the Consequences If the Public Declines to Obey Quarantine Orders? It is not clear how those quarantined would react to being subjected to compulsory confinement. Civilian noncompliance with these public health efforts could compromise the action and even become violent. Historical quarantine incidents have generated organized civil disobedience and wholesale disregard for authority. Such conditions led to riots in Montreal, Quebec, during a smallpox epidemic in 1885.[24] Some might lose confidence in government authorities and stop complying with other advised public health actions (eg, vaccination, antibiotic treatment) as well. The possibility also exists for development of civilian vigilantism to enforce quarantine, as occurred in New York City in 1892.[48] The rules of engagement that police are expected to follow in enforcing quarantine must be explicitly determined and communicated in advance. Protection of police personnel and their families against infection would be essential to police cooperation.

What Are the Consequences of Restricting Commerce and Transportation to and From the Quarantine Area? Halting commercial transactions and the movement of goods to and from quarantined areas will have significant economic effects that may be profound and long-term and reach well beyond the quarantined area. Much modern business practice relies on just-in-time supply chains. Shortages of food, fuel, medicines and medical supplies, essential personnel, and social services (sanitation) should be anticipated, and provisions must be in place to deal with such issues. Postquarantine stigmatization of the geographic location and of the population quarantined should be anticipated.

Conclusions and Recommendations

Public Health Disease Containment Measures Must Be Based on Scientific, Disease-Specific Analysis

The essential first step in developing any disease containment strategy is to determine if the disease at issue is communicable. If not, then no consideration of quarantine should be pursued. If the disease of concern is contagious, then the specific mechanism of disease transmission must drive the disease containment strategy (eg, spread by cough at close distances or possibly over longer range, as has occurred in smallpox outbreaks; infrequent spread by cough at close distance, as in some plague outbreaks; or spread through person-to-person contact, as in Ebola outbreaks). Some progress in delineating disease containment strategies for bioterrorism-induced outbreaks has already occurred in the form of consensus public health and medical recommendations,[56-58] though more diseases must be addressed and public health actions examined. Political leaders in particular need to understand that a single strategy for limiting the spread of all contagious diseases is not appropriate and will not work. The political consequences of public health actions such as large-scale quarantine must also be carefully examined and understood. Modern US disaster response has consistently focused on assistance to those directly affected; in the case of bioterrorism, response will focus on both those potentially infected and those actually infected. With implementation of quarantine, the perception may be that those potentially and actually infected have instead been secondarily harmed by response actions.

In an outbreak of a contagious disease, disease containment may be more effectively achieved using methods that do not attempt to contain large groups of people. As noted, persons with clinical or laboratory evidence demonstrating infection with a contagious disease should be isolated, separate from those who do not have clinical or laboratory evidence of that contagious disease. Depending on the illness, this isolation may be primarily respiratory, body fluid, or skin contact isolation rather than full physical separation from all healthy people.

Additional, population-based public health intervention strategies should also be considered. Depending on the context, rapid vaccination or treatment programs, widespread use of disposable masks (with instructions), short-term voluntary home curfew, restrictions on assembly of groups (eg, schools, entertainment sites), or closure of mass public transportation (buses, airliners, trains, and subway systems) are disease containment steps that may have more scientific credibility and may be more likely to result in diminished disease spread, more practically achievable, and associated with less adverse consequences. For clarity, these alternative disease control measures should not be termed *quarantine* or *quarantine actions.*

Invest in New Information Tools and Emergency Management Systems That Would Improve Situational Awareness During Disease Outbreaks

During large-scale contagious disease outbreaks, decision-makers would be critically dependent on the availability of timely, accurate information about what is happening and what interventions are desirable and feasible. Emergency management and public health officials will need real-time case data and the analytic capacity to determine the epidemiological parameters of the outbreak to make the most appropriate disease containment decisions. Clinicians will seek information about the natural history and clinical management of the illness and ongoing analyses of the efficacy of treatment strategies. Rapid communication between the medical and public health communities may be especially important and in most locales is currently not conveyed by electronic means or through routine, well-exercised channels.

Provide Incentives to Foster Specific Public Actions

Positive incentives may help to persuade the public to take actions that promote disease containment. The ready provision of adequate medical expertise, appropriate vaccines or antibiotics, or distribution of disposable face masks to the public in specific circumstances are examples of incentives that may positively influence population behavior to promote disease containment. Allowing family members to voluntarily place themselves at some defined, calculated risk of infection to care for their sick loved ones might encourage participation in a community's overall disease containment strategy. Assisting family members in these efforts by offering them some forms of protection against the disease could be a valuable aspect of an integrated disease containment strategy. For example, distribution of barrier personal protective equipment and education aimed at discouraging potentially dangerous burial rituals were successful interventions in controlling viral hemorrhagic fever in Africa.[59]

Devote Resources to Developing Robust Public Communication Strategy Commensurate With the Critical Importance of This Action

The development of strategies for communicating with the public throughout a disease outbreak is of paramount importance. Objectives of this strategy would include informing the public through multiple appropriate channels of the nature of the infectious disease and the scope of the outbreak, providing behavioral guidelines to help minimize spread of illness, and conveying details about how to get prompt access to effective treatment. Ideally, such messages would be conveyed by informed, widely recognized health experts such as the state health commissioner or US surgeon general. In a bioterrorist attack, the media's appetite for information will be limitless and health authorities must be prepared to provide accurate and useful information on a nearly continuous basis.[60] Advanced planning and preparation for such a media storm is essential. Once public credibility is lost, it will be difficult or impossible to recover. A well-informed public that perceives health officials as knowledgeable and reliable is more likely to voluntarily comply with actions recommended to diminish the spread of the disease. Effective information dissemination would work to suppress rumors and anxiety and enlist community support.

It is clear that public health strategies for the control of potential epidemics need to be carefully reevaluated. This process should ensure that civil rights and liberties are kept at the forefront of all discussions, as recently proposed by the congressionally created Gilmore Commission.[3] Further delineation of the authority to impose quarantine is required, and the political and psychological implications must be addressed. Given the complex multidisciplinary nature of this problem, further analysis of possible disease containment strategies would ideally include experts from the fields of medicine, public health, mental health, emergency management, law, ethics, and public communication. The process should specifically examine the various alternatives to quarantine that may be more effective and more feasible in addressing the containment of an infectious outbreak. Strict definition of terms such as *quarantine* must be maintained. With modern, in-depth understanding of specific diseases, more specific and medically valid response is appropriate than that used in the era of poor scientific understanding that established the practice of quarantine. The resulting work from this effort could provide a more comprehensive systems approach to disease containment in general.

References

1. *Improving Local and State Agency Response to Terrorist Incidents Involving Biological Weapons: Interim Planning Guide.* Aberdeen, Md: US Army Soldier and Biological Chemical Command, Domestic Preparedness Office; August 1, 2000.

2. *Road Map for National Security: Imperative for Change: The Phase III Report of the United States Commission on National Security/21st Century.* Washington, DC: US Commission on National Security/21st Century; January 31, 2001.

3. *Toward a National Strategy for Combating Terrorism: Second Annual Report to Congress of the Advisory Panel to Assess Domestic Response Capabilities for Terrorism Involving Weapons of Mass Destruction.* December 15, 2000. Available at: http://www.rand.org/nsrd/terrpanel/terror2.pdf. Accessed October 30, 2001.

4. Senate Government Affairs Permanent Subcommittee on Investigations. Global proliferation of weapons of mass destruction: a case study on the Aum Shinrikyo. October 31, 1995. Available at: http://www.fas.org/irp/congress/1995_rpt/aum/part05.htm. Accessed May 25, 2001.

5. Bioterrorism alleging use of anthrax and interim guidelines for management—United States, 1998. *MMWR Morb Mortal Wkly Rep.* 1999;48:69-74.

6. US General Accounting Office. *Biological Weapons: Effort to Reduce Former Soviet Threat Offers Benefits, Poses New Risks.* Washington, DC: US General Accounting Office; April 2000. GAO/NSIAD-00-138.

7. Zilinskas RA. Iraq's biological weapons: the past as future? *JAMA.* 1997;278:418-424.

8. Notice to readers: ongoing investigation of anthrax —Florida, October 2001. *MMWR Morb Mortal Wkly Rep.* 2001;50:877.

9. Centers for Disease Control and Prevention. CDC summary of confirmed cases of anthrax and background information. October 23, 2001. Available at: http://www.bt.cdc.gov/DocumentsApp/Anthrax/10232001pm/10232001pm.asp. Accessed October 24, 2001.

10. Carter A, Deutsch J, Zelicow P. Catastrophic terrorism. *Foreign Aff.* 1998;77:80-95.

11. Office of Technology Assessment. *Proliferation of Weapons of Mass Destruction.* Washington, DC: Government Printing Office; 1993. OTA-ISC-559, 53-55.

12. Cilluffo F, Cardash S, Lederman G. *Combating Chemical, Biological, Radiological and Nuclear Terrorism: A Comprehensive Strategy.* Washington, DC: Center for Strategic and International Studies Homeland Defense Project; May 2001.

13. Gernhart G. A forgotten enemy: PHS's fight against the 1918 influenza pandemic. *Public Health Rep.* 1999;114:559-561.

14. Mayor's Office of Emergency Management, New York City. *Draft After Action Report for Operation RED-Ex Recognition, Evaluation, and Decision Making Exercise.* New York, NY: Mayor's Office of Emergency Management; May 2001.

15. Horowitz S. B'nai B'rith package contained common bacteria. *Washington Post.* April 29, 1997:B2.

16. *Top Officials (TOPOFF) 2000 Exercise Observation Report Volume 2: State of Colorado and Denver Metropolitan Area.* Washington, DC: Office for State and Local Domestic Preparedness Support, Office of Justice Programs, Dept of Justice, and Readiness Division, Preparedness Training, and Exercises Directorate, Federal Emergency Management Agency; December 2000.

17. Inglesby T. Lessons from TOPOFF. Presented at: Second National Symposium on Medical and Public Health Response to Bioterrorism; November 28, 2000; Washington, DC.

18. Cumming H. The United States quarantine system during the past 50 years. In: Ravenel M, ed. *A Half Century of Public Health.* New York, NY: American Public Health Association; 1921:118-132.

19. *Oxford English Dictionary.* 2nd ed. Oxford, England: Oxford University Press; 1989:983.

20. Jackson M, Lynch P. Isolation practices: a historical perspective. *Am J Infect Control.* 1985;13:21-31.

21. Gostin L. *Public Health Law: Power, Duty, Restraint.* New York, NY, and Berkeley, Calif: Milbank Memorial Fund and University of California Press; 2000.

22. Merritt D. The constitutional balance between health and liberty. *Hastings Cent Rep.* December 1986:2-10.

23. Gostin L. Public health, ethics, and human rights: a tribute to the late Jonathan Mann. *J Law Med Ethics.* 2001;29:121-130.

24. Hopkins D. *Princes and Peasants: Smallpox in History.* Chicago, Ill: University of Chicago Press; 1983.

25. Chapin C. State and municipal control of disease. In: Ravenel M, ed. *A Half Century of Public Health.* New York, NY: American Public Health Association; 1921:133-160.

26. Act of May 27, 1796, ch 31, 1 Stat 474 (repealed 1799).

27. Act of February 25, 1799, ch 12, 1 Stat 619.

28. Freund E. *The Police Power: Public Policy and Constitutional Rights.* New York, NY: Arno Press; 1904:124-130.

29. Lee BH. Limitations imposed by the federal constitution on the right of the states to enact quarantine laws. *Harvard Law Rev.* 1889;2:267, 270-282.

30. Hennington v Georgia, 163 US 299, 309 (1896).

31. Gibbons v Ogden, 22 US 1, 205-206 (1824).

32. Compagnie Française de Navigation á Vapeur v Louisiana State Bd of Health, 186 US 380, 388 (1902).

33. Gostin L. Controlling the resurgent tuberculosis epidemic: a 50-state survey of TB statutes and proposals for reform. *JAMA.* 1993;269:255-261.

34. Conright K. TOPOFF 2000: lessons learned from the Denver venue. Presented at: National Disaster Medical System Conference on Lifesaving Interventions; April 28, 2001; Dallas, Tex.

35. 42 USC §264a (2001).

36. *65 Federal Register.* 49906 (2000) (in reference to 21 CFR §1240).

37. United States Government Interagency Domestic Terrorism Concept of Operations Plan. January 2001. Available at: http://www.fas.org/irp/threat/conplan.html. Accessed May 4, 2001.

38. *65 Federal Register.* 49906 (2000) (amendment in reference to: Measures in the event of inadequate control, 42 USC §70.2).

39. Gostin L. Public health law in a new century, II: public health powers and limits. *JAMA.* 2000;283:2979-2984.

40. Knight W. The history of the US Public Health Service. 1999. Available at: http://www.usphs.gov/html/history.html. Accessed November 4, 2001.

41. Centers for Disease Control and Prevention, Division of Global Migration and Quarantine. History of quarantine. Available at: http://www.cdc.gov/ncidod/dq/history.htm. Accessed April 28, 2001.

42. Centers for Disease Control and Prevention. *Public Health Screening at US Ports of Entry: A Guide for Federal Inspectors.* Atlanta, Ga: National Center for Infectious Disease; March 2000. Available at: http://www.cdc.gov/ncidod/dq/operations.htm. Accessed November 4, 2001.

43. 42 USC §243a (2001).

44. Gostin L. The future of public health law. *Am J Law Med.* 1990;16:1-32.

45. Parmet W. AIDS and quarantine: the revival of an archaic doctrine. *Hofstra Law Rev.* 1985;14:53-90.

46. Gostin L. Public health law reform. *Am J Public Health.* 2001;91:1365-1368.

47. Cole T. When a bioweapon strikes, who will be in charge? *JAMA.* 2000;284:944-948.

48. Markel H. "Knocking out the cholera": cholera, class, and quarantines in New York City, 1892. *Bull Hist Med.* 1995;69:420-457.

49. Eidson W. Confusion, controversy, and quarantine: the Muncie smallpox epidemic of 1893. *Indiana Magazine of History.* 1990;LXXXVI:374-398.

50. Risse G. "A long pull, a strong pull, and all together": San Francisco and bubonic plague, 1907-1908. *Bull Hist Med.* 1992;66:260-286.

51. Jew Ho v Williamson, 103 F1024 (CCD Cal 1900).

52. Defense Advanced Research Projects Agency epidemiology software used during presidential inauguration [press release]. March 9, 2001. Available at: http://www.darpa.mil/body/newsitems/encompass_release.doc. Accessed November 4, 2001.

53. Centers for Disease Control and Prevention. Supporting public health surveillance through the National Electronic Disease Surveillance System (NEDSS). Available at: http://www.cdc.gov/nchs/otheract/phdsc/presenters/nedss.pdf. Accessed April 14, 2001.

54. Ross I. The influenza epidemic of 1918. *American History Illustrated.* 1968;3:12-17.

55. Szanislo M. Plane quarantined due to passenger's illness. *Boston Herald.* October 25, 2000:2.

56. Inglesby TV, Henderson DA, Bartlett JG, et al, for the Working Group on Civilian Biodefense. Anthrax as a biological weapon: medical and public health management. *JAMA.* 1999;281:1735-1745.

57. Henderson DA, Inglesby TV, Bartlett JG, et al, for the Working Group on Civilian Biodefense. Smallpox as a biological weapon: medical and public health management. *JAMA.* 1999;281:2127-2137.

58. Inglesby TV, Dennis DT, Henderson DA, et al, for the Working Group on Civilian Biodefense. Plague as a biological weapon: medical and public health management. *JAMA.* 2000;283:2281-2290.

59. Outbreak of Ebola hemorrhagic fever—Uganda, August 2000–January 2001. *MMWR Morb Mortal Wkly Rep.* 2001;50:73-77.

60. Ball-Rokeach S, Loges W. Ally or adversary? using media systems for public health. *Prehosp Dis Med.* 2000;15:62-69.

INDEX